T0288576

A WORLD
BEYOND
MONOGAMY

EDWARD CRANE Esq.

GENTLEMAN of LONDON

PATRONO AESTIMATO NOSTRO ERVDITO
SAGACIQVE VIRO CVM GRATIA VERISSIMA

Our humble thanks also to Mistress Anita Cassidy, Mistress Julie
Schmidt Bowen, Master Angus and Mistress Nita Gulliver
and to Mistress Hazel W and Master Mark P

A WORLD
BEYOND MONOGAMY

*How people make polyamory and open relationships work
and what we can all learn from them*

JONATHAN KENT

Luminastra Press

A World Beyond Monogamy
How people make polyamory and open relationships work and what we can all
learn from them

Luminastra Press, LLC
5305 River Rd North, Suite B
Keizer, Oregon 97303
press@luminastra-press.com

Cover and interior illustrations ©2021 Luminastra Press
Cover by Irfan Yang with thanks to Shaun Streeter
Edited by Alan MacRoberts

Illustrations:
Frontispiece: Shaun Streeter, from a 16th-century engraving of Petrus Apianus by Theodor de
Bry (Wikimedia Commons; public domain).
P182: Frontispiece to Le Vite de' più eccellenti pittori, scultori, ed architettori by Giorgio Vasari,
1550 (Wikimedia Commons; public domain); Table of Geometry, from the 1728 Cyclopaedia,
Volume 1 (Wikimedia Commons; public domain)
P254: 17th Century Unicorn Woodcut from The history of four-footed beasts and serpents by
Edward Topsell (University of Houston Libraries Special Collection; public domain); English
unicorn 15th century woodcut (Wikimedia Commons; public domain); Frontispiece to The
Countess of Pembroke's Arcadia by Sir Philip Sidney, 1598 (British Library)

Publisher's Cataloging-In-Publication Data
(Prepared by The Donohue Group, Inc.)
Names: Kent, Jonathan (Jonathan Christopher), author. | Barker, Meg-John, 1974- writer of
supplementary textual content.
Title: A world beyond monogamy : how people make polyamory and open relationships work
and what we can all learn from them / Jonathan Kent ; with a foreword by Meg-John Barker.
Description: Portland, OR : Luminastra Press, [2021] | Includes bibliographical references.
Identifiers: ISBN 9781734658743 | ISBN 9781734658750 (ebook)
Subjects: LCSH: Non-monogamous relationships. | Interpersonal relations.
Classification: LCC HQ980 .K46 2021 (print) | LCC HQ980 (ebook) | DDC 306.8423--dc23

10 9 8 7 6 5 4 3 2 1
Printed in the United States of America

ABOUT THE AUTHOR

Jonathan Kent is a writer and journalist. He's been a political reporter, a foreign correspondent and a commentator, has reported for some of the world's great news organisations including the BBC, Reuters and Newsweek and written for many others including The Guardian and The Daily Telegraph. His 2012 series for BBC Radio 4, Our Daily Bread, was widely praised. He's currently working on a documentary about the experiences of young British-born Chinese people. He read philosophy and theology at Keble College, Oxford and lives in the High Weald in Sussex.

For S, for everything and then some.

"And now these three remain: faith, hope and love.
But the greatest of these is cake."
1 Corinthians 13, vs. 13 (alternative version)

TABLE OF CONTENTS

Section Three: Heffalump Traps

Section Four: It's Illogical Captain

Section Five: ~~Loves Kills~~ Love Skills

Section Six: It's Political, Innit?!

Section Seven: Hell is Other People

Section Eight: Appendices

Dr. Meg-John Barker

THERE ARE MANY, many reasons to welcome the arrival of A World Beyond Monogamy. First and foremost, it's a book about relationships and the skills we all—monogamous and non-monogamous alike—can use to relate better. It's an up-to-date, well-researched overview of the state of consensual non-monogamy (CNM). It's superbly comprehensive, covering everything from kitchen table polyamory to one-penis policies, from accountability to attachment theory, anxiety and insecurity to communication and negotiation, in engaging bite-size essays. And it draws upon a wide range of voices with a wealth of experiences of the good, the bad and the ugly of CNM relationships, including the voice of yours truly.

Here I want to focus on four things that I particularly loved about this book, and why I think they're so important:

- *The fact we hear from many, diverse voices,*
- *The inclusion of a wide range of relationship styles beyond hierarchical and egalitarian polyamory,*
- *The focus on what everybody can learn from each topic covered, whether monogamous or non-monogamous, whatever their relationship style, and...*
- *The fact that consent is at the heart of the book.*

BEYOND MONOGAMY, BEYOND THE US

OKAY, INSERT HERE my standard rant about how we were researching CNM in Europe back in the early 2000s, before it was even a twinkle in the eye of some well-known US poly-scholars. We had the first academic 'International Conference on Polyamory and Mono-normativity' in Hamburg in 2005, doncha know, and a special issue on polyamory in the Journal of Sexualities the following year! Yet reading many of the US books on the topic you would be forgiven for thinking the study of CNM begins and ends there. The wealth of previous work—from Europe, Australia and elsewhere—is often absent.

Also, as the resources at the end of this book attest, the vast majority of self-help-style resources on CNM come from a US context. That was certainly the case back in the 2000s, and it was one of my motivators for writing my own book about relationships, Rewriting the Rules. European poly-folks loved the bible, The Ethical Slut, but sometimes struggled with its Californian tone. So it is wonderful to finally have a book which focuses entirely on CNM and which has a distinctly British flavour (references to Monty Python and everything) and yet passes the mic to people from six continents so that their thoughts and experiences drive the narrative.

So, I would hope that this book will be highly accessible to people everywhere, rather than just to those in the UK or Europe. Jonathan has done an excellent job at drawing together people with CNM experiences from around the world and from many different cultural backgrounds. This is something that I haven't seen accomplished anywhere near this comprehensively in any other book.

Does it turn its back on the North American experience? Absolutely not. Folks from Canada and the States will find many interviewees and well-known voices from the places they call home. It was particularly great to see those of Black US polyamory experts foregrounded throughout, not just wheeled out to talk about race. Indeed around half the non-monogamists interviewed are people of colour. They include Christians, Muslims, Buddhists, Hindus, Taoists and Jews, as well as avowed atheists. Queer and trans people are very well represented as are neuroatypical and disabled folk.

RELATIONSHIP DIVERSITY

PERHAPS LINKED TO this cultural diversity is the relationship diversity of those included in this book. I've been doing what I can of late to get relationship diversity—alongside gender and sexual diversity—included in the training and resources which are provided to therapists and other organisations in order to be fully inclusive. But even then people often read relationship diversity as just relating to CNM, and often read CNM as equating to polyamory. As I try to emphasise in Rewriting the Rules, your monogamous relationship doesn't have to look like everyone else's either—it can look how you want it to look!

Jonathan does an excellent job in A World Beyond Monogamy of including the full range of relationship styles that can be understood under the umbrella of CNM. This includes many very common ways of relating, such as monogamish relationships, hook-ups, and fuckbuddies which could be encompassed broadly under CNM, as well as swinging, open relationships and Don't-Ask-Don't-Tell arrangements, which are often dismissed as somehow less legitimate than the various forms of polyamory in the CNM world.

It is particularly heartening that, of those Jonathan interviewed for the book, solo-poly and relationship anarchy were the most common styles of relating. These were exactly the two ways of doing relationships whose absence I noted—with sadness—in the last collection on CNM that I reviewed. It's great to see proper attention given to the idea of your relationship with yourself being your primary relationship (or at least one of them), to the potential for dismantling the cultural hierarchy which puts romantic relationships above all others, and to the challenging of the notion of people as property in any form (from interpersonal relationships to global politics).

WHAT WE CAN ALL LEARN

ANOTHER THING TO love here is the balanced approach that Jonathan takes to the range of relationship styles, common experiences in CNM, and other themes that he covers. I always try to ask the question 'what does it open up and what does it close down?' of everything, rather than the more usual binary questions of whether things are right or wrong, good or bad, etc. Many books on CNM explicitly, or implicitly, suggest— for example—that certain relationship styles are better than others, or that CNM is better than monogamy, or that being out about your CNM is better than keeping it private. This book takes the more sophisticated approach of asking what is opened up and closed down by each particular style, approach, or agreement. It examines the complexity of reasons why people—across different cultural, class, faith and other contexts—might feel more or less able to be openly CNM, to have certain kinds of agreements, or to practice certain forms of CNM.

Each chapter of the book also asks the important question of 'what can we all learn' from the style, or way of navigating relationship issues, which has just been covered. In my own work in this area my sense has always been that we should shift away from asking the standard psychological questions of why people engage in CNM, or whether it works, and instead ask what everybody might learn from people who could be seen as at the cutting edge of how to do relationships. Jonathan does a great job of pulling out—for all readers—what might be learnt from the conversations that happen in CNM communities, whether or not CNM itself is for them.

CONSENT AT THE HEART

Finally it is great to see a book which puts consent right at the heart of its exploration of CNM. Despite consent being the first word in CNM, many authors in this area focus on the range of non-monogamous styles and how they work, rather than fully unpacking what it means to be consensual, and how consent might apply across all relationships and relationship styles.

My own view is that consent is vital at all levels of human experience, from wider culture, down through our institutions and communities, our family systems and interpersonal relationships, and our relationship with ourselves. It isn't possible to have consensual sex if the wider relationship it is happening in is not consensual. And it's incredibly hard—if not impossible—to have consensual relationships if the wider systems and structures around us are non-consensual.

Experiences of the trauma of non-consensual behaviour—and the covering-up and gaslighting that surround it—are at the heart of most of our individual struggles including our mental and physical health problems. The same can be said of many of our societal struggles, from the imbalanced impact of Covid-19, through the racial injustice revealed by the #BLM uprisings, to the prevalence of sexual assault and abuse highlighted by the #MeToo movement.

For these reasons it's vital that a—or perhaps the—key question that we ask when considering how to do our relationships is how to do them consensually. We need to pay close attention to the complexities and challenges of this in such a non-consensual world, where many of us have been trained to treat ourselves, and others, non-consensually, where the cultural scripts we receive about how to do relationships are non-consensual, and where power imbalances are inevitably present in any relationship dynamic.

These are themes that Jonathan explores throughout this book, including grappling with how we collectively address situations when relationships in our communities are revealed to be physically, sexually and/or emotionally non-consensual. I expect that there will be many further conversations between Jonathan and myself on all these often highly contentious topics; neither of us has all the answers yet, nor pretends to. I greatly appreciate his courage and care in opening up these questions for us all as readers to explore and to relate to our own lives.

ONWARD...

This is a big book, no two ways about it! You will not necessarily read through from cover to cover in one sitting. Instead I imagine that it will become a welcome friend as you continue to navigate your relationships, whether you're new to CNM or an old hand. It contains helpful explorations and guidance to dip into to whet your appetite or get you thinking, to return to when a new issue crops up, and to reorient you in times of turmoil. I certainly hope that you enjoy it as much as I did and, as Jonathan says, do—please—be excellent to each other.

FIND OUT MORE:

YOU CAN CHECK out MJ's books and other writings at rewriting-the-rules.com and read their resource for practitioners on gender, sex and relationship diversity on: bacp.co.uk/media/5877/bacp-gender-sexual-relationship-diversity-gpacp001-april19.pdf

It's February 1st, 2015. I'm standing amidst a cluster of trees on the earth ramparts surrounding the great henge at Avebury, the largest megalithic stone circle in the world and one of Europe's ancient sacred places.

The day is Imbolc, the ancient Celtic festival that marks the beginning of spring, though at that moment spring seems a very, very long way away. It's seven in the morning, five below zero, the sun isn't due to rise over the stones for another 46 minutes and I'm bloody freezing.

There's a gaggle of people waiting for the celebrant to begin the handfasting ceremony. I've known the 'groom' nearly seventeen years and his partner for almost as long but only became aware that he was polyamorous three months previously when I met the woman to whom he's being handfasted.

When the sun finally drags itself over the horizon there are words of wisdom, poems are read and two people are joined together. It's a wildly romantic, beautiful ceremony that has me reflecting on the nature of love, the perfection of the setting and the loss of all feeling in my fingers and toes.

Polyamory isn't unknown in the UK at this point but it's still a curiosity, the stuff of three-in-a-bed tabloid fantasies and TV talk show exploitation. Most of those attending the ceremony are sympathetic, having met through a shared interest in tantra, but I'm the only one of the groom's work friends invited. In 2015 most Brits are still getting their heads around same-sex marriage and trans rights. In just over a year 17 million of them will vote to leave the EU, pitting traditional against inclusive values, a sometimes fondly remembered past against an increasingly fraught present, and little England against the world.

Five years later, as President Trump marks the dying days of his presidency with the patrician dignity of a man succumbing to rabies, Vivienne Vermuth and Jason

Perkins are married. America's newspaper of record, *The New York Times*, carries news of the happy event in its weddings section. 'We wanted to include our partners and their immediate family' in the ceremony, Vivienne told the paper.[1] She and Jason are also polyamorous. The story focuses on Jason and Vivienne's struggle, not for acceptance, but to get their extended network of lovers and lovers' lovers together as the coronavirus pandemic plumbs new depths of awfulness. If anything is remarkable about this story it's the degree to which readers are invited to empathise with their predicament, not disapprove of their relationship.

In the decades since the emergence of the counterculture in Sixties San Francisco, consensual non-monogamy has gone from being perceived as a fringe curiosity explored in cults or communes to an option that's becoming more mainstream across much of the world, and not just among the young.

The United States is undoubtedly the epicentre of this phenomenon, though elsewhere, such as the UK, Canada, Australia, Germany, it's starting to move in from the margins. Interest in polyamory and other forms of consensual non-monogamy, or CNM, has grown considerably, not least because the internet has made it far easier for people to find one another, exchange ideas and experiences and form communities of interest.

But only since about 2010 has the CNM movement gained the critical mass to take off in the wider world. Many journalists who approach the subject still treat it as exotic or titillating: the 'I made my excuses and left' school of tabloid reporting.

However that has been changing. From about 2014, particularly in the US, newspapers, magazines, television and other media started to cover CNM with increasing depth and sophistication. Nowadays, even mainstream publications give space to examine how the consensually non-monogamous make their relationships work, and the lessons their communication, negotiation and other relationship skills have for everyone else.

Consensual non-monogamy is still heavily stigmatised. People I've interviewed for this book have lost friends or jobs through coming out as consensually non-monogamous, and at least one has even had to fight to keep his children in the face of prejudice. As we'll see, research suggests that when presented with details about two exemplary and otherwise identical couples, one monogamous and the other consensually non-monogamous, many people judge the non-monogamous couple exceptionally harshly.

And yet it's a fascinating topic that deserves to be examined sensibly and sympathetically. One observation that you'll encounter over and over in this book is that there is indeed much that monogamous people can learn from how non-monogamous people run their relationships. It's not because they're better or smarter

---

1   A Blue Moon Wedding for Two Goth Romantics, *The New York Times*, November 13, 2020.

people. It's simply that in the absence of an overriding, culturally accepted blueprint for how CNM works, they have to consider what they'd like their relationships to look like. They find themselves having to communicate, negotiate where necessary, and manage their time and emotions much more deliberately and assiduously. Plenty of monogamous relationships could benefit from a little more of that.

In starting to write this book I'm reminded of Tolstoy's famous opening to his novel Anna Karenina, "Happy families are all alike; every unhappy family is unhappy in its own way." Being provocative, one might riff on Tolstoy that "Monogamous relationships are all alike; every non-monogamous relationship is non-monogamous in its own way."

And yet, despite the enormous variety of styles of agreed-upon non-monogamy, and the fact that one can find it being practiced from Sydney to Singapore, from Stockholm to Seattle, we tend to hear from quite a narrow range of voices, not a few of whom really believe that they have discovered 'the one true way'.

A majority of those voices seem to be from North America. They're disproportionately of European origin and generally middle class and they often offer very personal accounts; a 'This is how I did it!'. As a disinterested observer looking in from the outside you might be forgiven for thinking that consensual non-monogamy is a fashionable lifestyle choice for a privileged minority, some of whom are just a little bit pleased with themselves for being so very evolved.

That is why I set out to write this book. It's a journalistic endeavour to present a broad range of voices and perspectives. It's not a piece of academic research, though I've drawn on a wide range of research papers and the expertise of people in a variety of academic fields. What I hope to do is to show that there is no single right way of being non-monogamous. I also want to offer those exploring non-monogamous options and those looking to deepen their monogamous relationships some new ideas and perspectives, and a chance to find thoughts and experiences that chime with their own, from a diverse bunch of interviewees, some of whom will look like them.

Having joked that monogamous relationships are generally all alike I should make it clear I accept, of course, that they are not. However if one reads men's and women's magazines you'll soon realise that the same themes reappear on a twelve month cycle; 'how to keep your partner happy in bed'; 'how to rekindle the spark'; 'what to do if your partner cheats'; 'is it wrong to be attracted to other people?' etc. etc.

Clearly many of the problems that crop up in monogamous relationships do so pretty consistently. For so long as we've been presented with a model that eulogises lifelong fidelity and never-ending romance within the confines of coupledom, we've been trying to untangle the consequences of attempting to live up to a near unattainable ideal.

Consensual non-monogamy is a way of trying to rework the ideal so it accommodates and liberates the inclinations of many people to love widely rather than narrowly, instead of crushing them. There will, of course, be people who are deeply offended by this idea. Often their objections are rooted in faith or culture or fear.

For some it's not enough for their faith, their culture, or their fears to be personal matters—instead they seek to impose these things on others. Throughout history all these have been employed, often in parallel, to constrain and subjugate human sexuality, especially the sexuality and agency of women. Some forms of consensual non-monogamy, you may be unsurprised to learn, make considerable space for those who embrace the principles of feminism and for those who experience life in ways beyond the binary.

However this book will not be evangelising for 'ethical' non-monogamy. That can only be a matter of personal choice. CNM is not a panacea. Just as the problems that arise within monogamous relationships are quite consistent, so are those that crop up amongst the consensually non-monogamous. Quite often problems are common to both, though they may manifest differently in a non-monogamous setting. This book will explore those from multiple perspectives. To be messy is human, but we can learn from others' mistakes to avoid simply recreating them, leaving us freer to be messy, complicated and imperfect each in our own way.

Lastly, when it comes to ideas of right and wrong that are put out there by various advocates of consensual non-monogamy, I'd simply argue this: We don't need to reinvent the wheel. Throughout history, in various forms, faiths and philosophies, the same basic ethical principles have cropped up again and again.

The rabbi Hillel the Elder, asked to explain the scriptures, summed them up thus; "What is hateful to you, do not do to your fellow: this is the whole Torah; the rest is explanation; go and learn." This is often called the silver rule: Don't do to others what you don't want done to you. Following Hillel, just a generation later, Jesus taught the more positive version known as the golden rule: "Love your neighbour as yourself"; in other words, do do unto others as you'd like them to do unto you. Much more recent is the platinum rule: "Do unto others as they would actually wish you to do, not as you would wish in their place".

These principles are sufficiently universal that they transcend faith and encompass many styles of loving. It's not all that complicated. 'Be excellent to one another' and 'Don't be a dick' pretty much sums it up.

So when you work though the various topics in this book I'd invite you to bear those in mind. No ideas about love, no matter how lofty, should be used to belittle, constrain, punish or hurt. It's not about being somehow superior to someone else. It's about trying to meet one's own needs and those of the people around one in a way that's generous and compassionate. It's not always easy. Sometimes it's downright tough. However it's now down to you to find your own path. Don't just take my word for things. I make absolutely no claim to be expert or enlightened or perfect. Everything that follows is offered as food for thought and your own inspiration, not as prescription.

So in that spirit I hope that what you discover brings you and those around you happiness, and that you engage with kindness, compassion and a healthy dose of humility. May the wind be forever at your back, may the stars above you light your way and may there ever be biscuits in your tin.

NOTES ABOUT THIS BOOK

THIS BOOK RESTS substantially on more than 50 interviews I carried out between 2018 and early 2020. Some are with academics who have studied aspects of consensual non-monogamy or who are expert in areas that can shed additional light on it. Some are with activists who are happy to be known by their real names, while others are with consensually non-monogamous people across the world who were generous with their experiences and insights but who would prefer to remain anonymous.

I use the terms consensual non-monogamy and ethical non-monogamy largely interchangeably, but I prefer the former because what one considers ethical is subjective, but consent is not simply a matter of opinion: consent is either given or it's not. Ultimately it strikes me as less important whether one person approves of the way another organises their private life than that all those actively participating or directly affected by it do so freely—ideally enthusiastically, or at least consciously giving consent.

My interviewees are a pretty diverse bunch. There is a coterie of people, some of them linked, from the UK and North America. Others are from mainland Europe and the Middle East, and there's quite a large sample from Asia. Under-represented are black Africans (one of my interviewees grew up in Zimbabwe, moved to the UK at seven, then returned to school in Zimbabwe but is, frankly, as British as they come) and Latin Americans (a solitary Brazilian).

A lot of my interviewees are queer in some way. This doesn't surprise me. Once you've been forced to examine and think actively about your sexuality because it doesn't fit into the cis-het normative pigeonhole, you don't necessarily stop at the borders of monogamy/non-monogamy. People who have nuanced or complex sexualities often find consensual non-monogamy a place that accommodates nuance and offers solutions that embrace complexity.

When I interviewed people about their experiences I agreed to offer them anonymity but asked for barebones details of their backgrounds to give readers context: age, ethnicity, orientation, education, profession, relationship circumstances,

etc. These are set out in the bio section at the back of the book. Those marked with a *
are using a name other than their real one.

I do include some of their background in the text by way of an introduction to the
various voices. However other details I feel best are deployed only where I feel they're
immediately pertinent. There are many voices from many backgrounds in this book
speaking about a wide range of issues, adding to the sum of wisdom and insight I was
able to draw on. Where people speak English as an additional language I have occasionally, with their consent, edited their comments for clarity but left in some of their
more idiosyncratic phrasing because it gives a flavour of the person. However, in every
instance they speak English better than I speak their native tongue.

That said, I do have a *mea culpa* and that is that I contacted the three gay men I
interviewed, James Finn, Charlie Wilde and Simon Copland, when the rest of the book
was almost complete. As a result, their contributions were confined to the section on
non-monogamy and orientation. For this I can only apologise because all three are
intelligent and thoughtful interlocutors. My oversight was in part a reflection of the
fact that there's limited interplay between gay and other CNM scenes, but that's to
make excuses. We all make mistakes and that one comes under the heading of 'could
do better'.

Nevertheless, I hope that you enjoy what the many people who helped with this
book had to say. Interviewing them was an immense pleasure and I learned something
from each and every one. All are very circumspect about their expertise, as is the norm
with most intelligent people. Nor can I imagine that any would pretend they haven't
made mistakes. Most of us have.

There's a Whole Wide World Out There

CHAPTER ONE

What is Consensual Non-Monogamy?

WE ALL KNOW what monogamy is, as it's the script we're handed even before we have any real understanding of adult relationships. Whether it's Disney princesses and royal weddings, celebrity couplings, the staples of music, film, theatre and literature, or what most of our parents have done, monogamy is the cultural air we breathe when it comes to romantic and sexual relationships. It's what we're told is both natural and desirable. To break the rules is to risk being judged: home-wrecker, slut, slattern, wanton, slapper, strumpet, harlot, tramp, tart, trollop, vamp, floozy, whore, cheater, deceiver, sinner—there are plenty of negative labels ready to hand to apply to those (especially women) who deviate from the accepted and acceptable norm.

We all know, or think we know, what monogamy is. Just so we're on the same page, perhaps we should start with a formal definition.

In broad terms monogamy is the practice of only being in a romantic and/or sexual relationship with one person at a time. Most of us talk about couples. In sociological circles academics often refer to couples as *dyads;* two people forming a unit. It is this unit that monogamy is designed to encourage and support.

There is, however, a more austere definition of monogamy: someone only being in a romantic and/or sexual relationship with one person *ever.* Admittedly this rather puritanical definition is largely favoured by conservative religious and/or cultural minorities, the sort where daughters pledge to their fathers to guard their virginity until marriage. Those who subscribe to this very specific view of monogamy are likely to be pretty disappointed with the overwhelming majority of humanity. Few adults, especially in western countries, are romantically or sexually involved with just one other person ever. Most people who identify as monogamous are serial monogamists. They wait for one relationship to end before starting another. Sometimes they don't wait.

Needless to say, much non-monogamy is not at all ethical or consensual. In 2015 the polling organisation YouGov asked 1600 British adults[2] whether they'd had, or had thought about having, an affair. Some 20% of those who responded said they had cheated (another 4% declined to answer). When asked whether they'd *considered* having an affair one in three said yes. Another study by the conservative Institute of Family Studies in the US arrived at similar figures,[3] though American men admitted infidelity at a 50% higher rate than women, while in the UK numbers were fairly even.

Numerous similar surveys have been carried out over the years, and their results diverge wildly. This may be because that some are better than others at persuading subjects to answer honestly. Infidelity is still stigmatised in most cultures and it's hard to get people to be honest, even if given anonymity, if they struggle to be honest with themselves.

So, while cheating is certainly non-monogamous it's hardly ethical or consensual. However, others who effectively practice non-monogamy don't really fall into either the 'ethical' or 'unethical' camp. I'm thinking of those who date casually (sexually or romantically), and where neither party has discussed commitment or set out terms of engagement. Consent is often barely negotiated, if at all, but rather assumed—sometimes correctly, sometimes not. For a lot of people, getting to the stage of discussing such things is a big deal in itself. So, there's often a grey zone before (if ever) people agree on what basis they're dating. If they're seeing more than one person concurrently, they're non-monogamous.

For some people *cheating* is about covert physical intimacy outside their relationship, while for others falling in love or sharing deep platonic intimacy with another, is just as bad or worse. Technology offers even more grey areas. Does using a dating or hook-up app, flirting with other players in an MMORPG or watching porn constitute infidelity?

There's another, much less discussed form of non-consensual and thus unethical non-monogamy, and that involves coercion—whether for cultural or religious reasons or simply because one party uses their power over another to push them into a non-monogamous situation to which they don't consent. People cowed into remaining in a relationship while their partner sees other people, or pushed into non-monogamy, fall under this heading, as do people trafficked against their will for sex work. It should

2   '1 in 5 British Adults Say They've Had an Affair', YouGov survey for *The Sun* newspaper, 17-18 May 2015. https://yougov.co.uk/topics/lifestyle/articles-reports/2015/05/27/one-five-british-adults-admit-affair

3   'Who Cheats More? The Demography of Infidelity in America', Institute for Family Studies, 10 Jan 2018. From the IFS general social survey 2010-2016. https://ifstudies.org/blog/who-cheats-more-the-demographics-of-cheating-in-america

be superfluous to point this out but non-consensual relationships involve a degree of abuse. That abuse can easily reach the point of criminality and should be a call to action for principled people everywhere. This book isn't setting out to say that 'ethical' non-monogamy is inherently right; that's a personal decision for all involved. But it is absolutely clear that unethical behaviour in the form of coercion is inherently wrong. Let's commit ourselves never to look the other way or remain silent.

So, non-monogamy, though hardly uncommon, has very little formal standing in our society. Broadly speaking it's either dismissed as inconsequential (in the case of casual dating) or deplorable (in the case of infidelity).

But there's another wide category of non-monogamous relationships, the one that this book will explore.

CHAPTER TWO

The Naming of Things

Polyamory ˌpɒliˈam(ə)ri/*noun*
The philosophy and/or practice of maintaining intimate relationships with more than one partner with the informed and active consent of all those affected.

NAMING THINGS MATTERS. In naming things we give them an identity. In naming ideas we bring them into being. We give names to new-born thoughts just as we do new-born children.

It's easy to underestimate the importance of language in the spread or suppression of ideas, something George Orwell grasped well. He argued that cliché and verbosity drain language of meaning, providing cover for those who want to express anything other than the truth.[4] He takes the idea to its logical conclusion in *1984*, where citizens use Newspeak, a language so hollowed out that concepts the regime deems dangerous are eliminated one word at a time. If there's no word for something how does one communicate it, or even think it?

Conversely, giving a name to something gives it life. The word 'polyamory', for instance, is generally attributed to Morning Glory Zell-Ravenheart, a neo-pagan priestess and community leader in California. It's a mash-up of Greek (*poly-*, many) and Latin (*amor,* love). Framing the concept and giving it a name has made it much easier to share, discuss and develop.

The internet has helped bring into being countless communities of interest by connecting like minds who might be a minority of one in their own neighbourhoods but collectively number thousands or millions worldwide. One area where its impact has been huge is the realm of sexuality and relationships.

---

4   George Orwell, *Politics and the English Language* (1946)

Before the internet the public debate about sex and relationships was largely mediated by television, radio, magazines and newspapers, few of which dared venture much outside the mainstream. And when they did they tended to indulge in prurience, titillation or moralising.

The creation of shared, safe spaces for discussion was an essential feature of the second wave of feminism. Women wrote and published magazines for other women, for example *Ms.* in the US, *Spare Rib* in the UK and *EMMA* in Germany. Likewise, for same-sex-attracted men, the gay press played a vital role in creating a sense of solidarity and collective strength that allowed people first to come out and then demand and secure acceptance and proper legal and civil rights.

But now broadcasting and publishing channels have proliferated, becoming so accessible that the conversations are everywhere, and traditional media have been all but side-lined. Gender and orientation identities have also multiplied, and so too have the words coined to describe them. We have genderqueer, gender-fluid, pansexual, demisexual, heteroflexible, agender, bi-gender, two-spirit, gender nonconforming, sapiosexual and so many more.

It's hard to overestimate the importance of this for people who now have a vocabulary they previously lacked.

Something I heard time and again from those I interviewed for this book was that discovering there was a name for what they felt, that it was 'a thing', was a pivotal moment for them. Xena is originally from Indonesia, and her story is typical.

> I was in a relationship with my husband and another Danish guy and I was wondering why I have a feeling for him also and feeling for my husband and why am I able to love these two people, but it didn't occur to me that there was such a thing called polyamory or ethical non-monogamy. Then about three years ago my best friend messaged me saying I think you are polyamorous Xena! So I read this article about polyamory and it was like finding myself.

For Becky, a British trans woman, who was also questioning from a young age, discovering that there were those who had gone before was a little like finding other footprints in the sand of a desert island.

> My first girlfriend introduced me to the concept of poly and I went 'oh that's what it's called!' because I'd never understood this Disneyesque idea of *The One*. I remember having conversations with my mother about how will I find the one, this perfect person, and what if they died 50 years ago, what if they lived in India and I never go and meet them... you know? And so, my mum said 'well, okay, I guess

that there must be like more than one person out there' and I was like, natural question, 'what happens if I meet both of them at the same time?' It never seemed to fit and then, finally, Alex introduced me to the concept and okay, so it's okay to love other people, it doesn't make me a monster, it's fine and there are other people who identify as this, so I can probably find other people who will be into this and open to these experiences. So, discovering that poly is a thing and identity or concepts that other people relate to was huge, and I am eternally grateful for the poly community such as it is.

From our earliest years we learn how to behave by having our feelings and experiences mirrored back to us by adults. If we find ourselves in a minority of one, it's liable to lead to self-doubt or self-recrimination. It's isolating. For Nathan, a technician from Florida in the United States, finding people who could both mirror his experiences back to him *and* give him a vocabulary to articulate them was transformatory:

> In ninth or tenth grade my girlfriend at the time said, 'how could you possibly love more than one person?' And I thought to myself 'how could you not?' It seemed obvious to me and it was absolutely alien to her and I just kind of started following it. After that, I met Joreth [who introduced] me to the official concepts, 'here's all the terminology you need, here's how to do Poly wrong, so don't do it like that'. She's given me the vocabulary to describe a non-standard situation and it's delightful.

So the naming of things has its place in the discovery of self. It facilitates conversations and discussions because people aren't constantly having to lay out the basics for one another. There are broadly accepted definitions of different experiences and concepts, albeit you'll often find that these remain up for debate at the edges. If you don't know a word you can search for it online. It's fairly easy to do enough research to be able to take part in any number of conversations about any number of topics.

Later in this book I'll explore various ideas captured by the terms coined by the community. Some are for styles of non-monogamy: *monogamish, solo poly, relationship anarchy* and so forth. Others are for non-monogamy-related phenomena: *metamour, unicorn, new relationship energy, compersion,* etc.

But for now let's define some basic terms.

A number of the researchers whose work I've drawn on broadly divide the styles of consensual non-monogamy into three categories: swinging, open relationships and polyamory. If there is a clear boundary between each of the three I would struggle to identify it. Moreover, people can practice more than one of these. My definitions will thus be slightly arbitrary, and be aware that other people may invest terms with their own meaning. I'll be looking at each of these and their variants in more detail later.

Open Relationship: A primary-couple relationship in which, by mutual consent, one or both parties may pursue sexual encounters with other people. 'Open relationship' is sometimes used as a catch-all term for all styles of consensual non-monogamy, and before 'polyamory' entered the vocabulary it was often the default term for the practice of maintaining multiple relationships. However, most people, including many academics in the field, use it more narrowly to mean a situation where each person is allowed to explore sex separate from their partner. It's not uncommon for there to be a bar on *romantic* involvements outside the dyad, and sexual encounters are sometimes on a 'don't ask, don't tell' basis.

Swinging: a primary-couple relationship in which, by mutual consent, the couple meet other couples or groups for sex, often at parties within an established swinging scene. Many swingers have agreements not to have romantic involvements outside the dyad. A key difference between swinging and open relationships is that swingers often, though not exclusively, share their sexual experiences with their partners. Typically, swinger events are either couples-only or require men to attend only as part of a couple.

Polyamory: Polyamorous people maintain more than one intimate relationship, which may or may not be sexual, simultaneously. The difference between polyamory and open or swinging relationships is arguably that polyamory is predicated on ongoing relationships which tend to be as much, and sometimes more, romantic and emotional as sexual. In many instances polyamory connects not just individuals and their lovers but their lovers' lovers and beyond as an extended network. Some would say that this is a defining aspect of 'polyamory' and that relationships beyond the first degree matter even if they're not necessarily close, that ideally there is at least goodwill, somewhat like an extended family. There is no such expectation with 'open relationships'. Sometimes polyamory manifests as a tighter group relationship such as a **triad** or **quad**—occasionally an unofficial group marriage is even celebrated before the community with a ceremony and exchange of vows.

Ethical non-monogamy and **consensual non-monogamy are** umbrella terms for the various different forms of non-monogamy I will explore. In this book I'll use the two terms interchangeably though, as explained before, I much prefer the latter. 'Ethical non-monogamy' was presumably coined to distinguish polyamory, open relationships and swinging from other forms of non-monogamy such as cheating.

Everything I discuss in this book rests on consent, so before we go any further we should make sure we're all agreed on what that means.

CHAPTER THREE

Consent

I think that the definition or the proper understanding [of consent] is really problematic. The tendency is to focus on sexual consent. And it's just about whether someone consents to sex or not. So the rest of the relationship is not considered. And then there was this 'no means no' idea about consent, which is basically you go on and do whatever you want sexually and unless somebody actually says no to it, then that's all good. And I think these are just such simplistic understandings because I think that we can't actually have consent sexually if that's in the context of a wider relationship or a wider culture that is really non-consensual. If our wider relationship involves pressuring people to do things or trying to persuade and manipulate, then that's not all going to just go away as soon as we're in the bedroom.

And also consent is really important in wider relationships as well in terms of their emotional dynamics as well as the sexual dynamics. And then the 'no means no' approach is very limited because actually really often people don't use the word no. And also, are people really aware that when somebody says, 'oh, maybe, oh, I'm not sure,' that *does* mean no? That's effectively how we tend to say no in our culture.

So we need a more affirmative understanding of consent, which is about 'we only do things when everybody's really enthusiastic towards them'. And even that doesn't go quite far enough because a lot of people are socialised to be really enthusiastic about things that they're not enthusiastic about. We're taught that we should give granny a hug even though we really don't want to, or we should be delighted about a present that we don't really want or eat food that we don't really enjoy because it's been served to us.

So, my take on consent is we're living in a very non-consensual culture in terms of all kinds of areas, and doing consent in relationships is a much more complicated task than just waiting for 'no' in the bedroom and going ahead if we don't get one.

—Meg-John Barker

BECAUSE OF THE centrality of the question of consent, let me lay out the principles clearly at the outset. I hope everything in this book can be read in the understanding that consent is a non-negotiable prerequisite.

The concept of consent is simple: it is to give permission. The reality of consent is that people seem to complicate it or wilfully misread it.

Some people reduce consent to the fact that someone has said 'yes' to something or, more problematically, that they haven't said no.

But, as we'll quickly find, 'yes' doesn't always signal full consent. Not every 'yes' is given freely; a 'yes' cannot be divorced from the context in which it is given.

As consent is a potentially fraught subject let's confine ourselves to how it is understood and practiced in the context of sex and relationships.

The US-based organisation Planned Parenthood uses the mnemonic 'FRIES'. Thus, consent should be

Freely given
Reversible
Informed
Enthusiastic
Specific

The people who devised this *aide memoire* were specifically addressing consenting to sex. Let's explore these ideas a little.

Firstly, consent should be **freely given**: If someone isn't in a position to say no, then it's impossible for them properly to give consent. This could be for any number of reasons. If you are forcing someone to say yes with physical or emotional pressure, that absolutely negates any expression of consent you may get. A 'yes' with a gun to your head isn't yes. Nor is 'If you don't say yes I'm going to drive off and leave you in the big dark wood'. Nor is 'If you don't say yes I'm going to dump you as my girlfriend/ boyfriend'. Basically, if it isn't genuinely okay to say no, then it's not possible for consent to be freely given.

All too many people understand how difficult it is to say no to a boss at work. If your livelihood is riding on compliance then 'Okay' cannot truly indicate consent. A book could be, and almost certainly will be, written about the disgraced film mogul Harvey Weinstein and consent in the workplace.

If someone's judgement is impaired because of alcohol or other drugs they cannot, in that moment, negotiate consent. You cannot be sure that they would have said yes if they weren't under the influence. 'Oh, I am sure they would have,' you might say, 'because they have before'. Really? Are they actually Schrödinger's cat? Can you, thanks to the miracle of quantum theory, simultaneously compare their putative inebriated and sober states? Thought not. If it's not negotiated when someone is capable of negotiating, t'ain't consent.

If you know someone very well it may be possible to negotiate when they're sober and alert specifically what works for them when they're drunk or high or asleep. This is sometimes referred to as 'shelf-stable consent'. Be aware that being in a long-term relationship with someone does not inoculate you from possible breaches of consent, including those resulting from misunderstandings. All the FRIES rules still apply.

Legally, in most parts of the world, children are considered to be unable to consent to sex. This shouldn't need spelling out, but sadly it does. Different jurisdictions set different ages at which someone is considered able to consent. In parts of Europe that's as low as 14, in parts of the US it's 18. The fact that someone is of legal age isn't the whole story and shouldn't be sufficient of itself to assume they are mature enough to consent, especially when there is a very inequitable power dynamic, such as with a significantly older person.

As you may have gathered from the above, power dynamics affect the ability of people to consent freely. Ergo some jurisdictions will take a view that two children of a similar age consenting to sex with one another is a substantially different matter than someone young, but of legal age, ostensibly consenting to someone much older and/ or in a position of authority. There are a number of countries where it's assumed that sex between someone in authority and someone in their charge is non-consensual. It all comes back to whether someone can freely say no without fear of consequences. If they can't, it's not consent.

Next: consent should be **reversible**. Someone said yes twenty minutes ago and now they're saying no? That is their right. Consent is in the moment and for the moment. It's not a lease. 'I hereby give you rights over my mind and body for the next five minutes/hours/weeks/months/years/lifetimes'; that's not actually a thing. You can do that with property, but not a person. Treating a person as property is generally regarded as slavery. If you hadn't realised that slavery is not widely seen as a good thing then your research may need to go beyond this book. And before some smart aleck refers to slave/master BDSM relationships, once again; consent. It's as central to BDSM as everything else.

Some guys find the reversibility of consent a bit of an issue. That hot person who was hot for you and your hotness ten minutes ago has cooled? You were right in the middle of getting it on? 'Well I'm all horny and my penis will not be denied....' Stop there. Your penis will be denied. Your penis does not want to be banged up for rape. Yes it's frustrating. Relationships and the sexual dances we do with one another can be intensely frustrating. Welcome to humanity. We're complicated like that. You or anyone else can withdraw consent in an instant. If someone stops consenting then you stop too. Thank you.

The thing is, consent is a fluid thing. It exists in four dimensions, the fourth being time. It's not good to ignore signs that consent given earlier is growing more tentative or has actually been withdrawn.

Think back to the references to power dynamics above. If there is an imbalance, the person who felt able to say yes freely may not feel able to say they've changed their mind. Saying no to an amorous senior co-worker at the outset of an encounter may be a lot easier than saying no halfway through when you realise it's not working for you. Some people feel they can't change their mind because it would break an earlier 'agreement' or because they're worried about being labelled negatively. You really don't want the person you're with to feel that they have to go along with something. Not only does it have the potential to make you and them feel terrible, it may also close down the possibility of future encounters where things feel more natural.

So it's the responsibility of all involved to check in with one another periodically and to stay engaged.

Meg-John Barker is a psychologist, a former lecturer at the Open University and the writer of a number of books, not least the hugely influential 'anti-self-help book' *Rewriting the Rules*. They also co-presented the excellent *Meg-John and Justin* podcast with the sex educator Justin Hancock. The podcast often talks about 'the third handshake'. Spoiler: 'handshake' is a metaphor.

Handshake approach number one is spontaneous. You just shake hands. Most of us know what a conventional shaking of hands looks like. The trouble is that some of us don't like shaking hands like that at all. So the second option is negotiation. You talk through how you're going to shake hands before you shake hands. That would be pretty awkward if you don't know each other very well or if you find it hard to verbalise your likes and dislikes.

Meg-John & Justin posit a third way; the third handshake. It's a hybrid of the spontaneous and the negotiated. It involves dumping our preconceptions about how such encounters work, so we put aside the idea that we're both on the same page. Assume that you're not—and let things flow while maintaining constant verbal and/or non-verbal communication. Look at your partner/lover/friend/hook-up. Give them the opportunity to send signals: pleasure, distress, irresistible cravings for munchies... Give them gentle cues to signal that it's okay to change course. Check in with them.

Midori, a widely respected California-based kink/sex educator, is particularly insightful when it comes to negotiation. She can expound at length on how you can negotiate a scene. Examples went something like this:

'So if we play, how does it go....?'
'What are you wearing just then?'
'And perhaps at that point I could....?'
'And maybe a bit of x or would you prefer y or z?'

You don't want to break the spell, right? Well, stay 'in character' or 'in the moment'. You don't have to switch from lover to auditor or gynaecologist/proctologist when you ask 'How does that feel?' Maintain compassion. Be receptive. Be okay with answers you'd rather not hear: 'That's painful/gross/not my thing'. If both parties are remaining in the moment it shouldn't have to result in a slapdown.

'How's that?'
'Mmmmm, it's okay.' (Sounds equivocal)
'No good?'
'Not really my thing.'
'Is there something else you'd prefer?'
'Actually I really like it when....' Etc.

Informed consent means having all the information you need to decide whether you consent or not. The example that Planned Parenthood gives is actually a poor one: "If someone says they'll use a condom and then they don't, that's not consent." That's actually not about being informed. That's just a straightforward violation of an agreement.

A better example would be if someone agrees to unbarriered sex with a partner who says they were recently tested for STIs, when in fact they weren't. Another example: consenting to sex with someone who lies and says they're single. In both cases there is no consent because the thing that was consented to is not actually on offer.

Let's not pretend that men are the only ones who may ignore consent. If a man consents to unbarriered sex with a woman on the explicit understanding that she is using other forms of contraception and she's not, then consent has been violated. Sex, under those circumstances, is non-consensual.

In the UK the Crown Prosecution Service (the CPS is the state prosecutorial body in England and Wales) stipulates that someone must know the true identity of the person they are having sex with if the act is to be considered consensual. In recent years it has emerged that British undercover police officers had been having sex with environmental activists and, to maintain their cover, hadn't revealed their true identity. By the CPS's own criterion this would, on the face of it, have been rape.

If you persuade someone to have sex or into a relationship using lies, there is no consent. Be honest. If you don't like the reality you have to be honest about, then change your reality.

Next is **enthusiastic**. 'Mmmm, well, okay then' isn't a great start to an encounter and it's not much of an agreement to anything. Obviously, enthusiasm is expressed differently in different cultures; an American saying 'Yeah, that's awesome' might actually be a smidgen less enthusiastic than an English person saying 'Oooo, I rather like that'. If you give people a proper chance and full permission to say no, then you can be that much more confident that a yes is sincere and committed. There's nothing like hearing 'I really didn't want to disappoint/upset you' to leave an experience sullied by guilt or regret.

It would be so nice if we could just take a clear indication of enthusiasm at face value, but no. Again think of Meg-John & Justin's third handshake approach: In the moment take nothing for granted, and constantly be alert to verbal and non-verbal cues. That should help you to take the temperature of someone's consent more accurately.

One of Maxine's suggestions, that E could equally stand for **engaged,** stems from the fact that one *can* consent to something one isn't very enthusiastic about, such as a root canal procedure. Engagement, even if it's not enthusiasm, offers clearer options for people on the asexual spectrum and in certain kink settings. Jenny Wilson's Consent Culture Manifesto also suggests engagement, which they couch in terms of clear communication and positive agreement for things to proceed and continue.

Lastly, the S of 'FRIES' stands for '**specific**'. Consent to certain acts doesn't imply consent to others. 'Yes I'd like a massage' isn't the same as 'yes I'd like to see you suddenly drop your trousers and present me with your genitals'. Lying down for a kiss and cuddle doesn't mean that someone is necessarily ready for penetrative sex. Wanting sex with a condom is not the same as wanting sex without a condom. Wanting sex with the lights out is not the same as being comfortable having sex with the lights on. Even if someone is a happy slut and wants sex with lots of others, that doesn't mean they necessarily want sex with *you.* Meanwhile, in a kink context, consent to engaging in impact play (spanking, flogging etc.) doesn't infer consent for other forms of play or for penetrative sex.

There's a reason lawyers are paid handsomely to draw up contracts. A good agreement tries to limit, or ideally eliminate, the possibility of misunderstandings. When they're vague problems often follow. And no, you don't have to break the mood by putting in a call to a lawyer while you're just getting comfy on the sofa. Just try not to be a bad human... or as Jesus taught, 'Don't be a dick'. That covers most things.

Sex is important. It can often be fraught and presents the possibility of someone not being listened to and feeling, or being, violated. Because of this, as Meg-John Barker points out above, we tend to focus on consent for sex and neglect to apply it to the rest of our relationship(s) and lives.

Clearly consent ought to apply across the breadth of our human interactions and absolutely to all aspects of our relationships. In consensual non-monogamy in particular, a lot of extra negotiating is usually needed to establish people's boundaries. We would do well to remember that the ambient culture doesn't give us a set of widely-shared assumptions. Contemporary consensual non-monogamy is just beginning to develop a common culture, but for now we have to agree things deliberately as we go along, and that means talking everything through in each instance. (Indeed it may be a good thing if CNM doesn't develop too many shared assumptions, consent aside, so that the default is that people have to negotiate pro-actively what their relationships will look like. And if that approach filters through to monogamous culture as well better still.)

The principles of consent should equally be applied to negotiations about what people in a relationship feel comfortable with their partner(s) doing. Don't assume that your partner shares your ideas about how much you can, or cannot, constrain each other. *Talk.* There's a reason why people with experience of CNM tend to offer one piece of advice above all others: 'Communicate, communicate, communicate'.

And, inevitably, if relationships between two people are complex, relationships involving three or more people can become exponentially more complicated. Let me give a brief example.

Suppose that Angie and Badrul are a couple and that they've discussed Angie's desire for a relationship with Constantine. Badrul was fine with that at the outset and gave his consent. However six months on Badrul's relationship with his other partner, Dakshi, has come to an end and he wants more attention. He says he no longer consents to Angie and Constantine's relationship. Consent, after all, is in the moment and reversible, right?

This scenario raises a host of issues that I'll expand on in the course of the book, not least the whole issue of negotiating the opening of a relationship and the nature of involvements with others. Assuming that Angie and Badrul opened up their relationship consensually, the withdrawal of Badrul's consent has to be weighed against the fact that Angie and Constantine have developed a strong emotional bond and that both of them would be hurt by having to end their relationship.[5]

As you can see, there are circumstances in which issues of consent are simple and others where they become more complex.

There are also a few special situations where consent looks and sounds rather different as the result of negotiation, for instance where it's agreed that 'no' does not mean no but that it's replaced with another word, a 'safeword' that means stop. This is common in kink/BDSM scenes. Safewords are agreed in advance so that instructions such as 'slow down' and 'stop' can be explicitly signalled. More on this in the sections on sex and kink.

You'll find, as you read though this book, that consent will be referred to fairly regularly. Please bear in mind the principles outlined above throughout.

---

5   In this situation a lot of consensually non-monogamous people would argue that Badrul would be acting unreasonably to prevent Angie and Constantine from continuing to see one another but within his rights to withdraw from his relationship with Angie. Either way it's a bit of a 'no-winners-here' situation.

CHAPTER FOUR

The Road to Consensual Non-Monogamy

IF YOU'RE READING this, it's as likely as not that you're either already non-monogamous or you're thinking about exploring consensual non-monogamy. CNM takes many forms, and this book is intended to help you decide which, if any, is right for you. Or maybe you're wondering what you might learn from CNM for your own monogamous partnership.

In most of the world, monogamy is the relationship model that we're presented with. Culturally and institutionally the ideal of one lifelong, exclusive relationship between one man and one woman is treated not just as the ideal but as the default, or even only, option. Other options are implicitly 'lesser'.

Marriage owes much of its shape to religious institutions and secular marriage retains many of these religious features. For example, many governments view monogamy, as expressed through marriage, as a social good and use tax breaks and countless other mechanisms to promote it.[6] As Professor Joanne Begiato, a specialist in the history of emotions, the family, marriage, masculinities, material culture, and law at Oxford Brookes University, observes, the western, Judaeo-Christian view of marriage has long been pretty static.

> Within the Christian Church, marriage is somewhat similar across time. Scholars used to think that marriage could be entered into more informally in the past, but even according to that view, the unions were based on consent and it was their performance in certain locations that determined whether the Church deemed them regular or irregular. Generally speaking, the Church presupposed and dictated that

---

6   In an earlier age, the licentious 18th century, the church intervened materially; there's a story of a clergyman in the Forest of Arden in the English Midlands effectively bribing couples 'living in sin' to get married; the inducement, a pig.

marriage was between two members of the opposite sex and it would be expected to last for the lifetime of the spouse, and that definition was fairly typical across the centuries.

Beginning with the colonial period, Europe exported its model of marriage globally together with its trappings. Go to Paris these days and you'll doubtless see umpteen Chinese couples in full western wedding regalia, pursued by a small army of photographers and stylists, having wedding album shots taken against backdrops such as Notre-Dame, the Sacre Cœur or the Eiffel Tower. In Africa evangelical Christian mores have often supplanted local ones. In Latin America the profound influence of conservative Catholicism has made it hard to question or challenge conventional monogamy even from indigenous viewpoints.

Even popular and consumer culture weighs in. There are discounts for couples and families culminating in Valentine's Day events that are alienating for almost everyone not in the throes of new love. The depiction of couples in advertising is pervasive and remarkably prescriptive about what relationships should look like—it rarely ventures beyond the socially acceptable. Tellingly, traditional Hollywood romances seem to end when the fantasy ends. They pan away from the housework and the financial worries, let alone helping elderly partners with dementia or incontinence, airbrushing out the reality of relationships, monogamous and otherwise.

Only in recent decades have attitudes started to change: firstly to accept that relationships before and outside marriage are normal, and more recently that same-sex relationships are no less valid or valuable. But even as same-sex couples become recognised, the dominant model for them too remains monogamy: two people, exclusively, for life.

And how's that working out?

Well, that's hard to tell. Patently it's great for some but not brilliant for everyone. In the UK marriage and divorce statistics have fluctuated. Divorce rates have dropped sharply since the early nineties, but so has the number of people getting married; from over 346,000 in 1989 to 283,000 in 1995 to 232,000 in 2009. Of those marrying in 1995, two fifths had divorced by 2016.[7]

In the US, a country where religion looms far larger than in the UK, the American Psychological Association puts the divorce rate at between 40% and 50% overall. It's even higher for second or subsequent marriages.[8]

7   UK Office for National Statistics, https://www.ons.gov.uk/peoplepopulationandcommunity/
birthsdeathsandmarriages/divorce/datasets/divorcesinenglandandwales
8   American Psychological Association, https://www.apa.org/topics/divorce/

And then there's infidelity. Here accurate numbers are even more elusive. The famous Kinsey reports put infidelity in the late 1940s and early 1950s amongst American men and woman at around a half and a quarter, respectively, suggesting that either women were less inclined to report infidelity or that a smaller sample of women were unfaithful more often than most of the men surveyed.[9] The annual sex survey by condom makers Durex put the 2018 figure at 22% in the UK. That's a lot of non-consensual non-monogamy.

So no one should pretend that monogamy is easy. Many who claim to be monogamous aren't, and many who choose one person 'for life' come to regret their decision. But if forty percent of people who marry get divorced, then sixty percent don't. If a minority of people are unfaithful, a majority aren't. That, in itself, is impressive and it would be churlish in the extreme to suggest that most of those aren't happy.

At the same time, we shouldn't believe that society is monolithically monogamous. It's not. The fact that movies and magazines overwhelmingly equate good relationships with monogamous relationships only tells us how wary the media are of getting too far ahead of their audiences. The first consensually non-monogamous television programmes have already been made, and there are plenty of books and articles being written. But we're not yet at the point where consensual non-monogamy can be presented as normal rather than a curiosity.

And yet, deviation from the monogamous and the vanilla is far from exceptional. In 2015 a research team from the University of Indiana and the University of North Carolina produced the Sexual Exploration in America study. [10] It used a sample of just over 2000 men and women recruited through the GfK KnowledgePanel®. The panel claims to represent accurately the population of the United States and includes the correct proportions of people that surveys normally find harder to reach, including African Americans, Latinos and people without mobile phones.

It found that rather more Americans than one might expect had experimented with different forms of sex. For instance, some 10% to 12% of men and women between the ages of 25 and 39 had experimented with group sex. In the same age bracket some six percent of men, and rather more women, had gone to a swingers' party. Women in their late twenties seemed to be particularly open to experimentation, with 12% having attended a swingers party and over 10% having gone to a BDSM party or dungeon. As

9   Alfred Kinsey, *Sexual Behavior in the Human Male* (1948) and *Sexual Behavior in the Human Female* (1953)

10   'Sexual Diversity in the United States: Results from a national representative probability sample of adult women and men', Debby Herbenick, Jessamyn Bowling, Tsung-Chieh (Jane) Fu, Brian Dodge, Lucia Guerra-Reyes, Stephanie Sanders. PLoS One, 20 July 2017. https://journals.plos.org/plosone/article?id=10.1371/journal.pone.0181198

for threesomes, between 12% and 17% of men and women between 25 and 39 had had (hopefully) the pleasure.

As for consensual non-monogamy, another paper[11] suggested that it's far more prevalent than one might imagine. It reported that two studies, each based on a census-based sample size of around 4000 to 5000 people, found that 21.9% (of 3905) and 21.2% (of 4813) had participated in a consensually non-monogamous arrangement at some point in their lives. The survey was of single people, and the results have been questioned by some, but even if the figures are inflated by 100%, (which would be highly unusual for two academic surveys carried out by a reputable institution), that's still more than 10% of the US population that has experienced CNM. Other surveys put the number *actively* engaging in CNM in the States at around 4-5%.

Another study by Rubin, Moors, Matsick, Ziegler and Conley (2014) also looked at a broad cross section of available data and found that CNM was remarkably common. Among the research they looked at was Blumstein and Schwartz's 1983 survey of around 6000 couples. It found that between 15% and 28% of couples had an agreement that allowed extramarital sex. That's quite a wide spread, so it might not be a total surprise that other studies (i.e. Cole & Spaniard, 1974) have found lower figures (7% would consider CNM, 1.7% actually reported being in an open relationship), while a 2002 US National Survey of Family Growth (oh the irony) found that about 18% of women and about 23% of men were non-monogamous, albeit not necessarily consensually.

And, broadly speaking, within the United States at least (a culture with a keenly developed interest in the sex lives of others and thus a goldmine of interesting research), non-monogamy, and indeed CNM, seemed to cut across lines of race, gender, sexuality and class. People of colour are, in broad terms, equally likely to practice CNM while queer people are, if anything, distinctly more likely to do so. There were only small differences between socioeconomic classes and between different parts of the US. Where minorities and the less well-off are underrepresented seems to be in literature and media dealing with consensual non-monogamy.

The data certainly suggests that monogamy doesn't suit everyone. For some, deciding whether or not to be monogamous is gut-wrenching. For others there's no decision to be made. They simply view themselves as 'naturally' one way or the other. I'm suspicious of appeals to both god and nature because they're often attempts to stifle debate by invoking an uninterrogatable authority.

I'm not going to argue that monogamy is inherently unnatural or that non-monogamy is a 'proper' or 'natural' state. They are simply different choices that suit

---

11   'Prevalence of Experiences With Consensual Nonmonogamous Relationships: Findings From Two National Samples of Single Americans' M. L. Haupert, Amanda Gesselman, Amy Moors, Helen Fisher & Billie Garcia; *Journal of Sex & Marital Therapy*, Vol. 43, 2017, pp424–440.

or don't suit different people. If there's any appeal to nature to be made, it's actually that nature loves hedging its bets; rather than a single model for sex, gender and relationships, biologists have discovered countless varieties and far-flung outliers beyond the realms of imagination—from snails, jellyfish, and worms that have both male and female reproductive organs working in one body, to snakes, birds, sharks, and lizards with females that can breed by themselves, to a single-celled water creature that comes in not two sexes but seven (imagine writing relationship advice for *that* market), all of which are fertile with all the others. Mating and relationship *behaviours* seen in nature include not only homosexuality, what we might call kink, and polyamorous families collectively raising young, but the downright bizarre beyond even our human capacity for novelty and invention, such as fishes in which the male permanently attaches to the female's body, is engulfed by it, and digested. ('But officer it was completely consensual...') The rule of evolution, which is always blunderingly undirected, is simply 'whatever works', and the more variety the better the chance that some line will survive.

CHAPTER FIVE

Why Consensual Non-Monogamy?

CLEARLY, WHETHER THEY feel they have a choice or not, some people are inclined towards non-monogamy. But why?

'More sex,' yell the media, always eager to titillate. Except it's not that simple. How do we know? Because research. Amy Moors, Jes Matsick and Heath Schechinger asked 175 people practicing various forms of non-monogamy to list up to five benefits of their relationship style, and collated the results.[12]

The single most referenced reason was **being part of a bigger social unit** (45%) and all the advantages that was perceived to have, especially having a large social network (61%), greater financial resources (19%) and sharing domestic responsibilities and childcare (14%). One respondent described the feeling as that of 'being part of a big, happy, close-knit chosen family'. This may not be the first thing that springs to mind for people outside non-monogamy looking in, but feeling part of something larger than oneself is important to a lot of people.

Abraham Maslow, in setting out his famous hierarchy of needs, identified social belonging—something that includes friendships, intimate relationships and family—as the middle tier of five. Maslow argued that humans need a sense of belonging to a group, whether large or small. Given that humans are intensely social creatures and the wide body of evidence that we do not thrive on our own, this should hardly come as a surprise. And while humans' need to feel valued and loved includes sexual as well as non-sexual love, sex itself is listed separately by Maslow as a physiological need along with food, warmth, shelter, sleep, etc. as the foundational tier in his pyramid of needs.

---

12   'Unique and Shared Relationship Benefits of Consensually Non-Monogamous and Monogamous Relationships - A Review and Insights for Moving Forward' Amy C. Moors, Jes L. Matsick, and Heath A. Schechinger, *European Psychologist*, Jan 2017, 22(1): pp 55-74

The contrast between the monogamous and non-monogamous models can be quite stark. Of course many monogamous couples are very social and are plugged into a wider circle of people. However, at a more emotionally *and* sexually intimate level, that dyadic unit can put up a barrier around the couple. When children arrive you have the makings of the classic, self-contained, nuclear family.

Many non-monogamous models are far more akin to being part of a network than a unit. As we'll see, there are terms for your partner's other partner (if Angie dates Yusuf and Binyamin, then Yusuf and Binyamin are *metamours*), and your partner's partner's other partner. If Binyamin also dates Magda, then Yusuf and Magda are *meta-metamours*.

This is not to say that one approach produces isolation and the other social integration. That would be unfair. However, the monogamous model lends itself to self-containment and the non-monogamous model leans towards social connection and that's one of the qualities that non-monogamous people apparently prize most about it.

The second most popular set of answers is related to **trust** and to '**diversified need fulfilment**', in other words being able to have one's needs met by a bigger group. Both were cited by 42% of respondents.

Amongst those who mentioned diversified needs fulfilment, being able to turn to more people to meet one's needs and consequently having more of their needs met was overwhelmingly the key reason (55%). Sharing responsibility, or as one person put it, 'spreading the burden of having my and my partners' needs met', was also mentioned regularly (23%). This is also often framed as not having to be someone else's 'everything' or them having to be yours.

This is a theme that will crop up at various points. Traditional monogamous relationships are often sold as exclusive need-fulfilment vehicles: One person will be your lover, cook, cleaner, breadwinner and companion. Miraculously, they will also share your love of 1970s folk rock, your passion for the Tuscan countryside, your concerns about homelessness, and your love of 80s teen flicks, while being able to knock up breathtakingly good sashimi having already picked the perfect Loire white to accompany it.

Meanwhile, back in the real world, people generally feel lucky to have found someone who is able to meet a good proportion of their needs. In the context of a monogamous relationship they often make considerable allowances for their partner's likes and dislikes. And while people often have platonic connections who make excellent activity companions, sometimes our romantic partners can experience such close connections as a violation of the spoken or unspoken rules of a monogamous relationship. And all too often one or both partners simply give up on activities they enjoy because they're not shared interests.

However, for many consensually non monogamous people, being able to enjoy favourite things not enjoyed by partner A with partner B instead, is very appealing.

You and B both love the movie Ferris Bueller's Day Off. You both love sashimi. The idea of an evening cuddling up on the sofa with the movie while feeding one another slices of sashimi between kisses is appealing. Though plenty of people will argue that kissing doesn't add to the enjoyment of raw fish, or even vice versa, for some it absolutely does.

The other quality referenced, increased trust, is also something one hears a lot about when people describe their non-monogamous relationships. It boils down to this: 'If things aren't automatically out of bounds, we can talk about them and negotiate. We can know exactly where we stand because we don't have to hide parts of ourselves'.

Or, put another way, if it's okay for your partner to have sex with other people, it's a much smaller deal if they just fancy going out to the cinema with friends. There is no need to be wondering 'Did they have sex with someone else?' because if they did they'll just tell you (or ring to ask for an okay first if that's the agreement).

Trust is related to one's own openness and honesty. Of those who referenced trust as a benefit of consensual non-monogamy, 56% said it was because CNM allowed for honesty and reduced the need for deception. As we'll see, it's still possible to cheat in the context of a non-monogamous relationship. It's just that there are arguably fewer reasons to do so.

After trust and diversified need fulfilment came variety of activities, something mentioned by 40% of respondents. Just over half of those said it made possible more and different activities. Something over a quarter mentioned fun. The flip side of 'diversified need fulfilment' is that having more partners exposes you to more peoples' interests. After all, if one squeeze is keen on line dancing, perhaps another's love of jazz would offer a welcome change of pace.

Sex was mentioned by just shy of 40%. Yes, a greater variety of sexual options and more experimentation *is* a reason many people are drawn to non-monogamy. After all sex can be life affirming and joyous (though it's worth stressing that non-monogamy also creates considerable space for people who consider themselves to be asexual or demisexual). And it's something of a truism that monogamous couples very often lose interest in sex with one another as time passes.

Non-monogamy not only offers an answer to the gradual decline in the frequency of sex in monogamous relationships, it frequently reverses it. Many non-monogamous couples attest that having sex with other people revitalises their own sexual connection.

Other benefits cited by significant minorities of CNM people include a multiplicity of sources of love and commitment, more opportunities for personal growth and development, and better, deeper communication with those they love. As Moors and Co. put it:

> Whether CNM provides greater opportunities for social bonding and enjoyment than monogamy remains an empirical question; however, recent research supports the idea that those engaged in CNM embrace the nonsexual activities that are involved in their relationships.

> Perhaps, this benefit is particularly salient for people engaged in CNM because they may not be experiencing dyadic withdrawal. For instance, research on people in monogamous relationships has shown that as a couple progresses toward living together (and becoming more committed), they tend to withdraw from their social networks.[13, 14]

Meg-John Barker in their book *Rewriting the Rules* looks at various aspects of life, including relationships, for which we're handed scripts: essentially sets of assumptions and rules that we're supposed to accept and adopt 'as read'. It's not that we need to tear these up; it's that we should be, and indeed are, free to question them.

Clearly many social rules exist for good reasons, or did once. However, a lot of the time it's assumed wrongly that we know these reasons. Dana Zohar and Ian Marshall, in their book *SQ*[15], propose that humans function much better if they know the 'why' of something. They use the example of a team at a Japanese nuclear power plant that found a fantastic new shortcut that saved them time and hassle but that very nearly caused a major nuclear accident. The reason? The team hadn't been told the reasons *why* things were done the long way.

It's good to understand the reasons behind rules. They're often there to prevent harm to oneself or others. However, there are other rules for which the reasons amount to little more than habit, tradition, social control or codification of prejudice.

In either case, asking why is healthy. One either ends up with greater respect for the rules and an understanding of why they're there, or maybe one finds intriguing relics that have long outlasted whatever usefulness they once had.

If there was once a social need for monogamy, whether as a form of social contract or to try to guarantee paternity, (as the evolutionary biologist and emeritus professor

---

13   Ibid.

14   Moors references M. P. Johnson & Leslie, 1982; Kalmijn, 2003

15   Danah Zohar and Ian Marshall; *SQ: Connecting With Our Spiritual Intelligence*, New York: Bloomsbury Publishing, 2000. ISBN 0-7475-4676-2

of psychology David Barash posits) those reasons matter less now that we have contraception and DNA testing. In so far as consensual non-monogamy doesn't hurt others, then those rules can be questioned. And in rewriting the rules of monogamy we increase the number of options available, some of which may suit some people better than traditional choices.

A QUICK EXPERIMENT

LET'S ASK OURSELVES a few questions.

Start by writing down five things you like about relationships. This is *your* list so you should write down anything you like. I'm going to offer a few obvious ones to get you started. But list whatever makes sense to you. It could be 'someone to make me coffee and bring it to me in bed'. If it were my list it might include:

- *Support and encouragement*
- *Someone to explore new places with*
- *Great conversations*
- *A source of new ideas*
- *Sex*

For others it might be having:

- *Someone to build a life with*
- *Someone to have children with*
- *Someone to help pay the bills/mortgage*
- *Someone to cuddle*
- *Someone to watch favourite TV shows with*

It could be:

- *Someone to keep me on the straight and narrow*
- *Someone to cook for (or to cook for me)*
- *A good reason to stop dating*
- *A best friend*
- *A confidant*
- *A mentor*

And if people were really honest it could even include

- *Someone to clear up after me...*
- *...to make me feel better about myself*
- *...to put up with my shit*
- *...to make life seem less pointless*

Don't stop at five. Write down everything and anything that comes into your head. We can always knock that into some sort of order of priorities later. A list like this generally tells us as much about ourselves as it does about a person we'd like to be with.

Next let's consider things we don't like about being in relationships. Again, it's *your* list. Here are some of mine:

- *Arguments*
- *Feeling unreasonably constrained or obligated (for what constitutes unreasonable, see Arguments)*
- *A lack of mutuality—if someone is much more focused on me than I am on them, or vice versa*
- *Boredom*

Yours might include:

- *Having to pick up their socks/do their washing up*
- *Worrying if they're cheating*
- *Annoying habits*
- *My partner doesn't change*
- *I don't grow*

I'm loath to spend too much time listing the many ways people are awful. So, let's move on to monogamy and list some of the positives and negatives we associate with being in an intimate relationship with just one person.

Positives might include:
- *Security*
- *Predictability*
- *Dependability*
- *The chance to explore one person profoundly over time*
- *Commitment*
- *Familiarity*

Negatives might include:

- *Predictability*
- *Lack of sexual variety*
- *Decline in frequency of sex*
- *Lack of time to oneself*
- *Few opportunities for growth.*

Finally let's consider the advantages and disadvantages of being in a consensually non-monogamous relationship. We've discussed a few of the advantages people have identified above. These include:

- *Feeling like part of a bigger group/community*
- *Wider group to meet my needs*
- *More people to enjoy different activities with*
- *Opportunities for more honesty and intimacy in my relationships*
- *Greater frequency and variety of sex*

We will explore many of the negatives in the course of the book, but on many people's lists will be things like:

- *Jealousy*
- *Insecurity*
- *Commitment-related issues*
- *Sexual health*
- *Scheduling*
- *Task-sharing*

Some people may find it useful to list their preferences and reservations in order of priority. One useful method of doing this was proposed by the writer and lecturer Richard Bolles. Simply fill the options you're comparing into the grid below and examine them in pairs. For each pair, ask yourself which of the two scores higher. Give your choice 1 point. Once you've done that for every permutation of pairs, add up the total score of each option and you have your priority list.

You could do the same for pros and cons of monogamy, scoring on the basis of whether the pro outweighs the con. It might give you an early indication of whether you're inclined towards monogamy or questioning it. You might also want to repeat the exercise when you've finished reading this book.

You can find example decision grids easily online.

CHAPTER SIX

CNM as an orientation

So, WHAT LEADS people to consensual non-monogamy?

Some people explore CNM simply because it's intriguing. But for others it's more of a coming home. Many people who wrestle with their sexual orientation describe discovering that they're gay, lesbian or bisexual in similar terms—a realisation that they've found themselves.

That raises the question of whether some people are innately non-monogamous. Is being non-monogamous akin to an orientation?

Debate still persists about whether being LGBTIQA+ is innate. Some conservatives still insist on seeing it as a choice, because as a choice it assumes a moral dimension that is lacking if it's not. It's much easier to defend one's prejudices and to argue for discrimination if something is a matter of choice.

The best research at the time of writing, published in *Science* in 2019[16] and carried out using a sample of 493,000 people in the US, the UK and Sweden, suggested that there is indeed a genetic component but that our sexuality is also the product of our psychology and our experiences. 'Experiences', some further research suggests, may include exposure to hormones and other influences in our mother's uterus. In short, it's complicated. What the scientists couldn't identify was a specific gay gene, nor a specific straight one.

The study didn't address inclinations towards non-monogamy, but it wouldn't be a huge surprise if a similar array of influences—psychology, experience, genetics (perhaps many of the same genes), and epigenetics—determine whether we're more

16   'Large-scale GWAS reveals insights into the genetic architecture of same-sex sexual behavior', Andrea Ganna, Karin Verweij, Michel Nivard Robert Maier, Robbee Wedow, Alexander Busch, Abdel Abdellaoui, Shengru Guo et. al; *Science*, 30 Aug 2019.

or less inclined to form a sexually exclusive pair bond with a single partner and eschew all others.

There's no easy way in sight of resolving this debate, and even overwhelming scientific evidence is unlikely to sway those whose opinions aren't susceptible to facts. For some people who are determined to believe that homosexuality is evil or that non-monogamous people will burn in the pits of hell, no amount of science or rational argument is going to change their minds.

Some non-monogamous people insist it's just the way they're wired. It's like that classic retort to those who accuse LGBTIQ+ people of choosing their orientation: 'When did you choose to be straight?' McFadden is a forty-something American man from the US city of Philadelphia, works in IT, and has lived on both coasts. For him, being non-monogamous feels innate.

> I'm inclined to wonder whether non-monogamous is an orientation because I have a very clear recollection of having a crush on two girls at once in kindergarten. So, I would have been I think four or five years old and the two of them rode the bus to school together and they were best friends and they were adorable. And I wanted to be with either one of them or both of them together and I think I had no idea what I would do if I had ever gotten my hands on them at that age, but I mean that's sort of my earliest recollection of, you know, fancying a member of my, you know... chosen orientation was actually two at once.

Some people will trivialise McFadden's experience. That's hardly surprising. People trivialise the experience of women, people of colour, queer people, the disabled, the young and the old. That's simply a reflection of the privilege that some enjoy to discount the feelings of others with less power than themselves. But what McFadden felt is what McFadden felt. It's not a blueprint for humanity, but it's his experience of his own humanity.

Dr Liz Powell, author and psychologist and a fierce advocate of sex positivity, agrees. She came to non-monogamy instinctively rather than as the result of research or conscious exploration.

> I had my first non-monogamous relationship in high school. I was a part of a dating quad when I was 17. Well, four of us went to prom together which was quite lovely. And then I kind of was nominally monogamous on and off through until I got married at 23, and that was a monogamous marriage. And then we separated when I was 26 and I've been non-monogamous since then. And for me what I've

noticed is that I'm someone who is very slutty and I like to have a lot of sex with a lot of people and monogamy doesn't seem to offer me opportunities for that. And also, I tend to like, really like, a lot of people and feel very connected to a lot of people, and the monogamy model often limits the types of connections you can have with folks.

It's not just people growing up in liberal, educated western communities who, one might argue, are simply the product of a permissive environment. Shyam, an IT professional in his mid-thirties, grew up in a small village in the state of Kerala in southern India. Not only did he have no formal language for his feelings, there was nothing he can point to in his culture that might have prompted them. They were just something that arose 'naturally'.

Since I was young, I've been attracted to multiple people at the same time, even though I didn't know what it was. I kind of knew these terms only maybe four, five, six years back. So even when I was with my first girlfriend, I used to tell her, like that is completely okay for her to see other people, even though she was freaked out it was natural for me to tell her that, you know, it's okay, you can see other people, okay.

Some people simply don't need to have the concept explained to them. Despite all the conditioning in the environment that supports and encourages monogamy, for them there's never any question that that's just not them. However, Shyam, Liz and McFadden, at least anecdotally, seem to be in a minority. And even those who feel that non-monogamy is the most natural thing in the world are, at the very least, coy about the idea that it could be innate. Richard Temple-Purcell, Magick to his friends, is one of those who maintains a healthy scepticism.

It's a debate that I actually tried to avoid only because there are people on both sides of it and I feel like both sides, both sets of feelings, are valid on that point. I know people who are non-monogamous and who say 'I could give it up anytime I want, you know, I can leave this behind for the right person or whatever' and their experiences are valid. And there are people who were like, 'I could never give this up. I knew from age 12 that I was non-monogamous and that was just who I am as a person', and their experiences are equally valid. Honestly, I don't even know where I land on that spectrum. What I know is, whether it's behavioural or an orientation, I've structured my life around this to this point through where I couldn't go back if I wanted to and I definitely do not.

Treating an inclination towards non-monogamy as akin to an orientation does have something to recommend it. For a start there is emerging evidence that, while for some people sexual orientation is pretty static, for others it is fluid.[17] Some people who consider themselves straight unexpectedly fall in love with someone of the same gender, and some who consider themselves same-sex orientated fall in love with members of a different sex.

In much the same way, some people find themselves immovably inclined either towards monogamy or non-monogamy, while others are monogamous at one point in their life and then switch at another. And there are doubtless others who, in the absence of strong social norms and pressures, would simply weave between monogamy and non-monogamy as circumstances warrant.

---

17   Research in this field is relatively new and still evolving. Orientation seems to be fixed for many, if not most people, however for others it can change with time or in response to experiences. There is little or no evidence that orientation is open to change through what's euphemistically termed 'conversion therapy,' something that many people would categorise as psychological abuse.

CHAPTER SEVEN

Deciding to Explore Consensual Non-Monogamy

SOME PEOPLE DO not feel innately inclined to non-monogamy but simply reason their way there. In this it's unlike sexual orientation. People don't generally arrive at being gay or lesbian or bisexual because it seems logical. Maxine, a queer British artist and illustrator in her thirties, draws a parallel with the way that we form values.

> I don't really think poly is an identity as such. There's a lot of people argue with me on that, but for me it's about a belief. It's about the belief that it's actually normal and okay to have multiple romantic relationships. My introduction to non-monogamy was just asking the question; 'Well, why would I want to be monogamous, why should I be monogamous and why would my partners want me to be monogamous?' And I could never find a sensible answer to any of those questions so, I didn't do it. So, I just came in like that from the start.

Sandy, an American media professional born in the early 1950s was raised in a moderate Christian household. He was a young child when he too reasoned his way to consensual non-monogamy after a widowed neighbour remarried.

> Mom told me how happy she was for him, what a wonderful thing this was. But I wondered: When they all finally meet up in Heaven, which one will be the real wife and which will be left cruelly, tragically abandoned? The only logical answer, little me concluded, was that they would all love each other together. It just seemed natural and obvious.

For Eunice, a thirty-something events organiser from London, it was almost a research project, albeit when she encountered polyamory back in the late noughties, there were relatively few resources compared with today.

> I had broken up with what turned out to be my last monogamous partner. I hadn't actually been out of relationships since I was 15—I think the longest break I had was two months. I decided at this point that I would take some time, find out about myself. So, I gave myself a year of no dating to make sure that I wasn't dating because I was afraid to be alone or that I somehow desperately needed someone.

> In the UK there tends to be a fairly large overlap between the polyamorous community and a whole bunch of other communities; bisexuals, kinky people, geeky people, queer. It's a very queer-friendly space. I met a bunch of people who were polyamorous via one of those overlaps, talked to lots of people, read a lot. I read so much, everything I could get my hands on, and at the end of that year, I just turned around and went, "It turns out I'm polyamorous." There was no struggle. There was no trauma. There was no difficulty for me in accepting that, which I gather is not necessarily always entirely typical for other people.

For others, it's a reaction to the way they see relationships working or, more often, not working. For Mawar, an arts and culture administrator from Jakarta, it was partly not wanting to replicate what her parents had been through. Her relationship with her father wasn't close. The term she uses for him is 'lazy-arse'. She clearly feels her mother got a raw deal. So when her friends started dating she started to question what she saw around her.

> I remember in junior high school, around 14 years old, never had boyfriends before, I asked my mum what is like to be in a marriage, long-term relationship. Don't you get bored? My Mum said that after being in a looong relationship, partners tend to feel/act like family, like a brother or sister. And I asked again, is it how it's supposed to be? And she said, "Well, no. But that's what most people tend to become".

Later, having started a relationship with one guy, Mawar found herself attracted to a second.

> My boyfriend I found boring (a friend said he's like a milk, warm and comfortable, but that's it) and my affair was an artist; he was lively, knew what he wanted etc.

(My friend said he's like a wine, fun and intoxicating.) And I thought, is this what it should be? I have to choose between a milk and a wine? What if I want/need both? That's how I explored more about relationship in general and found ENM.

There are other reasons that people embrace consensual non-monogamy, not least because one relationship doesn't meet their sexual needs. Ivan and Yana married in 2010 but as Ivan puts it, "As time passes in marriage you realise that it's less and less the fairytale you have been promised." It wasn't that he'd stopped loving Yana, it was more that he found himself wanting other sexual relationships. Since they came from relatively conservative backgrounds in Russia, consensual non-monogamy was not something either of them had been exposed to.

> The dilemma is you either cheat or you try to control yourself. Or the third option is that you try to break out of this framework. So after some consideration and some talks with Yana, we have decided that we are interested both in opening our marriage so that was the first step. We decided that cheating happens not in the pants but in the head. So it is possible to have sex with someone else and not be a cheater.

For Kerilyn, a twenty-something, London-based, victim-services professional, it was her realisation that she was kinky. She was in a long-term monogamous relationship but her partner didn't share her sexual tastes, so she started exploring. Her interest in exploring her fetishes led her to the kink and BDSM website FetLife and to a realisation that she needed something that her then partner couldn't provide.

> I think if I hadn't encountered kink first I probably wouldn't have then come to non-monogamy. I was on a very stereotypical path prior to that. I think the first person I actually started talking to when I discovered FetLife was non-monogamous.... The more I delved into FetLife the more I realised at least that my existing relationship was not working, though it took a long time to disentangle ourselves.

Cooper Beckett, co-presenter of the *Life on the Swingset* podcast and author of *My Life on the Swingset*, argues that for many people a simple binary unit cannot contain or express the whole of two people's sexuality. In Cooper's case he is both polyamorous and queer as well as a swinger. In the past that tended to mean that people either suffered in silence or took the route of serial monogamy.

In my case, it was more of both my now ex-wife and I realising, sort of at the same time, that we hadn't had the opportunity to sexually explore before our relationship, because we got together and got married very young, and both of us wanted to have sex with other people and explore far more widely. And we thought, well, I guess we get divorced then. Because we didn't know that there was an alternative at all.

But a random comment from a friend of mine alerted me that there was still a swinger community and in fact it was a community probably far larger and more connected than it ever was in the heyday of the 70s. And that changed the world for me.

Without question sex is a major factor in people opening up their relationships. Novelty and variety both have their appeal, so is the desire to have specific physical needs met, whether they be within the realm of BDSM or different aspects of someone's sexual personality. Sometimes this leads to purely sexual connections and sometimes to additional relationships.

For others it's more about feelings than sex. They might find themselves attracted on a romantic level to more than one person or to the idea of a family of choice or being part of a group or tribe where boundaries are blurred. Some people identify as asexual or nearly so ('ace' or 'grey-ace'), and encourage their partners to find other people who can meet their sexual needs because they don't want to surrender their romantic connection.

IS CONSENSUAL NON-MONOGAMY FOR YOU?

'How do I know?' you ask. 'I've only just started reading the bloody book.' Fair point.

The first thing to say here is that 'no' is a perfectly good answer. Because consent. If someone has given you this book because they'd like you to be non-monogamous, please be assured that no one should expect you to do what doesn't feel right.

Most of those I've interviewed have embraced consensual non-monogamy for emotional, intellectual, sexual and/or social reasons. It jives with who they feel themselves to be. A significant proportion would say that they're simply innately non-monogamous and it has precious little to do with external factors.

Some, however, explore CNM because they feel they *should* be open to it, or to keep or please a partner or even to appeal to a would-be partner. If this is you, please pause.

No one should be compelled to be either monogamous or non-monogamous. Coercion happens. That's abuse. We'll look at that issue in detail later in the book.

However, I'd urge you to keep reading if for no other reason than that there are plenty of things we can all learn from consensually non-monogamous people that can help build happier, healthier, *monogamous* relationships.

This is probably a good point to ask yourself what actually interests you about non-monogamy. Is it something that feels 'right' to you, or are you just intrigued? Do you feel comfortable with the idea, or do you find it challenging? Is this what you want, or is it something you're interested in learning from?

If you were to map out your ideal life on a piece of paper, would the relationships part of that map include more than one romantic or sexual relationship? Would having two or more partners or lovers make you feel more secure, more wanted, more fulfilled, more satisfied, more connected—or less? Would you rather it were just you and one other forming a couple, conventional or otherwise? Or perhaps you would rather it just be a singular and single you, complete by yourself.

Outcomes tend to be poor for people exploring non-monogamy under pressure, to please someone else, or even just because it seems in tune with the times. I should stress again that nothing in this book invalidates monogamy as a choice so long as, like everything else, it's wholly consensual; it's what you and the other person in your monogamous relationship want.

Relationships are hard enough as it is without pursuing ones that don't feel right for you, and non-monogamy isn't always an easy choice. I'm a big fan of encouraging people to trust their instincts. If yours tell you that CNM doesn't feel right then at a minimum that should prompt you to slow down.

Just as the language of sexual liberation was co-opted in the 1960s by those who abused it for sexual coercion, so too will be that of CNM. If in doubt just check the section on consent again.

So, what do you do if you decide you'd like to explore non-monogamy? Below are some questions worth asking yourself before you start and reviewing as you go. Answering them honestly isn't necessarily simple.

It's hard to know how one might feel about something until one has tried it. Some people assume that having more than one intimate relationship will be easy and find it's not. Others think the insecurity or jealousy will be too much and then surprise themselves.

And having opened up a relationship, it may be hard to put the genie back in the bottle. It's worth considering carefully whether knowing that one's partner has been physically or emotionally intimate with someone else might make it difficult or impossible to go back.

There's no easy way around this. Even thorough research and deep reflection may not prepare you for the emotional impact of reality when you move from a thought experiment to a real one. There is no crystal ball.

It may be easier if one isn't in an existing relationship. There's much less at stake. All the same, taking time to mull over some of the issues you may encounter is unlikely to be time wasted. So here are some questions:

- *What does a relationship mean to you? Is it primarily about taking on life with someone, or about being emotionally and/or sexually intimate?*
- *Is being part of a couple a defining part of your identity?*
- *Have you ever been in a situation where you were attracted to more than one person at once and cheated or felt obliged to choose between the two?*
- *Have you, while in a relationship, repeatedly had fantasies about someone else?*
- *How confident are you of your ability to be 'fair' to two or more people and to meet both their emotional and physical needs?*
- *How easy do you find it to divide your time between close friends?*
- *Do you feel that important friendships sometimes get eclipsed to your detriment when you're in relationships?*
- *Do you fear that your partner(s) will like someone else more than you?*
- *How confident are you of your attractiveness?*
- *Do you have a strong sense of self-worth?*

If you're not ready to answer these yet there's no rush. In the chapters that follow we'll hear from many different people about their experiences of non-monogamy. They'll probably give you food for thought about many of the issues involved.

Come back to these questions whenever you're ready.

CHAPTER EIGHT

The Culture We're In

"A long habit of not thinking a thing wrong, gives it a superficial appearance of being right, and raises at first a formidable outcry in defence of custom. But the tumult soon subsides. Time makes more converts than reason."

—Thomas Paine, *Common Sense*, 1776

DISNEY PRINCESSES, ROM coms, special deals for two people, tax breaks for married couples—we live in a monogamous world, or at least one that maintains the pretence of monogamy. Failing to live up to the monogamous ideal is generally portrayed as, well, failure. Some ideas, and the institutions that support them, are just so pervasive that they pass largely or even wholly unquestioned. Even when the ideas are relatively recent, it can be hard to imagine what it was like to live in a time when people thought differently.

Young East Germans probably struggle to understand their own parents' and grandparents' attitudes living under communism. It can be much harder to inhabit the mindset of a culture separate from our own. Liberal westerners, monogamous or not, may still recoil from non-monogamy as it's practiced elsewhere: in southern Africa where some Zulus, such as former South African President Jacob Zuma, are polygynists; in much of the Islamic world where men can take up to four wives; or in the United States where some Fundamentalist Mormon men take 'sister wives', albeit without state approval.

We are, to a huge extent, the product of our environments. These may be environments partly of our own making or entirely of our culture's, but they can feel immutable and overwhelming. *They make us.* So, as Meg-John Barker says, the things we grow up with and live with form the very fabric of our reality.

> I think in a sense everything's a 'social construct'; it's felt in our body and is incred-
> ibly real because it's the world we've come into. It's all that we know. It's been writ-
> ten into our bodies and brains. For example, gender stereotypes are clearly social
> constructs; you know that it means this to be female, it means that to be male.
> But because we're immersed in them, and because we've repeated these actions
> so many times, they feel very real. And I think the same is true for monogamy, for
> romantic love. These cultural scripts get engraved on us and that's why it's incred-
> ibly hard to move away from them. Quite often they still play out in our lives even
> if we've started doing things differently.

Not only does nothing happen in a social vacuum, there has also existed, for a long time, predominantly one type of air. And it has been the oxygen of monogamy and marriage. As the therapist, writer and broadcaster Esther Perel put it in an interview with *The New Yorker*, the relationship-air we breathe "is an aggregate of multiple nar-ratives. It belongs to the people who are in it, but it also belongs to the people who are supporting it and living around it: family, friends, community. As I once said, and it became a kind of a saying for me, when you pick a partner, you pick a story, and then you find yourself in a play you never auditioned for."[18]

Perel isn't expressly questioning monogamy here, though she might as well be; she's actually talking about values that can cause friction—for instance whether peo-ple see marriage as a joining of two *people* or of two *families*. But she's absolutely right in so far as we are handed scripts and those scripts are overwhelmingly centred on monogamy. You can have any flavour you like so long as it's vanilla.

Challenging orthodoxy is inherently hard. We often seek out evidence to support our ways of thinking and that happens on a cultural level too. If actual evidence doesn't exist wishful or even magical thinking often fills the gap. The 18th and 19th centuries saw the rise of scientific racism, because what better than to prove 'scientifically' that people from other parts of the world were somehow inferior in order to justify nicking their stuff. And their countries. Likewise economics has become a 'science' that typically 'proves' that the free market is the answer to pretty much everything just as in other times and places it often 'proved' that socialist command economies were the one true way. And, as we've noted, nature has been plundered for examples

---

18 'Love Is Not a State of Permanent Enthusiasm; an interview with Esther Perel', *The New Yorker*, 9 Dec 2018. https://www.newyorker.com/culture/the-new-yorker-interview/love-is-not-a-permanent-state-of-enthusiasm-an-interview-with-esther-perel

of monogamy in other species to help validate our romantic ideal, except that the evidence really doesn't stack up.

History tends to teach us that being part of a large majority that's wrong rather than a small minority that's right, especially in matters of morality, gives one a better chance of retaining all one's limbs and, quite often, one's life. All the battles for civil and human rights that have shaped the modern world have been hard won, and many are still in the balance. The one over consensual non-monogamy has barely started.

At the time of writing, social attitudes towards non-monogamy are generally very negative, though they have become noticeably less so in some quarters in the last few years when the qualifier 'consensual' is added. Oddly, the fact that people will cheat on their partners has long been broadly accepted, though not generally approved of. The idea that people might *consent* for their partners to be romantically and/or sexually involved with others seems to upset a lot of people more than the idea of cheating, as though the problem is less infidelity than the sanction of sex outside the sanctity of the couple.

Dr. Dylan Selterman of the University of Maryland's psychology department is a social psychologist whose interests include the 'mechanics' of happiness and interpersonal relationships. He's also been investigating attitudes towards non-monogamy. His starting point was the good old-fashioned non-consensual kind: cheating. His work is informed by that of Jonathan Haidt, Craig Joseph, Jesse Graham, Sena Koleva and Ravi Iyer, who developed something they called 'moral foundations theory'. In very broad terms, they argue that moral judgements and choices are made on five main axes:

- *Care vs. harm*
- *Fairness & proportionality vs. cheating*
- *Loyalty to your group(s) vs. betrayal*
- *Respect and authority vs. subversion*
- *Sanctity and purity vs. degradation*

Haidt subsequently proposed a sixth parameter:

- *Liberty vs. oppression*

Dr Selterman has a strong sense that a lot of the qualms people have about CNM are rooted in feelings about sanctity and purity.

We gave people vignettes [stories] describing a character who cheats on their partner and [a] control [story] where they don't cheat. And then in both cases, the relationship ends. So ultimately the partner who was cheated on isn't actually harmed because their relationship ends either way. But people still think that the cheating is wrong, and the reason they do is because they feel it's more disgusting and impure and disloyal—not because it causes more harm.

And I think that kind of thing is underlying a lot of people's normative judgements about non-monogamy. That is, they feel that it's not necessarily harmful, but that it's impure, that it's degrading, that it's not consistent with the purity-sanctity foundation. And in some research we found that this is actually consistent across people's ideological beliefs. So, we tested it in one experiment for political views. Conservatives tended to be more judgmental toward that kind of behaviour across the board. But the *pattern* of results was the same for liberals and conservatives. Both liberals and conservatives say that infidelity is wrong and [for both,] it's driven by impurity rather than harms.

Amy Moors, assistant professor of psychology at Chapman University in California and co-chair of the Consensual Non-monogamy Committee of the American Psychological Association, is a feminist researcher who has looked extensively into attitudes within and surrounding consensual non-monogamy.

I think a lot about power dynamics, why things are set up the way they are, whose voices are on the margins, who's silent, and how to create inclusion and social change. So that's kind of how I operate within the worlds. And we all have different orientations as academics. So I think a lot about that. And when you just think about us as humans doing our thing in the world, love and intimacy is an integral part of most people's lives.

So finding sexual intimacy, finding romance—there's lots of different ways to do this. Yet in the media, even in our own personal lives, and particularly within the field of psychology, there's only one kind of relationship that's highlighted. And that's monogamy. And so, when you idealise or prioritise coupling and a monogamous relationship, and this even goes as far as legislation when we're talking about the institution of marriage, that has historically been for white people, that has been for people of the same religion, that has been for heterosexual people, and only over time has that changed, we keep reinforcing this idealisation of monogamy. Although there's lots of other ways to have relationships or not.

Her findings have been fascinating. For one of her studies she invented two characters in a relationship, Dan and Sarah.

> Dan and Sarah had, you know, these great careers, these boring hobbies. They've been together for a few years. They're monogamous and they really enjoy their relationship.

So far so dull. Then Amy invents another couple: an anti-matter Sarah and Dan (think 60s Star Trek here).

> Sarah and Dan have the same careers, the same boring hobbies, they really like each other, but they're consensually non-monogamous.

Oh dear. I can see trouble coming.

> So, then we have people rate, like what do you think of Dan and Sarah; what do you think of their relationship? Are they trusting? Are they lonely? Are they spreading sexually transmitted diseases? Are they happy? Are they reliable, paying their taxes on time? And so on... Like, tell me your thoughts about Sarah and Dan?

You know, Amy, I'm starting to wish you hadn't asked that.

> People overwhelmingly rate Dan and Sarah when they're in monogamous relationship as really, really positive. And just a word changes, monogamy or consensual non-monogamy, between the two vignettes. And they really like Dan and Sarah when they're monogamous; they're happy, they're secure, they're definitely not spreading diseases. They're really good at paying their taxes on time. But when a group of people read about Sarah and Dan being consensually non-monogamous, they are just seen as amoral, as bad citizens, as the worst sorts of relationship quality.

Sigh.

> Now when you think about how we're rating these things on a scale from one to seven, one being not trustworthy at all, seven being incredibly trustworthy, people

on average are rating the monogamous relationship as really close to seven and rating the consensually non-monogamous relationship as really close to one. So it was very clear this was a large effect size, basically a bi-modal distribution about the ways in which people had attitudes towards these two relationships.

Which is pretty extraordinary.

Right? Extraordinary for a lot of different reasons. These are hypothetical vignettes. Only one word changes. So, you can really get a sense of the this visceral... or you know, at least stigma surrounding consensual non-monogamy.

Moors says this is one of the largest effect sizes (i.e. causing a large A vs B split) that she's seen in her research career. The group replicated the study 12 times, showing one set of monogamous profiles to one group of interviewees and a second set of non-monogamous profiles to a different but similarly constituted group of interviewees. Sarah and Dan weren't alone. What Moors had chanced upon was a sure-fire, guaranteed way of completely tanking your reputation in the great public mind: being consensually non-monogamous. It's like kryptonite. Invade a neighbouring country (Putin), wave nukes around (Kim), shoot down a passenger airline (Iran/Russia, allegedly/US Navy), you might get away with it. Be in love and/or have sex consensually with multiple people, and in the minds of the moral majority you're toast.

Carrie Jenkins is a professor of philosophy at the University of British Columbia, author of *What Love Is: And What It Could Be*, and herself consensually non-monogamous. She thinks that the monogamous ideal has taken on a life of its own to the extent that we're judged by how well we navigate its challenges.

It's actually become a central component in how we understand what it is to live a good life. Life should include a central romantic relationship; just one and that, ideally, should be forever. Ideally it should be with a person who is everything to you. They should be your lover, your best friend, your confidant, your co-conspirator, someone you do laundry with, someone you play Monopoly with or whatever. This one person should literally be your everything. And that kind of vision of what it is to have a good romantic relationship has expanded into our sense of what a good life is, what a good person is. A good person is someone who lived a good life, and this includes having that kind of relationship.

(I have to confess, the moment when this picture of monogamous bliss fell apart for me was when Jenkins mentioned Monopoly. I can accept people have lifelong, fulfilling, soul-mate relationships, but play Monopoly together and still like one another afterwards? I remain distinctly sceptical.)

Jenkins has concluded that the world is divided into those playing happy couples and everyone else.

> ...not just [those who practice] non-monogamy, but also people who choose to live a single life. People who engage in serial monogamy intentionally. Anyone who intentionally has relationships with an end date attached to them. Anyone who's breaking that kind of script of the norm of a permanent, monogamous, sexual, romantic relationship. It also includes people who are in asexual relationships, people who don't choose to have romantic partners as a whole, who prefer to live with a network of friends and family and what have you—basically everybody in that camp is relegated to a secondary status, because this one way of living has been so exalted. At that point it's no longer just about who you put a wedding ring on, or who you have sex with or whatever. It's actually about whether you're a good person. That also explains the heat behind these kinds of criticisms. It is not a small thing. That is actually really getting into the existential hype of how people think about life and what it is to have a good human life.

And to think that for some people that includes playing Monopoly! Could it be that people *resent* struggling with monogamy (and Monopoly), *resent* accepting a lifetime of self-denial, *resent* living with the fact that the trajectory of desire within most relationships is a downward curve, *resent* seeing other people deviating from the rules, freeing themselves from social constraints, and come to *resent* the choices others made that perhaps they feel weren't available to themselves?

We know that an element of 'I've suffered so why shouldn't you?' is found in many cultures—not explicitly framed as such, but instead presented as a standard or ideal that must be defended rather than subverted.

Selterman's finding that this concern with the 'purity' of relationships seems to obtain across the political and social spectrum is fascinating. As mentioned earlier, other research has pointed to a much stronger disgust response amongst conservatives than amongst those whom Americans call 'liberals'[19]. But it's important to point out

---

19   'Disgust Sensitivity, Political Conservatism, and Voting', Yoel Inbar, David Pizarro, Ravi Iyer, Jonathan Haidt, *Social Psychological and Personality Science*, 6 Dec 2011. Also, 'Nonpolitical Images Evoke Neural Predictors of Political Ideology', Woo-Young Ahn, Kenneth T. Kishida, Xiaosi Gu, Terry Lohrenz, Ann Harvey, John R. Alford, Kevin B. Smith, Gideon Yaffe, John R. Hibbing, Peter

that this has been contested, and that other researchers have argued that disgust responses are evenly distributed across the values spectrum with regard to hypotheticals that are apolitical, such as, 'It would disgust me to stroke a cat with a skin disease'.[20]

So, is a negative response to CNM prompted by a fear of social norms being contaminated? Is it a fear of more literal contamination through the spread of disease? Or could it be a mix of the two? I'm struck by the way that when socially conservative institutions put out messages about sex they often seem to focus heavily on the risk of pregnancy and disease (sometimes, in US school curricula, accompanied by pointedly unpleasant colour photos), and not on pleasure, fulfilment, intimacy and love.

However, Selterman seems to lean not towards the contamination explanation but toward the idea that people are defending social conventions.

> Aside from what people are choosing to do in their own relationships, they're also concerned about stigma and judgment from others in society. And there's some work showing that when people have this kind of normative view of relationships—that they should be monogamous—they tend to want to enforce that. Like, if there's a neighbour of mine who's non-monogamous, that doesn't affect me in general, but the research shows people are very protective over what they consider to be a normative relationship arrangement; the same kind of thing that we've seen in people's negative attitudes toward marriage equality though that's changed a lot, especially in recent years.

There may be another factor at work: People wrestling with their *own* identities react strongly against stimuli that confront them with traits they themselves are conflicted over. Carrie Jenkins thinks such factors drive some of the hostility to consensual non-monogamy:

> Those who work with mental health issues will quite often tell you a common thing about how humans work is that they react very strongly or negatively against a trait in someone else that they themselves have but don't want to acknowledge, or that they have and wish they didn't have, or are trying to repress in themselves. And so, if you see somebody reacting very negatively to, let's say, watching an openly

---

Dayan, & P. Read Montague, *Current Biology*, 17 Nov 2014.

20   Clearly if you wish to upset people with a pronounced disgust response introducing yourself by saying 'I am consensually non-monogamous and I have been stroking a cat with skin disease' is likely to provoke a reaction.

gay couple walk down the street holding hands, I think it's not news anymore that quite often those most visceral and potentially violent responses are coming from deep-seated fear that one is oneself potentially attracted to the same sex.

And there's not just the issue of being confronted with one's own inner desires, but also with the fact that one didn't choose a more authentic path or didn't have the option.

Some people find monogamy easy. But I also believe there are a lot of us that don't. And those are the people that I suspect are wound up by the carrot being dangled. When the carrot is dangled in front of the person who's already, let's say, in a committed monogamous marriage and they have all kinds of entanglements—house, mortgage, kids, whatever, it's all set up for life—and then they see that they, in some sense, could have chosen differently, now they're confronted with the question: '*Should* I have chosen differently? Would I have wanted to have chosen differently?'—under conditions where they feel like they cannot do anything about it. Because it would literally destroy their lives.

And so now the suspicion that the answer might be, 'Yes, I would have preferred to have chosen differently if I'd had the option' and to know that now it's impossible unless you really kind of shake things up and at the risk of losing and destroying everything—so the stakes are very, very high in those kinds of situations—it also amplifies and exacerbates, it fuels the heat under these debates to some extent.

But even if part of the prejudice against non-monogamy comes from a fear of confronting repressed parts of the self, or even simply from jealousy of free people, we may find that, even if we see broader acceptance of consensual non-monogamy as a mode of living, the fear of literal contamination may well persist amongst the more conservatively minded.

This seems to be, in part, a fear of the unknown. In the UK, fear of immigration is strongest in communities with the fewest immigrants. Likewise prejudice against LGBT people often doesn't withstand a close connection with queer people. Indeed, US Republican politicians Dick Cheney and Rob Portman both added their voices to those calling for same-sex marriage; both had children in same-sex relationships. Once experience shows that contamination *doesn't* take place, that having gay neighbours doesn't encourage straight people to go gay, that there's no outbreak of disease—or that having people of African or Asian origin in one's communities doesn't lead to crime or family breakdown—those fears tend to dissipate. However, what having gay or non-monogamous people in one's community *might* credibly do is to persuade people who experience same-sex attraction, or who are attracted to multiple people, to embrace a more authentic version of themselves.

For Shelly, an Israeli academic based at a UK university, starting to question one orthodoxy led to her question others. Finding herself in a new place, with new friends with different attitudes, accelerated a process that had begun back home.

> I think there's a breakthrough moment when you understand that you were doing things in a specific way because of social constructs. And because this is what you've been taught is right and because this is what you've been fed for a long time.

> And when you choose to say, 'Oh, maybe this isn't the only thing', then all of a sudden you start asking that question about other aspects of your life. One of the areas where it happened to me was with politics, where increasingly you ask yourself, 'Oh, okay, so I've been fed this narrative.' Specifically, in my case this was like the Israeli-Palestinian narrative. I've been told stories and I've been taught these things in school and things have been framed in certain ways and this is the only way that I've heard those things. Can we look at things differently?' Of course! Taking a step away from where you are does that. Probably the journey into non-monogamy wouldn't have happened as easily if I was living in the same place as I was before. So being able to step away and kind of reinvent yourself gives you an opportunity to do that.

Perhaps that's part of the fear; that once people start questioning one thing they'll start questioning another and that non-monogamy could be a gateway into other unconventional ways of thinking. Look at the LGBT scene, once a byword for unconventionality and a harbour for the creative, the free-thinking, the unorthodox and the excluded; it's been interesting to see the attempts to co-opt the community. Once there was broad acceptance that being queer might not be a choice but was an orientation attitudes started to change. People started to talk more about the pink economy, as though the fact that some LGBT people, especially successful, child-free, (not to mention white) gay men and lesbian women, have substantial disposable incomes that might interest mainstream advertisers gave them a legitimacy that the marginalised *and* poor lacked. It's been argued that support for same-sex marriage grew not only amongst those with a sincere desire to respect the equality of LGBT people but also amongst those who wished to foist respectability on the gay community and obliterate its notoriously non-monogamous culture, something that has been explicitly expressed in conservative circles in the US.

After all the LGBT/queer community, not least bisexual people, were pioneers of non-monogamy and non-monogamous culture. Maxine, a British illustrator in her mid-thirties and bisexual herself, sees the role of queer culture as instrumental in the development of the UK's CNM scene.

> The majority of bisexual people live in monogamous relationships with a person of a gender, but there are certainly folks in the bisexual community who started questioning monogamy and developed a culture out of that. It's something I find quite interesting about the UK poly scene as opposed to the US poly scene. I've had folks come over from the US and say, "You know the scene [in the US] is very couple-centric, very heteronormative; it's very 'unicorn huntery'". That's something that's happening I think on the UK scene more recently, but when I started running Polyday, we used to get complaints from heterosexual couples that it was all too queer and they couldn't cope with it.

People have been remarkably inventive with the language of moral judgement and it's often heavily gendered. The most negative terms are overwhelmingly applied to women. Those like stud or player, more often used to describe men, arguably contain an element of grudging respect, admiration, perhaps even jealousy.

Some have attempted to reclaim such language, most notably 'slut'. Dossie Easton and Janet Hardy's 1997 book *The Ethical Slut* was the breakout publication about non-monogamy. It consciously embraced the term while arguing for exploring one's sexuality outside the confines of monogamy. There have been suggestions that other words be reclaimed. The Chinese academic Jess Zhu put forward 'cheater' as another candidate, though there seem to be inherent problems with the word. While *slut* encapsulates a promiscuity that many non-monogamous people would happily sign up for, *cheater* in English is about dishonesty and betrayal, which seems antithetical to consensual non-monogamy. Nevertheless, the intention is well meant. Just as the terms non-monogamous people have created make possible a different discussion about relationships and sexuality, those we've inherited are so laden with negative connotations that they wall people in.

We internalise the unspoken ideas that surround us. They shape our assumptions, our thinking and our actions to such an extent that questioning them starts to feel like questioning the laws of the universe. When one lives within a culture it is almost inevitably so pervasive, so all-encompassing, that there's almost no vantage point on which to stand in order to be able to look at it with perspective and consider it more objectively. It can be the intellectual equivalent of hanging off a sheer rock face by one's fingertips.

But the idea of the romantic partner being the one-and-all is actually a relatively recent construct. Go back two hundred years and many marriages were primarily economic or family alliances. Go back further and they were mainly for survival and procreation, procreation being partly about the hope that children would provide care in one's old age. Then a man might have a wife but have closer, more important relationships with his male comrades.

Western societies once took it pretty much for granted that men would often seek other sex partners elsewhere. Meanwhile a woman might quite happily enjoy herself with friends or female relatives while her husband just rocked up occasionally, provided for her economically, sometimes provided love, sometimes was just tolerated, and sometimes was an almighty pain in the bum.

Meg-John Barker says this accommodation was thrown into disarray in the West by the upheavals of the twentieth century.

> Stephanie Coonzt, the historian, argues that [the modern view of romantic, dyadic] relationships was really invented in the 1950s partly due to women doing so much [industrial] work in the war and then not wanting to go back to [being homemakers]. So then we started inventing all these spurious gender differences and this kind of romantic love [ideology] that's based on the nuclear-family couple model.

So, to some degree, was our current model born out of trying to reset American and European society back to where it was before the fundamental changes wrought by the first and then the second world wars?

> I think so. For that version of capitalism to work, apparently, you needed women to work unpaid in the home. So we sell women [who had worked in the wars] the idea that that's a super romantic, pleasurable thing to do, to work for your man and reproduce, boost the workforce by having kids. You can see the like in romance fiction now.

But that model has been breaking down. Women were drawn back into the workforce, sometimes out of a desire to have a career and self-actualise, more often out of financial necessity. Initially women met shortages in the labour market. However, as the 20th century wore on, dual-income households became the norm and prices eventually shifted to reflect this to the extent that single earners found themselves unable to afford certain essentials such as housing. As property prices across Europe continued to rise to the point that millennials couldn't even contemplate getting on the housing ladder as part of a couple, living in shared accommodation became the norm for many outside high-paying sectors such as finance and law. Meanwhile, the birth rate fell. A 'household' started to look rather different from the seventies norm of mum, dad and 2.4 kids. Might the 'family' of the future look like the crowded living arrangements of the present—multiple adults with a few children sharing a single property?

It's against the backdrop of these economic trends that we're seeing people increasingly thinking differently about relationship structures. It's something that Amy Moors has been tracking.

> I did a study where I looked at what people were searching for on Google. Google is the dominant web browser in the US and much of the world. It's also an anonymous context where we're sharing things and seeking out information that we might not ask someone we know. So it's a cool context to know what's on the public's mind or what the zeitgeist is. So I looked over the last decade [to see] what people were searching related to polyamory, open relationships and swinging. [And it was] things like, "What is polyamory?" "How do I open up my marriage?" "How do I get involved in swinging?" And I found that searches related to polyamory and open relationships markedly increased over the past decade, just rising year after year, with very large spikes some years, like a 59% increase in 2012 when the ShowTime series 'Polyamory: Married and Dating' came on.

Is there a trend? Possibly. I'm always slightly wary because if you study a single time period, something can look like a one-way shift when it's actually part of a longer cycle that will reverse. The 1890s were a time of licentiousness in Europe. The flappers and the denizens of the Weimar-era cabarets in the 1920s, and the hippies of the 60s and 70s, might all have reported more liberal attitudes towards sex. Not so the generations in between that suffered through the Great War, 30s fascism, 1950s' buttoned-down conformity, and the 80s' AIDS panic.

However, where we are now seems to point to more relaxed attitudes to relationships, something Mawar even noticed in Jakarta.

> It was very uncommon when I started this. Adam and I have difficulties in being in a relationship because whenever we went on a date and we explained to people that we are in poly relationship they back off. It's a deal breaker for them. But lately

in the last two years, I think people have been catching up. More and more people are exploring poly or they have been in a poly relationship, or basically exploring a non-monogamous relationship.

Even so, in a conservative culture like Java's, non-monogamous people have to operate more or less in secret. That's possible because of social media like Facebook, just as hook-up apps like Tinder have shaped dating.

Meg-John Barker says it's becoming hard to draw clear lines between monogamy and non-monogamy:

> [They] have become so blurred as to become almost nonsensical. A lot of people live their relationships these days through hook-ups, through apps, through friends-with-benefit arrangements. It's like, where do we even put all of that stuff in terms of monogamy/non-monogamy? And even monogamy, which much more usually takes the forms of serial monogamy, often with affairs and infidelities in there so it's secret non-monogamy; again, do you put secret non-monogamy on the monogamy side because it's pretending to be monogamy or do you put it on the non-monogamy side?

You know, it's shifting. There are gradations.; 'Don't ask, don't tell' for instance. And there are certainly versions of non-monogamy where people aren't behaving ethically, even though they're saying that they're openly non-monogamous. And you know, one might argue, most of us don't have complete awareness of all of our baggage in relationships and aren't operating completely consensually within this non-consensual wider culture. So where are the dividing lines? What does it mean to say that you are ethically non-monogamous?

That's a question that we can examine at some length. However, before we do, it's worth looking a bit more at some of the arguments people deploy against consensual non-monogamy.

CHAPTER NINE

God, Nature and Other Adversaries

IF BEING UP against a hostile majority isn't enough of a challenge for you, next there's God, germs and nature.

Let's start with the little guys first: germs.

As mentioned, an intriguing line of research[21] has opened up in recent years suggesting that those who identify as conservative may experience more visceral disgust than those who espouse liberal values. Some of the research focused on the brain's response to images showing, for instance, maggot-infested meat or someone touching the seat of a public toilet.

The researchers hypothesised that disgust acts as a protective response to perceived threats, not least to health, and found that the conservatively inclined are more fearful about, for instance, germs and the spread of disease. (This was before COVID-19, when a largely conservative group of contrarians across North America and much of Europe came out against masks while dismissing the threat from germs.) An instinctive fear of contamination might include fear of outsiders arriving in a close-knit, homogenous community. As Kathleen McAuliffe noted in a piece for *The Atlantic*, some 'scientists think germ fears piggyback on negative stereotypes about foreigners common throughout history—the notion that they're dirty, eat bizarre foods, and have looser sexual mores'.[22] As mentioned previously, this may feed into

21 Disgust Sensitivity, Political Conservatism, and Voting', Yoel Inbar, David Pizarro, Ravi Iyer, Jonathan Haidt, *Social Psychological and Personality Science*, 6 Dec 2011. Also, 'Nonpolitical Images Evoke Neural Predictors of Political Ideology', Woo-Young Ahn, Kenneth T. Kishida, Xiaosi Gu, Terry Lohrenz, Ann Harvey, John R. Alford, Kevin B. Smith, Gideon Yaffe, John R. Hibbing, Peter Dayan, & P. Read Montague, *Current Biology*, 17 Nov 2014.
22 'Liberals and Conservatives React in Wildly Different Ways to Repulsive Pictures', Kathleen McAuliffe, *The Atlantic*, March 2019.

some conservative narratives about sex that put great emphasis on the risk of STIs, even though these are largely avoidable with a modest degree of knowledge and care.

However, one of the studies used fMRI scanning to map brain activity while subjects looked at a range of images. Even stronger than the responses to images representing threats were those that reminded people that deep down we're just animals: "Disgusting images, especially those related to animal-reminder disgust (e.g., mutilated bodies), generate neural responses that are highly predictive of political orientation."[23]

This conclusion is still contentious and there are certainly those who think such disgust reactions are much better explained as simply being death-and-disease-related rather than animal-related. Nevertheless, could this help to explain why so many people who consider themselves conservative find sex so problematic? Christianity, in particular, is steeped in the duality of our earthly bodies weighing us down and our divine souls lifting us heavenwards, and consequently it sets up a conflict between our physical and spiritual needs; needs that are far better integrated in other faiths and philosophies. All that stuff kicking around our reptilian brains left over from our deep, dark, evolutionary past just freaks some people out. However, when they express this disgust they're much less likely to say 'I'm far more sophisticated than your average reptile, thank you,' and rather more so to say a thing disgusts them because 'It's unnatural' or 'It's against God's will.'

God and nature are both standard go-tos for people who want unchallengeable support for their beliefs. The effect is often to shut down any discussion. Often this appears to be the whole point. God rarely turns up at the lectern herself, nature only occasionally. Just as people pick and choose their quotes from scripture and put their own spin on them, witnesses from nature are almost always cherry-picked from the extraordinarily wide range of natural strategies and behaviours that biologists have actually identified. And even those are often wholly misappropriated and misinterpreted.

But let's start with religion. It's not generally the best guide on how to have sex and relationships, but it's an amazing resource for those who want to have an opinion about how other people should do it.

There's not a lot in any of the major religions that helps people who are consensually non-monogamous, but plenty to remind their critics that they might put their own houses in order before they start taking a pop at others.

Of the world's most widely practiced faiths, Christianity is probably the most hostile to sex, and yet the Old Testament is littered with revered figures who presumably had lots of it with lots of different people. Take 1 Kings 11:

23 'Nonpolitical Images Evoke Neural Predictors of Political Ideology', Woo-Young Ahn, Kenneth Kishida, Xiaosi Gu, Terry Lohrenz, Ann Harvey, John R. Alford, Kevin Smith, Gideon Yaffe, John Hibbing, Peter Dayan, and Read Montague,- Current Biology, 17 Nov 2014.

Now King Solomon loved many foreign women: the daughter of Pharaoh, and Moabite, Ammonite, Edomite, Sidonian, and Hittite women, from the nations concerning which the Lord had said to the people of Israel, "You shall not enter into marriage with them, neither shall they with you, for surely they will turn away your heart after their gods"; Solomon clung to these in love. He had seven hundred wives, princesses, and three hundred concubines; and ...

...presumably amazing stamina, not to mention a great deal of whatever passed for lube back in OT times. Solomon seems to have collected wives like some people collect superhero figurines, and practiced non-monogamy with knobs on. There have been suggestions that this was purely for diplomatic reasons; forging relations with other nations through marriage for instance. Even by modern standards that's one heck of a diplomatic service. And I still don't quite understand why a man with 700 wives would want 300 concubines as well but, clearly, I don't have the judgement of Solomon.

Solomon may have been outstandingly polygynous but he was hardly alone amongst Old Testament figures in having more than one wife; Abraham, Jacob, Esau, Elkanah, and dozens more, sometimes for 'diplomatic' reasons, sometimes because wife one was infertile, sometimes because why not? And of course there were the concubines, members of a man's household with whom he might have children but who didn't enjoy the status of wife and who, in many instances, were no more than servants or slaves.

When God pops up in Exodus he gives direct instructions (21:10-11) that when a man takes an additional wife, he must continue to have sex with his existing wife or wives: 'If he marries another woman, he must not deprive the first one of food, clothing and sex. If he doesn't provide her with these three things, she can leave freely without having to pay to do so.'

Most translations refer coyly to conjugal or marital rights, duty of marriage or even 'the price of her chastity', as in "wotcha darlin', want to come back to my place, check out me etchings and see what the Wall Street Journal has to say about the price of yer chastity, like?" The original Hebrew word is וְהָתְנָעֹ (wə·'ō·nā·ṯāh): sexual. As we'll see, Judaism is far more comfortable with the idea that as humans we have sexual needs.

At the same time there are strict rules about adultery: sleeping with a woman who is married or is pledged to be married (not necessarily consensually).

Deuteronomy 22 is often quoted in this regard.

If... no proof of the young woman's virginity can be found she shall be brought to the door of her father's house and there the men of her town shall stone her to death. She has done an outrageous thing in Israel by being promiscuous while still in her father's house. You must purge the evil from among you. If a man is found sleeping with another man's wife, both the man who slept with her and the woman must die. You must purge the evil from Israel. If a man happens to meet in a town a virgin pledged to be married and he sleeps with her, you shall take both of them to the gate of that town and stone them to death.

There's a lot of getting stoned in the Old Testament, and not a Jimi Hendrix album in sight. If there's a theme it's that having multiple partners is fine (for rich and powerful men anyway) but sex out of wedlock for women is definitely not.

The New Testament is rather different. Stoning puts in an appearance in the Fourth Gospel (7:53 onwards) when a bunch of Pharisees drag a woman accused of adultery before Jesus and ask if they can stone her to death.

Jesus, being a generally good geezer, doesn't seem overly impressed, suggesting 'Let he who is without sin toss the first rock'. There were no takers. The woman's accusers slunk away leaving her alone with Jesus, who just told her 'Go, and sin no more'.

Aside from the overarching Golden Rule, Jesus doesn't have very much to say about intimate relationships, absolutely zip about same-sex relationships, and very little about what relationships are supposed to look like. There's a passage in Matthew chapter 19 concerning marriage, but it's largely an admonition of those who trivialise divorce[24]. The model described is heterosexual and monogamous but it's couched as an 'is' rather than a 'should'. The passage goes on to discuss celibacy. Jesus makes clear that this is fine for those presumably born asexual or intersex, those who have been castrated, and those who are clearly inclined not to marry, but it's not an exhortation to celibacy. Indeed, in the light of the earlier verses it reads more as an endorsement of sexual union while avoiding shaming those who are not inclined. Claims about Jesus' own sexuality, extrapolating enthusiastically from a few passages in the gospels, have been hotly disputed.

On the other hand, St. Paul had lots to say about sex and relationships and arguably shaped Christianity more than the historical Jesus. Paul was from a conservative Jewish

---

24   Matthew 19: 4-6. 'He said to them, "Have you not read that He who made them in the first place made them man and woman? It says, 'For this reason a man will leave his father and his mother and will live with his wife. The two will become one.' So they are no longer two but one. Let no man divide what God has put together." '

religious background[25] and had received an education in Jewish law[26], yet his views about sex ran counter to those of most of his contemporaries. Judaism views sex as an innate positive, a gift of god, a blessing between a husband and wife (something that can be discerned in that passage from Exodus), while marriage was the fulfilment of a divine commandment to procreate and thus a matter of duty. Indeed rabbis normally married and had children. Paul, however, was having none of it:

"It is well for a man not to touch a woman. But because of the temptation to immorality, each man should have his own wife and each woman her own husband. ... To the unmarried and the widows I say that it is well for them to remain single as I do. But if they cannot exercise self-control, they should marry. For it is better to marry than to be aflame with passion." —1 Corinthians 7

There you have the root of much of Christianity's problem with sex and relationships. The church of Paul's time was expecting the imminent arrival of the Kingdom of God. Believers gave away their possessions and eschewed the material world. It's been argued that some of Paul's teachings were about elevating women to be equals in the new Christian movement, but that seems like wishful thinking given how the role of women in the early church was soon largely erased. I think it's more credible that they reflect Paul's deep personal antipathy to sex and romantic relationships.[27]

It's worth remembering that the world in which the early Christian church spread was not a particularly monogamous one. The first letter to Timothy, which though attributed to Paul was probably written in the first half of the second century CE, deals with the organisation of a growing church. The author stresses that church leaders, overseers (sometimes interpreted as bishops) and deacons, should be many things including honest, temperate, not overly fond of money, gentle, sober and 'married to one wife' (1 Timothy 3:2). This is conspicuously not prescribed for rank and file members.

---

25 Acts 23:6. 'Brothers, I am a Pharisee, a son of Pharisees.'
26 Acts 22:3 'I am a Jew, born in Tarsus in Cilicia, but brought up in this city at the feet of Gamaliel, educated strictly according to our ancestral law, being zealous for God, just as all of you are today.' Gamaliel was the grandson of the great Jewish teacher Hillel the Elder and was himself an authority on Jewish religious law.
27 A topic not much explored is whether Paul might have been drawn to Christianity by its 'world-rejecting' focus on the hereafter, something that gave him more latitude to avoid sex, given that in Judaism there's something approaching a sense of duty and obligation where sex and procreation are concerned.

What's clear is that of all the major religions, Christianity is, doctrinally, the most sex-negative. By the Middle Ages Christian theology had come to treat sex as a necessary evil, the result of the fall of man in the Garden of Eden. Without the original sin (snake-incited scrumping from the Tree of Knowledge) we'd have been immortal and wouldn't need to have children (and ergo sex) to please god. So, the mediaeval church essentially taught that sex was only for the purpose of procreation and that everything else was sodomy. Basically, don't have fun. Ever.

One doesn't have to be a psychologist to realise this is all a bit screwed up and that it may leave the faithful deeply conflicted about their relationship with their own sexuality and bodies. If one sees god as a caring father figure (and that characterises much of Jesus' teaching), he's given his children a compelling toy (their sexuality) and told them not to play with it or he'll throw them in a fire to burn. By any sane standard this is poor parenting.

It's hard to dodge the conclusion that either God is just not very nice (in which case why are we wasting our time?) or people have just gotten him wrong and that he gave us our sexuality for a reason. After all, it would have been quite easy to have us breed asexually, like parthenogenic sharks, or to make sex no fun. Take cats, for instance. Listen to them mating. It doesn't sound like they're having a good time. That could have been us.

If one was generous, one would say that the Bible is a rather patchy guide to intimate relationships; non-monogamy was apparently fine, at least for a while for some (mainly those aforementioned powerful OT blokes... *plus ça change*), but then again we're probably best off celibate. But whatever you do, don't enjoy it too much. Surely the best advice in the Bible is to love one's fellow human as oneself and to be compassionate. Everything else, consent included, stems from that.

Islam is a bit more sex positive (actually much more sex positive) than Pauline Christianity and sees sex as an integral part of a relationship between a man and his wife. There is a considerable body of scripture devoted to sex, what is allowed and what is not. Islam, for instance, is explicit about a man's duty to give his wife pleasure rather than focus on self-gratification.

More problematic is that Islam also permits sex with concubines and slaves. This is less well thought of now than it was fourteen hundred years ago.

Nor is marriage restricted to one man and one woman.

> "If you fear that you shall not be able to deal justly with the orphans, marry women of your choice, two or three or four; but if you fear that you shall not be able to deal justly (with them), then only one, or (a captive) that your right hands possess, that will be more suitable, to prevent you from doing injustice."[28]

---

28 Qur'an, Sura 4 (An-Nisa), Ayah 3

Again, men get to be non-monogamous, while women don't. Islam does, however, place strict conditions on taking more than one wife, though in practice these are often overlooked. Men are supposed to take multiple wives only if they can treat them justly (and equally), and then primarily for their protection. Far too often it doesn't play out like that.

Shia Islam also recognises *nikah mut'ah*, a temporary or 'pleasure' marriage that has been criticised as a means of legitimising prostitution but is also used to enable 'halal dating', mainly in Iran. It's basically an Elvis-free Las-Vegas-style marriage and divorce for people wanting to shag. Make of that what you will.

Buddhism's view of sex has evolved over time. In ancient texts you can find a condemnatory attitude towards romantic and sexual relationships, such as the Buddha scolding the monk Sudinna for having returned to his wife to have sex.[29] However with time this morphed into an emphasis on the philosophy of nonattachment, with the result that more modern forms of Buddhism are generally less proscriptive about love, marriage and sexuality. It generally advocates the middle way: nothing in excess. It also promotes unconditional love, and some interpretations of Buddhism that embrace Tantra treat the mastering of one's sexual energy as essential for enlightenment. None of these are antithetical to non-monogamy. Buddhism's main injunction is to avoid anything that produces cravings or attachments. Over-indulgence in sex comes under such a heading.

The Buddhist precept of *mudita*, taking happiness in another's happiness is sometimes cited by the polyamorous community as a precursor of *compersion:* happiness for your lover's happiness with another lover. That's a real thing, if pretty foreign to mainstream culture, and some describe it as life-changingly powerful when successfully cultivated.

Hinduism's pantheon of gods includes those that are non-monogamous. Shiva has countless wives. Historically the ruling class of princely states that made up India was non-monogamous, and Hindu temples sometimes celebrate human sexuality through erotic statuary. Some smaller western religions such as Unitarianism and Neo-Paganism also make room for non-monogamy; indeed paganism seems to positively embrace it.

On surveying polyamorous people in the US for her 2015 book *The Polyamorists Next Door*, writer and researcher Dr Elisabeth Sheff found that most weren't religious[30]. Those who were religious or spiritual followed, in descending order of popularity,

29 'The Buddhist monk who became an apostle for sexual freedom' Donald S. Lopez Jr, *Aeon,* 3 Sep 2018. https://aeon.co/ideas/the-buddhist-monk-who-became-an-apostle-for-sexual-freedom
30 Elisabeth Sheff: *The Polyamorists Next Door: Inside Multiple-Partner Relationships and Families,* Lanham, Maryland, US: Rowman & Littlefield (2015) ISBN-13:9781442253100

"paganism, Unitarian Universalism, Judaism, Buddhism, and some form of sacred sexuality."

IF PEOPLE AREN'T appealing to God often as not they're citing nature. Sometimes we're told, implicitly or explicitly, that monogamy is *the* 'natural state', which is rather hard to take at face value given animals. But then, if more children get their ideas about nature from biblical picture books depicting animals going two-by-two into The Ark than from zoology books then they'll probably grow up with ideas about nature that are divorced from reality. We were told much the same thing about heterosexuality, though homosexual behaviour has already been documented in around 1,000 animal species. Yet being non-monogamous or queer are cast as unnatural or, worse, 'crimes against nature'. Promoters of the monogamous ideal set about showing us umpteen glowing examples of creatures that maintain lifelong exclusive relationships. The problem with this is that the facts generally don't support those assertions quite as neatly as it's generally suggested.

First, we should distinguish between two different terms applied to creatures in nature: *sexual* monogamy, or genetic monogamy as it's sometimes called, and *social* monogamy.

Social monogamy, also referred to as pair bonding, is an attachment relation-ship. "In socially monogamous species, the adult males do something really different than they do in other species," says Karen Bales, professor of psychology at UC Davis and also core scientist at the UC Davis California National Primate Research Center. She's made a study of the behaviour of titi monkeys, forest dwelling primates found in South America. She contrasts their pairing behaviour with that of the bonobo, often considered (along with the chimpanzee) to be humans' closest relative.

> If you compare an adult male titi monkey to an adult male Bonobo, for instance, you'll find that the male titi forms a very close selective relationship with his pair mate. But you don't see male Bonobos forming those kinds of relationships. Likewise male rhesus monkeys don't, nor male rats. That's not to say that they [bonobos, rhesus monkeys, and rats] don't interact socially [with their mates], but they don't form that kind of selective [pairing]. And by selective I just mean that it matters who it is, this one individual.

Pair bonding clearly seems to have had evolutionary advantages for many species. In humans it's often linked to care of offspring because human children are so vulner-able for so long. This doesn't have an immediate corollary with titi monkeys however. Human males exhibit stress signals when their young children become separated from them; titis don't. The bond is with the mate, though there may be benefits from this that flow to offspring indirectly.

More to the point, pair bonding and *sexual* monogamy are very different things. 'I don't think that there's really any species,' Prof. Bales says, 'including the ones that we call monogamous, in which all individuals display sexual exclusivity.' Even famously sexually 'monogamous' creatures like swans aren't the paragons of fidelity they've been held up to be.[31] Since the advent of DNA testing, it has become clear that eggs in the nests of socially monogamous birds very often carry genes from other dalliances. Such genetic outbreeding is a healthy thing to keep any small, local population from becoming inbred.

Prairie voles come up frequently in discussions of animal monogamy. They are a focus of research by the former executive director of the Kinsey Institute, Sue Carter. Her research broke new ground in the study of pair bonding and social monogamy. Her subjects were small, cute, and furry, and tend to pair-bond for life. While it has occasionally been known for prairie voles to mate again if their partner dies, that's primarily been observed under lab conditions where the opportunity has been provided. However, as professor Bales says,

> "[as] socially monogamous rodents, they become very aggressive when they form a pair bond both towards animals of their own sex, but also towards those of the opposite sex. But having said that, Sue used to tell me that she's seen female prairie voles, in a partner preference test, which is a test where they're choosing to spend time with their partner versus a stranger, go over and have sex with a stranger while they're essentially making all these aggressive noises at him."

Haven't we all just been there...?

In short, no species in nature has been yet been discovered to be fully sexually/genetically monogamous.

What about humans? Well, what about us? The evidence tends to point towards monogamy being a social construct, perhaps a relatively recent one in our species' roughly 300,000-year history, much of which predated the advent of TV documentary crews.

Prof. David Barash is an evolutionary biologist, an emeritus professor of psychology at the University of Washington in the United States, and an early contributor

---

31 'Secret Sex Lives Of Swans Under Scrutiny In New Study', University Of Melbourne press release, *ScienceDaily* 8 June 2006. www.sciencedaily.com/releases/2006/06/060607170545.htm

to the field of sociobiology. He's written, co-authored, or edited dozens of books on many subjects including sexual behaviour in humans and animals. As he puts it:

> If you want to go interior in terms of the human mind, it helps to go anterior, which is to say, look at our ancestry, look at our own evolutionary antecedents.

Professor Barash's view is that humans are 'mildly harem forming'. We'll examine that suggestion in a moment. However his simple observation is that infidelity and other forms of non-monogamy have been a staple of human behaviour throughout recorded history and beyond. The genetic evidence tells its own story.

> If you were an observer from Mars looking at the human species, you would have no doubts that we are not, biologically speaking, monogamous. That's not saying we're not capable, or even that monogamy isn't a good thing, but that if you simply look at our biology, there's no question that monogamy is an imposed thing.

Barash and his partner, the psychiatrist Judith Lipton, both subscribe to the idea that women will tend to cluster around men who are more physically/ socially/ politically powerful (like King Solomon perhaps): those with access to more resources and, possibly, a greater ability to provide protection; hence the hypothesis that humans form harems. Monogamy, Barash suggests, arose in reaction to this, as a social compromise or contract.

> There are going to be a lot of men in such a system who are left out, [modern day]'incels' for instance. And so monogamy really is a democratising device whereby men are provided the opportunity to have a mate, [men who] would otherwise likely be angry, excluded horny bachelors.

Oddly this echoes, if distantly, the demand of some who identify as incels (a contraction of 'involuntary celibates') that women be 'redistributed'. Barash thinks it's possible this idea shaped humankind's earlier history.

> When you have a bunch of men who are horny and excluded, society is going to be very disrupted and disruptive, whereas in a monogamous society where everybody has at least the high probability of finding a mate, things are going to

be a lot calmer. And so it's a real possibility that monogamy was an arrangement whereby the more powerful men agreed to essentially withhold some of their harem-forming inclinations, in return for social peace.

This view is far from unchallenged. A study of contemporary hunter-gatherer tribes by anthropologists at University College, London, found that they exhibit considerable gender equality. Far from humanity in its pre-agricultural state being about who was the biggest and baddest, it was more about cooperation. As the leader of the study, anthropologist Vincent Dyble, told *The Guardian* newspaper;

> There is still this wider perception that hunter-gatherers are more macho or male-dominated. We'd argue it was only with the emergence of agriculture, when people could start to accumulate resources, that inequality emerged.[32]

Interestingly, the groups studied were ostensibly monogamous, but the idea of that being because of a social contract to counter resource-hoarding harem-forming males is clearly open to question.

I asked Lipton, a distinguished fellow of the American Psychiatric Association, her opinion on what role biology actually plays in these questions. Her answer was pretty straightforward.

> Biology will act so as to maximise the inclusive fitness of the individual who has the genes for that particular behaviour or trait. So, biology is always about making babies. Maximising inclusive fitness means making as many surviving and reproducing offspring as you can. And all natural selection does is this: every single biological thing you can think ultimately occurs because our ancestors who had that trait made more babies than ancestors who didn't have that trait.

So what's worked in the past is reflected in what we are today. Strategies that didn't produce more babies that inherited and passed on those strategies don't show up much or at all in our current behaviour. Those that did, do.

Obviously, as they say with financial investments, past performance is no guarantee of future success. Yesterday it was the Neanderthals, tomorrow it could be

---

32 'Early men and women were equal, say scientists', *The Guardian*, 14 May 2015. https://www.theguardian.com/science/2015/may/14/early-men-women-equal-scientists

us. But the genetic evidence suggests that sexual non-monogamy has been a feature of human existence pretty much forever, that it has benefited the species, and that it has co-existed with some degree of sexual exclusivity all that time

Social monogamy is slightly more complex. There is a clear survival advantage to infants having more than one caregiver. This is often reduced to an argument that women will use strategies to ensure that a man sticks around—not necessarily the biological father(s) but a man whose active participation increases the chances of a child's survival.

But why just one? As David Barash observes; "The more adults taking care of it, the greater the advantage to the baby."

One could reference the saying "It takes a village to raise a child"[33] at this point and argue that survival increases as the resources committed to a child's survival increase, and that elements for success in life improve as the number of interactions with different adults increases. The human experience teaches us that isolation is deadly to humans, far more in ancient times than now. It's been argued that shame evolved to protect us from being expelled from social groupings, which in prehistoric times was akin to a death sentence. So reducing social and sexual mating strategies to just ensuring that the father sticks around perhaps doesn't do justice to the complexity of the human social experience.

So why not a polyamorous family? One could argue that children with two fathers and three mothers would do even better than one raised by a dyad, or that a child with both a mum and dad but no community might fare worse than a child with a single parent in a close-knit tribe.

Purely anecdotally, I used to live as part of a close-knit community on the Oxford Canal in Oxford. The children were treated as small adults and, to an extent, the shared responsibility of their neighbours. Even from a young age they were very comfortable popping in and out of nearby boats and seemed to really benefit from having a large group of adults to interact with.

All I would argue is that perhaps we should conclude that there is no one right way, that nature generally pursues multiple strategies, in this case both monogamy and non-monogamy, both sexual and social. As Dr Meg-John Barker cautions:

> I'm never sure that any arguments to nature and evolution are that helpful. There are books that try to make the opposite claim, that non-monogamy is actually the more natural, normal way to do things, and I'm never too convinced about that either. Rather, relationship diversity seems to be the best approach. We're asking

---

33   This aphorism is often framed as an African proverb though it appears to be more a fusion of sentiments expressed in various African cultures than an actual proverb.

the wrong kind of questions. We're asking what's normal and what's natural. It's far better to ask questions like, Is it consensual? Does it enrich the lives of those involved? Is it ethical? That kind of thing.

If modern consensual non-monogamy does anything, it's to acknowledge a persistent and widespread human trait and to try to create a framework in which it can happen in an honest, open and consensual setting, rather than consigning it to a world of shadow and deceit. It takes the notion of right and wrong away from the 'what' and locates it in the 'how'.

Which 'what' and 'how' you subscribe to is very much a matter of personal choice. The next sections will look at the what and how of those who wish to venture beyond monogamy while asking what the rest of us might borrow from that world.

CHAPTER TEN

Dealing With Prejudice

As I WRITE this I've just returned from sitting in an Indian Muslim cafe on the Changi Road in Singapore listening to two white guys, one possibly Australasian, the other Eastern European, discussing polygamy... no, wait, polyamory. That's right. There's a difference. They worked out that much. But what followed, from two presumably intelligent, educated people, was a stream of misunderstanding and prejudice. The Australasian simultaneously trotted out his own history of casual relationships and, by inference, cheating, with apparent disdain for consensual non-monogamy, wondering why people agreed to let their partner choose their own path while speculating whether he might get to sleep with someone whose husband let them have sex with other people.

It wasn't the worst I've heard. But it was depressingly predictable. For many people there's a plain cognitive dissonance between their own behaviour and desires, which they readily admit to, and a casual, negative judgement of others' behaviour even if it is, by some measures, more honest, decent and principled.

In our avowedly monogamous culture, consensual non-monogamy, more than bog-standard cheating, represents difference, change and possible threat. And if you're consensually non-monogamous that possible threat is you. You bring change and new ideas. You could corrupt others, mentally and physically. As we saw earlier from Amy Moors' research, you can be a perfectly respectable and upright individual, couple or whatever in every other respect, but tell people you're non-monogamous and their opinion of you plummets. In going down the path of non-monogamy it's easy to feel you have to be otherwise blameless because 'anything you do say [or do] will be taken down and may be given in evidence' against you.

DK Green is a fifty-something trans man who lives in the English East Midlands and works as a counsellor, psychotherapist, celebrant and activist:

> I had to be so sure that my choices were not going to harm anyone, that I could stand up in a court of law and defend myself. Because we were very open and very public long before poly was a word in society, and generally used at all. I had to explain to schools and to doctors and to all those other busybodies what it meant; that my children had more than two parents. So I had to be absolutely unshakable because I had, at one point, a mean neighbour shop us to social services.

Of course it shouldn't be this way and sometimes it isn't. But you never know when it could be.

> I have had a full investigation into my parenting and ended up with a beautiful letter of apology from social services saying it was obviously a malicious call. '...and although your family is unusual to us, your children are obviously well adjusted and you're doing a fine parenting job.' So that was really cool. I've got a letter, I can frame it and put it on the walls.

This will be all too familiar to people of colour living in predominantly white western societies, to queer people, to disabled people, to people with minority beliefs, to the young, and to the old.

Heck, it's even hard to undertake academic research into the subject without coming up against a wall of prejudice, as Dr. Amy Moors and her colleagues discovered.

> Terri Conley and Jes Matsick, Ali Zigler and I, we did a lot of this research circa 2009 to 2014 together, and we first noticed that there was stigma. One of our first papers was that experimental study where we were looking at the ways in which people were evaluating consensual non-monogamy. And trying to get it published was just incredibly difficult. And it was just a very straightforward paper. We thought our research was rigorous. There were multiple different studies using different stimuli.

> When researchers try to get their research published, they submit it to a journal and the editor sends it out to anywhere from two to five [peers] to review and give comments. They decide, 'Does this belong in that body of academic literature or not?' 'Does this get published?' And so we would get reviews back that were often quite odd. Like; 'this topic seems very niche' or 'I encourage the researchers to look at x', or 'to think about their research program' or really harping on 'well, I'm not

sure how many people even study this' or 'I think the authors might have been conflating infidelity with consensual non-monogamy,' like telling us that the thing we'd been researching might not actually be the things we been researching.

Just pursuing an academic interest in the topic was enough for Moors to be targeted by an array of people who, possessed of a penis and a PhD, decided that her research topic made her fair game.

> I went to a conference once to present on my research. I was very young. I was in my mid-twenties. And for some reason the idea of attachment and consensual non-monogamy, I had a bunch of people, particularly men, particularly faculty members, coming up to talk to me and borderline if not explicitly hitting on me.

Being out as a public or semi-public figure can invite a degree of opprobrium that is enough to make many, if not most, non-monogamous people want to stay well and truly closeted. The philosopher Carrie Jenkins has written books and articles about the foundations on which we are able to build knowledge, including *Grounding Concepts: An Empirical Basis for Arithmetical Knowledge* and *Concepts, Experience and Modal Knowledge.* But in writing *What Love Is and What It Could Be,* an exploration of relationships beyond the traditional social constrains and in coming out, she's attracted not just comment but considerable abuse.

> You get all the very obvious kind of surface scum, which are the misogynistic trolls and racist trolls as well, because I have non-white partners, and all kinds of really disgusting stuff. Lots of slut-shaming; all of the words for non-monogamous women, I get called them. In pretty much any kind of public-facing forum that's happened.

> In my professional life as a philosopher it's harder to see exactly how things are patterning out because people aren't going to come up to me and just say that stuff. A lot of philosophers have been quite accepting, and I think it's actually been possible for me partly because philosophers like to have conversations and consider the pros and cons and really come to a conclusion. It's been more possible to have that conversation than it might have been in other disciplines or other walks of life. Especially because there are some really handy precedents that I can call upon, like Bertrand Russell argued for non-monogamous marriages.

Clearly it helps to have Bertrand Russell on your side in a scrap. A number of people I interviewed working in the professions actively fear being disbarred or prevented from practicing if their personal lives were to become public knowledge.

It's hard to overstate the degree to which the prejudice goes hand in hand with what are often referred to as the 'culture wars'. One comment on a YouTube interview with Jenkins, quoted by *The Cut* and apparently since removed, read: "This femme-pig is the spectral opposite of Trump; a far far left-wing freak that desires to completely overthrow western Christian Civilization."[34] And to contemplate how close Carrie Jenkins came to doing that single-handedly, makes you think, dun it?

It's hardly just non-monogamous people who face this degree of sex-based prejudice. In early 2020 Tilli Buchanan had to enter a plea deal with a court in the US state of Utah to avoid being added to a sex offenders register after removing her top at home in the presence of her step-children. If you can be dragged before a court for something so anodyne then what are the chances, as DK Green found, that you might face having your children taken away for your daring to have more than one relationship?

For many, prejudice is simply best avoided. Living in Indonesia, Penny is only out to people she trusts.

> I'm lucky that in my family, at least my sisters, they know about it and they understand [I'm] still happy and still the same; not you know, not really seeing me as a different person. So, I think as long as I'm in the good circle of friends, I'm in a good environment that allows me to be accepted for what we are and who I am.

> I think even though I live in a conservative society, my friends and family is quite supportive. And even though some of other people, if they know about it or finds out, why now they will talk about [me and I'll] be frowned upon. And I don't really care, as long as it doesn't affect my working capability, it doesn't affect my career, it doesn't affect my family, then I don't really bother, you know. As long as people who are close to me are not affected, then I'm okay.

Liam and Kate are a very engaging couple from Toronto. He's in his fifties, she's in her forties. He runs a company and has a separate creative career, she's an educator and writes. She's bisexual, he's heteroflexible. Together they started writing a blog called The Monogamish Marriage and kept the title when they turned more towards swinging. Neither of them is out. Far from it. As Kate, a teacher, points out, she could be targeted for the way she chooses to live, or even be fired from her job.

---

34 'Maybe Monogamy Isn't the Only Way to Love', Drake Baer, *The Cut*, 26 Mar 2017. https://www.thecut.com/2017/03/science-of-polyamory-open-relationships-and-nonmonogamy.html

Well, it would be pretty disastrous I think for me as a teacher. The two groups that cannot find out are my parents, who are deeply religious, and my colleagues who are deeply judgmental. I think, just on a global scale, people feel like if you're slightly into deviant sexual things, then you're going to be a predator. So, the fact that I'm working with children all of a sudden makes this so much worse, even though I never look at them in any sexualised way. I think some things are changing and, for instance, we're doing a very good job of being open to kids who are LGBTQ in class and we're accommodating the students. But I think we have a different standard for the teachers.

Liam's take on it is different. He feels that his lack of openness is letting people down.

I have very different feelings about this because I feel guilty sometimes. We've discovered this amazing thing and yet we're more or less keeping it secret from people who would profit from knowing about it. So if I think back to gay people, pre-Stonewall and post-Stonewall, who very courageously said 'This is who we are', and it was considered embarrassing but we're going to take the flak. Our society is unambiguously better for the sacrifices those individuals made.

And we're at a much safer level, we're not going to get beat up and killed for our preferences, but we're afraid to share this amazing thing. And I use that comparison to challenge myself and challenge some other people and challenge Kate, frankly! Should we not take a stand?

The mood of the times is hard to read. On the one hand it's possible to start conversations with people in unlikely places, such as a yoga centre in Kuala Lumpur, Malaysia, and find people who know exactly what I'm writing about. The conversation is growing. Some of the prejudices are fading. But as the psychologist, therapist and author Dr. Liz Powell said when I interviewed her in mid-2018, the widening culture wars that have emerged across Europe and North America have created a divide. A big slice of society is becoming more global, more interconnected, more broad-minded, less judgemental. But there's another world out there of people who feel disconnected, left behind and threatened. Globalism and growing inequality are fuelling insecurity and fear which in turn feed populism, and populists like nothing better than an easy target. As Liam says, it all combines to make life difficult for non-monogamous people just as it's making life hard for people of colour, women, queer people and so on.

To some extent the current political climate in the United States is a reflection of people's continued issue with the civil rights movement. I think that perhaps because of the greater religiosity of the United States, perhaps because of any number of other factors including historic prejudice, there is this difficulty the United States has [accepting] those things. There is greater support for folks who are queer than there was years ago; but there are still a huge number of people who are vehemently anti-queer and who argue for the right to deny queers any rights.

And when it comes to trans issues, we have some people who are very publicly trans but there are still bills being put forward in many states that say that trans people can't use bathrooms. I feel like the switches are just much slower for us. There's this perception that the States is this place of understanding and freedom and giving everybody rights and being welcoming to everybody, and I don't think it could be further from the truth in a lot of ways.

That's not most of Europe, yet. But it could be. In some places it's worse, like Hungary, Poland and Russia, whose authoritarian rulers and their followers show little tolerance for difference or diversity. In others, like China, the weight of social expectation is such that many people feel their primary duties are to others—parents, society—rather than to themselves. Individuality and authenticity can feel like indulgences in a society that doesn't value them as highly as, say, filial piety and obedience.

So how you present yourself to the world depends heavily on where you are and who the people are that you move amongst.

Thankfully, for most non-monogamous people, there's no obligation to be out. It's hard to tell by looking at someone that they're non-monogamous in the way that you can tell that someone is black or female or disabled or too young or too old. Even many gay people, particularly those from a generation or two ago, recall having to observe straight people carefully. Being able to pass wasn't something one took for granted.

When it comes to consensual non-monogamy people have wider choices. One of those is who you can hang out with. People have a workplace persona (or a persona for school or university) and one for friends. Similarly, it's understood that circles of friends can be segmented. Some might be receptive or even encouraging. Others might expect you to behave more conventionally. Lots of people have found out the hard way that they've come out to the wrong group.

Vincent's friends in Singapore would rather make light of his being consensually non-monogamous than be seen to be taking an interest:

When you communicate with people on a one-to-one basis, they may want to find out more or they may think 'This is something I want to explore'. But when you are in a group setting there is peer pressure. Right now is just a joke; they never want to be seen as someone who is interested in it.

Charlotte is in her mid-thirties, a graduate who works in the property sector. She's also neuro-atypical and a lesbian. Her solution has been to make sure that she has a tribe of people who get her in all her complexities and who appreciate her for it.

Normal people are very odd to me, I don't understand them. I usually frequent very 'not normal' subcultures and these are sort of easier. Subcultures are easier because they tend to be more defined. And I am NOT normal and I find myself much more comfortable with the other weirdos.

There is no 'one size fits all' solution to dealing with the monogamous world. But there are some useful questions to ask oneself.

- *Might coming out compromise my safety?*
- *How would I cope if I out myself or am outed to people who are not sympathetic, and would there be consequences?*
- *Would I lose friends or family relationships if I came out?*
- *Could coming out lose me my job or my home?*
- *Am I feeling isolated?*
- *Do I have the support I need?*
- *Do I need to have people I can talk with about my experiences?*
- *Do I feel I should stand up for my identity and be seen to do so?*
- *Am I comfortable?*
- *Are there situations in which I'm expected to talk about relationships with people who may not understand the way I live?*
- *How can I find like-minded people?*

One thing one can certainly do is actively seek out other people who are, in one form or another, non-monogamous. There are Meetup groups for discussion, support, and socializing, and 'munches' that tend to be simply social gatherings. Organizers usually aim to create a comfortable environment for everyone and that generally means they specify that these are not pick-up opportunities. Sometimes it's enough to be in the company of people who accept you for who you are.

In the United States where the sheer number and variety of people practicing CNM lends itself to greater diversity, there is generally a good choice of different groups. If you don't feel comfortable in one, try another. Many will advise people to avoid groups dominated by one guru figure in favour of those run more collectively. In other places, even in global cities like London and Singapore, there's generally far less choice.

You'll probably find a distinction between polyamorous people and swingers— sometimes the groups intersect, sometimes they don't. Take your time to figure out which particular social scene feels like a better fit for you.

In the broadest terms, at the time of writing, people who identify as poly skew towards being educated, geeky, left of centre, and more likely to embrace queer and alternative cultures than the general population. Swingers probably better reflect the population as a whole: regular people with familiar lives and mainstream attitudes except when it comes to sex. Many, if not most, are very discreet about the parties they go to.

Having found people with whom you can be authentic, and who form a supportive network that understands what you're dealing with, it may be easier to decide who else to tell: family, friends, colleagues.

KamalaDevi McClure, star of the Showtime network's 2012-13 reality series *Polyamory: Married and Dating*, was asked at a retreat for her most important piece of advice for making a success of polyamory. 'You need a tribe,' was her immediate reply. *'You need community.'*

That sense of community, of interconnection, of being part of something bigger than oneself, bigger than a modern, western, nuclear family, was something that many of the people I interviewed identified as an important if unanticipated benefit of consensual non-monogamy. If it is a path you choose, the tribe that you gather around you will doubtless play a key role in the experience.

CHAPTER ELEVEN

Opening Up A Relationship

ONE OF THE most common scenarios in consensual non-monogamy is a couple deciding to open their relationship. Why common? Because the couple is the default configuration in our society and because of all the reasons mentioned earlier—people feel the need to grow, they and their partner's sexual needs have diverged, they realise they're still attracted to other people, they yearn for emotional and/or sexual novelty, they want to explore other people's worlds or a sexual kink or orientation that can't be expressed in their relationship, or they fall in love with someone new. People often reach a point at which they find themselves rattling the bars of their monogamous cage.

Once the choices were stark: suffer, cheat, or split. Yes, there have always been people who've had unconventional arrangements, but they've barely been on the radar of their contemporaries. If you were part of the Bloomsbury set in the 1920s you might have been aware of other options, but if you'd been living in a quiet cul-de-sac in Purley or Peoria or Puchong you'd be forgiven for not thinking 'Why don't we form a triad or a nice cosy poly family?'

But you're here, reading this. Perhaps that has something to do with the vastly increased public awareness about consensually non-monogamous options. That's at least partly due to an increasingly vocal poly/CNM community and a more engaged media. People have discovered that other choices exist, and work, at least for some.

This is not to discount the value of maintaining a monogamous relationship while trying to address any stresses. If monogamy is your choice and you're willing to work at addressing your or your partner's desire(s) for novelty, growth, and freedom within a monogamous framework, it's clearly possible to make it work. Nor is opening up a cure-all for monogamous relationships under stress. As Eunice, a professional in her thirties living in London, points out:

> You've been with [someone] for 20 years and you want to open up that relationship. The first thing you need to do is make sure that relationship is stable, because 'relationship broken, add more people' is sort of an in-joke. But people do it, in the same way that they do 'relationship broken, add a baby' and that does not work. Relationship broken add more partners is a bad approach because you briefly duct-tape over the cracks and then sooner or later, the underlying issues seep out.

I'm going to maintain a sceptical tone throughout this book: sceptical about monogamy and sceptical about the alternatives because sceptical is what you should be too. Just as fools rush into monogamous relationships, they also rush into non-monogamous ones. The feelings we experience when we meet someone new and feel very attracted to them have evolved to make us (forgive me, I say this because like many people I've been there) temporarily stupid—because evolution is shaped by individuals who reproduce even more than those who survive. None of the relationship options we have are perfect and few are simple, except perhaps simply bonding together for survival and just being grateful for being alive. Humanity has gone a long way on that. But if it's self-actualisation through personal relationships you're after, steel yourself.

So, first of all, what can go wrong with opening an existing relationship?

Let's start with the bleedin' obvious and proceed from there.

As Eunice explains, often one person in a couple wants to open the relationship and the other doesn't.

> No two people feel the urge to do a particular thing with exactly the same amount of enthusiasm. Even if both are enthusiastic, one is just a touch more enthusiastic or maybe one is just a touch more determined or maybe one is a touch more likely to find the sorts of new partners they're interested in than the other. And this is not to say that it's going to be a major issue with every couple. But it happens.

> It particularly has a potential to be a problem if one partner is opening up almost on sufferance in order to keep the other partner, which does occasionally happen. I will go polyamorous because if I don't...

...my partner may leave me.

It comes back to consent. If both partners do not wholeheartedly and enthusiastically consent to opening up you have a problem. Either the person who is less into the idea goes along with it to keep their relationship alive, or they decline to do so. In which case the other partner either accepts remaining (possibly unhappily) within a monogamous setup, or they put the idea to one side in the hope of a better moment or change of heart, or they end the relationship.

Joreth Innkeeper is a poly activist from Florida and has seen this sort of dynamic play out numerous times with similar results.

> It's usually a train wreck. In my experience what then happens is the person who is not so keen on [opening up] tries any number of tactics from the overt to the sub-conscious to sabotage the attempts, and pretty much everybody gets hurt that way.

Franklin Veaux, who co-authored *More Than Two*, one of the most widely read books about consensual non-monogamy, agrees strongly[35].

> Oh man! I've seen this happen so many times. Usually we grow up steeped in this culture that says 'There's one right way to have a relationship and that is monog-amy'. So as soon as somebody says, 'Well, we've been together for however many years but I would like to be polyamorous now', that person is wrong.

> And it becomes very easy for the person who wants the traditional relationship to blame them, to shame them, to enlist the help of their friends and say 'Look at this terrible thing my partner is doing to me'. And so, you start off with this framework of shame and blame, a good guy and a bad guy. And even when that doesn't hap-pen, you've got an inbuilt tension within the relationship because the two people want two fundamentally incompatible things.

> It's not like you can meet halfway; you can't have a relationship that is simultane-ously open and closed. Either it's going to become open, in which case one partner will likely be unhappy, or it's going to remain monogamous, and the other partner will be unhappy.

> I've seen people hold it together for a few years, but I don't know that I have ever seen any relationship that went polyamorous because [only] one person wanted it manage to last longer than a few years. You will get situations where people will try to compromise. So, they will be non-monogamous but they'll place fences around the relationship—for instance a rule that you can shag other people but you can't

---

35   Since I interviewed Franklin Veaux, allegations of emotional abuse have been made against him. He denies the allegations.

fall in love. If you could pass rules on how someone feels, that might be nice, but it doesn't quite work that way.

So, I would say that usually such a relationship is doomed. Compatibility in relationships matters. People have this idea that love conquers all and love is the answer, and it's bullshit. *Compatibility* matters, and when people grow and change in ways that make them incompatible sometimes the relationship ends, and it doesn't mean that anybody is a bad guy.

And the thing that is really kind of fucked up, is that you will inevitably get, when the relationship ends, a tremendous amount of blame for the person who wanted non-monogamy. Sometimes it's okay to just acknowledge 'We really loved each other, we were great for each other for however many years we were together. We want fundamentally and irreconcilably different things now.' It is heartbreaking, but it happens. And the ability to grapple with that directly and say 'Look, we don't want the same things anymore,' is part of being a mature human being.

The author Anita Cassidy is in her early forties, lives in London, and runs a website supporting alternative relationships. She found herself in exactly this position. A few years earlier she reached a point in her life where she wanted to explore non-monogamy and her then-husband didn't.

Basically 'Sam' and I agreed in our eighth year to open the marriage up to my dating, essentially. It was something that I think he felt at the time would meet some of my different sexual needs. I'm bisexual as well, so, certainly I was dating women that year and still am now. We spent a year and a half basically with my dating and him not really wanting to, which is absolutely fine, but the further I explored the path of openness and polyamory, the more I read, the more I learned about myself, the more it became clear that his and my relationship, whilst it was a very functional one as co-parents, really didn't work on a romantic and sexual level anymore.

And we agreed to separate in September 2017 and we are in the process this year, 2018, of getting divorced, and very amicably most of the time. We remain friends and great co-parents. I think what I learned is that you can't ever really control the consequences of choices you make. I chose to open things up and chose to make changes not realising quite the size and the scale of what I was opening myself up to, the degree to which everything about myself and my world would change and transform from that one moment. And I guess in terms of advice—we made so many mistakes and I'm still making mistakes now—what I say to people when they're talking about opening an existing relationship and just exploring any kind of alternative framework is, 'Take your time, take it slow, take it steady and take care of each other's feelings.'

I was very thoughtless at times, I was so keen to explore something that I was super excited about. But I trampled over 'Sam's' feelings on a daily basis, I would say for a long time, and I'm not proud of that. I think getting support is helpful as well. I would have gone about it very differently if I'd had a professional to talk to. I would definitely recommend seeking out the likes of that through something like *Pink Therapy* or an open-relationship or poly-friendly therapist or support person to help navigate those changes together.

Joreth Innkeeper argues that in those circumstances there is a tendency for the couple (though this could apply to a relationship with more than two people in it) to put their existing relationship first and defend it against external threats.

It comes down to the fact that everyone has subsumed their identity into the relationship. The relationship becomes its own entity which needs to be fed and nurtured, often at the expense of the people who are in it. So, what these people tend to do is do whatever it takes to keep the relationship from ending at the expense of everybody else's own wants, desires, needs and even their own existence. So, the goal there seems to be just keeping the relationship intact.

That often makes things very hard for an outside person who finds themselves in a relationship with one or both members of a troubled couple (something we'll come back to later). All too often they're not having two relationships with two autonomous individuals. They're having a relationship (at least in part) with a two-headed, four-armed quadruped called SamandDimphna or TrevandDave or whatever, and it's hard for that to be a relationship of three equals. Joreth thinks that dynamic is hard to break down without first deconstructing the original relationship.

In my observation, they have already given up their bodily autonomy and their emotional autonomy and they have merged into one unit. And so, their forays into non-monogamy tend to act as if they are one unit, which means that they can't have ethical relationships because they're not respecting anybody's autonomy including their own.

So, my recommendation is that people don't 'open up', because [that makes] people tend to think that their relationship is its own entity and all they have to do is expand it to include a third person. And then it is still a single entity comprised of three people, and that dismisses the agency of everybody involved. So, I recommend that people [in a couple] deconstruct and then reconstruct their relationship as one made of individual people who are relating to each other. And then go out and have individual relationships with individual people.

If you're part of a couple, that may make you blanch. It's hardly unusual that the longer a dyad—a couple—has been an entity the more it takes on a life and identity of its own. The two people are already bumping up against the things that led them to want to open their relationship, and now they're being told they have to break it apart and start again with another person involved? Of course they may feel apprehensive. Just as they're making this foray into uncharted territory, they're being asked to take apart the source of comfort and security that was supposed to underpin this adventure.

However, even if unlacing an existing relationship in order to remake it seems like a big undertaking, it's still a useful thought experiment. Just think about all the things you do as a couple that give your relationship its identity. Perhaps you have pizza night once a month, or you go together to each new superhero movie as it comes out. Relationships are often built around these things. But as well as being small rituals that lend form and strength to a relationship, they can also exclude.

So, do you keep your traditions to the two of you, invite your third in, or invent new ones? What if they hate pizza and superheroes? Or suppose dates clash with pizza night or one of you wants to see a Marvel movie with a new squeeze?

These ostensibly trivial problems point to rather more serious ones. If you already live with one partner, what will be the status of a new partner (or partners) in your home? Are they your guest(s) at dinner, or are they part of the family and expected to contribute groceries and help cook? Do they treat it as their home too? Do they contribute to the mortgage expecting to gain equity in the house, or do they pay rent instead? Who gets the best bedroom? Who can bring guests back?

There is no right way that suits everyone, but this is intended as a taster for some of the practical issues that might get in the way of a romantic adventure. If you're single it may matter less who pays for dinner, but if you're consensually non-monogamous and your cohabiting primary partner sees their other lover(s) only once in a blue moon while yours is around two or three nights a week, clearing out the fridge, you can probably see the potential for resentment. Once again, you see why so many consensually non-monogamous people put so much emphasis on open, honest and kind communication.

Eunice found CNM having consciously stayed single for a year after a breakup, figuring out what she wanted. She very quickly found herself in a number of relationships, three of which lasted the next ten years. With the benefit of hindsight she advises being very clear about what one wants.

> There's not one single checklist that works for everybody, but [there are] things that pretty much everybody needs to have considered before going into this type of change. Because it is a big change. If you are opening up your relationship and it's not in some way a little bit scary and a big change, then you're not really opening up your relationship.

> Things like thinking about what a really ethical relationship looks like. What does that mean, and especially what does that mean to you? How would you show this? How would your actions show that you are gaining the consent of everybody around you?

> How can you make sure that you are not treating your current partner, your future partners, their future partners in ways that will disempower them? Another thing you need to consider is what is it you're really looking for? What would be the minimum, at least, that you need in a relationship to be happy and fulfilled?

Eunice has a really good, if not exhaustive, list of questions.

> Some people think, 'What am I not currently getting?' and again, I would like to say that there are very few poly-specific issues. Even if you're monogamous, you can think, 'Oh, I'm not getting to do x. My partner doesn't share this interest. I will just go out and have friends who do this.'

> I don't necessarily suggest looking for a new partner with a checklist of 'You must do this, you must be this, you must have this'. People are not there just to fulfil your needs. I like to think of it as a more holistic, 'What do I need from my relationships?' Because every partner that you will have will mesh with you in slightly different ways. They will fulfil slightly different needs whilst you're fulfilling slightly different of their needs to any other partner they have.

> So it's good to think, 'What are my deal makers in a relationship?' Everyone has things that they require in order to be happy and fulfilled and satisfied. If you

didn't, that would be very unhealthy. It isn't saying that the only types of relationships are these big, romantic and sexually intimate ones where you see each other every day and you talk every day. But if you're the sort of person that needs y in a relationship, that needs to be something that comes out pretty quickly, if you're talking to a new person.

Also, when you are checking in with your current partner, which you should be doing on a regular basis anyway, if this revelation about exactly what you need in your relationship comes out, this needs to be a topic of conversation.

Shelly and her husband also took their time. They got together around the turn of the millennium and, for the first eight years or so, had a fairly standard monogamous relationship. Then they started reading about non-monogamy together and then, over the course of three years, discussed what opening up their relationship might mean, to the point of writing a new set of vows to complement the ones they made when they got married.

Others dive in having found a degree of mutuality from the outset. Philadelphia-based Kevin Patterson is author of the superlative *Love's Not Color Blind* and co-author of the *For Hire* series of SF novels. For him and his wife, the issue came up early in their relationship and it turned out that they were very much on the same page.

It was sort of a joke. My then-girlfriend, now-wife, and I had only been dating for a few months and we were going on a road trip with friends to party in Toronto. I made a joke that something wild might happen between me, my wife and a friend of hers. I didn't really specify what I meant, but my wife took it a little bit more seriously than I did. So when the opportunity happened for the three of us to hook up we all went for it. We spent the whole trip back trying to figure out whether or not exclusivity was important to us and it just sort of wasn't. After that we were just off the path and we stayed there.

Sometimes things working out is more luck than judgement. Kevin and his wife were at a stage of their relationship when it could flex and adapt. Perhaps it was intuition that told them it would work, but their relationship has certainly remained strong.

Vincent and Mia were, perhaps, even more gung ho.

Mia: At the start we didn't really go in depth into what we wanted to do. We just jumped straight into it and off we went on our adventures. And we came back and reconnected, and that's where we started finding out that there were a lot of things that we were uncomfortable with.

Vincent: When we started the whole open thing we didn't establish what the boundaries were. We didn't really know what we were doing, so we had different notions about what having an open relationship meant. At the core of it I think we both realised we both wanted to be emotionally exclusive and work outwards from that. Still kind of in the dark, but as time goes on you have a clearer picture of where the boundaries are.

For Seb, a forty-something international corporate lawyer originally from Johannesburg, opening his relationship was the unexpected consequence of a drunken evening. It was luck, rather than judgement, that non-monogamy suited both him and his wife.

It happened accidentally with us, although we had discussed it in the abstract before. We had a very unexpected threesome, very definitely my first—I had a conservative sexual upbringing in South Africa—and after that, when I realised that it wasn't going to spell the end of the relationship, we had the conversation about polyamory ex post facto. But the lessons that I'd want to share would definitely apply if you're having a more sensible conversation in advance. And that is to start with as much honesty as you possibly can, because you're going to need that in the open relationship going forward, including as clear an articulation [as you can manage] of your goals and your reasons for wanting to do this, so that your partner fully understands what you want from your side. That can only make the process of opening up the relationship easier. It's much, much better in my own experience to start off communicating absolutely everything. Then it's always possible to dial some of that down at a later stage, if you decide that you're comfortable with and trust the other person on matters of communication.

Ivan and Yana are from Russia but now live in South East Asia. Ivan works in IT, Yana is a barber. Their journey into consensual non-monogamy lies somewhere between that of Shelly and Kevin. It wasn't wholly spontaneous, but it hadn't been deeply discussed. But again, it worked. I sat down with them and asked how they set out on the path to opening up their relationship.

Ivan: So basically the story goes like this; so we are married for a very long time, I think it's eight years this year. I have developed certain urges, and I have talked about this... well I don't talk about sex very often so I hide my embarrassment by making jokes. So basically the milestones of our journey are that [first] we have decided to open our marriage, [then] we, so to say, fucked around, and then, when we have figured out that there is more to it than just having other people in your pants, we looked up polyamory on Wikipedia, learned new words, realised you can love other people too, created accounts on dating sites, looked for other people and with varying degrees of success have found our partners. So I have found Alexandra on tinder, and we have been happily together for three years now. I would say that I am a happy polyamorous person now, where I have two partners in my life and I love them both and I think that has improved my life greatly.

Jonathan: When you first started talking about this, had you already reached the same conclusions?

Yana: it actually happened during breakfast, oatmeal porridge with blueberries, that was our usual breakfast during that time. So, it was just like; "Is it okay if we start seeing other people?" "Yeah I think that's okay, yeah let's do it." "Yeah let's try it." "Okay good. Then I'm off to work." "Yeah sure."(Laughs) Yeah so that's about it.

And I think for Ivan it happened faster than for me because he had someone on his mind and that person was coming over. I was supportive and happy for them. I was looking forward to it and I remember making jokes and asking questions; so guys when are you going to do this? Don't be so shy in front of me. And stuff like that. I think that made them feel super awkward and uncomfortable. But because it was our first experience we made a lot of mistakes, no I wouldn't call them mistakes but there were things that could have been done better. It was a learning process.

Ivan: I would like to add that in my opinion it wasn't as spontaneous as Yana says. Indeed the decision was made over breakfast, but we did have conversations around that topic for a little bit before that. More like a theoretical exercise.

Yana: I don't really remember that though. But I remember the porridge. The porridge of fate.

DO RELATIONSHIPS YOUR WAY

SHELLY AND HER husband and, with time, Ivan and Yana, arrived at some of the best lessons of consensual non-monogamy, lessons that could be usefully applied to all sorts of relationships, not least monogamous ones.

Back in 2013 *Scientific American* published an article suggesting just that. It quoted Bjarne Holmes, a psychologist at Champlain College in the US state of Vermont, saying;

> "People in [non-monogamous] relationships really communicate. They communicate to death. They are potentially doing quite a lot of things that could turn out to be things that if people who are practicing monogamy did more of, their relationships would actually be better off."[36]

And that's why I've subtitled the book as I have; *'How people make polyamory and open relationships work and what we can all learn from them'*. Because, in many ways, in the absence of generally accepted blueprints for how to do non-monogamy well, non-monogamous people are continually creating, debating and refining them. There's much less room for the assumed and the unspoken in consensual non-monogamy because, as we'll see, it has so many different permutations. Two people who think they are on the same page may be assuming different things

If you have expectations that a new partner will want the same as you and you don't bother to check in about it with them, don't blame them for your eventual disappointment. Of course monogamous people want different things in a relationship too, but in monogamy there's a clear, heavily signposted cultural path all the way from first date to full commitment. This well-trodden route is often termed 'the relationship escalator'. You get on at the bottom with a first date, and if you stick with convention, it carries you all the way up through that first kiss, sleeping together, moving in, marriage, mortgage and children to umpteen anniversaries and death (though not necessarily in that order, especially if you're into vampires). People are free to get off the relationship escalator anywhere along the way, but that typically involves a breakup, a painful tumble down the stairs, and then hopping back on at the bottom to start again with someone new.

Non-monogamous people don't have the luxury, or perhaps the constraints, of such a well-worn and widely understood path. They've ventured off-piste.

---

36   'New Sexual Revolution: Polyamory May Be Good For You', Stephanie Pappas, *Scientific American*, 14 Feb 2013.

In one episode of journalist Tim Harford's (excellent) podcast Cautionary Tales, he considers the creative impact of unsettling environments. One example he draws on is of jazz pianist Keith Jarrett's 1975 Cologne concert. Jarrett, a perfectionist, had driven 350 miles from Zurich, was sleep deprived and suffering from back pain, only for the Cologne Opera to present him with a terrible piano; neglected, out of tune, and way too quiet. Jarrett only performed because the 17-year-old promoter begged him to. Harford's hypothesis is that being off-balance, not having a road map, having to deal with adversity and new circumstances forces us to be creative. In the event *The Köln Concert* was only recorded because the engineers had already been hired and paid. It arguably produced Jarrett's greatest recording, and it became the best-selling piano album of all time.

Consensual non-monogamy forces people to think like that; to be creative in adversity. And, in reinventing relationships to accommodate non-monogamy, perhaps these people are helping to reinvent relationships, full stop (or 'period' as people on the desolate shores of North America would have it).

Many monogamous people are still recovering from the idealised portrayal of the 'modern' marriage that became idealised in the 1950s as part of the drive to persuade women who'd broadened their horizons during the war to get back into the home. And oh, that home; suburban and nuclear, all faux-contentment, white goods and mind-numbing domestic drudgery, deadening gender roles and no room to confess to feelings and desires that fell short of that confected ideal.

Well, listen up mono people; it doesn't have to be that way. In the chapters that follow we'll look at different ways of doing things. Some are more compatible with traditional coupledom than others. But the big 'go-tos' of non-monogamy—communication and negotiation and the ability to write the rules of your relationship your way—are absolute gold for anyone.

Ultimately some of the best advice out there is to talk to people who've already walked the road. When Dr. Meg-John Barker talks about 'holding it lightly' (and possibly sniggers at this point...) they mean that by knowing there are options out there, one doesn't cling quite so tightly to a narrow traditional set of possibilities when they're not a good fit.

> Whether you're talking about bisexuality, about kink, about trans and non-binary and about non-monogamy, a lot of the time people have already been wondering about this stuff and it can really liberate somebody to find somebody else who's talking about it openly.

It actually helps to start one thinking about it and maybe moving into doing things differently, because remaining in a straitjacket of monogamous, heterosexual cisgender-ism, that's pretty hard for a lot of people. That doesn't necessarily mean they're going to be bisexual or polyamorous or kinky or trans, but they might start to hold those things a bit more lightly or do things a little bit differently. And so this whole concept of "monogamish", for example, and opening up the space between monogamy and non-monogamy, is something that people are starting to do.

For instance, even if you're monogamous, knowing that the whole 'till death us do part' thing isn't the only way might mean that you can be a bit gentler on yourselves. You might agree with your partner at the outset that, while you won't go looking for other relationships or encounters, it's something that could happen and that your relationship shouldn't stand or fall on whether it does or not.

Lots of us have been socialised to feel that exclusivity should be not just assumed, but a requirement. But to declare and live up to such ideals should be a positive, active choice for both parties if that's what they explicitly agree they want. Knowing that some people do things differently, and do different things successfully, makes it easier, I think, for two people in a more traditional relationship to agree to something that suits *them,* rather than only being able to choose an off-the-peg arrangement.

Kevin Patterson notes that CNM offers people dealing with very human feelings a wider range of responses:

> When you're monogamous, there are sort of expectations on behaviour. If I have feelings for somebody outside of my monogamous relationship, I'm expected to either push that away or to cheat and to lie. If I'm non-monogamous, that's a conversation I have to have as opposed to something I have to let go.

In some monogamous relationships, even 'thoughtcrime' is a violation. There are those for whom 'You looked at her, I saw you!' and 'I know you flirt with that guy at the office,' is a prelude that ends in a coda of smashed crockery. But you'd be amazed how intimate some people in monogamous relationships find being able to be real about being attracted to someone they saw and sharing that with their partner, even though there's an understanding that neither will act on their attractions.

A lot of consensually non-monogamous people, like Penny, a senior media professional from Jakarta, say that it has forced them to engage more deeply with their partner(s):

It's a continuous learning process. It's learning of giving trust or gaining trust, of gaining and giving respect in the much deeper level of each other as a partner, as a partner in life. We've been opening this relationship for almost seven years now, and it's still a process. There's always up and down, but what I can advise helps a lot, is communicate a lot, and if you want to get mad or you want to say something that is on your mind, if you've already having this deeper level of trust and understanding and respect, then it's easy.

That will be a recurring theme throughout this book: the depth of intimacy one can achieve through being honest and vulnerable. Again, this isn't something that needs to be the sole province of the consensually non-monogamous.

So here's a takeaway for the monogamously inclined: Talk about what intimacy means for you both at the point where your relationship starts to feel serious. It's important. The feeling that one can share anything and be accepted for it is powerfully bonding. Ask if there's anything they don't want to hear. If nothing else that will give you an idea of what struggles they might be having with insecurity or anxiety—two things we'll talk more about when we look at jealousy.

CHAPTER TWELVE

First Steps

OH! MY! GOD! We're Actually Doing This Thing! What Do We Do Now?

There are two things that couples often do when opening up their relationships, one very useful (but not always done) and the other potentially fraught (and done rather too often).

The first is that they talk about what their changed relationship will look like. It's an excellent thing to do however you relate.

The other thing they do is address the worry that their relationship may not withstand outside involvements by putting *rules* in place.

We'll look at all of this—communication, negotiation, rules, agreements, boundaries etc.—in much greater detail later in the book. For now though let's have a sneak preview.

Let's assume that you're currently monogamous or you're starting out on a relationship with someone and you're trying to reach a mutual understanding of the parameters. Let's try a few questions. Score each of the following from one to five, with one meaning disagree strongly, five meaning agree strongly, and three being neutral.

- *A long-term emotional connection is important to me*
- *A long-term sexual relationship is important to me*
- *I like novelty in romance*
- *I like sexual novelty*
- *Relationships are more exciting early on*
- *Sex gets boring with time*
- *I need more than one relationship can offer*
- *I want multiple relationships*
- *I can feel trapped or stifled in a traditional monogamous relationship*
- *I like the security that a committed relationship has to offer*

It's useful to compare answers. For some people this can be scary. After all, there's always the possibility that you'll discover that what your love wants isn't what you want.

Some people tell themselves that they prefer not to know. Even if that were possible, you still face a fundamental choice: Do you want emotional and intellectual intimacy with someone you're in a relationship with, or not? Do you want real, mutual trust, or not?

As the British thinker and educator Alain de Botton put it in a wildly popular essay for *The New York Times:*

> We have a bewildering array of problems that emerge when we try to get close to others. We seem normal only to those who don't know us very well. In a wiser, more self-aware society than our own, a standard question on any early dinner date would be: "And how are you crazy?" [37]

We may choose not to know now, but the chances are that we'll find out sooner or later. The longer we leave honest discussions the more we risk investing in a relationship on a mistaken premise, and the more we risk breaking another's, or our own, heart. Honesty is a risk. It invites disillusionment. It invites loss. But it also opens the door to intimacy.

As for rules, agreements and boundaries, I'll repeat the distinction later but I use the terms in the sense that *rules* are what one person or group imposes on another (with corresponding punishments for failure), *agreements* are mutual, consensual and arrived at by negotiation that involves all those affected, while *boundaries* are set unilaterally but relate to oneself—they are borders one places around one's own person or possessions.

There is a common-sense element to setting out expectations and what it means to treat each other with respect and consideration. However, in many cases *rules* (and even some agreements) are an understandable but misguided response to the fears of one or both people involved. Misguided because rules will not keep those fears at bay.

For instance, it's not unusual for couples to specify things like:

- *Neither of us is allowed to spend the whole night away*
- *Dates can only be sexual, not romantic*
- *You can only sleep with any given person once*
- *You can't see anyone else during 'us' time. You have to create time for other people from other parts of your schedule*

---

37   'Why You Will Marry the Wrong Person', Alain de Botton, *The New York Times*, 28 May 2016.

- *Nothing is allowed that takes away from 'us'*
- *If our own sex life suffers, the arrangement is suspended until we fix it*

As you can see, it's possible to come up with a lot of rules that boil down to 'anything that threatens us is forbidden'. This is completely understandable. However, it can be both unrealistic and create a host of additional problems.

Firstly, it's very hard to create hard-and-fast rules for the human heart. You can perhaps constrain actions but you can't make rules that constrain feelings. People fall in love, get obsessed, grow and evolve, discover new aspects of themselves, re-evaluate existing relationships, and so forth. There's also a whole load of chemistry that goes on when we have sex with people, and I'm not talking the 'must be chemistry' requirement that appears in dating profiles. When we have sex, especially when we orgasm, we release lots of oxytocin. As you may know, oxytocin is a peptide hormone and neuropeptide that plays a major role in social and personal bonding. It's part of why we feel connected to people after great sex. All the rules in the world can't be relied upon to keep hundreds of millions of years of evolution at bay. We can intellectualise our relationships until the cows come home but at some point we have to acknowledge that the 'humanimal' side of us has a life of its own.

Secondly, in a healthy relationship, people don't police their partners. That's effectively coercion. Healthy relationships are firmly based on freely given, informed and enthusiastic consent. That means we rely on a partner to abide by an agreement of their own volition.

We'll look in due course at the sorts of agreements that people practicing CNM typically make. They generally get pared down to things like 'use good judgement', 'practice safe sex', 'communicate', 'talk to me early', 'no surprises', 'be kind'. Agreements are the space where we get to ask for the things we feel we need. We'll also look at the boundaries that people set to protect themselves.

Thirdly, rules and agreements that couples decide upon often fail to take account of the feelings of the third (or more) parties involved (not least because the third isn't involved in making them because they haven't met you yet)—and if the third isn't involved in the negotiation then what to the couple is an agreement is, to the third, a set of rules. This issue will come up again when we talk about hierarchical polyamory and 'unicorns'. It's sad to have to say it, but some people have a tendency to treat those outside their dyad as little more than playthings. There are, of course, people who like nothing more than to be treated as a plaything. However, all too often, the 'plaything' aspect of the job description isn't highlighted and people end up feeling short-changed, disregarded, manipulated, or worse.

That said, the point where you are starting to talk about opening up your relationship is a good one to set out your wishes and desires for the relationship as they are right there and then, to establish where you all are now and where you *expect* to be in the future.

What if one party says 'I want to be free to date who I want' while the other says 'I'm not really interested in dating other people, but if one of us should happen to sleep with someone else, I don't want it to wreck our relationship'? Those two things are quite different. If you have different expectations it's worth finding out.

Accept that where you are now may change. Having explored, one of you might wish to go further, the other might want to return to the *status quo ante*.

Bear in mind that part of the rationale behind opening relationships is being open to change and growth and it's both unreasonable and unrealistic to try to bind someone to a permanent contract. In healthy non-monogamous settings, agreements generally hold until they're mutually renegotiated. And negotiation, in many CNM relationships, is a constant because when one no longer feels an existing agreement fits then all need to find a new equilibrium. This may or may not be for you.

Sometimes there are unspoken truths at work in the background: 'I'm no longer in love with you and I want a way out', 'I don't like the idea of being alone. Maybe this is an easier way for me to jump from one relationship to the next.'

To reiterate; adding more people to the mix is not a solution for a relationship that needs work or that has run its course. Nor does using consensual non-monogamy as a Trojan horse for another agenda do anything but risk causing even greater hurt and heartbreak.

And yet, few relationships are ever perfect (nor are many humans), so, by the same token, waiting for everything to be ideal so you can make a change risks meaning that change will never happen.

So, a quick summary:

1. ***Check you're on the same page:*** that you either broadly want the same thing from opening your relationship or, if you want different things, ask whether you're genuinely comfortable with what the other wants.

2. ***Be clear about what sorts of things are unacceptable to you,*** and make sure your partner knows that. If these need to be spelled out in the form of an agreement (written or unwritten), spell it out. Certainly keep notes. Memory is unreliable. Having what you wrote at the time to hand can help. If nothing else it can reduce disagreements later about what was actually said.

3. ***Recognise that any relationship agreement needs ongoing mutual consent.*** That doesn't mean just deciding to ignore an understanding without discussing it, but it does allow that people and circumstances change.

4. Think about the others who may get involved. For instance, if you've agreed 'no falling in love' (and best of luck with that...) this needs to be communicated early to anyone else either of you gets involved with. Behaving in such a way that encourages someone to fall in love with you, only to say later 'Sorry, I promised my partner I wouldn't fall in love with anyone' is just deeply rubbish behaviour.

5. Be compassionate. Assume the best possible motive until you have evidence otherwise. Allow for people being human (or possibly Vulcan in some cases).

6. Don't forget: your connection with one another is unique. No one else can replicate that. The lack of sexual or romantic exclusivity need not make it less special. Try to locate the specialness within your connection, not in the things you do. For instance, the classic 'I don't want you dancing with him/her/them to our song' is probably rather less about concern for the new love's toes than it is insecurity.

CHAPTER THIRTEEN

Coming Out

ALMOST EVERYONE FROM a sexual minority seems to have a coming out story. In many places those stories have changed markedly over the last half century. One hears less of people being disowned for being gay or lesbian and more about declarations of love and acceptance by parents, friends and colleagues. More people are accepting certain queer relationships as the equal of straight partnerships[38]—more so, perhaps, since the trappings of monogamous respectability were made available to same-sex couples.

Obviously queer people still have to contend with severe prejudice in many parts of the world where you can still face persecution or even death for loving someone of the same gender.

Consensually non-monogamous people also have their coming out stories. I'll share some to give you a flavour of their experiences, then I'll look at some of the questions you might want to ask yourself if you're considering whether to come out. I'll also suggest how to start preparing should you decide the time is right.

It's hard to predict how people will react to your coming out, but it is possible to prepare for some of the possibilities.

First, however, let's hear how it went for some of those I interviewed.

The most difficult thing for many is coming out to parents. Dr Liz Powell had to come out to her mother repeatedly.

> All of my coming outs have been somewhat fraught. My mother, I think, does the best she can with what she has, but she has not reacted particularly well to any of the coming outs that I have done. These days, you know, I live my life very publicly.

---

38   The progress made by gay and lesbian people hasn't necessarily been mirrored by that made by bisexuals or asexual people and, despite some superficial changes, in the case of trans people high levels of stigma, discrimination, economic marginalisation and poor mental health remain an issue.

I talk about my sex life on the Internet, I'm completely and fully out all the time and my mother will still tell me she hopes I find the one man for me.

And in fact, like when I came out as bisexual, I had to come out to her three or four, maybe five times. And each time my mom would throw this big fit and scream and threatened to divorce my dad. The final time that it finally, like, stuck with her that I was not going to give up this bisexual thing, she asked me if I had sex with trees or animals because clearly if you have sex with more than one gender, you have sex with literally everything. It's such a slippery slope.

So, that was challenging. And then I came out to my family about my non-monogamy about three years ago and you know, I offered to give them books to read about it or to have conversations. And my mom especially didn't really come around on any of that until just this past November, when I was telling her about the book that I was writing about non-monogamy and she made her displeasure and her disapproval very clear.

She ended up sharing with me that, like, she just doesn't approve of anything that I'm doing with my life, and we were able, out of that, somehow to have a really good conversation about the ways that her disapproval and displeasure is about her sadness that I'll never have the kind of happiness that she had; that she was very happy in her monogamous marriage and she's sad that I won't have that. And my sadness is it feeling like the only way I can live my life is the way that she did, otherwise she's going to think that it's the wrong choice.

And so, we're working on it, we're still working on it. She knows I have two partners and I've mentioned both of their names to her and talked about the things I've been doing with them and she just kind of glosses over it, but you know she eventually comes around. A few years ago, I was marching in the Pride Parade with my genderqueer, assigned-female-at-birth partner, and my mom wished us both a happy Pride! So, it just takes time. It takes time.

Liz's story makes me smile. There's so much in there. As parents we allow ourselves hopes and dreams for our children. Perhaps we imagine them playing cricket for Sussex and England (Google it, American folks, you used to be pretty good at cricket once), or having a hit single, or lecturing at Oxford, or settling down with an opposite-sex partner and breeding us a small mountain of grandchildren.

Most parents don't nurture dreams of their children growing up to be appalling sluts and, worse still for some, sluts with a liking for the wrong shade of skin or the wrong genitalia. But hey. It's all part of learning to let our children be their own people, and allowing those we love to change and to grow into their true selves. Seeing someone as they are, rather than how we want them to be, is one of the greatest gifts we can give them.

Liz lives in California, and in California (I have this on excellent authority) you can be prosecuted for being insufficiently kinky. Singapore on the other hand is not what one would call a liberal environment, except perhaps in the economic sense. Conservative evangelicals hold considerable sway. The annual pride event, Pink Dot, is stringently policed to prevent non-Singaporeans from attending. It's a fairly tricky place to come out.

Vincent and Mia are both Singaporean-Chinese. They're graduates, professionals, and in their early 30s. Both have friends in the queer/kink community with whom they can be themselves more easily. Of the two, Vincent is the more relaxed about being honest with his mono friends.

On that night my friends found out, there was a group of them and it was awkward and they joked about it. I try to be honest with them and tell them it was just where we are. It's what we do. But I didn't explicitly explain. I actually gave a lift home to one of them and she asked me privately what it was like. She also said that she did think about this. So, I think on an individual level if we were to extrapolate to [Straits] Chinese society on this small sample size, when you communicate with people on a one to one basis they may want to find out more, or they may think this is something I want to explore, yes, or maybe not, but not when you are in a group setting

So, is Mia out to her friends?

No thankfully, because I used to be quite religious so most of my friends are Christians. God forbid! My friends don't know and that's why I get on his case when he is very loose and not careful with information pertaining to us. When it comes to us interacting with others we always use this topic to test the boundaries, how open people are in getting to know us. Once they answer certain questions, tick certain boxes we are like 'Okay! This is us.' We give them a peek and once they're okay we are like 'rah rah', we are out in the open. But that usually doesn't happen very often, and when they do these people then become very close friends eventually.

In many people's experience there remains a quantifiable difference between the reactions that men and women get. That may explain why Vincent feels able to be the braver of the two.

> Despite the peer pressure and despite the way society might view us I think it's good to be radically honest with people you meet, with your friends, with people outside of your social circle. I feel that in theory it is good, it is the right way to do things. I may feel awkward or afraid to do it but that is society's problem. It is not my problem that you make me feel this way. I think we should all be more open and more honest with each other. But having said that, it's difficult of course.

Those close to them were often supportive, but both lost some friends over their choices. Colleagues, generally less invested in a particular story of someone they work with, were often sympathetic if they knew at all.

It's one thing to come out to the people one chooses at a time of one's choosing. It's quite another to find oneself outed. Ivan, our IT expert from Russia, found himself in just that situation.

> I am part of a small online community, about 100 people. It's not related to poly-amory. It's just like an old bunch of friends. It's like a small Facebook group. We have a small website for ourselves and we think that it's fairly hidden and obscure and no one knows about it. I felt we were pretty much unknown.

> We had an event like a videoconference kind of thing. We staged a video chat where people were invited to speak about topics that they feel are important, just to present themselves, just to put some faces to our names maybe. I chose the topic of polyamory; that's about one year into our relationship, me and Alexandra. So I made a video about polyamory, I talked about what is polyamory, how it's working, why it is good, why it is bad—so on and so forth. I briefly showed Alexandra on camera as well, introduced terms and then spent like 40 minutes answering ques-tions from the crowd, and everything went well.

> A couple of days later I received a WhatsApp message from my mother who appar-ently was following me on that website. I thought our little group was impossible to find. I had relied on its obscurity, and I didn't think that it would actually be a problem that someone would find something that I said there and somehow use it against me.

So, my mother... she's absolutely a normal mother, she has no special hacking skills. I'm pretty sure, I grew up with her. She was very displeased with me and things that I talked about. She called me names. She said that these things that I was talking about were a verbatim copy of what my father told her when he told us he was leaving us. So my father left the family when I was three. I haven't heard from him for a decade. I don't even know if he's alive now.

So my presentation clearly hit some pain points for her. She was very upset and she asked me to take the video down because—I don't know how to properly translate from Russian to English—but basically she didn't want to be held accountable for my actions. That is how I understood. So I didn't really press into her, I didn't really have the mental strength to understand her. So I complied.

I told her 'You have been a more or less perfect mother to me all this time, and out of respect for you being this good to me I will comply' and I went and I asked for these videos to be taken down and I removed them from the internet. But I then went and closed everything, every profile that I had I locked into private, I kicked her from my Instagram, because I felt really upset, I felt that my boundaries were violated [that] I didn't know that she was there and that I should have filtered my output maybe. So yes that was pretty painful. So I closed myself and I think that probably has been painful for her, because we don't contact that much. We are 8000 miles apart so she was following me on Instagram and various other places to see if I am still alive and what I am doing. Like a motherly thing which is understandable, but I kicked her out of everything. Maybe it is a petty thing but I felt like it was important to gain some sort of control.

And more than a year later... we never talked about this thing again, we never truly resolved this, like I never had a talk with her as in 'I am an adult and I can take responsibility for my own actions...' but one day she asked me to be put back on Instagram which I took as an apology ...

It's a weird situation but I don't know if I want to go into resolving it, like properly having a conversation with my mother about my lifestyle choices. I didn't have this conversation with anybody in my family because I don't think they need to know that. I think they wouldn't really understand me. No, I know that they wouldn't understand me.... to be judged by my mother... being compared with my own father did hurt...

Ivan's story has everything: humour, agony, reconciliation. We shouldn't forget how the things we express about ourselves can be very confronting for people. Sometimes they trigger uncomfortable memories; in the case of Ivan's mother, her own marriage breakdown.

Xena too found that being honest with those around her carried a price. She's in her 40s, from Indonesia and works in training. She has lived in Europe, is married to a Scandinavian engineer, and doesn't conform to the stereotypes some people entertain about South East Asians.

> I lost a lot of friends for [being consensually non-monogamous] because I guess my opinion about relationships has always been different. Mostly I lost girlfriends. I lost some friends because they think what I am doing is not normal. Or they think it's ruined the image of the fantasy of the perfect life, the perfect relationship, so they think I encourage... affairs.

> *Jonathan:* And you explain to them that the point of ethical non-monogamy is that you're open and honest so you don't have affairs?

> *Xena:* They still don't understand. Every time they when I try to explain it they think I'm being defensive of this non-monogamous [lifestyle. They're mostly] French and Asian, quite mixed. The women reacted worse than the men. The men, they believe that men can do that but that women should not, that or their partners shouldn't do it. But what's the difference? Why are men allowed to do that while women are not allowed to do that? And especially when you do it openly in a relationship?

I put it to Xena that perhaps the way she chooses to live her life, challenging the monogamous ideal, makes her an active threat to what her friends have invested in, even to the sanctity of their relationships. A woman who doesn't stick with one man might steal theirs.

> I think this is maybe why they don't want to hear the truth. Like if this is the reality, if this is what the world would actually believe deep down, I think everyone would want the lifestyle that I have. They just don't want to recognise it and they don't want to admit it. I can tell from their faces sometimes that they would really like to have that kind of relationship like what I have. I could just tell from the face because it's the idea of free love, the idea that we don't hurt anybody in this scenario

and everybody knows, everybody is aware, instead of cheating behind peoples' back—and this is why it challenges people, why my friends don't like this idea that challenges their normality, their monogamous life.

People look at me with suspicion because they know I'm that way and maybe they are afraid that I will do that [with] their man or whoever, or their woman whoever sometimes. I can see from their body language and feeling protective and afraid that I am going to take them...

Shyam and Rati grew up in the southern Indian state of Kerala, moving abroad to study and to pursue careers in IT and psychology. They married in 2019 after almost five years together as a non-monogamous couple. Both are pansexual. Rati says that her friends and acquaintances are normally fairly accepting of her being non-monogamous, albeit in a rather dismissive way, until she hits turbulence in one of her relationships whereupon they're quick to point the finger:

I've come out to some, some of my family members as well, younger cousins and things like that. And of course they give me the 'Oh yeah. Just going through a phase, you know... everybody's tried these things at some point in their lives and it doesn't work'. You know, that those are the usual reactions. Or when I say, 'I'm having trouble with my partners', they're like, 'Oh, what did you expect?' You know, it's three of you guys. It's not a couple, it's three. There's a lot of negativity. I mean, a lot of them are accepting in the sense that, 'Hey, you know, it's your life so you can do whatever you want. It's fine.' They're okay to hang out with my partners and all of that. But the moment I start talking about issues I'm facing, things that I'm dealing with, they'd be like, 'Oh, what did you expect?' or 'Of course, it's a poly relationship that's not normal.'

Shyam for his part has had to be judicious about who he tells about the way he lives. Even so, in these days of pervasive social media and dating apps, it can be hard to maintain a discreet separation between the more and the less conventional aspects of his life.

I have not opened up to my family about anything about me, basically because I pretty much lived on my own since I was really young. So they have no idea about my life, my sexuality or relationship, all that. With friends? I think I kind of [compartmentalise] some friends. Like there are some friends that I cannot avoid, because they have known me for ages since I was like young, we came [abroad] together. To them I'm a very normal person. I don't talk about anything. So I filter everything out in front of them. So they have no idea about my life at all.

But those other friends who actually reject [my choices] or show negativity, I just try to avoid them. The moment I feel that they don't accept me for who I am, I try to find new friends. So, I started making new friends who accept me for who I am.

Obviously, there are a couple of friends who are very close to me with no idea about me. Like recently one of our friends, she was whispering to Rati when I wasn't round that, 'Oh wow, I want to tell you something. I saw Shyam on Tinder', because she has no idea about us. So, there are people who still, you know, talk behind my back saying that all 'Oh, I found Shyam on Tinder or Bumble or OKCupid'. Obviously, I have heard people calling me names, like he's a playboy, he's a slut and I can't be bothered. So, I'm like, I have fun.

Kevin, the Philadelphia-based author and educator, really prepared when he felt it was time to come out to his mother. That probably says a lot about him, and a fair amount about his mother.

It didn't go really well for me. My mother wasn't interested in hearing anything about it. But what I did was I prepared my ass off. My mother was an academic. So, when I said, 'Hey, this is what my life looks like,' I didn't come there just to talk. I came with books, I came with resources, articles, YouTube videos, you know. So, I had everything. I knew everything. For every response I knew my mother would have I had an equal response that would resonate with her. I mean, ultimately it did not, but not through lack of trying. My coming out didn't go well strictly because of stubbornness on the part of my mother, but had she been willing to learn about and accept me, I did everything I could to make that a reality.

My friends, on the other hand, didn't care at all after that initial threesome that opened up my relationship. I'm a cisgender guy. I was then identifying as straight. All my friends were straight, cisgender guys. They were just excited that I had a threesome.

Even if preparing thoroughly didn't make coming out to his mother an unmitigated success for Kevin, it might have gone worse had he not. Preparation is about mitigating risk; reducing the downside. Thinking in advance how people might react, thinking about the questions they might have, the thoughts they might throw out, allows you to be more emotionally prepared, better able to meet surprise, shock or even hurt, calmly and with reason.

So, if you find yourself preparing to come out—and I suppose this broadly applies to revealing one's orientation, being non-monogamous, or even telling your stupendously conservative parents that you want to smash capitalism ('only at weekends mum!')—what might preparation mean?

I guess the first question is, 'Why come out?'

Everyone will have their own reasons, but top of the list for many people will be a desire to live authentically and to be valued for their true selves rather than an edited version.

Some people who feel they have to censor their lives, often with good cause, long to be not just accepted but loved for the person they feel they authentically are. That's probably even more the case for people who harbour fears that they might be rejected if it was known who they really were. It can be positively damaging for some people to live a lie, though there are many parts of the world where the upsides of being true to oneself are hugely outweighed by the negative consequences.

Another factor for a lot of people is a desire to show solidarity with those who have come out and who have been discriminated against unfairly. The sense of 'That could be me' is very powerful. That, obviously, cuts both ways.

There's also the matter of one's partners. Coming out allows one to introduce the significant people in one's life to parents and friends. Non-monogamous people will often talk about the times they were invited to events and were asked to bring a plus-one. That often leads to uncomfortable choices. Sometimes it means that one or more partners are excluded. It also means tracking which friends know about who.

Weddings can be a particular nightmare. Inviting a non-monogamous person to a wedding might freak some people out. There they are trying to psych themselves up for a lifetime of 'to have and to hold' just each other, definitely not having and holding anybody else, and there you are turning up with your plus-three making their decision feel less like pledging a lifetime to a special person and more like giving up dessert for Lent. And let's not forget that they have to pay to feed and water all your lovelies. For a newlywed couple worrying about the cost of their nuptials, poly people are a cost centre. Offer to bring a packed lunch maybe?

Joking aside, events like weddings or even dinner parties (assuming anyone has those any more) are a big reminder how things are set up for couples. Single people find much the same thing, albeit they're cheaper dates. Being out at least allows one to discuss your reality with friends, and it makes it easier for you to introduce them to those you love.

And then the family can invite all of you to the wedding or not, as they please.

WHY NOT TO COME OUT

MOST WRITING ABOUT consensual non-monogamy has come from North America, only a small portion of which reflects the experiences of people of colour. Even in the United States, a society that defines itself around the notion of liberty, there are practical reasons why people choose not to be openly consensually non-monogamous. As we've heard it could cost some people their jobs or their families. Even in America, liberty, it seems, has its limits.

But what of other societies? In the West people take their freedoms for granted. But the ethical norms we've established can be utterly unworkable in very conservative or traditional societies, likewise in many countries ruled by oppressive regimes.

This has long been implicitly understood by much of the LGBT+ community, who know only too well what it's like to be actively persecuted by the authorities or by a hostile society. As the Szechuan-born academic Jess Zhu says, our seeming obsession with honesty in freer societies could be potentially deadly if put into practice by people elsewhere.

Opacity is an ethical necessity for queer people in societies hostile to both gayness and dishonesty. There, the eagerness of the public to know more 'truth' about gay people, especially the married ones, is as oppressive as, if not more than, the direct verbal or physical homophobic violence that keeps them in the silent closet. The assumed existence of such 'truth' is related to the essentialisation of (homo) sexuality. As an optical spectrum that covers the ambiguous in-betweenness, opacity displaces the binaries of gay/straight, closeted/out, shamed/proud, visible/ invisible, and fake/truth—binaries that have produced and reinforced the double bind on gay people. This helps us to understand various forms of camouflage, be it 'cooperative marriage' or mixed-orientation 'fraudulent' marriage, the ethicality of which should be evaluated on a case-by-case basis.[39]

For queer and gay in China we could equally substitute poly or monogamish in any number of countries, let alone those like Iran or Saudi Arabia. Both partners

---

39   ' "Unqueer" Kinship? Critical Reflections on "Marriage Fraud" in Mainland China,' Jingshu Zhu, Leiden University; *Sexualities*, 12 Sep 2017. https://journals.sagepub.com/doi/ full/10.1177/1363460717719240

might decide the consequences of being out are extremely serious. It's better, they decide, that each of them know as little as possible. That way if they're caught the other can deny all knowledge. To poly people in Portland or Paris that might seem terrible, but to someone who wants to protect themselves and their partners in a repressive environment, it may seem like the obvious decision. Adulterers in Iran have rarely been punished by stoning (at least since 2002), flogging is a more common consequence, but what people in Berlin and people in Tehran visualise when you mention flogging are probably very very different.

We'll delve further into being open in the section on 'don't ask don't tell' arrangements within relationships. The pertinent point here is that being out is not necessarily an unmitigated positive. For some people discretion is the better way. However, discretion works best when everyone involved in the relationship is happy with that.

OKAY, SO WE'RE GONNA COME OUT! BUT TO WHOM? WHEN? HOW?

ASSUMING THAT YOU decide to come out, where might you start?

The first point to make is that you don't have to come out to everyone at once, and you might never come out to some people. Yes, people may talk and word may spread, but it's still possible to keep our various circles of birth family, chosen family, friends and colleagues separate to some degree (though it can require careful management of social media). It's your choice, presumably in consultation with your partners.

As with all things non-monogamal (I made that word up btw) it's good to talk with your partners. How out you are may well have a direct effect on them. What might, for instance, be the effect on a married partner of your posting photos on social media of the two of you holding hands if they and their spouse are not out? Hear and understand their concerns. Negotiate. Walk at the pace of the slowest person. This may be at your pace, but if your partner(s) want to go even slower, or don't want to be exposed at all, respect that. After all, once someone is out they're out. Ever tried putting toothpaste back into the tube? How did that work out for you?

It's no great surprise that non-monogamous people, just like the queer community before it, tend to build mutual support networks. A cursory search of internet sites like Meetup.com should direct you to groups in your area and you should find those that are about socialising or discussion rather than cruising. Obvious search terms are *polyamory, polyam, poly*[40] or *open relationships*. Much the same can be found online. At

---

40   There has been a debate about using poly as a dating term because it has been suggested some Polynesians apparently also use it as a short form.

the time of writing polyamory.com, reddit/r/polyamory, countless Facebook groups and umpteen CNM bloggers provide focal points for chat, support and advice.

You might take your first tentative steps in your own circles by considering, amongst those you wish to tell, who might be most sympathetic? But it's sometimes difficult to judge which friends might be receptive and which might recoil in horror. This may be one of those moments when you find out who your real friends are. Starting with those who know you best is not a bad idea, especially if you know they have a fairly open-minded attitude towards sex and relationships.

Don't discount the subtle approach, where you sound friends out for their opinions about things related to CNM without actually coming out. You could always go with, 'I saw this really interesting show/article/book/movie about this couple who opened up their relationship. I'm not sure what to think of that but it doesn't seem so terrible if they're both happy. What do you think?' Gauge the reaction. If you get an unexpectedly negative response you might want to pause.

If someone is struggling with their own relationship, especially if it has involved a partner's infidelity, you might wish to exercise caution. Your happy news might hit uncomfortably close to home, not least because, increasingly, one comes across those on the dating market passing themselves off as consensually non-monogamous or as polyamorous when they're either simply cheating or not interested in a serious relationship. As CNM becomes more common it's almost inevitable that it will provide cover for the unscrupulous, and that's not likely to make life easier for those who are genuinely consensually open.

Likewise, and this is hard to quantify, ask yourself who clings most tightly to an idea of you that the truth might dent or shatter. Parents are often heavily invested in their children (yes, financially as well as emotionally). They allow themselves hopes and fantasies for their children that are their own, not those of their offspring. Going back to weddings again: How many times have your friends' weddings been dominated by their parents and the people they choose to invite, rather than by those the bride and groom want around them? Some parents are properly accepting of who their children are, others aren't. If parents are likely to prove tricky, perhaps leave them until you have established a support network. That way if some of your (hypothetically) nearest and dearest are less than sympathetic you'll have others who are more understanding to fall back on.

And, of course, family doesn't just mean parent and siblings. Many of us consider those we choose to have around us to be as much family as blood relatives. Just bear in mind that sharing a secret with some people can lump them with a burden and it may be neither kind nor safe to do so.

In all things, be compassionate. If your parents' hopes for you are likely to be dashed by your revelation, be as gentle as you can. That may mean making your peace with never being able to tell them, especially if they might be so upset that they will go to court seeking custody of your children (it happens) or write you out of their will.

People need time to absorb momentous news and to adjust. It can be a journey for them too, especially if they have negative attitudes towards sexual minorities and/or have a very traditional view of relationships. By and large it's far easier to dislike or hate people because of difference if you've never met them. Confronted by someone you know and love who has come out or has forged a relationship with someone from a different background, you have to work hard to maintain that antipathy. By and large the path of love is an easier one to walk. But very often people need time to embrace acceptance.

And watch out; anger cuts both ways. It's rarely a good idea to act in anger, especially hot anger. If it's possible you're coming out in order to hurt someone, pause and wait for things to cool. Indeed if you've decided to be non-monogamous to hurt someone you might ask yourself if you're doing the right thing for the right reasons, and what the consequences might be. Surely your relationships should be about choosing who you love rather than who you wish to punish.

Be ready to deal with a whole range of responses from the overwhelmingly positive to the positively hostile. Some of those I interviewed lost friends as a result of coming out as non-monogamous. Many of them made good friends too.

As Kevin Patterson says, preparation is important. Think about the language you're going to use; say 'I'm polyamorous' and some people will hear 'I'm a swinger'—they may not be listening properly or they may simply not understand. Pick your terms carefully and explain them, so people Google the right things. Better still, put together resources for them. That way they'll read things that you feel best shed light on your circumstances and choices. If it would help to have something off-the-peg the very knowledgeable Dr Elisabeth Sheff has written *When Someone You Love Is Polyamorous: Understanding Poly People and Relationships*.

And of course, talk to other people who've been there before you. Quite often they'll tell you 'Be relaxed about things'. Try not to give the impression that you expect your disclosure to be seen as shameful or a big deal; act the opposite. You might start by just dropping mentions once in a while, easily and casually. 'Linton came with us on our camping trip. He's a good friend we've become very close with.' If you don't act like your disclosure needs or warrants a response, the less people will feel that they have to give one. People are quite responsive to body language and non-verbal cues. (At this point I want to say 'just relax' but I know that if someone tells me to just relax that can stress me right out.) So if you come across as 'mum, dad, we have this really massive thing to tell you' mum and dad may feel obliged to treat it as a massive thing.

So here's a quick checklist—the TL;DR version of questions you may want to consider:

- *Do I actually need to come out?*
- *Why should I come out? If I need to, is this the right moment?*
- *If not now, when?*
- *Why am I coming out? (A question distinct from 'Why should I come out?')*
- *Who do I want to come out to, and who not? Will this be possible?*
- *Who first?*
- *Who may be the easiest to tell?*
- *Who may be the hardest?*
- *Where does everyone else sit between those two poles?*
- *How do I describe my style of CNM? Be ready to be specific.*
- *How do I identify?*
- *What books and articles have I read that I'd like to recommend to people I'm going to tell?*
- *Who can I ask for their own coming out experiences?*
- *What does my support network look like?*
- *Am I ready for very negative reactions? (Or what happens if your best friends suddenly respond by revealing that they've been non monogamous for years? It happens!)*
- *What's the worst that could happen? (Carte blanche right there for all you catastrophisers! Try to rein yourselves in, just a little.)*

It Ain't What You Do,
It's The Way That You Do It....

CHAPTER FOURTEEN

Relationship Styles

RELATIONSHIPS ARE A bit like going travelling. Once you ditch the itinerary, you can head off anywhere. That suits some people but not others. There are always those who would prefer to take a bus tour or a cruise. Others like a package holiday. Some will do their research, plan their own trip, and book flights and an Airbnb. And others still just get up one morning and set off without a destination in mind.

Consensual non-monogamy can be pretty much any of these in a way that monogamy typically isn't. As the writer Franklin Veaux puts it:

> Monogamy is pretty straightforward, the rules are pretty simple: you don't shag other people. But non-monogamy is everything in the world that is not that. So, the varieties of non-monogamy are far greater than the varieties of monogamy, and it is possible for two non-monogamous people to be non-monogamous in ways that are absolutely at odds with each other [even though they call it the same thing].

Part of the purpose of this book is to help you find what works for you. In the chapters that follow we'll look at various different styles of consensual non-monogamy. These examples are wide ranging but not comprehensive. Nor should they be treated as prescriptive. The whole point is that you get to write your own rules—whether you're single or doing this together with a partner or partners. Dr Liz Powell:

> I like to think about ethical non-monogamy as a way to explore and experiment and figure out what is actually genuine for me when I remove the axiom of monogamy. So, if I don't have to do these things the way that other people do, if I don't have to do them the way our culture tells us to do, what is left and what actually works for me?

I can't stress too much the importance of treating this book as a resource and not a workshop manual. This is all about what works for you and those you're intimate with. If something doesn't feel right, don't do it. Certainly, don't conform to a certain model because you want to tell people you're in a triad, or solo poly, or a relationship anarchist (don't be a conformist relationship anarchist, it defeats the whole purpose!).

Some people adapt the language to suit themselves. Maxine was involved with someone who did just that:

> I had a relationship with a lovely chap a few years ago who wasn't poly, at least not by his definition. He was seeing a number of people, he was having a number of sexual relationships, being very open about it. He was definitely non-monogamous.

> But as far as he was concerned he described all of these things as intimate friendships, which could possibly have been a point of contention, except as far as I was concerned his definition of friendship matched almost word-for-word my definition of love. So, I was quite happy to treat him in the way that I would treat my partners but call it an intimate friendship because that's what he was comfortable with. As far as he was concerned it wasn't a 'relationship', so I went with the term that he was comfortable with.

Some, like Dr. Amy Moors, argue what we call something is really only relevant when it comes to communicating: Labels, schmabels. Save them for parcels. For instance, what in the fifties was dubbed 'wife-swapping' and by the nineties 'swinging' these days is starting to defy neat categorisation:

> I think young people are doing it, they're just calling it a different name. I think it's hookup culture. I think it's threesomes. It's not just paying [to go to a swing party] or having a membership at a club. I think people are having house parties and even cuddle parties or some sort of poly parties. There's a lot of swing-type activities.

Others will say that the language we use to frame concepts and the meaning that gets attached to those labels can have a profound effect on our thinking—it's why minority groups so often move to defang once-derogatory terms and seize the linguistic agenda. It may seem trivial but it can profoundly shift the debate.

A lot of what follows are ideas about what you might want and what you might not. Some people love the idea of putting together a tiny tribe where everyone loves everyone else. Others absolutely want their own space (physical and personal) and want to invite people into it only on their own terms and when it suits them.

Moreover you're allowed to change your mind at any point, bearing in mind that this may have consequences for those you're involved with. You may start off liking the idea of being monogamish but end up being deeply in love with three people, each of whom has a quite distinct role in your life. Heck, you might experiment with them all and then decide that you'd rather be monogamous with someone who you just want to furnish a nice cottage with. If there's consent, real consent, it's all okay. Your own wholehearted consent is vital.

However, as has been said, it's really quite hard to break away from the ways we've been taught to do relationships. As Dr. Meg-John Barker notes, it's all too easy to fall back into established patterns:

> I think often non-monogamy is [approached] just like monogamy squared or monogamy cubed; people just trying to do monogamy but with two partners or three partners, and often that comes a cropper. But if we can really get away from those scripts, if we can instead really embrace this multiple script, then I think non-monogamy can open up the potential to do relationships at different paces that really suit the people involved.

> Comet relationships are a really nice example of a different way to do relationships that comes up in some non-monogamous settings where you have somebody that you maybe see once or twice a year, but then you have a really intimate time when you are with them. So it does open up this potential for variation, but again, it's really hard not to find yourself being drawn back onto the relationship escalator or the normative cultural script of 'This is how we do love'; 'Now we're called partners, that means X, Y, and Z in terms of how we have to commit to each other.' It's just so hard to go against the grain of the wider cultural script.

I should add another caveat here about the chapters that follow. Having decided to question one set of scripts that we've been socialised into following, there's no point leaping into a different cultural setting and swallowing all of *its* scripts, different though they be, wholesale. It's easily done. You escape one world view only to become a convert to another.

In his book *Freud and Christianity,* the theologian R. S. Lee observed that the experience of sudden and overwhelming conversion, such as that of St Paul the Apostle (or St Paul the sanctimonious blooming nuisance depending on your point of view), often produces someone who is more devout than the devout; in short, a fanatic.

If you find yourself reacting that way to anything you read about non-monogamy, pause. Not because you'll necessarily do anything crazy; you probably won't. Rather that because if something appears that suddenly fills a hole in your existence, the salient thing to examine is almost certainly the hole itself, not the potential filling.

Moreover I really don't want people emailing me and complaining 'But you told me to do it like that'. No I bloody didn't. This is all very much offered in the spirit of 'This is how a bunch of people do things, now go figure out your way for yourself'.

So, to relationship styles. We'll start with 'monogamish' because, as we'll see, it's a common entry route into opening up an existing relationship. The principle, if not necessarily the practice, is also fairly straightforward. Then, after having looked at swinging and other similarly open relationships on the way, we'll move on to variations on the theme of polyamory.

CHAPTER FIFTEEN

Monogamish

"We agreed long before marriage that faithfulness for us meant honesty, not exclusivity. My husband knows that if he wants to fool around, he can—so long as he's safe and honest (with me and with her). The same goes for me."

—Invisible in Canada, writing to Dan Savage[41]

OH, DAN SAVAGE what did you start?! Back in July 2011, in answer to a woman in Canada who set out her relationship agreement in the terms above, he wrote: "So I've got a new word to describe relationships like yours, mine, and your mom's, IIC: "monogamish." We're mostly monogamous, not swingers, not actively looking. Monogamish."

And just like that he opened a little door in the back of the wardrobe that led to Narnia... except with less Turkish Delight and more sex.

Dan Savage is often described as America's best-known sex advice columnist. Morning Glory Zell-Ravenheart may have coined 'polyamory' back in the day but she didn't have a following like Dan Savage's. Not only does his Savage Love column appear in several dozen alternative weekly papers, his spinoff Savage Lovecast podcast is, by some measures, one of the most listened to in America. So when he coins a useful term, it can take hold.

41   Monogamish, Savage Love: Dan Savage, *The Stranger*, 20 July 2011

And add to that heady mix the fact that monogamish is, if you like, a common 'gateway drug' (one for which there was previously no word), it was not a complete surprise that the term developed a life of its own. As the polite Canadian wrote; "We look monogamous and probably will always look that way." And as Dan Savage replied; "I'm convinced that there are a lot more PTBMCs out there than people realise; that's 'Perceived To Be Monogamous Couple', a married/partnered couple with an understanding about when outside sexual contact is permissible." He rather hit the nail on the head. He understood both the tensions within monogamous relationships and he grasped the price of being identified as non-monogamous. As he put it: "Tell an AMC—'Actually Monogamous Couple'—that you're non-monogamous, and they'll assume you're a couple of huge sluts, i.e., that you're actively seeking outside sex partners or that you're swingers." Or as Cooper Beckett, presenter of the Life on the Swingset podcast, puts it, "Monogamish is the thing that polite society would be shocked by if you told them. It's not full on swinging, but it's shocking."

This is the dilemma at the heart of non-monogamy for millions of people. You have desires well within the range of normal human experience but you can't tell anyone about them. Remember Amy Moors' research? Be upstanding monogamous Dan and Sarah and people will hail your sheer upstandingness. Be upstanding non-monogamous Dan and Sarah and people will rush to get the ducking stool or burn you for witches. Savage offers a tempting solution: You can deviate from the norm and not make exclusivity the touchstone of your relationship, but you don't have to make a big deal about it.

Author and therapist Dr. Liz Powell sees *monogamish* as being interpreted in either of two ways:

> What it means depends upon who says it. It's either that you have a recognition within your monogamous relationship that actual complete hundred-percent monogamy is unattainable over a lifetime cycle, so there will be occasional indiscretions and that's okay. Some other people use it to mean that occasionally they have outside sexual dalliances with the knowledge and consent of their partner.

It's a subtle but important distinction. The first acknowledges the challenges of being truly romantically or sexually exclusive over the course of a decades-long relationship and says occasional 'failure' is okay. It essentially says; 'monogamy is a fine ideal, we're going to try to live up to it but we don't want it to be a deal-breaker.' The second is more active: 'We're free to have other involvements. It's just not a big deal. Our primary commitment is overwhelmingly us.' The first is essentially two people cutting one another some slack to be human. The second is a big step towards what might be called an open relationship.

Once you've questioned one set of rules and decided to do away with them, any set of rules that you've agreed to guide your monogamish relationship will be open to, and indeed require, discussion and negotiation.[42] You may start off by simply agreeing that sex or romantic feelings outside the dyad aren't a deal-breaker, but then find that these additional involvements become quite important to you.

Swingers Liam and Kate from Toronto called their blog The Monogamish Marriage, because that was their starting point for CNM. So why Monogamish? First Kate, then Liam:

> *Kate:* Initially it was that we are committed to each other and anything we do is just extracurricular. It was meant to augment our own sexual relationship. And it wasn't all that frequent. It wasn't something that defined us.

> *Liam:* Also, I think it captures the centrality of our relationship with each other to everything that we do. So that's not an intellectual ideal for us. That's just how it works out. We look at it and we love spending time with each other. So right now we're in Montreal together enjoying a trip. So we like including other people, but the monogamous part of monogamish really captures our connection with each other, I would say.

> For me, throughout our relationship I've come to appreciate with Kate how utterly unlikely I would be to ever find someone to replace her. So if I look at the long list of things that makes her a great partner for me, the likelihood of meeting someone else who is as low drama, sexually adventurous, intellectually curious and such a great practical partner is so low that I feel I can expose myself to any situation with another woman with no fear that I'm going to get carried away into another relationship.

> *Kate [laughing]:* Yeah. So, right at the beginning, I was very concerned about him being drawn away by someone else. But we've been doing this for eight years now, right from the beginning of our relationship. And I've seen him have sex with other women. I've seen him grow emotionally connected to other women. So having very deep friendships, long text conversations, you've even gone out separately with some of our friends and but I'm never worried because I know him and I know the strength of our relationship and I know these women. And I know that they don't want to steal my man away, they are also as committed to their spouse as I am.

---

42   As indeed should be the case in any healthy relationship, monogamous or otherwise.

So we try to be helpful, I guess, to, to be with people who are similar to us—people who are crazy about each other first. And then who want to have these social sexual connections as an addition to their already wonderful relationships. So that creates great security...

Kate and Liam found that their being monogamish soon led them to re-examine the sexual side of their connection together and explore the swinging scene. That's not a necessary progression; however it does illustrate the fact that relationships do evolve.

I joked earlier about monogamish being a 'gateway drug', the same way that you start with cheap Liebfraumilch and before you know it you're swigging Château d'Yquem, right? Well probably not. It's more that one of the biggest steps with consensual non-monogamy is deciding to put the rules we've been handed to one side and design our own. That, and realising that it is possible to love and desire someone and be loved and desired in return even if one's relationships aren't exclusive. Monogamish seems to offer a gentle way to clear these hurdles.

CHAPTER SIXTEEN

Swinging

SWINGING IS OFTEN overlooked when people talk about consensual non-monogamy. In some ways it stands separate from other choices. For a start swinging's precursors can be found at various times and in various places through history; Saturnalian orgies, Beltane rituals, wife-lending in ancient China and more.

Its modern origins are debated but chroniclers often point to a live-for-now culture at US Air Force bases in the years after World War II that later spread to the burgeoning suburbs. If it had started out amongst anthropologists then we'd probably know more. In the early decades it was often called wife swapping. That term went out of fashion during the 1970s, the decade when swing culture became widely known to the public and mythologized by the media. It was almost a totem of the expansion of the more sexual, more liberated atmosphere of that decade, beyond the counter-culturalism of the hippie free-love movement. Thriving venues for swingers sprang up in many cities, such as the legendary Plato's Retreat in New York. The North American Swing Club Association (NASCA) formed to support and promote the movement, which by then had also spread to the UK and Europe. If 70s swinging had an avatar, he probably looked like Will Ferrell as Ron Burgundy in *Anchorman* and possibly had attitudes to match.

Then came the early 1980s and the AIDS epidemic. Plato's Retreat was closed down by Mayor Ed Koch in 1985 along with New York's gay bath houses as part of the response to the epidemic,, though the popularity of such venues was already in steep decline and many were going out of business. The 80s are remembered by many of that generation of swingers as a time of fear, paranoia, infection and loss. The public mood seemed to turn decisively against the permissive culture of the previous decade.

The tide turned again when the HIV virus was established as the cause of AIDS. Fear gave way to pragmatic caution and safer-sex practices such as default condom use and regular STI and HIV testing. The swing world spent the 90s picking itself up, dusting itself down, and getting its glad rags back from the dry cleaners.

As swinging has gained in popularity it has also become much more diffuse, as the seedy under-the-counter magazines were replaced by websites, and later as dating apps like Tinder opened the door to the hook-up culture, without the need for clubs, associations, or in-groups at all. But swinging is definitely deep into its renaissance—more widespread, more popular and better organised than ever.

Swingers tend to refer to it as 'The Lifestyle'. Researchers find high levels of sexual satisfaction amongst swingers, quite possibly because they put a lot of effort into their sex lives. For most, however, it's still something that happens in the shadows because of social stigma. Of all the forms of consensual non-monogamy, swinging is arguably the most unabashedly driven by sex, the most mainstream in its demographics, the most couple-centric, and the one that overlaps least with other alternative social movements.

Clubs remain a big part of swinging, as do organised events. At one end of the spectrum are huge happenings like Naughty in N'awlins, where more than a thousand couples sign up for a four-day event in New Orleans and thousands more turn up to take part in satellite activities. There are dedicated cruises and tropical resorts. At the other end are group-friendly dating sites like Feeld and OKCupid and niches sites where couples often post ads and arrange meetings with other individuals, couples and groups. There are club venues in most large cities in the western world and, more discreetly, across Asia. There are even places, like the Cap d'Agde on the French Mediterranean, that have mutated from naturist (nudist) colonies to swingers' enclaves, often to the great disgruntlement of the naturists.

The author Cooper Beckett lives in Chicago. A genial and charming fortysomething, married and bisexual, he has presented the podcast *Life on the Swingset* since 2010.

> If you break it down to its most basic, swinging is generally a couple who have decided to have sex outside their relationship. Usually it's done together, usually it's with another couple, and usually it's what used to be called wife swapping where the couple basically switches around the partners. Now, that's a very base-level look at swinging.

You may be aware of the popular stereotypes: the key parties of swingdom's early years, where the husbands at the party would put their car keys in a bowl and the wives picked a key at random; you took whoever you got. The darkened disco den full of heaving bodies. Even people who practice other forms of consensual non-monogamy often look askance at swinging. The author Franklin Veaux, who writes about polyamory, sees swinging as a throwback.

> While people are like 'Oh! Swingers, they are really far out there,' my experience with the swing community is that it tends to be extremely conservative and to really focus on protecting the core couple against any and all threats. And I've actually seen swing clubs that forbid their members from forming emotional attachments with other members and in one extreme case there was a swing club in Tampa that actually had rules that would forbid you from seeing other swing club members outside of the context of the club and if you did, they threw you out.

Such perceptions come as no surprise to Beckett, who is both a swinger and polyamorous, and who in turn points out that some swingers have similarly negative views of polyamory.

> The swinger communities tend to think of the poly communities in their 'logical' (albeit not actually logical) final form, which is the weird, creepy communes of San Francisco in the 60s, which seems to be polyamory pure, you know, that's where it ends. But the rest of us are really just somewhere around the middle, just discovering friendships while poly people are having casual sex and there's a lot of overlap that people just refuse to acknowledge. And it's a shame because we, as communities, really need each other.

So, does that mean that the stereotypes about swinging are just wrong? No, says Beckett. As with many stereotypes there's often a foundation in truth but at the same time they distract from the wider reality.

> In practice it's a little bit more fluid, a spectrum. There is definitely 'the scene'. The hardcore traditionalist swingers are the ones who go and meet people and probably don't have conversations beyond first names and probably don't have advanced sexual health discussions with them, unfortunately people like at Plato's Retreat, that had all the stigma of swinging surrounding it, just everything that you don't want swinging to be represented as. There's nothing wrong with that but it's not the majority by any means.

For many, Beckett included, the social side of swinging is very important. This is true of a lot of polyamorous people as well. It's not all about hooking up or finding partners. Hanging out with like-minded people is a key part of the appeal.

> Here's where I start to get in trouble, because I practice both swinging and poly-amory and I am of the belief that they are far more similar than they are different. Most swingers I know establish relationships of some kind with the people they swing with. Very few of them are anonymous swingers, and 'relationship' doesn't need to mean 'romantic', it can mean friendship. It can mean close friendship. Some of the best friends I ever made were the people I met early in swinging.

As Beckett says, swinging is couples-focused. In that respect it's more a shared experience than typical open-relationship or monogamish agreements. At the same time, the idea of privileging the core couple and defending it against 'external threats' is, if anything, often more pronounced than in other styles of non-monogamy.

Part of the appeal of monogamish setups, open relationships (in the narrow rather than the catch-all sense), and swinging is that they all allow the doors and win-dows of relationships to be opened to let in a little more fresh air. Perhaps becoming parents has meant that a couple has come to see one another more as co-workers at the job of life than as lovers. Maybe they miss the thrill of a new encounter, maybe things have become a little stale and the sex has become repetitive. These forms of consensual non-monogamy hold out the possibility of finding pleasure, adventure and excitement in a way that limits its impact on the relationship. 'Yes we'll have sex with other people, but our relationship will still be sacrosanct'. The door may be open and guests can come in, but they don't get to redecorate. So, for two people who feel that commitment doesn't need to include sexual exclusivity, swinging can be a safety valve, an exciting hobby, and maybe a means of continued growth and exploration. Cooper Beckett again:

> It's what generally draws people to swinging, and monogamish even more so. I look at it as a sort of gradation, because monogamish feels like an entry level. You know, we're kind of figuring this out and it also goes with the 'don't ask, don't tell' kind of thing where if you met someone while you were at a convention for work, it's okay. You know, go ahead.
>
> When I started I was reading Tristan Taormino's excellent book *Opening Up*, and that sort of became my non-monogamy bible. But early on when I started swinging, I read the poly chapter and it scared the shit out of me because relationships,

romantic relationships, love seemed so difficult and advanced and scary, you know? And if you're coming from monogamy, like full on real monogamy, directly into this—that's a whole new world, you know. Sex can be just sex and that's easy for people to understand. If you can disconnect sex and love, it's sort of understandable that you could swing, and that's easy, we can do that. And I think monogamish is even easier. We can do that.

But while, for some people, monogamish and swinging are a route into consensual non-monogamy, others travel in the opposite direction. Both Alain and Laura have experimented with various forms of CNM, even dabbling in polyamory. But, as Alain says, that wasn't really satisfying for either of them.

> I think play is very important for us. Sex is very much this centre of our relationship in a way. I don't believe on a personal level that shelving urges or interest is very good because we could die tomorrow and I don't want to regret anything.

As for polyamory...

> I'm very comfortable letting it go. I don't see myself necessarily going back. I've discovered a lot of different things sex-wise and in terms of dynamics, so if we can find this happy middle where it's about us looking for something else together outside, that's what I really like because I feel it's kind of the best of both worlds. I think it's a lot easier and maybe a lot healthier way to manage our relationship, a couple still enjoying kink and having that extra space in life.

The way Alain tells it, he was never particularly comfortable with polyamory. He suffered from jealousy when his former partner saw other people. Laura, on the other hand, had good connections with a number of lovers.

> I've learned that I'm probably a lot more emotionally monogamous than I thought. Previously I thought that I could equally love different people, but I found that I channel all my focus to the one person that was giving me the most happiness or return of affection and attention, the one who made me feel the most desired. And that's also because one of my main love languages is intimacy. So I would only respond to that one person after a while. And even though I had feelings of tenderness for my other partners, gradually I channelled my attention to one person.

Nor is Laura, a pro-domme, particularly wedded to sexual non-monogamy. It's a nice-to-have rather than a must-have.

> I would genuinely be happy being sexually exclusive. But I've always been able to segregate sex from emotion. So for the purpose of having fun on an occasional basis, it's something that I am totally comfortable with and I would enjoy so long as it's not trying to build a relationship with another person.

WHY SWING?

WHAT LEADS PEOPLE to swinging? If the appeal of a monogamish agreement is that it offers a safety valve for people to look occasionally for fulfilment outside their largely monogamous relationship, the appeal of swinging is far more about sex as recreation.

As with much of non-monogamy (which we'll see when we get onto the topic of 'unicorns' and 'hot bi babes') a fairly common starting point is a woman in a couple wanting to explore her bisexuality. Female bisexuality is openly fetishized even by parts of male society that purport to deplore anything that amounts to sexual deviancy. The British tabloid press loves a 'three-in-a-bed romp', which is most often about fulfilling male fantasies of bedding two women. For Kate and Liam, our Toronto-based monogamish-couple-turned-swingers, it was a path she'd already started down.

> I started having sex with my best friend who is a woman before Liam and I got together. And that was a very organic thing. So we've been friends for several years and we got drunk one night and one thing led to another and, and we ended up in bed. I guess I wanted all of my sexual encounters to feel that organic and easy and not be planned out and not have lots of rules around them. I just wanted to have the freedom to go with the flow. And if I met someone who I was attracted to and wanted to sleep with, I wanted to have that freedom to explore it. So I didn't want there to be labels or rules or too many restrictions around it. And I guess it's kind of a, a hippie kind of motivation in the way just to, you know, have free love.

Initially, Kate and Liam's relationship was shaped more by wanting to avoid barriers to the possibilities that life offers rather than positively wishing to seek out new sex partners.

I think the term monogamish worked for us because, you know, we were open to doing whatever felt good for the two of us and that happened to turn into swinging. And I think we're open in the future to there being other versions of what monogamish is for us. But I guess the thing at the core of it is us and whatever we feel like doing, whatever we're comfortable with, then we can be "ish" about it just to do whatever we jointly decide is good for us.

It would probably be fair to describe Liam and Kate as romantically monogamous but sexually open. They see their core emotional relationship as strong and external threats to it as minimal. The journey from being monogamish to swinging unfolded gradually and naturally. Kate and Liam enjoyed sex with a third. Initially it was the two of them with another woman, but then something happened to ignite a spark for Liam.

At one point Kate told me a story about her sister getting involved with another man at the invitation of her husband. And it was a completely dysfunctional arrangement that went awry spectacularly, but it planted the idea in my head of seeing her with someone else. Something I never thought of before. [Her] being with another man... it became an obsession. And so, we figured it out that her ex-boyfriend was probably a good candidate. So, we did that; first time was a disaster and the second time was a bit better. And then it got really, really good until we wrote an article called 'the greatest threesome in the history of the world'. And it was a 10-hour marathon. So, seeing her with another man was something I came to with lust in my heart.

Kate: Eventually.

Liam: Yes. And so that, now I, I think of it this way, if some magic fairy came to us and said, Kate, you can have sex with other men in the future, or Liam, you can have sex with other women in the future, but you can't both have it. Only one of you can have it. I would immediately say she can have sex with other men. I don't even have sex with other women that much. But seeing her with other men is amazingly fulfilling for me.

So why was the first time a disaster? Well, by every measure Liam describes Kate's ex-boyfriend as no kind of threat. He was, after all, her ex. Liam saw himself as younger, in better shape, better looking, very much more secure and comfortable in himself. The only issue was that while the ex performed admirably, Liam simply couldn't get an erection. It left him, on that occasion anyway, feeling crushed. It's a reminder that the scenes people choreograph in their heads don't always play out in reality the way they do in the soft-focus of the imagination. Liam realised that he has an almost Stoic desire to face his worst fears and make his peace with them.

> I think part of it is I still have an adolescent conviction that women don't really like sex. And I was married for 26 years to a woman who really *didn't* like sex. So, every time I see a woman enjoying sex and when she's with another man who's not her husband, there's no social payoff for being with this man. It has to be lust. And seeing a woman's lust in up-close and contradicting that negative conviction that I had, it's really powerful. And then I feel really happy for her.

> So, we have our fantasy that there's a particular kind of man that I just know would be her kind of ideal. An English accent is part of it. But there's a long list of characteristics that I think would be perfect for her. So that man is probably a little bit taller than me because Kate's tall. He is probably a bit younger than me, has a fuller head of hair than me is, all of this long list of things that I'm not, I'm very scared about the things that I am. The better, the more threatening he is as a prospect, is more sexually satisfying for me.

> *Kate:* Liam is very generous and giving. But I think part of it has to do with some sort of competitive fear because he knows at the end, even if I go and have amazing sex with the world's most gorgeous English men, I'm still gonna come back to him and I'm still going to love him the most. So, it's kind of an opportunity for him to prove his dominance.

> *Liam:* So, if you can go to the edge of that abyss and peer into it, but not go there, it's very exciting. And I'm doing the same thing by my worst nightmare, which is being completely bested by another man. So, I'm going to be peering into it when I see her with another man. And the better he is, the more viscerally exciting it is.

A female partner's bisexuality is a common route into swinging, but Cooper Beckett challenges two 'myths': that male swingers are necessarily straight—he believes far more are bi than readily admit to it—and that women swing because guys push them to do it.

The mythology of swinging, that it's always a guy pressuring [his female partner] to open the relationship, is just not borne out in modern swinger culture, at least not in what I've explored and experienced. Among the people I've talked to over the last 10 years, most of the swingers, at least the people who are successful at it, are opening up for reasons of exploration. And exploration is different than just wanting a fuck.

The point, says Beckett, is that a woman's bisexuality is often the starting point for a conversation that leads to exploration that leads to more conversations that leads to more explorations.

'Like there's this whole thing that we haven't tried yet,' and then you add, 'Okay, well now we've done the threesome and what if we tried this?' Or 'What if I had two guys at one time?' or whatever, and then it opens up from there.

His advice to those wanting to explore swinging is to accept that while there may be a wrong time, there will almost certainly never be a perfect time.

When I first started I was listening to all these podcasts that basically they boiled down to 'swinging is amazing, but it's probably not for you'. You know? And, and they would say, well, you can't go into swinging if you have any problems in your relationship. And honestly, nobody I know ever has had a relationship with no problems. That's impossible. So therefore, right there, they're setting an unbearably high barrier to entry to swinging, and it's because they want to protect their fantasy that it's perfect, then we'll do this thing. It makes everything better and there's never any problems.

The advice you'll hear again and again—'relationship broken plus more people [does not equal] fixed relationship'—holds true. It's good to be in a solid place of trust. It's good to have positive reasons to want to explore. It's good not to be looking for any form on CNM to plaster over the cracks. If you go into swinging with that in mind and it satisfies a need for intimacy and sexual variety without diluting your romantic connection, it may well work for you.

CHAPTER SEVENTEEN

Open Relationships and Don't Ask Don't Tell

I'VE LUMPED TOGETHER open relationships and 'don't ask don't tell' (DADT) partly because they often go hand in hand. As I mentioned earlier, 'open relationship' can be a catch-all term for CNM but people who research and write about the subject tend to use it to mean a relationship where, by agreement, both parties can experiment sexually and romantically with other people.

The broad assumption is that, unlike swinging, one or both of a couple will explore separately. Unlike a monogamish fling, this will be a more deliberate pursuit rather than something triggered by circumstance. And unlike polyamory, these other connections are either not sufficiently committed to warrant everyone getting to know one another or the couple prefer to manage the situation by looking away.

Yes, this definition is rather arbitrary and no, the poly police aren't on patrol to make sure you stick to one side of the line or the other. Things blur.

One interesting finding from research by a team led by Terri Conley, associate professor of psychology at the University of Michigan, is that couples in open relationships tend to have lower levels of relationship satisfaction (though comparable sexual satisfaction) than people in monogamous, swinging or polyamorous relationships.[43] Why that's so isn't clear, but if people are playing separately and not telling, it would tend to increase novelty but decrease closeness and intimacy. Knowing that your partner is, or may be, up to things of which you're unaware—and you can't ask about it—is distancing. Perhaps for that reason, many couples in open relationships never even consider a don't ask don't tell arrangement.

---

43 'Sexual satisfaction among individuals in monogamous and consensually non-monogamous relationships', Terri D. Conley, Jennifer L. Piemonte, Staci Gusakova, Jennifer D. Rubin, University of Michigan; *Journal of Social and Personal Relationships* (2018), Vol. 35(4) pp 509–531.

Seb, who is polyamorous and knows his metamours, has a quasi-don't-ask-don't-tell arrangement covering only the more casual encounters:

> The reasoning is probably best summed up in a word-for-word quote from my wife; "After this amount of time I trust that you're not going to get into bed with somebody stupid. And so, I'm comfortable with you making your own decisions about things." That's one half of the reasoning. The other half of [it] was that, at the beginning, we were following the advice we'd heard, which was to communicate 100% of everything that had happened with a metamour. And even though I have become a very open-minded person over time, there were some aspects, I mean, just physically what her and partner would get up to, that felt uncomfortable, intrusive and sometimes unpleasant to hear. But I think as things progressed, it starts to become a two-way issue. There was a push factor; neither of us really wanted to hear certain grisly details about what the other got up to with another partner, but also there was a pull factor, which was that a level of trust had developed where we didn't think that the other would abuse the freedom that that kind of arrangement gave. And it certainly was a lot easier for both of us not to feel this ongoing pressure to kind of over-communicate everything about all aspects of seeing somebody else.

> It's tended to just evolve. Given that number one, we are married, and number two, we share an apartment, it would be quite difficult for either of us to truly conduct anything long-term or of any value without the other knowing about it. And I don't think either of us would really want to. So it's evolved into very much a qualified don't ask don't tell. What we've dispensed with is, mostly, just the need to get an informed consent in advance of doing anything with anybody else and to trust the partner to make the decision without having to check in specifically. That's one thing. And then also the need to communicate all aspects, particularly physical ones. Given that I travel a huge amount and both of us, while very close, live fairly independent lives, that also fits in better with our lives.

The phrase 'Don't ask, don't tell' was the mantra (and part of the official policy title) that the Clinton administration offered the US military in 1993 as a means to manage the presence of gay and bisexual people in its ranks. At the time, Americans' opinions were still fairly evenly split on whether gay relationships should even be legal.[44] The deal forbade openly gay, lesbian and bisexual men and women from serving, but it also stopped the military from pursuing those who had not come out. In other words, we won't look too closely so long as you don't make it an issue we cannot ignore. It was classic Clinton: not particularly high minded but a pragmatic workaround that reflected the divided views of the time.

There's also something of the practical workaround about DADT in a consensually non-monogamous setting, albeit, as we'll see, for a lot of people it can be a red flag. Meg-John Barker takes a nuanced view.

> It works for some people. A lot of cultures have that. There's been quite a lot of writing about French culture and how there's often an understanding that somebody will have a mistress or whatever and there's a 'don't ask, don't tell', 'everybody knows, but we don't really talk about it'. Again, downsides: obviously if you're not communicating, then things can go pretty badly wrong as we know. But at the same time, if that's the cultural script, it potentially offers a normative way of doing something that benefits people.

> But it can enable very dishonest kinds of relationships, so I guess I would always come down on the open-communication side of these things. But, again, that's not always that easy. So we've got to recognise where people are, rather than try to force them to be somewhere they're not. And in terms of the wider culture, again, if it's a culture where it's actually really dangerous to do this stuff, then the 'Let's be open about it with everybody' may not be so freely available to all cultures and all classes or all locations.

Xena is a forty-something Indonesian woman married to a Scandinavian man not quite fifteen years her senior. They've been together for two decades. She's long felt inclined to be non-monogamous; her husband doesn't. There have been times during the course of their relationship where sex simply hasn't been important to them. Xena feels able to disassociate sex from her primary relationship. It can be a physical need that is met elsewhere or it can be something that finds its voice in the early stages of a romantic relationship, when sex becomes more than sex. For most of that time, when Xena has taken lovers, her partner's attitude has been 'I don't want to know'. The arrangement worked well. At least it did for a long time.

---

44   A 1992 Gallup poll found that 48% of those asked favoured 'gay or lesbian relations between consenting adults' being legal, while 44% opposed. In 1996/7 another Gallup poll found the numbers almost reversed with 47% against and 44% in favour. https://news.gallup.com/poll/1651/gay-lesbian-rights.aspx

It wasn't very open with us because our rules are don't ask, don't tell. He doesn't want to know. I don't want to know. As long as we are still together, as long as we still love each other, as long as we still valued the same things together that's how it works with us. And then I started to open up to him two years ago and I told him this is what I want. I just never recognised what it is. I just found out about this term 'non-monogamous' and this is what I strongly believe. At the beginning he wasn't sure about it because before we had don't ask, don't tell kind of rule. He never questioned me or anything ever in the past 19 years of our life. Whatever, if I don't go home or if a guy picks me up for example he never questions me or anything.

There are clearly advantages, at least for Xena, in not talking about things. It avoids facing difficult feelings. It avoids uncomfortable discussions. It avoids quite a lot of things.

Everybody is different. What works about it is that there is no jealousy, like very open jealousy. Sometimes ignorance is bliss. That works for us because we don't need to feel jealous, we don't need to feel insecure about the whole situation, 'are we good are we not good?' because we pretend that the other persons do not exist. That I think is the good thing.

DADT is a viable arrangement for some people. However even Xena found that there were downsides.

The disadvantages: lying. It is kind of killing, you feel that you 'lie' to this person you love or you are with. I say 'I'm going to go out,' but it's a white lie, or 'I'm not going to come home don't wait up to me', that sort of thing, it's more like a very subtle hiding of the reality. For me that is not really freedom. That's the downside I guess.

I suppose, semi-seriously, you might call DADT a sin of omission. It's all about what you leave out. It's not that one necessarily has to tell one's partner everything. Not everyone wants a running commentary on the minutiae of someone else's life, even someone they're fond of to the point of loving deliriously. It's more that when there are things that one wants to tell a partner but can't, or feels unable to, then there's an issue.

For Xena not telling was problematic, even though there was a tacit understanding that her husband didn't feel the urge to know.

> So basically, only the last two or three years, I told him about this poly thing and this non-monogamous thing. He never made a comment, but this is his personality. He never makes a comment about things and I started being open to everyone, my friends, him and that's when it all started to be in the open. I think when you're together for 19 years you sort of know that you are solid. I felt more freedom when I could tell him 'That's okay I'm going to see Paul now and I'll see you in a day, so call me when you want'. That gives me more freedom. That's how I feel.

A lot of consensually non-monogamous people see DADT as inherently problematic. Many people certainly feel it's at odds with much of CNM's ethical underpinnings.

Why is this? Well, let's take a look at some of the commonly expressed reservations.

WHAT HAPPENS TO CONSENT?

Earlier in the book I set out some of the basics of consent. Among them are the notions that consent should be active and informed.

Consent isn't a one-time-only thing. Consent given at the outset of a situation cannot and should not be taken to cover all permutations thereafter indefinitely. Indeed, consent really should be both specific and conditional.

Nor can consent be informed unless the consenting party is in full possession of the facts. 'It's fine, whatever, I don't want to know,' isn't so much engaged consent as a mixture of denial and avoidance. For some people this may be easier than dealing with reality, but that suggests that perhaps they don't like the reality.

It also puts the onus on one partner to interpret what the other is comfortable with. Aside from the issue of whether someone is able to do that faithfully there's also the question of whether it's fair to ask them to do so. Some people will guess way too cautiously and others way too loosely. Either way it's hard to be responsible not just for someone else's feelings, but for second guessing them while you can't ask.

Suppose things change. How does one renew consent in a don't ask, don't tell? That would involve both asking and telling. Not doing so means assuming consent and, sorry to have to repeat this, assuming consent is what gets all sorts of people into all sorts of trouble.

NEGOTIATION

Is it possible to negotiate DADT properly? Much of the same argument applies as above. Negotiation really ought to be ongoing and properly informed. It is possible to imagine a situation where two people sit down and say 'Here are my red lines. Here is what I would just prefer you not to do. And here's what I'm okay with.'

There are certain problems with this. Firstly there's the fact that it's often impossible to predict all the possible situations that may need to be covered. Have you ever tried reading though one of those Byzantine user agreements that technology companies foist on their customers, the ones that give them your firstborn and first dibs on your spare kidney (check the squint print)? They're incredibly long 'because lawyers', and the lawyers' job is to try to foresee every unforeseeable circumstance and cover it—because this agreement is their only chance to do so. Do you really want to specify everything your partner should or shouldn't do in some circumstance they can't tell you about when it comes up? Do you really want to specify every single sex act that is and isn't acceptable in advance, just in case? What if the medical science behind the safer-sex precautions you specify changes in the future? Do you want to make a list of places you'd rather they not go on dates, and things you'd rather they didn't share?

As has been said and will be discussed in more detail later, CNM relationships normally involve considerable ongoing negotiation. Not only do we not always think of everything in advance, but it's also it's hard to predict how we'll react to situations we've not experienced before. People think they'll be okay with something and find they're not, and vice versa. And, as time passes, people simply change.

SOMEONE BECOMES A SECRET... OR NOT...

To be fair this is a not-uncommon issue in consensual non-monogamy. There's sometimes a genuine need for secrecy. You may find yourself in a relationship with someone who is unable or unwilling to make it public. Given negative public attitudes towards consensual non-monogamy on the one hand, and the practical realities of everyday life on the other, deciding to come out and who to come out to can be a difficult decision. So it really helps to be able to talk frankly.

Sometimes that just means not letting yourself be seen by a partner's friends. Sometimes it's more difficult, for instance if you're having a crisis and your partner can't explain that to their other partner because they don't want to know you exist. Or perhaps your own primary partner is worried about something concerning another partner you have, or even a casual involvement, but they're neither supposed to ask nor tell.

Or what if your primary partner is dating someone who knows you? Your partner can't tell you, and your acquaintance may feel they can't tell you either. It has potential for awkwardness especially if the other party(ies) involved know more of the story than you do and talks about it with mutual acquaintances. Your partner may have agreed to a DADT arrangement, but the people they date may not have signed up for that. People talk. To be the last in one's social circle to know is an unenviable position to be in. It invites pity.

IT ENABLES CHEATING

IF YOU GET into a relationship with someone who has a DADT arrangement with another partner, how do you make sure that their other partner(s) has actually consented, that they're telling the truth? And if they're lying and the truth comes out might you not find yourself being apportioned, justly or unjustly, some of the blame? People lie. People who cheat are often good at seizing on plausible excuses and CNM provides plenty. At least back in the 1950s when someone told you they were married, you could be pretty sure that their husband or wife would not look kindly upon your being wined, dined and bedded.

Being able to say 'We're in an open relationship' sounds all open and above board. It allows for a degree of disclosure—you know they're partnered—but all of that gets kicked into touch when they continue 'but we've got a don't ask, don't tell arrangement—I don't want to know who they're dating and they don't want to know who I'm dating.'

Sounds pretty straightforward, right? Except, right there, they've just nixed your ability to check that their partner is indeed okay with things. It would be perfectly normal in most CNM situations to say 'your partner sounds great, I'd love to meet them.' It's a very healthy instinct and, as we'll see when we discuss metamours—your partner's other partner(s)—it often leads to a better understanding of one's own partner(s) and, quite often, to friendships between metamours in their own right. DADT puts up a barricade. You are left to take everything on trust and, as is evidenced by countless tales of people ill-used in relationships, many complete scumbags are thoroughly believable. Strangely the two often seem to go hand in hand.

Early in Kerilyn's exploration of consensual non-monogamy she started dating Tim, who was married. Kerilyn made a point of speaking to his wife just to check she was okay with the arrangement. These days, though she's become more relaxed, she's still wary of DADT.

I wouldn't necessarily be cool going out with someone who is in a don't ask, don't tell, it's more just I would hope if you're seeing someone you do tell, you know. I'm trusting that person, but if they were to tell me I'm in a don't ask, don't tell, I would find that slightly weird and uncomfortable.

Subsequent experience underlined Kerilyn's reservations. She briefly dated an entertainer she met on a dating site who ostensibly had a DADT arrangement with his wife, who suffered from a severe degenerative condition. Kerilyn took that as read, because 'He seemed like a nice, genuine guy.' Then he became very defensive when she asked where he lived. He framed it as 'Why do you want to know my son's address?' and said he was worried about people turning up and causing a scene. She ended it at that point. DADT is open to abuse because most of us want to believe the best of other people and there are those who will take advantage of that.

One thing that you hear time and again from people who've been cheated on is that 'it's the deception rather than the sex that wounds them most'. As someone I knew who'd been cheated on put it, 'It was the fact that she [the third party] knew all about me but I didn't know about her. They had all the intimacy, we didn't.'

There are possible solutions of course. In an age when video is ubiquitous it would be pretty easy for two people in a DADT relationship each to record a video for the other in which they give their consent so it can be shown to anyone who might wish to know. This may not suit everyone. You might feel you're exposing yourself quite intimately to unknown strangers. It's one thing to record a video saying 'Hi, I'm David. If you're watching this you're presumably dating Kavitha. I just want you to know that's fine with me. We don't get involved in each other's dating lives. Hope you understand. Have fun guys!' But, for Christ's sakes, don't do it if your partner is an utter dimwit who forwards the video rather than simply playing it on their own phone to someone, or the next thing you'll know is you've become the latest YouTube sensation. All in all, an old-fashioned phone call would be safer.

And that's something you could reasonably ask your date to provide on a similar digital-privacy-aware basis. If they're unable, or if you end up talking with someone who gives their okay with all the joy and boundless enthusiasm of someone suspended over a tank of ravenous piranhas, you can take a view.

SAFE SEX

THINK ABOUT THIS: What does one do in a DADT arrangement if a condom breaks or, as has been known to happen where Homo not-terribly-sapiens is involved, passions trample common sense and bypass barrier contraception in the heat of the moment? What happens then if you're fluid bonded with another partner? Or what happens if one half of a couple practicing DADT finds they have an STI? Not being able to discuss this with your partner increases risk of transmission, and potentially onward to anyone else they're seeing as well.

IT'S A STICKING PLASTER

FOR SOME IN the CNM community, don't ask, don't tell is seen as a sign of a relationship in trouble. The first thing to say is that one shouldn't generalise. Some people work just fine on this basis. However, it would be healthy if it prompted a little reflection.

One question to ask is 'Why don't you want to know?' It's a good question. It could be the pain of thinking about one's partner being romantically or physically intimate with someone else. Lots of people who suspect their partner is having an affair prefer not to think about it. For others it may be the difficulty of controlling the amount of information they receive. To know a little is to invite the imagination to provide the rest. Or it could also be a reluctance to face up to problems within the relationship.

Only those involved know how good a state their relationship is in, and sometimes not even then, especially if there's not enough communication and/or honesty. Franklin Veaux, who's been writing about CNM for two decades, is very sceptical about DADT as an approach.

> To date, I have never seen a successful long-term don't ask, don't tell relationship. [I'm] not saying it's impossible, but I've never seen it work. If someone cannot handle knowing about a partner's other partners, something's going on. On some level they're living in denial or have jealousy issues they refuse to address, or they don't really want polyamory but think they have no choice. Something is going on that makes them unwilling to acknowledge the truth directly. Healthy relationships require communication. Deliberately blocking communication is not a good long-term strategy.[45]

There's a profound difference between being in a relationship that is fundamentally in good shape, with a life built together and a well of mutual affection, and being in a relationship one where one or both parties are looking for ways to get out. If DADT is your way out, what's keeping you? Is it the mess of disentangling your

---

45 https://www.quora.com/Can-a-dont-ask-dont-tell-polyamorous-relationship-work-in-the-long-run

finances, having to give up a home and find somewhere new to live? Are there children involved? These are not things that DADT (or any other CNM arrangement) can fix. It's a situation that needs *more* honesty, *more* communication, not less, and all of it compassionate. If you're hoping that DADT might allow you to find a new relationship that acts as a life raft to escape your sinking one, that might be understandable; being alone can be scary. However, adding more hurt to an already sensitive situation isn't likely to make any breakup smoother, rather the opposite.

Or if everything is pretty cool, you're in a good place together, but you just fancy some recreational dating to recapture the thrill of the new, ask yourself—why not talk about it? Is it because one of you likes the idea and the other doesn't, feels powerless to prevent it, and acquiesces for a quiet life? Maybe they want to pretend it's not happening? That doesn't sound exactly great.

By and large when people are in healthy relationships and want to experiment with non-monogamy, they don't shut down communication, they open it up. However, there are circumstances where that really isn't the best option. Read on.

CONTEXT IS IMPORTANT

Picking up on Jess Zhu's observations in the chapter on coming out, there's another discreet don't ask, don't tell dance that she notes in China's queer community.

China is a country where there's enormous social pressure, typically from parents, to marry and produce grandchildren. Filial piety, the obligations of children to honour, respect, obey and care for their parents, is far more important within Chinese culture than in most of its Western European and North American counterparts.

Thus arises the phenomenon of gay men marrying straight women without the woman knowing about the man's orientation. This is sufficiently common that there's a word, *tongqi* [同妻], for a woman married unknowingly to a gay man. There's also its corollary, *tongfu* [同夫], for a straight man unaware he's married to a lesbian. There's also a huge amount of angst and outright anger about what's known in China as *marriage fraud*.

However, Zhu also interviews people who suspect but who simply don't want to know about their spouse's orientation. Those people recognise their partner's good qualities. They are being provided for. They don't want their illusions shattered. They can live with the unspoken truth of the arrangement. The wife of one gay man Zhu interviewed had probably discovered traces of his double life on the internet, yet she was, in his words, "very smart not to 'poke the paper window'", i.e. not to make explicit what he believed was tacitly understood. That seemed to be confirmed by an exchange the husband described between him and his wife. Zhu quotes it thus:

'Let's just suppose, what if I were [gay]? What would you do?'

She said, 'I couldn't do anything with it'.

'But you could divorce me.' I suggested.

She replied, 'Well, even if I divorced you and married a straight man, he might still have affairs with other women. Yet, if I've already had a responsible husband, what's the difference?'[46]

Hard cases, they say, make bad laws. Zhu's *tongqi* example is a hard case, especially by the standards of most western countries. In most cases a minimum level of telling and knowing is preferable to none, for all the reasons listed above. Zhu shows that there are exceptions.

---

46 Graduate Journal of Social Science, January 2018 (14/1, pp 57-78). http://gjss.org/sites/default/files/issues/chapters/papers/GjSS%20Vol%2014-1%20Zhu.pdf

CHAPTER EIGHTEEN

Polyamory

POLYAMORY TAKES A wide range of forms. At its heart is quite a simple proposition: that it's possible to love many people with the knowledge and consent and to the contentment of everyone involved. This emphasis on ongoing emotional connections arguably distinguishes polyamory from the monogamish, swinging, and common or garden-variety open relationships we looked at in the previous chapters.

It would, of course, be simplistic and misleading to say that swinging, monogamish and open relationships are all about sex while polyamory, in its various permutations, is all about the romantic feels. Moreover, there are people who quite happily describe their poly relationship as an open one, or identify as a polyamorous swinger (albeit they might delineate their romantic/poly relationships from their purely sexual swinging relationships, seeing the latter as purely recreational). Plenty of poly people have one or more relationships that are predominantly sexual. There is a big intersection between polyamory and kink, so one quite often meets someone who has two loves—a life partner who shares romance and lust, not to mention lashings of ginger beer—and another with whom they have a D/s relationship that they wouldn't describe as romantic but that does matter to them intensely.

So grouping different relationship styles together or demarcating and separating them is somewhat arbitrary. But it's a way to explore the different ideas in play. If you want to call your relationship style blue-bubblegum-poly be my guest. If other people understand what you mean by that, it's a useful term.

Broadly speaking, the emphasis in all poly styles is on relationships rather than on encounters. Some of these relationships may be fairly brief and superficial, but plenty of people I've interviewed for this book have maintained multiple romantic relationships for years and decades. Their relationships are as enduring, or more so, than many marriages.

It would be a mistake to think of polyamory in predominantly sexual terms. Many of the polyamorous people I interviewed had one or more partner where the connection between them was largely or solely romantic or affectionate. Sometimes this reflects a diminution over time of the sexual spark in a relationship. Sometimes that spark was never there or it was much less significant than the emotional aspects of the relationship. And sometimes one or more of the people involved are asexual, demisexual or on the ace spectrum. As we'll see later, polyamory opens up plenty of options for people who either consider themselves ace or demi or whose partner(s) identify as such.

Other poly people have observed that the sheer availability of sex removes the sense of scarcity around it and, when resources are plentiful, people are less driven to secure their own supply. Do we need to remember the desperate hoarding of toilet rolls during the COVID pandemic? There may be attics still full of bog roll even as you read this years later.

All in all it means that, though some people's styles of polyamory may be highly sexual, there's never a lack of space for romance and platonic love. Yet even sexual polyamory takes very heterogeneous forms. Some groups seem to bear more resemblance to Mormon or Muslim polygyny than to the brave new egalitarian ideals for which many poly people evangelise. On the one hand you have many poly women arguing that polyamory offers a more truly feminist framework that further challenges the idea of woman-as-chattel by liberating her from the possession of one man. On the other you have some men instituting a 'one penis policy', i.e. their penis, whereby anyone in the group can have sex with anyone so long as they don't have a penis, unless it's The One Penis.

Once again I find myself with a strong foreboding that as the precepts of consensual non-monogamy gain greater acceptance, they'll offer cover to some deeply unethical people for whom consent is window dressing. Be warned. Yet so long as people remain sceptical they have the tools to put charlatans to the test and to expose them.

Anyway, enough of that for now. Let's look at the various forms polyamory takes. Some are far more common than others. Perhaps you'll find something that resonates with you.

CHAPTER NINETEEN

Hierarchical Polyamory: 'Couple-Plus'

Hierarchical polyamory, or 'primary-secondary,' is pretty much what it says on the label. It's an arrangement by which people have multiple relationships but some of them take precedence over others by default. Charlotte, a thirty-something professional from London, has a neat way of summarising it.

> The way I've heard the definition of hierarchical poly put is if you get a fabulous job but it's in, like, Glasgow your primary says 'When are we moving?', your secondary says 'Well, when can I visit?' and your tertiary says 'It's been nice knowing you'. And that's basically sort of the way I've always heard it [expressed], it's like some of your relationships are much more committed than others.

Or, Eunice suggests:

> Hierarchical poly is when your primary's wants are more important than your secondary's needs.

Much as with monogamish agreements and swinging, there's usually a core couple at the heart of hierarchical polyamory. It doesn't have to be a couple. It could be a triad or a quad. The point is, however, that in a hierarchical situation there is something of an assumption that some people's needs and opinions will take priority over those of others, while the others' responsibilities may be correspondingly less.

This can make perfect sense to a couple who have a life together with children, property, joint finances, careers, etc. If one of them starts dating someone outside the dyad, the notion that the new person is entitled to an equal say in whether the couple refinances their mortgage or buys a new car or invests in certain stocks would be ridiculous. But it's all too easy to conflate practical and emotional priorities—'we share a mortgage, the practicalities of our lives are entwined therefore we prioritise one another emotionally.' That sort of thinking, while comprehensible, can lead to the emotional needs of those outside the dyad being treated as lesser.

And yet the world we live in is built for couples. Marriages, two parents typically sharing legal responsibility for children, joint bank accounts, even the design of available living spaces... we've already seen how the dominance of a couple-centric culture shrinks the spaces and even the thought processes available for people who organise their lives differently.

I'll consider the problems that can stem from this in a later section. Suffice it to say for now that 'couple-plus' polyamory, while both pretty common and also much sought-after, is especially prone to unhealthy expressions of hierarchy. Forestalling this often requires a lot of fearless discussion and negotiation from the outset, where all involved are actively engaged and actively listened to but particular attention is paid to the new arrival.

Many of the various poly relationship styles can be operated hierarchically. Equally they can be pointedly non-hierarchical. Hierarchy or the lack of it is a choice. Just make sure everyone fully consents.

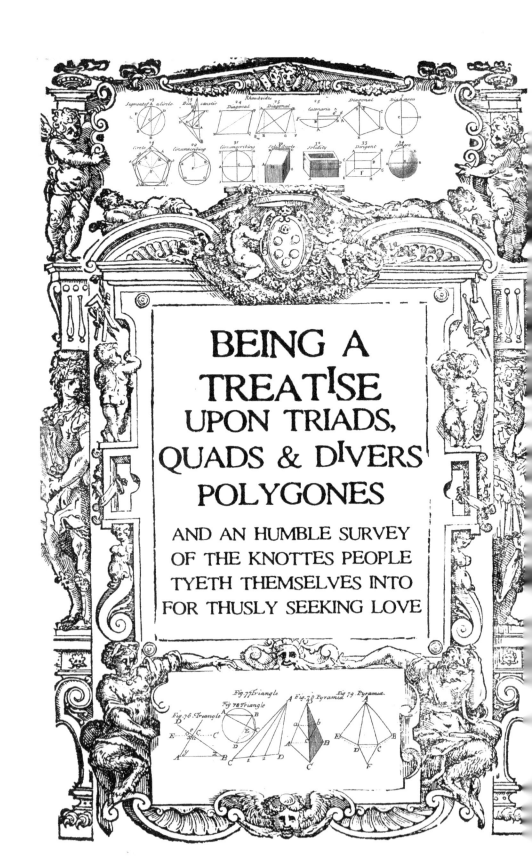

BEING A TREAT^ISE
UPON TRIADS, QUADS & D^IVERS POLYGONES

AND AN HUMBLE SURVEY OF THE KNOTTES PEOPLE TYETH THEMSELVES INTO FOR THUSLY SEEKING LOVE

Triads, quads, squares, Vs, Ws, and so forth are different relationship configurations that are fairly common within consensual non-monogamy, polyamory in particular. You might call it polygony.

Frankly, boundaries blur and there are a lot of crossovers with other styles of polyamory. So, for instance, you could be solo poly and find yourself in a 'V' or a 'W'. Let's quickly run through some broad definitions.

A triad, sometimes called a throuple (please be nice to the English language, people) is three people in a relationship where there's a sexual and/or emotional bond between each of the three people. A 'V'(or 'vee') is where one person is dating two others but those two are not romantically or sexually involved with one another (but could easily be close friends and part of the unit). Triads sometimes evolve organically as the result of the metamours in a V developing feelings for one another—if not sexually, which orientation often precludes, then chosen-family.

A quad is similar to a triad but with four. Commonly it's A dates B dates C dates D dates A; in other words, everyone in the configuration is dating two but not all three of the members. This is not uncommon in situations with two straight couples: both women date both men. I'd call this a square rather than a quad; another term is 'cross-coupled quad'. Typically it works best where everyone gets on pretty well even if they're not dating.

You could also have a square or quad where there were sexual and romantic bonds between everyone bar two of the members. Because of the remaining stigma around male bisexuality, a configuration of two women dating two men and one another, while the two men don't date, is not uncommon. And there are quads where it's just one happy pile of love and hormones all round.

An 'N' is like a square where the ends don't join, so A dates B dates C dates D but D and A don't date. A 'W' is a similar chain of five. Then there are larger chains and networks forming complex polycules. Some of those I interviewed for this book are members of a polycule called 'The Amorphous Squiggle,' partly because if you plot it on a piece of paper that's how it looks and partly, as Joreth Innkeeper puts it; "it was a reminder built right into our name that nobody was the 'gatekeeper' of our 'family' and to accept and welcome others and to embrace the inevitable change that the universe would throw at us."

How these configurations fare often owes a lot to how they form. Triads commonly arise when a couple adds a third to their dyad or, as mentioned, when metamours become involved. Quads sometimes result from a triad adding a fourth but equally because two couples have decided to fuse into a single unit. Indeed, while there are doubtless examples of spontaneous constellations forming all at once from hitherto unattached people, that seems relatively rare.

The problems that tend to arise within these configurations often seem to come back to the fact that couples generally already have a dynamic that predates the new relationship. It's for this reason that Joreth advises people who are thinking of adding others to an existing partnership to remake their relationship from scratch in a new context.

Charlotte says the situation is often exacerbated by inexperience.

> A lot of the time it's a couple opening up to a third person; they tend to think of it as adding to their original relationship, rather than thinking about the fact that they've got to break down their original relationship and recast it as a new thing because they now have this extra person in there. A lot of them don't confront what's called their couple's privilege, which is basically like this assumption that the original couples are the most important and they and their relationship must be protected over people.

> Also triads are really hard because there are four relationships in a triad; person A to person B, B to C, C to A, and the relationship of all three of them. So it requires a lot of communication and thinking. Especially since it's the type of poly that most people first do when they first become poly, it goes wrong a lot of the time.

Singaporeans Laura and David's experience is a good example of how tricky it can be taking on a third when you and they have different ideas of how things will work. Laura says she was clear from the outset that she wanted their thirds to feel like equals.

> I think we were very conscious of that with all women that we saw. I personally always made it a point to have them feel included. So, when we went out together,

for instance, we would never do coupley things. I would never hold his hand. I would encourage them to walk together and I would hold her hand so she didn't feel that she was the third wheel in that sense and in anything that we did. Even in the bedroom the focus was always on her. Not on me or on us. That was how I tried to ensure that the other woman never felt excluded. I don't think we ever had any complaints about them feeling excluded except for Emily, and I think that was because she was not very upfront about her expectations from the start.

Those complaints stemmed, at least in part, from Emily wanting a say in Laura and David's domestic matters.

Laura: We started to raise our issues with her, which were mainly the money and time and all that. She wanted to meet every other day, and for us to stay together, but we have a lot of things to see to like housework, our cats and all that. For us seeing her once a week or every two weeks is probably all we could commit to because we still have family and other commitments to do, but she wanted to come over really like every other night, once every two days also. So we gave in to her in the beginning, but...

David: To be fair, I think I've always been very bad at fulfilling the emotional needs of the other party. So I would try to have a role for them. I would say to them 'okay, you dom her' or 'you humiliate her' [the humiliation was consensual] or I would buy her a meal, or there might be some kind of monetary reward. I find it very hard to [get emotionally involved] with the other person, because I see it as kinky. Okay, she's fulfilling that role, but for me to fall in love with that third person takes a lot out of me. I don't even know if I'm capable. I like to think that I can. I mean if the stars are aligned and the person is right, but I think I've been facing some issues.

Clearly David and Laura had very different ideas about how the relationship would progress than did Emily. They already had full lives. Emily wanted a full life too, one that centred around her relationship with the couple.

In retrospect it seems that it would have been better to have discussed everything up front, right at the beginning. But before you rush to judgement, bear in mind that in some cultures being so direct is not the norm, and for some people, especially introverts like Laura, it can be doubly difficult.

TAKEAWAYS

- *Be clear in your own mind(s) about your needs, wants, expectations and boundaries.*
- *Listen carefully to the needs, wants, expectations and boundaries of the others involved.*
- *Communicate these early, ideally at the outset.*
- *Ensure they're compatible. Try not to let desire and excitement drown out your concerns.*
- *Be prepared to deal with the situation if these change.*
- *Be kind, compassionate, respectful and fair.*

CHAPTER TWENTY-ONE

Polyfidelity

POLYFIDELITY, OR POLYFI, takes the constellations we've encountered in the last chapter and closes the door behind them. In most triads, quads, squares, and the various polygons, people can also date outside the group. If they all agree not to, the arrangement is called *polyfidelity*. This adds a familiar dimension to a less familiar arrangement. As Eunice puts it:

> With 'closed' or 'polyfidelitous' relationships, people choose to date only within a group, say, three, five, six people, however many in are in that group, and *only* date the people within that group. Even though some people [would like to and others actually do] make those sorts of agreements, it tends not to be very typical.

Or as a rather sceptical Charlotte puts it:

> Polyfidelity is best thought of as monogamy with extra people in, or monogamy-plus. You will have three or maybe four people who are all in a relationship with each other, but don't date at all outside that relationship. So, it's basically monogamy with more people and it has all of the same issues that monogamy has and all of the same ickiness. Of non-monogamy styles it's the most monogamy-like one.

Polyfidelity has a long history, often within cults and religious communities that encouraged free love within the group. Some early Christian and Zoroastrian sects, for instance, rejected property (and marriage because it was seen as a form of property) and encouraged sexual freedom within the group. Radical and millenarian cults in the mediaeval and Renaissance periods often embraced free love. Better-known examples sprang up in utopian communities of the 19th century, most of which also espoused religious or socialist ideals. Perhaps the best known was the Oneida Community in New York state, which lasted from 1848 to 1881 and at one point counted more than 300 people living and working together. Members considered themselves to be group-married.

With the coming of the 1960s counterculture free-love communities became more numerous, more secular, and even more diverse. A particularly influential one was the Kerista community, which operated in the San Francisco area from 1971 to 1991. The terms *polyfidelity* and *compersion* were coined by Kerista members (the latter with the help of a Ouija-board-like device). The Keristans' lasting influence stemmed in part from their habit of documenting their doings in detail and dispersing vast amounts of this material in the form of flyers, newspapers, and comic books.

However, from a contemporary perspective a lot of these groups were highly problematic. It was quite common to have a strong, charismatic, male figure at the centre and, in some cases, sexual relationships were directed by the leader or leadership. Kerista was a case in point. The scope for these not being truly consensual was huge.

It's well noted that the 1960s free-love movement was overwhelmingly led by men. The current polyamory movement, such as it is, started to coalesce in the late 1980s and 1990s and was largely led by women from the outset. At the start of the 2020s women do most of the organising, provide faces for the media, plan conferences, write books and blogs and dominate polyamory's evolving thinking far more than men.

Polyfidelity's history, the propensity for the almost exclusively male founders of cults to encourage free love and polyfidelity within their groups for their own purposes, somewhat colours some people's view of polyfi even today. However, for some inclined towards non-monogamy, perhaps coming from a particular religious or cultural background, polyfidelity might feel more familiar, more traditional; as Charlotte says, 'monogamy with more people'.

Shyam and Rati, the professional couple from southern India, experienced issues with their partner. She was not untypical of monogamous people who find themselves experimenting but who want to retain aspects of monogamy. It was one of those cases where expectations and reality simply clashed.

> *Rati:* Our previous partner... we were a triad. She was strictly monogamous in her previous relationships. She was experimenting, but to a very large extent, she knew she was monogamous. And, we started to see the signs within our relationship as a triad as well.

> It's okay for a monogamous person to want to experiment but I think we needed to be more clear about our future plans and the possibility of seeing other people

in the future; even if this particular relationship is strong and ongoing, there will still be maybe [other people], and also individual plans, because you don't lose your individual identity. So that was important to make clear as well, because her idea of monogamy is two individuals become one, so everything gets aligned, and for us, even though we wanted to have a future as a triad, we still wanted to have a strong, individualistic lives as well.

Shyam: She kind of considered the triad to be very monogamous. To her this was an accidental love. She was a very monogamous person, so much, a very straight kind of very straight. And then she fell in love with us, both of us. And then she had this idea that okay, now it's just three of us so we are still monogamous, the three is fixed. Nothing more, never going to open up, that kind of thing. And one thing I learned from that was some people are just really monogamous. They are monogamous and very good in bed and they may not function in any other kind of relationship.

Rati: We were very egalitarian, we were clear from the very beginning that we didn't believe in hierarchy, everybody has the right to equal opportunity and things. The only thing we were very particular about is privacy, which was a huge problem because he and I had already come out as a couple way before we even had planned to date her. So there were a certain amount of people like his friends and my friends who already knew that we were polyamorous, but because of the nature of her friends, them being conservative and her family being conservative as well, she couldn't disclose that we were in a triad, she couldn't even disclose that she was in a couple. So that was quite a tough thing to handle.

Shyam and Rati's partner was uncomfortable with the fact that they continued to date other people. What she wanted was a closed polyfi triad. However, even that wouldn't really have addressed all of the issues she faced.

One interesting aspect of Shyam and Rati's triad was that their partner was frustrated by the fact that she felt unable to be out. It's the flip side of the more common situation where an existing couple are reluctant to include their third in social situations because they're unable or unwilling to come out to friends and family.

Shyam: Her family really liked us. We all would be sitting with the family, laughing, and they really care for us, but at the same time she has this feeling that these are people I really love and I want to be open to my family, but she can't, for her own reasons. Sometimes the arguments and fights will be about 'You are a couple and

I can't be, what am I like?' So she didn't have any identity in the relationship. That was what she felt, which spilled over to the relationship into arguments and which we didn't know how to adjust because that was her conservative side of the family.

Rati: We also did give her the option that, of course, she's welcome to tell her friends and whoever she wants to tell. And she did tell a lot of her friends. She even lost a couple of friends because they were completely unaccepting of the idea. So we told her that it's up to her, but there are a lot of consequences that may come along with that, that can be a bit dangerous situation.

Shyam: At one point I even suggested that I don't mind coming out to her family as me being her boyfriend, if that will help. But obviously she didn't want to.

Rati: She didn't want that. She said that she thought it was a very dangerous situation because my parents already knew that he was my boyfriend, and she was just not happy with the idea that we were a couple and she couldn't really come out and be taken seriously by her family if she said that they were a couple.

Clearly the problems that Shyam and Rati faced with their partner aren't specific to polyfidelity. However polyfidelity, by combining restrictions with more people, does have the potential to be a worst-of-all-worlds style of consensual non-monogamy for some people. You still don't have the freedom to date who you please, and you have more relationship combinations to manage.

In a quad there are six individual relationships to deal with (A & B, A & C, A & D, B & C, B & D, C & D), three pairing relationships (A&B to C&D, B&C to A&D, A&C to B&D), four where one person is relating to the other three jointly, and one collective four-person being. That's 14 relationships. Many of those 14 lines of connection may exist only very faintly, in terms of their importance and the attention they require, but still, that certainly makes monogamy look simple.

This probably partly accounts for why polyfidelity is quite rare. However, as I said above, if it works for you and everyone involved is wholeheartedly consenting, it might just be a joy.

Let me raise one particular red flag. For some polyfi groups part of the rationale is that everyone can be tested for STIs so that sex can happen within the group without the need for barrier contraceptives.

The received wisdom is that this often doesn't end well. Polyfidelity suffers from some of the same issues as monogamy. If someone breaks the agreement and has sex outside the group without using barrier contraception they don't always rush to fess up (indeed the group dynamics can exacerbate this—having to admit to *x* partners that you've messed up is potentially harder than having to admit to just one because everyone in the group then would have to use condoms until everyone gets the all clear). That means the entire group can be at risk of infection. And if people don't come clean it can lead to feelings of betrayal and even paranoia, not least because it's unclear how the problem arose. It can destroy groups. The best advice in CNM tends to be that everyone should be responsible for their own sexual health rather than to count on others to keep them safe.

CHAPTER TWENTY-TWO

Poly Families and Poly Networks

THE YEARNING TO have a family, to be part of something bigger than oneself, is a deeply human trait. We are social creatures to the core of our beings. In our distant past, belonging equated with survival. We don't thrive in isolation, which is why it's used as a punishment.

Even as the bonds of the traditional nuclear family have weakened, in the West at least, our need for others has remained strong. These days people talk about 'families of choice'.

The poly family is one expression of this need. Just as families the world over take different forms, so do poly families. For some it's the idea of mutual support, loyalty and trust, the naming of others as part of your inner circle. Family bonds are strong. It's not that parents and children or siblings don't fall out and cut ties, it's that we recognise the depth of the fissure when that happens. We don't do it lightly.

Families of choice are, perhaps, about drawing on the ideal of the family as an enduring and very personal institution and creating that amongst people we choose rather than those allotted to us by way of biology. As an adoptee, this resonates. We hold those most important to us close. We survive together.

The classic image of a poly family might be several adults all living under one roof, the relationships between them primarily founded on affinity rather than sexual intimacy, perhaps on bringing up children together, and acting as a unit at the centre of a wider social web.

However, poly families do not have to be like this. It's not essential to co-habit. It's not even necessary to be close by. Blood children and siblings can move halfway around the world and remain family. By the same token a poly family can be international. Familial bonds are stronger than distance.

Not only do people build families of choice, they can, to a considerable extent, decide how theirs works. As Meg-John Barker points out, such structures give people access to a whole range of essential support that they might not get elsewhere.

> Certainly any kinds of families of choice and systems have a lot to offer in terms of child rearing and having multiple parents or in terms of systems of care, the more people we have around who can care for us when we're sick and through [difficult] times in our lives. There's a lot that family-type models really open up in terms of financial sustainability, environmental sustainability, access to intimacy, all of that stuff gets us away from this very nuclear-family model or everyone as an atomised individual living alone.

Indeed for anyone who looks at 'the mum, dad and 2.4 kids' model and can't picture themselves in that situation, a family of choice is an important alternative, and not just to being alone. DK Green did go the conventional route, but that banged up against his reality as a trans man:

> I did the whole what you're supposed to do in society and culture, which is find your one true love, get married, have kids, buy a house, all that kind of guff. I wound up with the children out of that, because funnily enough, my husband at the time wasn't gay, and as presenting and as socialised as I [was], I [was] trying desperately to be a married woman. And you know, I'm neither really. I had the kids already, they were mine, neither of my partners have had children. When I left that particular lifestyle choice, which is the cultural norm, so to speak, the one we're expected to do, I thought, well, that was absolutely rubbish and didn't suit me at all. So I explored and I thankfully set out to systematically create the lifestyle I really wanted, not the one that I'd fallen into doing as I was told, and that's how I found poly.

> I decided to explore what was possible and I created this life for myself, which is exactly what I wanted. My children were raised by a village, to use the old term. We had my two primary partners and raised a family. Back then nobody used the word queer really, but certainly now it would've been recognised as a bunch of queer misfits getting together.

I don't know about you, but I find DK's phrase 'a bunch of queer misfits getting together' unexpectedly uplifting. Unexpected because I suspect, like many of us, I hadn't quite thought of it that way until he framed it. At the heart of what DK has described is acceptance. Acceptance is an amazingly powerful part of the human experience.

A few years ago I went to Leipzig to report on the world's biggest dark-music festival, Wave Gotik Treffen. Goth subculture, I discovered, offers much the same thing. It's a place where outsiders can get together to be their own sort of weird and be accepted. It's probably no coincidence that there's a big intersection between the Goth and CNM communities.

Families of choice, such as poly families, offer a haven for people who don't fit in elsewhere.

Olga Khazan, author of *Weird: The Power of Being an Outsider in an Insider World*, thinks being on the outside can be liberating, especially for our creativity. Freed, by not belonging, from any need to conform to stay part of a group, we can let our minds and our imaginations range free.

She makes reference to an experiment by Sharon Kim at Johns Hopkins University in the US that engineered a situation where a few people from a study were arbitrarily told that they were not 'part of the group'—there was actually no group. Then when all the participants were asked to draw a Martian, the 'not part of the group' people came up with far more imaginative images. Not only are people on the fringes of society typically more creative, Khazan argues, but they're also freer to innovate and challenge social norms.

However, as she observes:

Unfortunately, though, when people stop being "weird," these benefits go away. When people who were once in the minority become the majority, research shows that they tend to become more closed-minded. Weirdness has its perks, but nothing is weird forever.[47]

And yet it remains open to us all, misfits or not, to form our own tribes. That way we can belong somewhere even as we don't belong most places. Charlotte, who is neuro-atypical, sees in poly families not just a place to belong but a mirror of the sprawling familial networks that she grew up with.

I know a lot of solo poly people who are part of a poly family, it's just that things are a bit extended, which I actually find very comforting as I come from a recovering Catholic family. So, I'm used to enormous loosely connected families where some

47   Olga Khazan, *The Perks of Being a Weirdo*, The Atlantic, April 2020.

family members you see every day and some of them you see like once every three months.

So, poly families largely tend to be a more flexible thing than people would expect and also they are not as weird as people expect, because I think pretty much everyone has an auntie who or an uncle who you're not actually related to, they're just your parents' best friend or something. So, my auntie Jojo who I'm not actually related to, she's just been best friends with my mum, like since they were 11.

DK and his partners share a house and, when his children were growing up, they shared it too. Now that they've moved on, the house still functions as somewhere for them to come back to. It's almost a community hub where people connected to the family meet up.

It's a heart-warming image, but, says, Charlotte, in her experience it's the exception for poly families rather than the rule.

You might live in the same house, but there's a lot more where people visit occasionally or maybe they live round the corner or whatever. But there are a lot of complications with living in the same house both emotionally and relationshippy and also in legal terms, because there are laws [in the UK], meant to prevent slumlords, that actually just make it really difficult for multiple adults to rent the same house together or own the same house together, although the government's working on that.

Essentially your family and your support network are going to be more or less the same thing especially if you are including chosen family, which I always do, because a lot of my family are chosen family. I find it very calming because it's very like the family I grew up in. It's just like this enormous network of [people] being there for each other and always having someone who can help you and always being around to help someone.

As Charlotte says, for the most part poly families aren't the result of people setting out to construct a family, although that does happen. They generally happen organically.

However, some people absolutely love the idea of gathering all their favourite peeps under one roof. This is far from impossible but it can bring complications. So here are a few thoughts:

As with monogamous relationships, moving in together is a big deal. If it's a big deal for two people in a relationship to share a space, then the deal grows exponentially as you add people. Sometimes it's easier if the relationships are well established, so that living as a family is driven by logistics rather than passion.

In many countries property rental and ownership are organised around the assumption of no more than two adults per household. Sometimes it brings legal and financial complications if things don't work out. Or, if they work out too well. In some places local or national laws can limit the number of unrelated adults sharing a single property. This is common where a community wants to limit population density and traffic and, in particular, it can be a move to restrict student and immigrant households. Of course people often ignore the rules but it does invite the possibility that your happy poly family could be tossed out on its ear.

It's always worth checking first whether your plans for your living space and companions runs afoul of local laws.

WHAT WE CAN ALL LEARN FROM POLY FAMILIES

SOME PEOPLE HAVE enduringly positive memories of family that they have lost, and they want to re-create that environment. Others have had terrible experiences with their 'assigned' birth families but long for something that meets their needs for belonging, acceptance, and support.

Of course, families of choice don't have to be non-monogamous. Indeed they don't have to be anything you don't want them to be. As we'll see in the chapter on relationship anarchy, many people have friendships that transcend any 'mere' romantic attachments, and so their friends essentially become part of their family.

So just because you're monogamous it doesn't mean you have to buy into the whole nuclear family trope. We all get to decide who we want to include in our *de facto* families. You don't have to stop with the people you're biologically related to. It's a bit morbid, but think about who you'd want at your bedside if you were dying. That's a good reference point for knowing what your family of choice might look like. The rest is down to you.

CHAPTER TWENTY-THREE

Kitchen Table and Parallel Poly

THE KITCHEN TABLE is one of those powerful images, certainly in the West, that conjures up family and togetherness. In contrast, the dining table seems formal. People have serious meals and discussions and even disagreements around the dining table, but in the morning they stagger groggily downstairs still in their pyjamas or in T shirts and boxers to plonk themselves blurry-eyed and in desperate need of coffee at the kitchen table. We may do no more than grunt or stare at our phones, but the kitchen table is where we rub along, for better or worse, wearing our authentic rather than our public personas. The kitchen table is intimate and casual, somewhere to lounge and chat, especially once that first coffee has dispelled the fog of sleep.

The term *kitchen table polyamory* draws on that social informality. It also plays on the idea that various people have spent the night under the same roof, in the same or separate beds, and are starting the day together. It also evokes the idea of the family meeting where everyone sits down and works things out over tea and biscuits—that's probably milk and cookies in some far-flung corners of the world.

The term kitchen table poly was coined to encompass situations where the members of a polycule or an extended network are socially close and comfortable enough to share their morning selves. It isn't, after all, when many of us look or feel our best.

In sharp contrast there's also *parallel polyamory,* where metamours are aware of each other but have little or no contact with one another. Parallel poly blends into common-or-garden open relationships, with no clear dividing line between the two.

If there's a distinction between kitchen table poly and polyfi, triads, quads, poly families and so forth, it's that that KTP, as it's sometimes abbreviated, doesn't necessarily mean that people in the network live together or have multi-nodal relationship webs (which is possibly how Spiderman would do poly).

People do occasionally use the kitchen table label for a cohabiting poly-family setup, as is the case with DK and also Franklin below. When I refer to kitchen table poly here, it's specifically to give a sense of this ability to be together informally and communicate as a group, rather than to suggest cohabitation.

It implies that metamours know and generally like one another enough to want to spend time together socially, or are at least pragmatic enough to be able to sit down with everyone and try to find common ground and solutions to common issues.

In some situations there's considerable mutual support. This might be two or more metamours working together to support a lover in common, or to provide one another help through difficult times, or lend a hand when there are tasks to be done, or give advice on a subject they understand (or even on subjects they know bugger-all about but have an opinion on anyway...).

Take Ivan, Yana, Alexandra and Billie. They live in South East Asia; Ivan and Yana have roots elsewhere. Yana is married to Ivan. She also dates Billie while Ivan also dates Alexandra. Billie is planning to move in with Yana and Ivan while Alexandra lives separately.

'I would really love for Alexandra to move in with us,' Yana says, 'but because of her family and other issues she cannot do that, and that makes me really sad because I think she and Ivan are not spending enough time together.'

Ivan doesn't feel the pressure to cohabit. Indeed he wonders if that may be why everything works as well as it does.

> Maybe the secret to our success is that our arrangement is that we see each other on Saturdays, and one day of the weekdays, and I think that works fairly well for us. We [he and Alexandra] both have our own personal space. We talk a lot online. And we make an effort to spend time together. I think we have found a balance and I am not sure that upsetting this balance in favour of something that might be better is worth it, so I'm quite happy where I am right now.

However the four of them do make a comfortable unit.

In my interviews with poly people, I find that this sort of arrangement often evokes a degree of envy from those who don't have something comparable. For many people with more than one partner, there's a desire for everyone to get along and even be close friends to the extent that this ideal of closeness is often highly prized in the poly world. After all, if you love two, three, four or more people, isn't the best thing having everyone in the same place, enjoying each other's company?

Well, that depends. It depends on everyone *wanting* to spend time with one another. Naturally this raises again the issue of consent, and though consent is valorised in poly circles it isn't always practiced. Franklin Veaux:

I've always wanted to live with multiple lovers, but I've become disenchanted with that idea because I see the ways that it can be dysfunctional, I see the ways that people who pursue it and who deliberately set out to create kitchen-table polyamory end up creating these very coercive structures; if you're not, you know, part of the in-group then you're not really one of us, and there's some really fucked-up stuff that can happen when you have an expectation that anybody in the network must be like this, must be part of the family, must be willing to live with other lovers, must have close relationships with everybody else in the network.

There's a fundamental coerciveness that is baked into the foundation of that idea, and I see that so often among people who subscribe to a kitchen table model of polyamory that it has kind of put me off a little bit.

I would like an extended network of people who all get along, but it doesn't have to be that way. It's okay if people do not want to live with me, it's okay if people in my poly network don't get along with each other and don't particularly like each other. People are adults and they need to be free to decide for themselves how they relate to the other people in the network.

We'll return to the subject of coercion at various points. Suffice it to say that non-monogamous people are as capable of being as manipulative, bullying, coercive, and non-consensual as monogamous people, and group dynamics can amplify that.

The key point is, as ever, consent. It may make you sad that Pete, Kwame and Haruki aren't best friends, but if they're not big on one another's company forcing them to spend time together is unlikely to produce happy results. Personalities can jar with one another even if none of those involved are bad or unreasonable.

It may also be difficult for metamours faced with the whole 'What do you *see* in them?' issue. If someone we love patently loves someone we cannot relate to it may prompt questions. Those questions may include 'Do they really understand me?', 'Do I really understand them?', 'Do we really share as many values as I thought we did?' and so forth. I'll explore some of these questions in the chapter on metamours.

CHAPTER TWENTY-FOUR

Solo Polyamory

AMONGST THOSE I interviewed, the two most common styles of consensual non-monogamy are solo polyamory and relationship anarchy (I'll look at relationship anarchy in the next chapter).

That these styles seem to predominate may reflect a number of things—that one interviewee would introduce me to another with a similar outlook, for instance, but also possibly that CNM relationship styles have changed over the last twenty years. In Singapore where more of my interviewees were connected through the kink community, there was often a central 'primary' couple. In the UK hierarchical poly seems broadly to have fallen out of favour, especially with younger members of the community.

So, let's start with a definition of solo poly from Dr. Liz Powell.

> Solo polyamory is a form of polyamory where you are your own primary partner or where you operate as an individual rather than as someone becoming coupled. I *do* have a veto over myself, and I often use it where part of me is like 'I want to go on a date' and the other part of me is like 'You haven't gotten enough sleep this week and you need to sleep. So, I'm vetoing your date.'

> What solo poly means for me is that nobody gets to tell me what to do, with my heart, my mind, my body or my time. That doesn't mean I won't consider what other people want or need, but it means that the final say is always mine.

This idea that one's primary relationship is with oneself is central to solo poly. It sounds, superficially anyway, like a recipe for selfishness. Read another way, however, it's a charter for personal responsibility.

It may seem rather contradictory given everything I've said about humans being fundamentally social creatures. However there need not be a contradiction. Being solo poly and being your own primary in no way precludes other relationships whether committed or casual, serious or light hearted. It doesn't even preclude interdependence. What it does do, though, is put the emphasis on developing a good relationship with oneself. Meg-John Barker:

> I like it for recognising that we need a significant relationship with ourselves. It recognises, and it's a very clichéd idea, that in order to love others you need to love yourself. But there's an awful lot to that. One, we're not always aware of our own stuff. Again, we can just play [that stuff] out on other people in ways that really hurt them and hurt us. The more self-aware we are, the better. And, two, if we don't love aspects of ourselves we can project those onto other people, or we can go looking for them in other people. So, solo poly has built in that potential for really enabling more self-aware people who are okay with their own solitude to forming relationships from that basis of self-love.

In our relationships, a critical distinction can be drawn between (at the extreme ends of the scale) *co-dependency* and *interdependency.*

Co-dependency doesn't have a single definition, but the American psychiatrist Dr. Timmen Cermak proposed a set of criteria including:

- *The sacrifice of self-esteem to maintain relationships despite adverse consequences*
- *Seeing to the needs of others to the exclusion, not just the expense, of meeting one's own*
- *Poor boundaries*
- *Issues with separation and anxiety*
- *Over-attachment to people in chaotic situations, often resulting from substance abuse and addiction*
- *Often co-dependent people try to control one another to get their needs met.*

Interdependency, in contrast, can be very healthy. A key part of relationships is the role we play regulating one another's emotions. With co-dependency this can get badly unbalanced, while with healthy interdependency people offer mutual support. Those involved get the closeness and sense of attachment they need, have good self-esteem and are self-supporting, and while everyone contributes to the relationship there's no attempt to control anyone. Boundaries are very much in play. Everyone keeps their independence and maintains a strong sense of self. Dr. MJ again:

Intersectional feminists and others would point out we are all interdependent, and we do require systems of care around us to be part of those systems both for other people and for ourselves. It's whether we do it in a fiercely independent way that neglects the fact that we are going to be disabled and struggling with our health at some points in life when we do need systems of care—or are we doing it as a way of building our [support] system whilst also retaining our sense of self, so that we don't get lost in other people.

Eunice, thirty-something, British and an event organiser, describes herself as solo poly. After a dating-free year following a breakup in her early twenties she met a number of people who were consensually non-monogamous and began three important relationships. Six years later she had five partners (one of whom was strongly inclined towards monogamy) and two 'intimate friendships'. Five years on from that, her monogamously-inclined partner had found someone to be monogamous with, and she'd separated from a second who'd married a new partner with two children (as well as having a child from an earlier relationship). And yet she remains close to them both and the other relationships endured, two of them for well over a decade now and two others for more than five years.

Eunice remains very much her own person. She has her own flat in London and is phenomenally busy organising a variety of events, some professionally and some voluntarily for groups in which she's an active member.

So what is it that makes sense for her about solo poly?

It lets me explore authentically my own ethics and who I am and I think that exploration will never really stop. I've come to realise that I consider autonomy (my own, my partners' and my extended polyfamily members') to be vital for un-coerced and informed consent. It's one of my highest principles. Being solo poly allows me to really live that fully. It also compels me to be more proactive in my relationships—it's harder for me to be complacent if I can't just rely on seeing a 'nesting partner' at home all the time. I need to reach out actively, communicate, and connect. I feel like my relationships are healthier for us having our own private spaces and time apart. I'm an introvert, so that time alone to recharge is vital to my mental health.

Eunice and most of her network also embrace a kitchen table approach.

Being solo doesn't mean isolation or lack of support. We've all gone on holiday together, done creative projects together, shared joys and fears and hopes. That won't be the case for every solo poly person, of course, but it certainly has been the case for me.

I'm aware that I have a huge amount of privilege in being able to do this, as I'm able-bodied and have typically been financially stable enough to travel to see partners. Also I don't want children. If I did, that might have forced me to think deeply about whether I could care for them properly on my own.

Eunice makes a good point about being in a position of privilege having the resources she needs to be solo poly. She's not wealthy, not very highly paid, but she does have a home and a modest income that covers her needs.

In so far as solo poly is possibly the most common way consensual non-monogamy seems to be practiced, it's perhaps a reflection of the times we live in. Relationships, like most other human social spheres, are shaped by forces that include economics and technology. If marriage in the West was, until at least the 19th Century, more often a practical alliance for reasons of finance, family and survival than a romantic one, then relationships today reflect modern economics, greater opportunities to self-actualise than earlier generations enjoyed, and the changed status of women in particular.

Where we're at now is built on a century and more of social change that arguably began with the suffragettes, the drafting of women into the workforce during the two world wars, the pill and other forms of effective birth control, and the second wave of feminism that emerged from the political upheavals of 1968.

Women's social and sexual liberation has gone hand in hand with women's growing economic independence. If you're able to earn the money to pay for your own place, your food, and other basic necessities, then you can live independently. If you have access to contraception and medical care, you have a higher degree of control over your body than if you don't. If you're financially dependent *and* lack the means to prevent or terminate pregnancy, then your social and sexual independence is fundamentally compromised.

All this helps explain why consensual non-monogamy is most visibly (though by no means only) practiced by educated, middle class, professional and able-bodied people. To be solo poly, it helps enormously to be able to afford a way of life that allows for romantic and sexual independence. It's tough if you and your partners can't afford your own space or if you rely on assistance because of disability.

The changes we've seen aren't limited to the West. Modern, urban societies with independent people of both sexes dating for pleasure, rather than out of a social necessity, can be found from Shanghai and Sydney to Stockholm, Sofia, Shimla, Singapore, Santiago, and San Francisco.

These trends also filter through social and economic groups. Though it may be easier to be solo poly if you have the means, it doesn't stop those who don't. Emma, a twenty-something Singaporean from a Muslim background, isn't consciously solo poly. She doesn't own her own place, she doesn't earn a great deal of money. Nor does she call it solo poly. It's just the style that describes most closely how she conducts her relationships. I first interviewed her in early 2018.

> I wasn't into the idea of having boyfriends or regular relationships. Maybe I'm just not ready for it. But me being twenty-five I do like the idea of having options as well as the freedom to see other people and do what I want. So the guys that I sleep with or the guys that I date do know that I see other people.

> I am sleeping with two people. And have one long-distance relationship. Two of them are in Singapore, one local, one Australian, and the one that is overseas is Dutch.

> The Australian guy and I have passed the two-year mark which is incredible because I didn't expect to be with him that long. As for the local one it's kind of on and off. They are all older, the Dutch one hasn't even moved here to Singapore but he will. We will see where we go from there. The others have been going for about a year and a half.

> If you say you have been seeing someone for 2½ years and you see them two or three times a week, then that's pretty much me and the Australian guy, in a non-committal way. There are times when we cannot meet for a prolonged period of time, which can be from a few days to a couple of weeks. I think I'm more of a live-in-the-moment sort of person and I think just talking about the future or plans, even just for the next few months, is a bit much.

Emma may sound a little like a commitment-phobe, but two years on she and her Australian lover still see each other regularly. Emma just doesn't get the idea of boyfriends. She dislikes the term. 'It's boring' is her dismissive response. Birthdays, anniversaries, Valentine's Day, the furniture of committed relationships, simply don't mean anything to her. 'I'm just happy if he buys me flowers not on a special day,' is how she puts it.

Relationship styles in CNM circles do go in and out of fashion. A decade or two ago hierarchical poly was more common and closed triads were less of an oddity. What seems to be happening—with the passage of time, as apps like OKCupid and Tinder encourage retail dating, as CNM becomes more talked about, and as the community of consensually non-monogamous people expands and becomes more confident—is perhaps that there's less pressure to mirror the monogamous world. Dating simply becomes more fluid, less about appearances, more about the commitments that those involved want to make. For a lot of people, that means maintaining their independence and a degree of self-sufficiency but choosing to share that with the people that matter to them, whether romantic or sexual partners or not.

The downside may be that, for some people, the language of consensual non-monogamy is just a convenient way of dignifying casual dating by draping a philosophical fig leaf over its earthier aspects. There are surely plenty of people who talk a good CNM game who are simply players trying an angle, just as the term 'sapiosexual' (meaning people who find intelligence sexually attractive) has been appropriated by some who use it just to make their dating app profiles sound less superficial.

There's a lot of superficial out there. For Shyam, the IT professional from Kerala, being solo poly didn't give him the stability he needed. He wanted a committed ongoing relationship; to be part of a couple.

> With the people I dated I realised that I was easily dispensable. So whenever they wanted they will call me, and when I need them none of them were there. So I felt pretty much rejected. I think being solo poly, I did meet a quite a lot of people, but I realised that while a lot of people who liked me as a person, enjoy spending time with me and all that—but at the end of the day I felt really lonely because I am alone. So, there was a realisation that even though I had so many wonderful people around me, I am alone. That was kind of a realisation for me to learn that I need someone in my life. I could do poly, but I can't just have multiple people and no steady partner.

Kelli, a DJ from Seattle who is also neuroatypical, compares getting 'nested,' 'entwined' and hierarchical poly couples to understand her situation as a solo poly person, to getting neurotypical people to understand her autism. In many ways it comes down to the 'Who'll be the one who turns up at the hospital?' issue again.

> I prefer dating other SoPos, when I say SoPo I mean solo polyamory. Because there's just so many little tiny like microaggressions that happen with hierarchical people and nesting people and whatnot that you know enough of a build-up and it's really, really painful, and it can really put me out.

For example, like, who takes care of you when you're sick? I've been dealing with the biggest health crisis of my whole life in the last year, where it's pretty much invisible unless you're around me all the time. And it was very, very difficult for me to get help, beyond my anchor partner, because everybody else just assumed, one because they see me and my anchor partner as a unit, even though we're each of us are solo polyamorous, and we live separately, but we're visibly, the way that we act in the community, people just couple us together, and then they think, oh, Kelly's taken care of Kelly has help, even though I'm like asking them begging I'm on my knees begging people and like almost nobody came to help me, one because they couldn't see me, and two because they didn't believe me and three because what they saw was that I was already being taken care of, you know, it's just like it was horrible.

I had another SoPo that I had met at a conference, who lived two states away from me, called me twice a week to help me with stuff, and it was the most amazing thing, but it was another solo person who understood.

There are other Solo Poly niggles like people failing to distinguish Solo Poly from casual dating or even trotting out the old 'well you just haven't met the right person yet'. As Eunice points out there's a difference between single, 'single and poly' and solo poly. Waiting for the rest of the world to cotton on can grate sometimes.

Nor has the coronavirus pandemic been easy for a lot of SoPo people. Most don't live with a partner and the effect for many has been to leave them feeling isolated. It hasn't helped that governments have taken the opportunity to push a mono-normative narrative in the name of disease control—understandable certainly but it's added the issue of erasure to that of isolation.

Solo poly is, like everything else, not for everyone. But it does reflect the way that people are increasingly forming their relationships and running their lives.

WHAT CAN THE REST OF US LEARN FROM ALL THIS?

WHAT DO SOLO poly people do that monogamous people might want to consider? That depends on what you want out of a relationship. Some people like nothing more than to merge themselves with another, to subsume their own identity within that of the unit. Other people want a partnership where they remain themselves but work in tandem with a partner towards life goals.

Let's return to the idea of the 'relationship escalator' that's so culturally prevalent: in approximate order, you meet, date, kiss, have sex, date some more, move in, get a mortgage, get married, have kids, tick off anniversaries, die. Solo poly is a reminder that you can stay committed without staying on the escalator. The relationship doesn't have to end if it doesn't continue to progress through all the steps. It's not compulsory to live with someone. It's not compulsory to share your finances. You don't have to have children. For many people, living with someone is as much about the practicalities of splitting costs and labour. (I know! Many of you still live in hope of an *actual* equitable division of labour.) If they could afford to, more might choose to live on their own. There's a lot to be said for adjoining flats—the expense aside.

Maintaining one's independence and a healthy relationship with oneself is hardly the sole province of non-monogamous people. Monogamous people get to rewrite their rules too. That said, being able to stand on your own two feet doesn't mean that it isn't nice to lean on someone from time to time, or to let them lean on you.

CHAPTER TWENTY-FIVE

Relationship Anarchy

The idea of not prioritising romantic relationships over other kinds, that was always my entry point. I always had a really close relationship with my sister and now I do with both my sisters, and I hated this idea of 'the one' because nobody was going to be more important than my sisters. And it felt like in every monogamous relationship I was getting, and even close friendships, there was a sense of people wanting to be the one for me and of me really struggling with it. I was saying to people 'I won't be 'the one'', but I think actually it was more complicated than that, I was probably giving them the impression I could be, but actually I was trying to do it for more than one person at a time.

—Meg-John Barker

RELATIONSHIP ANARCHY, OR RA, is one of those ideas that seems to have come out of a clear sky. The person who coined the phrase, Andie Nordgren, is a Swedish video games producer who worked on the massive multiplayer online space opera EVE.

In 2006 Nordgren posted an essay titled 'The short instructional manifesto for relationship anarchy'(originally in Swedish). It was indeed short, but its impact was far out of proportion to its length. Perhaps that's because, being an anarchist manifesto, it suggests rather than prescribes. People seem to pick and mix the bits they like and leave those they don't in the box.

What the manifesto does is systematically pull to pieces our established notions of romantic relationships not by attacking them, but by offering thoughtful alternatives.

There are nine short sections in the original manifesto. Some are less than revolutionary, albeit common-sensical and important: the advantages of trust and of assuming no malice for instance (though Nordgren does put it rather beautifully: "choosing to assume that your partner does not wish you harm leads you down a much more positive path..."). Others are the need for good communications and the 'fake it till you make it' approach. Trust and good communication we will explore elsewhere; they're not specific to RA.

Nor is relationship anarchy static. RA has continued to develop since Nordgren first published her thoughts in 2006 and a new translation in 2012[48] but the manifesto remains an excellent starting point.

Relationship Anarchy doesn't have fixed rules. It's anarchy, innit! But there does seem to be broad agreement on principles. One that Meg-John alludes to is that relationships needn't be ranked in the way that we're socially programmed to rank them; for instance romantic relationships over birth-family or vice versa, or either of these over friendships, or those based on shared interests or work. Instead, each relationship between people should find its own level of value and importance based on what the people in it want, societal relationship rankings be damned.

The word *anarchy* winds some people up, but it's etymologically appropriate: It's from the Greek for *no ruler* or *leader* or perhaps no *order* in the sense of *ranking*. The RA symbol takes the anarchist A and places it in a heart rather than a circle.

Those who subscribe to RA generally believe that romantic love needn't be restricted to monogamous pairs and that love for one person doesn't necessarily detract from that felt for another, and another. RA recognises that there are many kinds of love and encourages people to ask whether romantic love has to trump all the others. In that respect one could see elements of RA in early Christianity which often seems to celebrate agapē (ἀγάπη) or unconditional love as love's highest form. And it is also worth stressing that you can absolutely be RA and be monogamous or even single and ace!

As we've seen, some forms of consensual non-monogamy are either hierarchical or seek to make the wellbeing of one particular dyad paramount. Thus you have arrangements whereby a primary partner explicitly or effectively wields a veto over their partner's other relationships. Things happen only with that person's permission. Relationship anarchy rejects that approach, cautioning against ranking or comparing relationships or necessarily seeing one relationship as a 'primary'. Nordgren's manifesto stresses the autonomous nature of each individual connection.

This need to respect the autonomy not just of connections but also of individuals permeates RA. Within the core cultural script that most people are handed and

---

48   https://log.andie.se/post/26652940513/the-short-instructional-manifesto-for-relationship

absorb from childhood is the idea that people in relationships are bound to one an-other in restrictive ways. People are taught that, as part of a couple, they are entitled to certain expectations of a partner. This generally boils down to 'You made me this promise, now act as you're supposed to.' The promise may never have been verbalised, but the expectations that come with coupledom are so strong that people often assume certain promises or commitments have been made simply by virtue of entering into an intimate relationship. 'Now we're dating you shouldn't be doing x or seeing y,' for instance.

Why, asks RA, does an intimate relationship between two people give either person any right to tell the other what to do? Even if those two people have a shared history, why is there an assumption that it's okay for one party to compel the other to behave a certain way?

Relationship anarchists rip up the rulebook. Anarchists generally like ripping up rulebooks (but because deep down they're cuddly and environmentally conscious they put them in the recycling). RA instead puts an emphasis not just on autonomy but also integrity and authenticity. Love, it says, should not seek to restrict but should rather be an act of generosity that seeks to help the beloved be their best authentic self—and obviously it allows them to determine what that best authentic self is. Compromise is fine if freely agreed, but compromise simply because of cultural or societal expecta-tions isn't really compromise, it's a surrender to programming. If you find yourself hearing, or using, the word 'should' it's a bit of a red flag. Phrases like 'because that's what people/couples/boyfriends/girlfriends do' are less a red flag and more of a huge distress flare. You don't need the rulebook. You're Adam and Eve in your own garden. No God, no snake, just a blank page. What you write on it is an exercise in love and imagination.

When the RA manifesto first appeared negative attitudes towards queer and trans people were more widespread than now, so Nordgren explicitly took to task cultural assumptions about heterosexuality. These days some may think that it shouldn't need saying that writing one's own rules of course includes throwing out old assumptions about gender and orientation.

Sadly, it's unlikely there will ever be a time that inclusion and equality won't need stressing. There's no point ripping up one rulebook just to create another for its own sake. You're two, or more, autonomous thinking people. You can determine what val-ues underpin your relationship for yourselves and which people you want to include in your relationships based on your own values rather than those foisted upon you. If you're building your dream chosen family, you get to choose; that's the point. So long as those you choose consent to be chosen and choose you back, you're grand.

That said, there's absolutely nothing wrong with setting out your own boundaries and expectations. But in any setup, it's wise to do this each as an individual in your own right. It may be that your values are incompatible in some ways and it's better to find that out sooner rather than later. Compromising these may seem like an act of love, but compromising at a core level makes it hard to love deeply and authentically and sustainably because you haven't brought your true self to the relationship.

Three other thoughts in the original manifesto really stand out. The first challenges the notion love is somehow scarce. On the contrary, relationship anarchists believe it is abundant. Yet for something that's a renewable resource, costs no money, and is widely available given personal openness and intention, love is strangely protected and guarded by society to make it scarce.

Second is an injunction that Nordgren frames as 'Build for the lovely unexpected'. In some ways this is another expression of the idea that we are unduly bound and restrained by 'shoulds'. But I prefer to see it as an acknowledgement of the fact that life produces unexpected opportunities for joy that conventional relationships often preclude. The most obvious are those chance meetings with others where there is immediate chemistry and the means to explore.

The famous British film *Brief Encounter* is almost a case study in the consequences of being bound by duty and expectation. The movie follows two characters who meet in a railway station waiting room through a brief unconsummated affair, whereafter they eventually part, clearly consumed by feelings for one another but denied the chance to explore them. It's high on the list of the most British things ever. Upper lips are starched and possibly reinforced with small lip-bracing girders.

Instead, relationship anarchy asks 'Should we deny ourselves or others these rare and fleeting magical moments, or are they the stuff of which a full life is made?' In conventional, monogamous relationships we're expected to deny ourselves these moments. RA recognises that the decision whether to pursue the lovely unexpected should rest with the autonomous individual. It embraces the unpredictable and the spontaneous and encourages us to wish it for those we love.

Thirdly, the manifesto ends with one of its most powerful thoughts: the idea that we should 'customise our commitments'. Far from discouraging commitment, RA offers the possibility of making commitments we truly subscribe to and doing away with those we don't. We'll have a look at the form that some of these bilateral (or multilateral) agreements take later in the book, but their scope can be as wide or as narrow as those agreeing them wish.

You can, for instance, commit to having children and to bringing them up together, or to a mortgage or to spending a life together. It's just that these things are not the preordained milestones of date, kiss, fuck, move in, mortgage, marry, reproduce, retire and die along the relationship conveyor belt. A commitment could take the form; 'We commit to spending a weekend each year with one another' (what might be termed a comet relationship).[49] Or, 'We commit to being there for one another whenever we're needed but not when we're not.'

The writer and therapist Esther Perel makes the inspired suggestion that we should say to our partners and friends 'I choose you' rather than 'I love you', seeing relationships as an everyday opt-in rather than stasis. Any commitment rests on the ongoing consent of those involved. One of the things contractual marriage does is bind people together long after one or both want out. Marriage can easily become non-consensual and the cause of endless unhappiness. Relationship anarchy fundamentally takes issue with the idea of enforced coupledom.

It's another of the scripts that we've been handed: that without coercion we wouldn't stay together, children would be abandoned, and Sodom and Gomorrah would reign. But is that true? Most people do their level best to make their relationships work and make huge sacrifices for their children. You can legislate responsibilities—child support for instance, education and child protection among other things—but you can't legislate commitment. Those we make for ourselves are surely stronger than those foisted on us.

For many of my interviewees a key part of RA's appeal is that it goes a step beyond most other forms of CNM by suggesting that romantic relationships shouldn't necessarily be prioritised over non-romantic ones. As Dr. Liz Powell puts it:

> The monogamy model essentially tells us that the person you've been dating for two months can have greater say over your time than the friend you've had for ten years. I've had so many friends who have disappeared when they start dating because the date person is the most important person in their life, not the friend person.

This idea isn't explicitly expressed in Andie Nordgren's manifesto. What she actually says is:

---

49   Comet relationships are so named because, like comets, the beloved appears periodically, even regularly, but not necessarily often. It might be the person who lives on the other side of the world and you recouple when they're in your hemisphere, or vice versa, every year or two. The ubiquity of free global communications and video calls means that more people are able to maintain meaningful long distance relationships where physical encounters are relatively infrequent.

Don't rank and compare people and relationships—cherish the individual and your connection to them. One person in your life does not need to be named primary for the relationship to be real. Each relationship is independent, and a relationship between autonomous individuals.

But RA has continued to evolve. The writer Anita Cassidy is another who sees the removal of any romantic hierarchy as a big plus:

> For me, relationship anarchy is about prioritising and seeing a lot of value in all types of connections. So, I don't just prioritise my romantic and sexual relationships, as most mono or heteronormative people do. Other people that I'm friends with still are really important to me, and I invest as much time as I'm physically able to in the periphery of my friendships, but also in the kind of non-sexual friendships that I have as well as my family connections.

Perhaps the prioritisation of romantic relationships is linked to the fact that, in many western cultures, two people who form a romantic bond routinely set up their own separate household. In many other cultures couples remain in an intergenerational family home and are thus much more connected to, and integrated into, a wider social group. In traditional village settings the same thing often applies. Couples are less separate from the wider community, possibly barely separate at all. And historically, even in Western Europe, husbands and wives were not necessarily each other's main social relationship. Indeed many marriages were for practical economic and reproductive purposes. You only have to turn to the novels of Jane Austen to see that even Fitzwilliam Darcy and Elizabeth Bennett, caught up in the irresistible tide of romance, had eyes and ears for their regular social circles. And you can bet that Charlotte Lucas, who pragmatically marries the boorish cleric William Collins for security, will absolutely cling to her circle of family and friends.

The cultural messages with which we're flooded these days flow against the weight of our social history. How many warm, sustaining and emotionally intimate relationships wither when people buy into the idea that, as part of a couple, they no longer need close friends and family in the way they once did? Perhaps we should ask ourselves whether it's actually the modern nuclear family that's the aberration.

Relationship anarchy, ironically, rather than simply smashing everything up, offers us the chance to reclaim a very traditional take on our connections. Above all it urges us to decide for ourselves which relationships take priority and encourages us, once again, to write our own story. No wonder it seems to resonate so widely.

This seems such a simple and obvious idea that it leads many people to ask why it's not universal. This idea of charting one's own course also colours many other forms of consensual non-monogamy and is one of the things that tends to set CNM apart from monogamy. CNM accepts that relationships can be valuable even if they're not able to meet our every need. More importantly still, the idea that relationships should be allowed to find their own level helps us avoid wrecking them by trying to force them to be what they're not.

However, it's worth adding a few caveats. As Liz Powell recalls:

> I don't use the label because the majority of the folks that I met who identified as relationship anarchists when I first learned about it, were assholes. So, I just have a very bad taste in my mouth.

It's becoming a bit of a recurring theme, but how many people have each of us met who've been very deft about dressing bad behaviour in ethical or idealistic language? There's the free-market-championing capitalist who uses their power to shut down competition. There's the socialist who abhors private property until they have private property of their own. There's the anarchist who hates rules but is quite happy to be controlling towards others.

RA is absolutely open to abuse, just as we'll see in due course with 'radical honesty'; radical or anarchic doesn't necessarily coincide with ethical. So let's consider some of the things to watch out for, so as not to be, as Dr. Liz would have it, an arsehole.[50]

While each relationship may be its own entity and the connection autonomous, that doesn't mean the relationship exists in a vacuum. Excitement or difficulties in one relationship can affect others. A connection may be autonomous, but that doesn't mean that saying 'It's none of your business' cuts it if the ramifications are causing someone else pain.

There is an inherent tension in the notions that, as Nordgren puts it,

> Staying away from entitlement and demands is the only way to be sure that you are in a relationship that is truly mutual. Love is not more "real" when people compromise for each other because it's part of what's expected.

---

50   As the Campaign for Real Arses says: 'On Palm Sunday Jesus rode into Jerusalem on an ass, however the part of Jesus that was closest to said ass was his arse. Plus arse (from Old English *ears*, *ærs*) is just a much better word than ass and far more piratey.'

and

> What are your basic boundaries and expectations on all relationships? ... Find your
> core set of values and use it for all relationships.

Freedoms and boundaries may indeed conflict. Some people find it hard to distinguish between defending their own boundaries and controlling another person. Sometimes those two things are genuinely in tension. Communication is one way to tackle this. Talking things through honestly and open-heartedly generally helps. However, it can also require compromise.

We may face a choice between compromising and ending a relationship. At that point it becomes an equation of, 'What sacrifices am I prepared to make for all the good things this connection brings?' So when Nordgren says 'Rather than looking for compromises in every situation, let loved ones choose paths that keep their integrity intact, without letting this mean a crisis for the relationship,' it's all too easy for this suggestion to be wielded as a cudgel against those trying to maintain reasonable boundaries. And, even when people are trying to accept their partners' autonomy in good faith, sometimes that does require Buddha-like powers of non-attachment.

If abused, relationship anarchy, like so many things, can be a charter for the mean, the manipulative and the unscrupulous. So just be aware.

But let's dwell on compromises a little longer. We make them every day. They're a means of parlaying differences in almost every area of life. If you meet another car on a narrow road, one of you has to back up. If someone has to cover the New Year's Eve shift at work, occasionally it may be your turn. If you can't afford both a new washing machine and the weekend getaway you were hoping for, you make a choice.

But in non-monogamous relationships compromises can come thick and fast. You partner hasn't seen another of their partners in a while, but you're having a rough time and could really use having them around and circumstances don't allow them to be with both of you... Again, compromise is inevitable.

Nordgren doesn't suggest no compromise, she simply cautions against compromising our essential selves, against constant, often one-sided compromise, and against compromise because it's expected of us. Rather she urges us to respect our partners' (and surely our own) integrity. It must be stressed again at this stage that clear boundaries are healthy, ideally communicated early in a relationship. Respecting someone's integrity doesn't just mean respecting their right to be free to do something, but also their right to be free *from* certain things.

Next it's worth restating that people inevitably prioritise. That's not unreasonable, indeed it's an almost inevitable consequence of letting relationships find their own level. Someone can easily be a priority without necessarily being a primary. Thirdly, while love may be abundant and even infinite, time, emotional bandwidth, and money are not. Love may not be a zero-sum game, but when someone new comes on the scene and someone is already has considerable commitments, something may have to give. Reality sometimes impinges on one's ideals. Then it's back to compromise or even to the acceptance that however lovely a potential connection may be, there's simply not the time or the resources to sustain it.

The key however, is to distinguish between not having all the things because we've been told we're not allowed them, and accepting we can't have all the things because maintaining a dozen relationships in a dozen time zones is beyond our capacity.

As the therapist DK Green puts it:

> Don't take on and don't bite off more than you can chew. It's a lovely idea that you can have all these multiple different relationships, but if you spread yourself too thin, nobody gets a healthy dose of relationship. So actually you have to be really damn sure that your life with its work, with its hobbies, with its other stuff, can fit in another human being and that they will not suffer or lack because you haven't time and space to give them.

WHAT CAN WE ALL TAKE FROM RELATIONSHIP ANARCHY?

HERE'S THE THING: You don't need to be non-monogamous to be a relationship anarchist. As Dr. Liz puts it:

> You can be a relationship anarchist and polyamorous, you can be a relationship anarchist and a monogamist. It doesn't necessarily dictate how your relationships go.

Likewise, the central tenet of solo poly, that your primary relationship is with yourself, is a great premise for a successful monogamous pairing. What it means is that you're happy and at ease with yourself and you give your own needs due priority.

There's no entrance exam to be a relationship anarchist and there's no membership card. You don't even have to sign up for all of it. It's all about what works for you.

So, here are a few questions that relationship anarchy might prompt you to ask yourself:

- *If I were to dream up my ideal/fantasy life what would my romantic and non-romantic relationships looks like?*
- *Who (if anyone) would I live with or share financial commitments with?*
- *Do I feel the need to have a say in the lives of those closest to me?*
- *How important to me is control over the commitments I make?*
- *Which are my most significant relationships? Please include relationships with parental figures, offspring, friends, colleagues and pets.*
- *Are romantic relationships necessarily my priority?*
- *What compromises am I prepared or not prepared to make?*

Heffalump Traps

CHAPTER TWENTY-SIX

Managing CNM Relationships

POLYAMORY ISN'T UNIQUELY difficult as a way to approach relationships. It simply presents people with a different set of challenges. A few of those will be novel while many others will be much the same as those we encounter in monogamous relationships.

Polyamory can relieve some of the potential frustrations of being intimately involved with just one person but replace those with the task of managing multiple romantic/sexual relationships at once. Most relationship problems however, monogamous or not, just come down to people.

That said, there are issues that are particular to at least some forms of polyamory that, being brought up in a predominantly monogamous society, most of us aren't exposed to. Forewarned, as they say, is forearmed. Not all of these are 'problems' as such but they are things to bear in mind.

What we don't inherit from the culture around us are solutions and strategies for CNM problems in the way that we absorb solutions and strategies for traditional relationships from the monogamous ether. This is both a good and a bad thing.

Bad, because we can be unprepared for what we encounter and at a loss for how to deal with it. Good because rather than just accept the script we're handed we can take time to look more closely at what's going on and ask ourselves what would be *our* ideal solution. Think about the impact on monogamous relationships of all that advice that runs 'if *x* then it means they don't love you...' when *x* can be 'doesn't like your cat' or 'isn't particularly keen on going on holiday with your best mates' or 'doesn't want to get married'.

Neither polyamory nor any other form of CNM is a cure for the human condition any more than monogamy is. However, sharing the experiences of some of my interviewees about the bumps in the road they've hit will hopefully prove helpful.

CHAPTER TWENTY-SEVEN

Poly/Mono Relationships

SOMETIMES A MONOGAMOUS person and a non-mono person will meet and fall in love. It happens. Humans have a propensity to fall in love with all sorts of other humans, even really terrible ones. Heck, some humans even fall in love with inanimate objects, like their car or, worse, someone else's car.

Monogamous people do date non-monogamous people—and vice versa... obviously. It's not as though there's any fundamental reason they shouldn't, but mono-poly relationships are often especially difficult. Knowing how others have worked it out, or failed to do so, may help you avoid stresses and conflicts. The author and poly activist Franklin Veaux is one of those who is once bitten, twice shy.

> God, I've done that. Don't do it. You build a relationship on a stressed foundation, you bake in this fundamental stress from the very start. Best-case scenario the monogamous person says, 'Well I don't want multiple partners myself but I don't care if you have multiple partners, that's totally cool with me', and in that case things can be wonderful.

> Where things run off the rails is when that person says, 'Well I'm monogamous and I only want one partner and I will grudgingly accept that you don't, but I will never truly be happy with it'. Because you get this conflicted relationship where the monogamous person will engage, [perhaps] not even consciously, in all these mate-guarding behaviours to try to maintain a separation between their partner and other lovers. At worst you will get somebody who actively undermines or sabotages [your] other relationships. I have been [the poly person] in both of those situations, it's miserable.

Joreth Innkeeper is likewise wary.

> I've seen it and I've also been there, done that, and every single time it's been a mistake. It's possible to really and truly love someone and still not make good partners for each other. And we really need to learn that lesson, because we get all of these feelings and these hormones and excitement and we want to dive into a relationship with people without paying any attention to how compatible we actually are. And then everybody wonders why their relationships blow up in the end, when from the start they've based their relationship on a conflict of interests.

Many people think that compatibility is primarily about how well they get along. You meet someone, find each other ridiculously attractive, make one another laugh, find that you both binged on the same box sets last year, and you're like 'Where have you been all my life?'

All that certainly helps, but so do shared values and goals. If one person has dreams of retiring to the French countryside to tend to a small vineyard and the other wants to be in the heart of London or New York so they can go to performances and galleries, then you have a problem. By the same token, if one person pictures their ideal life as being them and their (one) partner in front of the fire together and the other dreams of having their three lovelies drifting in and out, then you'll be calling Houston again.

As a practitioner on the UK's 'Pink Therapy' list, DK Green has long experience of working with LGBTIQA+ and consensually non-monogamous people. He's seen monogamous people make their peace with a partner being non-monogamous, but equally others who, however hard they would like to be okay with it, struggle.

> There are those who can learn for themselves that it can be okay; that they can be enough in a relationship with someone who is poly when they are not. Often what you find is the mono person makes an attempt to be poly too in a way of "Okay, I get it. This is a better way. This is going to work. I can do this too." And that has intrinsic failure points. If they're not actually wired for polyamory, it's just not going to work.

> So in client terms, what often happens is a mono person may come to my door and say, "But I'm in relationship with this poly person. Help!" I do my best to give them the space to see if they can move through that. In some cases they can and it's a win, right? And in some cases they can't, and I have to help them realise that actually this is wrong for them because it's actually making them intrinsically unhappy.

Generally speaking it's about unpicking jealousy for them. However, psychologically, if it's actually about a baseline of 'being uncomfortable with my partner being with somebody else', then poly is not for them. Poly is not evangelical, it's not more evolved. It is a different way of doing things. It is a choice. And if that choice makes you utterly miserable, then it probably isn't the right choice.

One fundamental mistake that we can make with one another is wanting to change someone else into someone they don't want to be.[51] Another is hearing what we want to hear and not what is being said. So, when someone says to us 'I'm not really into being monogamous/non-monogamous' we instead tell ourselves 'Actually I'm sure, deep down, they want what they say they don't want.'

Maxine has encountered this on a number of occasions.

> I have had several partners who went oh! Whoa, brilliant! Hot bi babe! We'll have all of the threesomes and it'll be amazing. And then, you know, when the relationship got serious they'd be a bit upset that I didn't settle down and become monogamous and that I stayed the same person that I always was, because apparently they'd had some underlying expectation that the relationship would become serious and serious meant monogamous, and that would all change.

This is all too familiar to sex & intimacy coach, psychologist and writer Dr. Lori Beth Bisbey. The inherent tensions in mono-poly relationships account for such a high proportion of her caseload that's she's writing a book about it.

> "Many couples come in with the monogamous person feeling betrayed because although their partner said from the outset they were non-monogamous, at the beginning they were so focused on their new partner that it felt a lot like monogamy. Many people come to see me believing that a person can 'give up' non-monogamy for the 'right person' and they'll point to that NRE-filled early nesting phase of the relationship as evidence that a person can give it up."

I don't want to give the impression that it's impossible for monogamous and non-monogamous people to date one another successfully or even form an enduring, long-term partnership. Consent in relationships shouldn't be mostly about what you can tolerate, but rather about embracing what you want.

---

51 Frankly even if someone wants to change the best we can do is generally to support them while they go through their own change process.

Sometimes the relationship is what all concerned want and it's just about learning to meet one another's needs. Debbie, who lives in Florida, works in IT and is essentially monogamous. She dates Nathan, who is not. I asked her what she struggled with.

> I think it's like just the normal; occasionally jealousy. I'm still learning how to deal with that and because most of the time I've realised it's just me being irrational about things that I shouldn't be concerned about. But at the same time I kind of like [the setup] because, him having somebody else to spend time with means that I get more of *me* time, and I like not being social sometimes and I like not having to worry about what someone else's concerns are at that moment. I like being able to just get lost in either video games or whatever else I'm occupying myself with. And it makes it easier for me and a little less stressful at times.

Debbie struggles occasionally with things but Nathan is supportive and helps her though it. Billie, meanwhile, a photographer from Singapore who dates Yana from Russia, seemed perfectly happy dating just her despite the fact that Yana is also happily married. The only thing that threw him was the fact that when he met Yana he had no idea at all how consensual non-monogamy might work.

> At the start there were a lot of rules that I didn't understand, especially when she was going back to Russia or something and I remember I texted her because I wanted to send her off and I found out that Ivan was going to be there too, and then I was crazy nervous about it. And then I asked if it was okay if I could hug and kiss her goodbye and she was really really quite nice about it. I remembered she said you cannot only do that but that is actually encouraged in front of Ivan. From then on I was figuring out the rules... We went out for about a month without kissing or holding hands, because I didn't know what the boundaries were because I was too afraid to ask and I was enjoying the relationship too much to care about the physical aspects of it. So it was only after some time that we sort of figured it out, well not so much for her but more for me. Because it was all new to me.

Luckily Yana was very supportive and her husband, Ivan, very encouraging. She remembers when some of the barriers finally dissipated.

> It was so cute. I remember our first kiss which happened, an accidental kiss on the MRT [metro]. I just wanted to hug him goodbye but his face was in the way. He didn't expect that so it just kind of happened and we were both so shy about it.

This isn't perhaps the image that many people would have of consensual non-monogamy. But CNM dating looks a lot like monogamous dating. People can be shy or self-conscious, or just into a person's company and holding hands.

COWBOYS AND CUCKOOS

THERE ARE MONOGAMOUS people who find themselves in a relationship with a consensually non-monogamous person, realise it's not for them and end things. Then, as Maxine says, there are those who take the opposite tack, consciously or unconsciously.

> A *cowboy* is someone who sees a person who is currently polyamorous and wants them to become monogamous with them. Cowboys [may] be quite honest about their motivations and be open about trying to rope someone off from the herd and persuade them into monogamy. And I'm sort of alright with that. People want what they want.

But not every cowboy wears a white hat. Some are less honest, hiding their intentions from their prospective partner, perhaps even denying them to themselves. Some monogamous people approach the non-mono person with everything from scepticism to outright emotional blackmail, from the patronising 'They just haven't met the right person' and 'They're just going through a phase' to the more coercive 'I'm sure I could change their mind' and the potentially abusive 'I'm sure, once we're dating, I'll be able to tell them it's me or non-monogamy and by that time they'll give in.' It's absolutely no better than someone planning to pressure someone who is monogamous into being non-monogamous. Neither respects the integrity of the other person.

Cowboys are so labelled because their tactic is to spot a straggler in the poly herd and attempt to lasso them and lead them away to the pastures of monogamy or brand them with the mark of the Dodgy Bastard Ranch. As Maxine says, they're often quite upfront. They often turn up at poly munches thinking that non-monogamous people are less discriminating so it'll be easier to get a date, and then once dating, they'll be able to turn the relationship into what they want: conventional coupledom.

Cuckoos, on the other hand, are rather less direct. Maxine again:

> Cuckoo behaviour is a little more insidious. They might not even know they're doing it. It's more a case of, I'm saying I'm poly but actually I want this person all to myself, so I'm going to try and make everybody else so uncomfortable in the

situation that they leave. So, it's not necessarily malicious intent, at the same time it's quite toxic within polyamorous relationships.

Becky knows from hard experience that it can get ugly.

I have seen it. I don't think it's intentional but they struggled so much with poly, they needed so much extra time from the partner that they were particularly in-volved with, that all of the other partners got pushed away. They would have emo-tional needs and demands above and beyond what everyone else did, so the part-ner was just naturally forced to focus on them. And in time everyone just got bored of the behaviour and moved away and out of the relationship until it was just a monogamous core left, and it didn't go well.

There are instances where cuckoos act more out of habit than conscious malice. For example, there are anecdotal instances of people in unsatisfactory relationships using non-monogamy to get their own needs met and then, when they find a better re-lationship, leaving the first and pushing the new one back towards monogamy. Good communication and clear boundaries are very useful in defending against these sorts of situations.

WHAT WE CAN ALL LEARN FROM THIS

A LOT OF the success or failure of any relationship is simply down to good mate selec-tion. Some of us like to think that love conquers all. All too often it doesn't. The allow-ances we make in the first throes of love can come, with time, to grate. Selecting a mate who is *compatible* with you is far more likely to determine how long the relationship lasts than how madly you love them.

Yes, people can change. Absolutely. But personal change, when so much of the personality is formed in childhood, is a huge task. Trying to persuade someone who is very comfortable with the way they are to be the way you want them to be instead is mostly doomed to failure and turns you into the bad guy.

Just remember the old joke, 'How many psychotherapists does it take to change a light bulb? One, but the light bulb has to want to change.' People change because they want that change, and even then it's hard. It's often made harder still by people around them resenting and resisting their changing because it reminds them of their own failure to change. One of the greatest gifts we can give someone else is to support them to choose and achieve the changes *they* want to make.

So rather than pick someone superficially compatible and setting about moulding them into your perfect person, better to find someone who is fundamentally in tune with your tastes, values and goals—and accept that we all have rough edges that may or may not be smoothed with time.

CHAPTER TWENTY-EIGHT

The Thing About Couples...

AT THE HEART of hierarchical polyamory there's possibly, nay probably, a couple. Couples are definitely a thing. If you're prepared to brave their natural habitats (the labyrinthine halls of IKEA for instance), you can even study them in the wild.

IKEA aside, the structural social bias in favour of couples sometimes carries over into polyamory in ways that can be unhealthy. The instinct of many consensually non-monogamous couples, to protect their existing relationships more or less at any cost, often heavily colours hierarchical relationships in particular.

In some it's but a mere hop, skip and jump away from the Victorian gentleman and his mistress; his wife and the gardener. Yes, with polyamory you're acknowledging that the mistress and the gardener exist in your emotional landscape but they're still the mistress and the gardener, with all the incumbent lack of access to the privileges that the man and the woman of the house enjoy.

Becky, a trans woman from the UK, has little patience for it.

> The way I would sum it up is that it's the concept that some people's emotions are more important than other people's. I have a friend in a hierarchical poly relationship and there is the husband, the wife, and my friend, and she gets a raw deal all the time. She's the one who has to travel to visit. She's the one who's relocating when they buy a house at the other end of the country. She's the one making all of the allowances and the exceptions and the wife and the husband never seemed to make any kind of compromise, and I think it's a terribly raw deal for her.

At the root of the problem is often the issue of who gets to set what rules.[52] On occasion these can amount to restrictions aimed at limiting the freedom of a partner

---

52   See the chapter on Rules and Agreements for key distinctions between rules and agreements.

to engage fully in a relationship with someone else—akin to some of the rules that sometimes come into play in monogamish and swinging relationships. It's the impossible law of 'Nothing can be allowed to affect us'. That's something Magick has had first-hand experience of.

> Most of my poly relationships in the past have been hierarchical. It's been a case of some negotiation and where it's come from, is like I'm with somebody initially, meet somebody else, and [person number one is] like 'Okay, well that's cool, but here's my conditions,' and that becomes a hierarchical thing. I was never especially comfortable with it and, as someone who's done it several times, I certainly would not want to do it again. I completely second what Becky says. You're still making rules about someone else's behaviour based on your feelings and not how they feel. And so it's got all the same issues as monogamy and I've run into all the same problems really. I'm very, very clear now with anyone I'm involved with, if I meet somebody else that's an entirely separate thing and you know, if in some way it all works together that's great.

However there's also an argument that hierarchical polyamory is a pragmatic reflection of the world around us. Not everyone is equally committed to, or responsible for, a mutual lover, and there are plenty who feel that time and investment put into a relationship can and should be recognised and that hierarchical poly is a way of doing so.

In polyamorous circles a distinction is often drawn between *descriptive* hierarchy (for instance recognising that a long-term married partnership is in fact a weightier thing than a new entanglement), and *prescriptive* hierarchy. 'Prescriptive' describes setting up an arbitrary hierarchy that someone has decided *should* exist: for instance, 'I can date whoever I want, but you can only date those I approve of.'

Quite a number of the people I interviewed reject all hierarchy, not just between romantic partners but between different relationships. Those who identify as Relationship Anarchists (RA), have often embraced philosophically the idea that romantic relationships shouldn't inherently be privileged over non-romantic ones, as we have seen.

Rather more poly people rely on discernment and negotiation to clarify the descriptive hierarchies that exist, arbitrary prescriptive hierarchies that strike them as unfair or manipulative, and what to do about them.

PRIMARIES AND SECONDARIES

The closer toward 'like-monogamy' that you move, the more there is an illusion that your relationship is safe. And I think it is very tempting, particularly if you're newer to non-monogamy, to trend towards these theoretically safer structures. The majority of folks I see who do hierarchical structures are newer to non-monogamy. They have had fewer structures, fewer partners and it's this idea that if I can say 'you're my primary' and you will say 'you're my primary' and we agree that we are always going to be first for each other, then nothing can come between us.

And that's not real. That's not even real in monogamy. The reason I choose non-hierarchical structures, the reason that I choose solo poly, is because I would rather have a harsh truth than a pleasant illusion. I recognise that part of doing things the way that I do them is that right now if I was in the hospital, I genuinely don't know who other than close friends of mine who would come. I assume that my partners would come, but I don't know that and we haven't had those explicit discussions.
—Dr. Liz Powell

It's quite common for people to apply labels to different relationships—friend, boyfriend, workmate, fiancé—by way of signalling their nature to their intimates and to their wider social circle. Given the diversity of CNM relationships, this is even more common among non-monogamous people. The terms one uses are significant not just in what they say about the relationship but also how they're perceived and how those you're talking about presumably feel about it. Imagine someone introducing their partners with the words; 'This is my husband and this is my boyfriend.' Most people would infer certain things from this, perhaps incorrectly. The word 'husband' implies not just a legal bond (and all the legal hassles that tend to accompany its dissolution) but also a degree of solidity, commitment and practical entanglement that the word 'boyfriend' doesn't.[53] If one was trying to reduce or eliminate the implied hierarchy one might use 'husband and partner' or even just refer to both as partners. Language has weight. It matters, particularly as social signalling, including signalling to ourselves.

---

53   'Boyfriend' and 'girlfriend' are pretty questionable if applied to anyone who considers themselves to be an adult. The French use *petit ami* and *petite amie* which are, frankly, just as infantilising. At least the Mandarin *nanpengyu* and *nupengyu* are better: man friend and woman friend.

This is why the terms primary and secondary (and even tertiary) in consensual non-monogamy are far from universally welcomed. It's not so much that someone might actually introduce their partners as their primary and secondary (though it doubtless happens), it's that this language risks undermining the intrinsic worth of another person. Arguably it demeans everyone involved. Even if someone is never going to co-sign the mortgage, this will strike not a few people as unacceptable. Down that path can lie exploitation and abuse.

It can become a pecking order, a fowl situation where one takes precedence over another or even orders another about. There is always a danger that if people are ascribed rank, they will at some point pull rank and try to exercise implicit or explicit power. Sometimes secondary partners feel their interests are being treated as being of secondary importance.

For this reason less loaded terms than primary and secondary have gained currency. These include 'anchor partner' for the one you expect to spend a life with, 'nesting partner' (or roosting partner if we're going to continue the chicken theme) for the person you live with, 'sweetie' or 'OSO' (other significant other) for what some might call a secondary, and 'comet' to describe a distant love who only swings into your orbit once in a blue moon.

Meg-John Barker says it's important we think carefully about the dynamics involved.

> There are dangers in treating people as secondaries. We need to ask what we mean when we talk [or think] about someone being secondary? Does it mean a bit less time or a bit less control over the rules, or does it mean actually we're treating you as a secondary human being and you're disposable and, if something comes up in the primary relationship, then the secondary has to just deal with the fact that they're let go or whatever.

Others, like the therapist, activist and educator D. K. Green, point out that it's also risky pretending that all relationships are equal when in reality they're not.

> I know a lot of people don't like the words primary and secondary and tertiary because it implies a hierarchy of importance to a person. I think that's not true. I think some of my tertiary relationships are just as important to me, but in a completely different way. To me, my partners and I are a family and we've been a family for decades. I've got five kids and six grandkids. So that relationship, for me, simply takes priority over other things, and ultimately I guess my kids take priority even over them. So you could say my kids are my primary relationship because if they call me, I'm there, it doesn't really matter what else is going on.

The idea that people have different *priorities* is one that I think will probably find wider favour than talking in terms of primaries and secondaries. Most people have a range of priorities and have to make choices. Do you put satisfaction over money when applying for jobs? Do you put your children ahead of yourself and your partner when making spending decisions? Do you choose to spend your weekends with the friends your partner approves of or the ones you prefer? Parents will readily recognise the priorities they arrive at with decisions regarding their various children. Priorities are not inherently a measure of love.

Likewise, in consensually non-monogamous settings, choices still have to be made. Even the consciously egalitarian often find themselves having to prioritise even as they try to be fair.

That's different than assuming a primary's needs will automatically take precedence over a secondary. Often such an arrangement is made plain from the outset: 'Clarence is my husband. We have a life together. You're just my...' (insert your term of choice here. I favour the very 70s Brit sitcom standby, 'bit o' fluff').

Ultimately it all comes down to consent. Many people make a positive choice to be a secondary because they don't want to make a bigger investment of time or emotion or to take on greater responsibility. Others will turn down a relationship that feels secondary. But that requires enough honesty on the part of primaries that everyone knows what actually *is* on offer.

Some people choose to be secondaries because there are clear boundaries limiting expectations for all involved. I asked Meg-John what the positives might be.

> Knowing your place, I guess; having a clear sense of where you stand with people. And some people really love being a secondary. Again, I've read really interesting things about Muslim women who are choosing to be secondary partners because it enables them to have a career in a way that being a primary partner within that particular micro culture of the UK Islamic community doesn't. So, there are reasons why people may prefer hierarchical arrangements or particular places within a hierarchy. And also it can be more honest.

> [But]a lot of people will pretend to operate an egalitarian poly model when actually it is hierarchical and somebody is getting more time or somebody does have a bit more control over the rules or whatever.

The author and Poly.Land blogger Page Turner came up with a rather nifty term for hierarchy that slips in via the back door: *sneakyarchy*.

So what does being a primary actually mean? It could be the person or people for whom one has the deepest feelings, or to whom one has made the most serious commitments, or in whom one has invested the most.

It could be the relationship that those involved have decided to put before all others. 'We can do what we like so long as we put one another first whenever there's a conflict of interests.'

It could be that 'primary' is being used descriptively, i.e. as a description of circumstances—the degree to which two lives are bound together by common history and enterprise; the cottage in the Cotswolds (or the dacha outside St. Petersburg), little Rufus and Titania, the Spode dinner service.... (substitute culturally appropriate detritus here...).

Sometimes, indeed most of the time, being a primary partner comes with responsibilities—more on those in a mo'.

Another distinction in some cases is that a primary is someone who has a power of veto over their partner(s)' choices, especially romantic ones. Such formidable power over another and their relationships is clearly open to abuse and can lead us down some very dark paths, though D. K. Green argues this needn't be the case.

> In some relationships they absolutely have power of veto, in some relationships they do not. In mine, I believe initially both [my partners] had power of veto and in fact, to be fair, even to this day, if one of them was unhappy or uncomfortable with a relationship I wanted to pursue, then it wouldn't happen. So essentially they kind of have a veto, but it's not built in as a structure, as an intentional thing. It's just that actually that happened. Their happiness is my primary importance, you know, secondary to my children, I guess.

> I think for me them being my primary partners means I'm always coming home and that's really our definition. I am always going to come back.

SOMETIMES HIERARCHY ISN'T even a conscious thing. Sometimes just being 'a couple' means that, even after you stop being *just a couple* in certain important regards—i.e. you are both coupling with other people—you still behave like a couple, or more to the point *the* couple. And, given understanding and consent, the implied boundaries may serve all concerned well.

For instance, if Ana has run up a £50,000 credit card debt, that might mean very different things to her primary partner Rachel than to her secondary Dmitri. Dmitri gets to enjoy the fun Ana. Dmitri can take Ana out for dinner and drinks because the

£50,000 debt isn't his problem. Rachel, on the other hand, sees the home that she and Ana have made for themselves as being at risk. She doesn't feel able to blow £100 on dinner and drinks because they have to find £2000 by the end of the month. As a primary you take the rough with the smooth, the '82 Château Margaux with the '22 Château Thunderbird.

As a secondary you, at least in theory, have the luxury of not having to deal with the difficult stuff. I say 'in theory' because in practice plenty of people who might be considered 'secondaries' or 'tertiaries' also have to do the emotional heavy lifting when their partner is having a bad time. Indeed, quite often problems in a 'primary' relationship get dumped onto the others, particularly if the primary couple wants someone else to blame in order to 'protect' themselves.

Consider also this: It's one thing for a couple who own a house to choose not to consult their other partners about spending £25,000 of their money on an extension; it's quite another if the issue under consideration is their moving 200 miles away. That has a material impact on people outside that dyad, for instance parents, children, and friends as well as any other partners. If something affects others, the question is 'Do they or don't they get a say about it?' Sometimes in hierarchical poly relationships they don't.

What makes things more complicated is that it's not uncommon for people to agree to an arrangement, such as being a secondary, that leaves them with 'buyer's regret'. Perhaps the reality of being a secondary doesn't live up to what they envisioned. Perhaps their wants, needs and feelings change. Nor is it unknown for someone to agree to be 'a secondary' when what they really want is a relationship on more equal terms but decided to accept 'second best' where the alternative was nothing. There is something of a tendency among consensually non-monogamous people to rationalise this either as something that can be resolved with good sensible rules, lots of communication and negotiation, or simply to say 'Well, you knew what you were signing up for.' Meg-John Barker again:

> I think that's a really risky thing that we tend to do. Again, and I'm including myself here, we like to take this kind of geeky approach to this whole area; if we could just find the right bullet point list of how to do relationships, or the right set of rules for poly or whatever, we could get rid of all the pain and only have the pleasure. Right. And it just denies all of the unconscious stuff we're bringing, all of the really emotionally loaded stuff; all our fears of rejection, all of our yearning to belong that is all in there when we're talking about human relationships, often particularly erotic and romantic relationships. So yes, I think there's a real tendency to go along with something that doesn't feel quite right to us and maybe not even

realise it for some time because we're just yearning for that particular person or this particular kind of love or some kind of belonging.

COUPLE PRIVILEGE

THERE'S A BIT of a debate in CNM circles about whether there is such a thing as *couple privilege* (sometimes rendered *couples' privilege*). At times it comes across as a bunch of well-meaning sociologists getting bogged down in semantics and too much bargain sherry.

Privilege is quite a touchy subject, not least because a lot of people who enjoy some social and economic advantages, like many of us, focus on what they don't have rather than what they do. You can enjoy considerable privilege and not feel at all privileged. If you're worried about your job, your relationship, your debts and the fact that your children are having a tough time at school you probably don't think much about how lucky you are to be white, male, educated, heterosexual, and able to walk unaided. Somehow thinking about what it would be like to have all of one's existing problems *and* be black and gay as well doesn't seem to help people realise how relatively lucky they are to just be dealing with financial and personal worries. Ideally we would all be a little more aware and count our blessings more often and more carefully.

A lot of people don't want to acknowledge the structural advantages they enjoy perhaps because they fear they'll be required to give them up, or they feel guilty or ashamed. None of this helps. What helps is awareness and compassion. No guilt, no angst, just gentle, positive action. Every time.

Anyway, couple privilege... It's when your assumptions are still guided by the assumptions you took into your original relationship. There's a simple 'sauce for the goose is sauce for the gander' test.

Does a request, or even a 'demand' from one partner, get treated in the same way as an equivalent request from another? I wonder how many times the words 'But he/she is only your boy/girlfriend. I'm your...' have spilled from people's mouths without them realising how dismissive that word *only* is of the other partner's needs and feelings.

Sometimes couple privilege comes into play without anyone quite being aware of it.

Kerilyn found herself in the position of secondary when she started dating Tim. Tim was married to Poppy, so, as we've already heard, Kerilyn made a point of speaking with Poppy beforehand just to check that she was happy with how things were developing. At first it seemed fine but, after a while, it became clear that Poppy wasn't comfortable with things and started exercising more control.

That's when problems began to crop up.

I'd actually spoken to his wife before; just a conversation over the telephone before we went out for the first time. He and I met, we started talking on a kik group, we met at a munch just as mates and then when we were talking about seeing each other, I spoke to his wife. And I mean it was sort of strange because she was quite heavily pregnant at the time but she sort of expressed that she had no issues with it and that it was an egalitarian sort of open relationship and if she wanted to do something she could do it, and that they'd been doing it for a while.

Poppy started to assert a degree of control that Kerilyn found uncomfortable.

There were things like having to sort of check in [with Poppy] before we could sleep together. For example; there were rules about spending the night certain places. So, if we were on a date, things were going super well and we were getting really hot, he couldn't necessarily go back to mine. He'd have to go back that weekend, make sure things are okay and then maybe next weekend we could have sex. And we, because they have their own place and I suppose I can understand not wanting someone in your space, I can't remember what the exact rule was, I just know that we weren't allowed in certain parts of their place. But it felt random, especially because there were so many rules about whether he could come to my place and they just felt restrictive.

After a while I started to get fed up with our not being able to decide between the two of us when we could have sex, for example, and just sort of feeling like there was someone else making decisions about our relationship—when we could see each other, how often we could see each other—and it felt arbitrary. Just because, I don't know, maybe it was that we were spending too much time together. Perhaps I should have been more understanding of the fact that she was heavily pregnant and probably not doing a lot of dating.

Kerilyn's experience illustrates a number of potential issues with hierarchical polyamory.

Firstly, whether or not it was explicitly understood and accepted, Poppy felt able to make rules about Kerilyn's relationship with her husband. There was no question of Kerilyn laying down rules for Tim and his wife.

Sometimes Kerilyn experienced these rules as arbitrary. It must have felt to her, at times, that Poppy was setting conditions simply so she could have a sense of retaining control. Some of the rules she set seem more intrusive than others.

On the one hand, setting rules for how Tim and Kerilyn could behave in Tim and Poppy's home might be understandable. As Franklin Veaux says, it's not uncommon for couples to agree that neither of them should have sex in their bed with anyone else.

> It seems reasonable to me to be honest, because it's about autonomy and it's about boundaries. And the difference between boundaries and rules is also something that people often confuse. But boundaries are things that affect access to yourself, your person, your mind, your emotion or your property. And it is reasonable to say, I will set boundaries on who can touch me. I can set boundaries on what you can do with me, like don't touch me there, don't do this thing.

> I can set boundaries on what you do with my stuff. I can say I don't want this person in my house and that's completely reasonable. I am not one of them, but there are people who feel very territorial about their bed. Their bed represents their sanctuary and they feel like the presence of another person in that sanctuary space is an intrusion. I don't feel that way myself but I understand it and I think that is a reasonable kind of boundary.

The poly activist Joreth Innkeeper agrees.

> I'm one of those people. I'm very territorial about my possessions mainly because my experience is growing up with bullies and people who would steal my things and use my attachment to objects as another form of torture. Plus I'm also an introvert. I need a long time to recharge and so, my personal space is where I go to retreat and recharge. So, I'm one of those people who would view my bed or my house or my room as my space and other people coming into it as an intrusion, so you have to have my explicit invitation to enter into my space.

On the other hand there's the issue of what Tim and Kerilyn could and could not do and when, such as the requirement that Tim check with Poppy to get the go ahead to have sex with Kerilyn. That's not setting rules for one's own person, space or possessions, that's controlling someone else's relationship. Yes, one can sympathise with Poppy. She's heavily pregnant and could reasonably be expected to look to Tim for support. What appears to be problematic is not that she and Tim agree what time they should spend together, it's that Poppy is setting rules for when Tim can see Kerilyn and what they can do during that time. It's not just that Kerilyn has no direct say in the matter but also that her feelings are apparently not being taken into account.

This is absolutely a point at which someone is being treated as secondary. Poppy, in essence, has a veto. Her behaviour is also quite controlling.

If you think that's an extreme example, it's not. Shyam was just starting out in consensual non-monogamy when he was drawn into a dysfunctional relationship.

> Before I met my partner I was pretty much solo poly. I dated a couple for a while. They were quite abusive even though they identified themselves as kinky, like in a D/S relationship. Basically the husband was using his power as a dom over his wife. And, it took me a while to realise that. He would push her towards me and then he would constantly message me saying, you know, why didn't you ask her out? Will you consider it? But at the same time, what he was doing was cheating on her meeting multiple other people. And then when she questioned him he would simply say 'You are my sub and you can't question' and things like that, which became very toxic and I had to pull out.

Shyam's experience is another reminder that hierarchical forms of polyamory (and indeed all relationship models) are open to abuse. It's not rocket science. It's just about consent.

If everyone concerned can gladly sign up to whatever is proposed, then fundamentally things are good. If coercion is involved, they're not. So with that in mind go enjoy being primary, secondary, tertiary, quaternary, quinary, senary, septenary, octonary, nonary, and denary. Heck, use ranks; Colonel, Chief Superintendent, Eternal Majesty, Scrubber of the Cupboard Under the Sink—whatever. If it makes you all happy good luck! But do, please, try to remain aware and keep your eyes open.

CHAPTER TWENTY-NINE

If You're Thinking of Dating a Couple

IF *YOU* ARE the prospective third, if you've met a couple and there's the possibility of dating them both, there are several things you might want to think about before you leap in.

The first is this:, though having a very long talk before ending up in bed with people may not seem like the most exciting option, it probably makes sense—unless everybody's goals begin and end at jumping in and out of bed.

The couple you've met may be very experienced, or they could be very new to everything. Either way they may have very specific ideas about what they want that may, or may not, mesh with your own.

Having a proper conversation allows you to find out what they really have in mind. One common issue that runs through consensual non-monogamy is that people can have a shopping list of traits and features they're looking for and then expect someone to conform to them.

There is a real possibility that the couple you've met will have already made that shopping list. When couples open their relationship they often talk extensively about the what and the why and the wherefore before they do anything about it. Talking is good. The downside is that they may have arrived at a clear understanding of what's going to happen before they've met you. Inevitably you weren't involved.

There are some common wants. One is 'someone who will date us both'. That could mean 'someone who will join us for sex (singly or together)' and it could mean 'someone who will be romantically involved with us both.'

Then there are expectations that 'You should be into us both equally'.

Let's stop there a moment. Can you think of two people you like equally? Most of us like our friends a lot but some we can imagine spending more time with than others, just as we would probably choose to do different things with different friends.

Finding a couple where you like both people *equally* is quite a tall order. Moreover, depending on the expectations, if we're talking about an opposite-sex couple, then the third may be expected to be *perfectly* bisexual—equally romantically and sexually attracted to both men and women.

Even if this isn't an issue because either everyone is the same sex or the third is bang-in-the-middle-of-the-spectrum bisexual, you still have the possibility of liking one half of that couple as a person more than the other.

Complicated huh?

So very early on, it's a good idea to scope out the couple's expectations. Often their expectations are born of wishful thinking (always a powerful cognitive error in humans) combined with naivety. Most relationships evolve naturally. Planning out in advance how your relationship will evolve before you even meet someone invites problems. This is also a chance to let the couple know where your sexuality takes you and why.

As we've seen, couples opening up their relationship for the first time often put lots of rules in place to guard that relationship. It's understandable, but that means you could be expected to obey someone else's laws without having had a vote. You need to be sure that you want to sign up. Are these the guidelines you would have chosen if you'd had a say? If it's an 'our way or the highway' situation, are you okay with that? Will you be okay with that after the initial fever has broken?

You also need to make your peace with the fact that you've stepped into a situation with two people who already share a bond and, for better or worse, a history. You may be hoping for an egalitarian setup. They may have told themselves that's what they want too. But when push comes to shove the couple may function as a two headed beast and, as with the two headed beasts of myth and legend, they're a lot more imposing than a mere hero with two arms, two legs and one head. That thing is bigger than you, like it or not.

And there's that shared history—it's worth knowing more. If you're wandering into a fractured relationship and they're eyeing you up as potential glue, that can be difficult. As we've seen already, stressed relationship plus one person does not equal mended relationship.

These things tend to work better when the couple has a sufficiently strong and healthy bond that no other person could represent a threat. It means they have more spare energy for another and are more secure in welcoming them in on equal terms. They're more likely to treat you as a human, and as a special one at that, not as a wish-fulfilment object; as a person with moral value and agency that is naturally and obviously equal to their own.

If in doubt, talk to them both. Always talk to them both if possible, separately and together. Finding a couple where one party is hot, bothered and determined to bring a new lover into their bed and the other is struggling to get lukewarm about it is not exactly unusual. Then there are considerations such as what role you'll end up playing. You may join as sex toy or lover or equal partner or friend, and end up being mediator, go-between, cook, housemaid, diary secretary, nanny.... People often end up in situations they wouldn't have chosen at the outset.

If all this is making finding a perfect couple to date look like hard work, that's because it generally is. More often than not it's a minor miracle that any two humans like one another enough to form a relationship without adding an additional layer of complexity to the process.

However, if you are inclined to be a unicorn then the laws of supply and demand work in your favour. Think of it less as a couple looking to find a third than as you select-ing a couple. You're in a stronger position to lead the interview process than they are.

People do date couples happily and successfully. Once again it helps to agree—all of you—on clear boundaries and expectations (don't leave expectations unsaid or unexamined), and to allow enough give and take to encompass people's being human and their propensity to grow and change. Do that and you stand a fighting chance of having a warm, life-affirming connection with two special people.

SIC... FLAMMA CORR... SCAT

UNICORNES
AND THE HUNTINGE
THEREOF

CHAPTER THIRTY

ONE PARTICULAR SCENARIO in consensual non-monogamy repeats itself so often, and with such predictable results, that it's become an in-joke.

Just as the writer and podcaster Cooper Beckett observed that the gateway to swinging is often a woman's bisexuality, that's often true of other forms of consensual non-monogamy. It's almost a cliché that a man in a relationship with a bisexual woman will think; 'Yay, I bet I can use this to get some hot girl-on-girl action and an endless supply of threesomes'.

It's hardly surprising. Research suggests that the threesome fantasy is one of the most prevalent and, if everyone consents enthusiastically, why not?

So the conversation starts possibly a little like this: 'Hey sweetie, you know you have a thing for girls. What would you think if we found someone we'd both really like to date so rather than it being the two of us there would be like three of us?' Of course one can dress up this stunningly original idea in the language of consensual non-monogamy so it's not just hot but hip. 'I mean, polyamory is really cool right now so people probably won't think it's weird at all. So why don't we find another hot bi babe like you and it'll be amazing?!'

And so begins the hunt for the hot bi babe of myth and legend: the unicorn.[54]

The next step is often for this newly liberated couple to launch themselves on the CNM world. Having had their eureka moment they rock up to their local meetup or approach polyamory groups online and it's 'Ta da, we've arrived and we've had this amazing idea....' Cue a collective head-in-hands moment amongst all others present. 'Here we go again....' As the author and educator Kevin Patterson says,

> Every Facebook polyamory group in existence gets an influx of couples who show up and say, 'This is what I want. We've just started, we're new to polyamory, we're

---

54 Unicorns are so called because the demand for them so far outstrips the supply that they are practically mythical.

new to non-monogamy. We want a closed triad. Are there any single hot bi babes available?'

And they get destroyed by the regulars of the group because they've seen that before. They've run into this a thousand times. A lot of the 'hot bi babes' in the polyamory groups are the jilted ex-girlfriends of broken closed triads. So, if you go in with a bunch of expectations, or a structure in mind, or a game plan, that plan is going to get trashed in about five seconds and it's going to leave you reeling. So leave that stuff alone.

As poly activist Eunice says, it's a well-worn path and one all too familiar to people in CNM circles. One can often count in seconds the length of time it takes for someone in the group to point the new arrivals to the excellent website unicorns-r-us.com.

It's so typical that this happens, especially with new poly couples, that there is actually a term: 'unicorn hunting'. They try to find this person that will fit both of them and join their family and be their third. However they are, number one, very new to polyamory and number two, they have immediately gone for the most difficult configuration as their very first step.

So imagine that you have somebody who has decided that they maybe want to try doing some sports to try getting fit. They decide they will go swimming. So the first thing they do is go and challenge Michael Phelps. It's the hardest form of configuration to find and the least stable to maintain unless you know what you're doing.

So why so much scepticism about people new to consensual non-monogamy trying to find that elusive unicorn, that hot bi babe?

The sheer maths of it should be enough to give most people the fear.[55] Let's suppose that as a single person in your 20s or 30s you find one in a hundred people attractive. If that seems conservative, start eliminating people by gender, age, orientation, body type, educational level, interests, politics and so on and genuine matches become somewhat rare. Let's also suppose that a potential match is similarly fussy. The chances of you both being one another's one in a hundred may not necessarily be 100 squared—we're often attracted to people with shared values for instance—but there is definitely a multiplier on the odds. Then add a third person to that, and one in

55   Polyamory and Statistics, or "Why haven't we found our third yet?" Maxine's Journal: Adventures of the Polka-Dotted One https://emanix.livejournal.com/28752.html

x hundred or *y* thousand quickly becomes one in tens of thousands if not necessarily one in a million. And let's not forget that only somewhere between one in 50 and one in 20 women in the UK tell pollsters they identify as bisexual[56], and the proportion of men is even smaller. Numbers in the US are similar.

It's simply inherently more difficult to find a third who will date both people in an existing relationship than for each of those people to find someone to date separately.

I've set out a list of essentials points to remember that apply to most areas of consensual non-monogamy. They certainly apply to people hoping to date a unicorn. However there are a few additional points for people who have come to consensual non-monogamy and are fervently hunting for their hot bi babe (or dude).

Don't be prescriptive. It'll be hard enough finding someone who likes you both without demanding that someone is perfect for each of you.

Even if you're looking for a plaything, never forget that they're *a person with their own wants, needs and dreams* that are no less valuable than your own.

Manage your expectations. You've set out to do something difficult; don't be surprised if it isn't easy.

If you're new to consensual non-monogamy think about *exploring less challenging arrangements first.* Ask yourselves whether it's essential that you date as a couple.

Learn from other people's mistakes before you make your own. Find out about other people's experiences. If you search for 'polyamory' and 'unicorn' you'll find plenty of opinion and experiences.

Don't be surprised if not all the consensually non-monogamous people you meet *aren't entirely supportive.* They've probably seen it all before. And if so many people are sceptical it's generally with good reason.

DAVID AND LAURA—LOVELY, INTREPID UNICORN HUNTERS

Two of my interviewees, David and Laura, have experimented with triads. You might say that they were unicorn hunters. They even talk about their third being a unicorn. In South East Asia, where they live, there's less scepticism about unicorns compared with North America and the UK, where people arguably have had more chance to learn from previous generations tumbling into heffalump traps. In South East Asia there's more of a sense that people are still having to make it up as they go along. The non-monogamous community in Asia seems much less concerned with the politics or the philosophy of CNM than the doing of it. You might call it naïve, but you might also call it more to-the-point.

---

56 https://www.ons.gov.uk/peoplepopulationandcommunity/culturalidentity/sexuality/bulletins/sexualidentityuk/2018

David and Laura had been married for some time when I interviewed them. Sadly they've since separated. What you should know about them is that they're both smart, educated, kind, considerate and caring people. I hope you'd like them. I did. However the interview I did with them is quite telling, because, for all their good intentions, you might think that they perhaps didn't handle their thirds as well as they might.

And this is the point. Even really good people can get some of this wrong. Heck, good people make mistakes all the time. And you're probably an awesome person too. But—and this is where we all need to be on our toes—being good and caring doesn't insulate us from making mistakes and possibly hurting other people.

So let's hear from David and Laura. I started by asking David how they started looking for a third to join them.

David: I think the advent of all these dating apps kind of helped. So we would create couple profiles or a female slave profile saying 'Looking for another woman' kind of thing, and profiles would respond though most of the time they were trolls or fake accounts.

OKC[upid] was the first [dating site] we had success with. There were a few responses but we had to weed out all the funny-funny ones. I think there was one genuine one we set up a meeting for and it turned out that it was a cuckold sort of relationship that girl was in[57]. They thought that it would be a fit for what we were doing so we met in a public setting to get to know each other. I spilled wine all over her accidentally...

Laura: The wine spilled on her LV bag so he didn't make a very good first impression, but he did make a lasting one.

David: So one thing led to another and we met up a few more times. Everything started to happen. The male from the other relationship encouraged us to play without him, or even openly in front of him in public when we were having drinks, to kiss her or to bring her to the toilet and make out with her, take some photos, and stuff like that. It was all very exciting in the beginning.

Laura: I was very involved in this relationship because she was probably the first woman for who I felt something more than sexual attraction. I liked her very much

57   Cuckolding is a fetish where a man is sexually excited by the 'humiliation' of watching his partner have sex with someone else (the female equivalent is 'cuckqueening'). The term cuckold, a man whose wife cheats on him, has mediaeval origins (from cuckoo, a bird that lays its eggs in other birds' nests) and 'cuck' has become a standard term of abuse used by neo-Nazis.

also because she was very dominant. I had a thing for very dominant personalities, and she dominated me in the bedroom. I don't really identify as bisexual. I never felt this way to any other woman before but there was a connection for sure. So I did fall quite hard. She was the first person we saw who made me think we could possibly aim for a triad, to explore that kind of arrangement with someone else. That was quite nice. We saw her for quite a few months. The fact that her partner was in a job that took him away, very often and for long periods of time, helped. So she saw us apart from him and we were the only people that she saw frequently. We dated her for about two or three months before her partner actually got very jealous and then he put an end to everything.

I think he was just starting to explore his cuckold side so we were probably the most stable avenue for her to express that, and when she started to use that to humiliate him it came to a point where he couldn't take it anymore. He saw it as a direct insult to his manhood and it wasn't play anymore, it was too real, so he put a stop to that.

David: It was very difficult. We took a long time to get over her.

Laura: This was about four years back and it took us a good year to get over. Even until now, when I see her pictures online I still feel a bit upset. I think we were more invested than she ever was though.

Far from making Laura and David more wary about finding a third, it simply gave them a better idea of what they were looking for.

Laura: It definitely made me more open to finding someone who could fill her shoes. I suppose you could say that we did find a number of other women who were willing and interested to be a part of our relationship, but I never felt that same way again. I couldn't access that part. I couldn't see them as more than just a friend or a play partner in the bedroom, and sometimes when you don't really, really like a person that much and that person is around all the time, it becomes very irritating. So it became a burden, an annoyance, more than someone we wanted to have around. Successfully we saw someone else for quite a period, somewhat shy of half a year, and we even went on holiday with her. So she was supposed to be a proper third, a proper part of the triad. And we were exploring our emotions with her, but I suppose we weren't clear about our boundaries and she wasn't either, and she had a lot of expectations that she didn't make clear from the start.

This included us paying for all her meals, our paying for everything everywhere that we went, such as having David send her home at all times even if it was late on a weekday night. So to me if you love someone you try to be a bit more understanding. Like if you ask to come over on a weekday night after work you should see yourself home. Because if you want to see us you need to play your part as well, lah. That didn't come to fruition, so there were a lot of those unspoken expectations and when we tried to bring it up with her nicely she said she was traditional. That was just her excuse. So I think I couldn't accept that. I think I saw it as her being too princessy, and we were not willing to give that much.

We tried to be very fair to her, I would say. And [David] saw her separately. He would see her alone and I tried to have some sort of relationship with her. We went to the same gym so we tried to have a relationship apart from when it's just the three of us. Relationships-wise she is very much into the idea of something non-traditional and emotionally perhaps she's not as mature as she thinks that she is. So it didn't actually work out.

We saw two women after that. They were both a lot better, a lot more respectful but I think they were both using us as an intermission before they found someone else more permanent. But we respected that. It was perfectly fine. We're still friends so that's good.

Laura and David feel that their experiences made their expectations more real and also alerted them to the potential pitfalls.

Laura: I think we are a lot more conscious now about the boundaries. Actually from the get go we start off by telling them that there will be no emotions involved. We put it on the table basically what we're interested in, and if that person wants to engage with us it's on these terms. I don't really know if we will ever meet anyone again that we want to date, will be emotionally involved with; definitely open but we are not seeking.

David: I should add that what we are looking for is quite out of the ordinary as well. It's quite niche. So when we were looking we were actively seeking that sort of person and it got quite tiring. It always ended up in failure because you can't find the perfect one. So now we just let it happen as it happens. I mean we open our doors, we are open to meeting new people but we don't actively seek 'the one' anymore.

The lesson learned is that what you read in fantasy does not always apply to reality. I think a lot of life gets in the way. I think when you look for someone a certain basic attraction must be met, at the wavelength of communication with the person rather than the physical.

Laura: I think because it is so difficult to find a unicorn many people have no standards. They will just lower their standards to a baseline; so long as someone is willing to fuck you, you're like 'Yeah, please, come on in'. And that is a problem because if you're looking to someone to date or to play with alone your standards are a lot higher, but when you go out there as a couple you tend to be a little bit more blind, lah. Very thick beer goggles on in that sense. And that can be a problem because you don't really connect with the person you invite into the bedroom.

Laura has a point. Sometimes people do lower their standards. But equally, sometimes, people have unrealistically high standards. And they do this even if they're monogamous and going on dates.

One problem that people hit when dating as a couple with a view to a relationship, as opposed to something purely physical, is that a date can turn into a job interview. If it's just you and your date you form your own opinion. If it's you, your partner and your date, then it can all too easily result in lots of verbal or nonverbal communication between the couple. That's quite intimidating for the third. Put yourself in your unicorn's position. If that were you, you'd just want to relax and have a nice evening with two attractive people you'd just met. So, if you are in a couple and need to confer you can always do it afterwards.

The basic message from those who've seen it all before is don't run before you can walk. Perhaps date separately rather than jointly in the first instance. It may help if you avoid going out looking with a shopping list of requirements in your pocket. Perhaps better simply to spend time with lots of other similarly-minded people, making friends and creating the opportunities from which things can happen. Unicorns can be found in the wild. It just takes time, patience, widespread genuine friendships, respect, a certain humility—and a goodly amount of luck.

CHAPTER THIRTY-ONE

The One-Penis Policy and Its Discontents

I think one penis policies are the height of misogynistic entitlement. I think they're evil and I want them to die in a fire. That's as gentle as I can get, and I didn't use a single swear word.

—Joreth Innkeeper

I don't understand why we only want one penis. I want lots of penises attached to all parts of my body so that I can be the Hedgehog of Sex.

—Maxine

FEW AREAS OF consensual non-monogamy are as challenging to write about as the one penis policy. To say it divides opinion is a bit of an understatement. Amongst those I interviewed for the book, however, as well as in online CNM communities, the division of opinion isn't particularly even. The idea of a one penis policy, by and large, attracts a mixture of ire, ridicule and contempt.

A *one-penis policy* is an arrangement where a man stipulates that everyone he is in a relationship with is fine to have sex with anyone else they choose so long as that person does not have a penis. The only penis permitted is that belonging to the instigator of the one penis policy.

As Elisabeth Sheff points out, this is just ancient, religious polygyny with a makeover. We don't know for sure what relationship styles predominated for most of our species' 300,000-plus year history, when humans were nomadic hunter-gatherers. But some anthropologists have hypothesised that before people made the connection be-tween sex and childbirth that not only did women enjoy more power but there was less, if any, stress on female fidelity. It's also argued that this changed when human society became settled following the invention of agriculture about 11,000 years ago. Settlement meant that resource hoarding was no longer limited by what one could carry. This may well be the origin of systems that resulted in hereditary inequality.

Some, such as David Barash, believe that polygyny, or harem forming, is a 'natu-ral' social tendency as high-status men use their control of power and resources to attract mates, and women congregate around those with resources that enhance their own and their offspring's chances of survival.

We do know that polygyny was very common by the time writing was invented around 5,000 years ago; it's well documented in the Old Testament and other ancient texts. It's recognised still by Islam and by some conservative Christian sects (including fundamentalist Mormons).

Polyandrous societies—where it's normal for one woman to have multiple hus-bands—do exist but are much rarer as they have been throughout recorded history.

However, in the context of modern consensual non-monogamy, polygyny causes sharp differences of opinion. You can make a case that this reflects the contemporary culture wars that have widened the gulf between those of a conservative outlook and those who consider themselves liberal/left/progressive.

Given the networked nature of CNM, one tends to find a certain, superficially at least, uniformity of opinion within networks insofar as like attracts like. And many, if not most, of those I've interviewed would identify as liberal/left/progressive rather than conservative. Consequently not only do egalitarian ideals and antipathy towards a one penis policy predominate, but it proved very hard (but not impossible) to find people who will defend operating one.

So I will start with a word of caution from Dr. Meg-John Barker about rushing to judge those who think differently than yourself.

> The minute you're looking at somebody else, at the way they're doing this stuff, and laughing, then you have got a problem because, just look at yourself; this desire to judge others for how they're doing things usually comes from a defensiveness of not wanting to look at our own shit.

It's common in marginalised groups for people to look for someone else to treat as even more marginal, so that they themselves won't feel like they're at the bottom of the ladder. Meg-John again:

That's because we are outside of the norm where we're already on the defensive, we're already being not given rights, and we're in a precarious position in all kinds of ways. So unfortunately there just seems to be a human tendency to find somebody else to sort of say, well, at least we're not as weird as those guys. Or at least we're doing it more ethically than those guys, or actually flip it so that somehow we are morally superior to the norms. All of these strategies just fetch us right back into suffering.

During the course of my research I found two examples of a one penis policy. The first was at one remove. I interviewed Vincent and Mia, who were involved with a woman and her male partner who had vetoed her having sex with other men. I'll let Vincent and Mia take up the story. They're a professional, thirty-something couple in Singapore. Vincent identifies as straight and Mia as bisexual. The situation came about because Mia was looking for a female play partner and met a woman on the dating app OKCupid.

> It's been two years since we matched on OKC. Our first meeting was a bit strange because she was passing through Singapore and she wanted to do some touristy stuff. So I suggested that Vincent come along and we went to the zoo and she later confided in me that she [mistakenly] thought I was angling for a threesome. She was slightly turned off but things moved on from there. So we have seen each other on our own, and our partners have been introduced, and since then we have gone on holiday, the four of us, quite a number of times.

So Vincent, Mia, her lover and her lover's partner have built a relationship as four. Vincent and the other man have become friends. However, the other man will not allow Vincent to have sex with his partner even though both men have sex with Mia. They have sex as a foursome but, Mia says, within clear boundaries.

> In fact the four of us have fucked but Vincent hasn't fucked her, so the three of us have fucked. Her husband has fucked me but Vincent hasn't fucked her. So this guy is quite jealous but I think the fact that he gets to fuck me takes the jealousy off a bit that I get to fuck her.

So the other man's jealousy extends to his partner's relationship with Mia, which he seems to self-medicate for by having sex with Mia as well. Vincent says it seems to make it easier for him to accept his partner's sexuality.

I think there is a lot more to it than that. One, he gets to fuck her, so that takes the edge off the jealousy. Also amongst all the other women that girl is dating, Mia is the one that is in a committed relationship, and he's met me and we consider ourselves friends so I guess there's a bit of trust.

I suggested to Vincent and Mia that the other man in their informal quad seems to be quite insecure.

Vincent: I mean he's a friend so it is an issue to deal with. I don't judge (laughs).

Mia: I think objectively he is quite jealous, yes. I don't know why though, because she assures him, even in front of us she reassured him, that there's nothing I'm going to do with them in a romantic sense or I don't want a life with them, and she told him this quite often enough in front of me as well until I'm like 'okay, thanks'. But I'm fine with it because I'm on the same page as her and our relationship. It's very strange but it really has worked out in the past two years for us.

The other person I've met and interviewed is Alain, a French tech engineer and entrepreneur in his 30s working around South East Asia. He's had ostensibly monogamish relationships with two women, both of whom I've interviewed. But in the first case he prevented his partner from dating other men while he continued to pursue other conquests, and with his second he stipulated that she couldn't have sex with other men without his being there.

His ex-partner Alice recalls how their relationship first opened up.

In the beginning, it was more of an open relationship as opposed to a poly one. It all started when he wanted a threesome; he always kept Tinder despite us being monogamous. When he finally found someone who was interested in having a threesome with him and myself, he used his birthday as an excuse to try to get me to say yes. I met the lady, was not interested at all but thought if it makes him happy, we should go ahead and open our relationship up.

For Alain the situation was very confronting.

Three years ago, I starting exploring and it really challenged my beliefs in the sense that I used to always think I was quite progressive. For the first time ever, I think I found myself in situation where I really had to manage my own feelings. And it's the first time I hit a wall. And even though some aspects of it made sense on paper and shouldn't be an issue for me, what I felt was very strong and very, very difficult for me to manage.

Alain is an interesting character. His family is liberal to the extent that they often wander round the house naked. However consensual non-monogamy really threw him. He found himself dealing with a panoply of unexpected feelings that he struggles to explain.

What's interesting is that what made it difficult for me was not the fact that I was afraid that she would meet someone better than me, or someone that I would perceive as better, and therefore that I would be threatened in the couple dynamic. I think it's more of a very basic, animalistic type territorial feeling, honestly. Saying it out loud it doesn't make much sense, but I think that it felt very difficult for me to just fathom the fact that someone else would play with or will have fun with my female, if that makes sense.

Jonathan: So deep down you're sort of like Conan the Barbarian?

Alain: I think every man is to some extent. Honestly, I think the difference is, I mean, I'm willing to say that out loud, but I believe that. Or let's say it another way; I haven't met a single man that is not like that at some level, I've seen men that intellectualised very well, the dynamic of polyamory and that are very happy, putting it all over the internet and these sort of thing. But I've never met a guy that really doesn't put up a front and really is willing to share how we feel deep down, et cetera, that doesn't at some level to some extent equals this type of feeling.

It was a relationship that ended badly, so it's perhaps not surprising that his ex-partner Alice doesn't exactly see him as Conan the Barbarian, more as Conan the barbaric horde of unresolved issues.

He was very insecure that I would find someone else better and run off, basically. And that's what he told me as well. So yes, he wasn't sure of himself. He wasn't sure of the entire relationship as a whole, while I was more the stable one that says, 'Well, you go do whatever makes you happy doing'. Which was why he actually said, 'Well, let's try this, but let's try it my way, which is you can only date women.' Fun times.

'Fun times', it has to be pointed out, was saturated with irony. In retrospect Alice doesn't see those times as anything of the sort. It's not as though she thinks of herself as bisexual.

He was basically out, every week, three to five times even, seeing different women all the time. And I was just freaking busy with work, with my studies, completing my dissertation, managing three performances. So, while he had all this fun, I wanted someone to go back to, to have fun as well, but I'm not getting that.

I mean I consider myself heteroflexible, so I wouldn't mind having sex with women. But not necessarily to date them because I think that one woman in a relationship is more than enough to be honest. So that really sucked.

And, to be fair to Alain, he was wrestling with the unexpected feelings that consensual non-monogamy brought up while trying to maintain a relationship with someone who was dancing with their own demons. Alice again:

I've always been a creative person and worked in the arts so whenever I get in and out of depression, I just called it a creative cycle. Every single creative I've known and spoken to about this all suffered with some form of anxiety or mental health issues at one stage of their life. I was just incredibly high functioning; I was able to hide a lot of what I went through even from my partner. At my worst, I wanted to self-harm, was suicidal and the music didn't make sense to me. Looking back, I was not the best person to be with whenever I got to the lows in my creative cycle. I would become incredibly insecure with irrational fears, with thoughts coming into my head that I was not good enough or would be abandoned.

The lesson Alice learned from that was that more honesty is better, certainly in terms of being prepared to state one's needs. She feels, in retrospect, that she should have made it clear that hers weren't being met. Whether that would have improved matters or simply hastened the denouement is impossible to say, but it might have brought about a resolution. Eventually Alice and Alain moved beyond the one penis policy, though even after separating, both of them continue to wrestle with being pulled in different directions by their needs for emotional stability and, at the same time, their desires for sexual variety.

Ultimately, as with all things non-monogamous, it ultimately all comes down to consent. As Magick points out, people will sometimes enter into very unequal relationships (and it's generally women getting the short end of the stick). Sometimes these are consensual, negotiated master/slave dynamics, or dominant/submissive relationships, or restrictions-by-gender of whom people in a relationship can date.

> First I would say I've never had a one penis policy and I never would and I think it's a bizarre concept in general. I can't see a situation where I think it's entirely justified other than within a serious D/s relationship, where it's as justified as is any other rule if everybody is agreed with that. And I know people who have patriarchal D/s families who have a one penis policy and that's as a D/s thing—it's not about jealousy, and it's not about poly and it's not really about gender, because I also know female-headed households that have similar restrictions.

Indeed many people who have issues with a 'one penis policy', or who are uncomfortable with the idea of female slaves[58]and submissives, seem less likely to be as critical of male slaves and submissives and of one vagina policies. This may be because the latter overturn rather than reinforce prevailing gender inequalities. A lot of the social discomfort around one penis policies seems to stem from their continuation of patriarchal models. Also, because men are broadly speaking better socialised not to consent to things they don't wish for, there may be greater confidence that the consent is genuine. Lastly there is a perception that where a one penis policy operates it's less about catering for the needs of the other parties (a lot of practitioners would argue that BDSM is primarily about the needs of the slave/submissive) and more about the insecurities of the proprietor of the sole penis at the party.

As a trans woman, Becky sees the whole idea as ridiculous.

---

58 Slaves in the context of BDSM means someone who has chosen to be a slave in a relationship with a master just as a submissive means someone who has negotiated their role in a dominant/ submissive relationship. Consent is just as necessary for BDSM relationships as it is for CNM or monogamous/vanilla relationships. Where consent is lacking abuse strides in.

It's not about genitals, it should just be about people, and I say if your penis is so fragile that it can't go near another penis then you need a better penis.

Becky, Maxine and others all object to the one penis policy not only as a patriarchal tool but also for trivialising relationships between women and being transphobic to boot. I suspect none of these objections will ping the meter of those who operate one. There's a cultural gulf within consensual non-monogamy, just as there is within society, between conservatives and progressives. Unless it just reflects a particular kink, most promoters of one penis policies seem to be firmly on the traditionalist side of that divide. And never the twain shall meet.

CHAPTER THIRTY-TWO

A Consensually Non-Monogamous Person's Bill of Rights?

OF ALL THE posts on the popular, early polyamory website 'More Than Two', one generated more discussion over the years than anything else. It was originally called 'A Secondary's Bill of Rights'[59], later generalized to 'The Relationship Bill of Rights'. It's a great starting point for exploring what rights and responsibilities people have within all kinds of relationships, monogamous or consensually non-monogamous. You may or may not find yourself agreeing with all of them. However, if they prompt useful reflection and discussion then they've done their job.

Later in this chapter I'll suggest my own list of CNM principles. But first I'll take a look at those proposed back in 2003. I've included some of the author's original comments with them, edited and condensed, then mine.

A SECONDARY'S BILL OF RIGHTS

- **I have the right to be treated with honesty, integrity, compassion, and sensitivity to my needs.**

Ideally this would be how everybody treats everybody else in any sort of relationship. Obviously much of human history is brimming with examples of people failing to treat others with honesty, integrity, compassion and sensitivity—because people are flawed or they were socialised to accept flawed notions of how to treat people, hence the need to spell this out.

---

59   A Proposed Secondary's Bill of Rights, More Than Two - https://www.morethantwo.com/polyforsecondaries.html#bor

- **I have the right, and responsibility, to understand clearly the rules of a relationship.**
  When I enter a new relationship, I have the right to have rules and the reasons behind them clearly explained and to have my questions answered. "Because that is how things are" is not an answer; if I do not understand the reasons for the rules, then I may unintentionally violate the spirit of those rules even if I remain within the letter. Rules should not be added or changed without explanation. I cannot be expected to discover the rules governing my relationship when by breaking them accidentally they blow up on me

This goes to the heart of much that causes relationship problems, and not just in consensual non-monogamy. People want different things from relationships, and it often takes time for us to figure out what we want and what the other or others want.

Sometimes this is clear from the outset. One person might say, for instance; 'I've just emerged from a very bruising separation and right now I'm looking for company, fun, someone to relax with and someone to have sex with. But I'm not in a place where I can think about planning and commitments.' Another might say; 'I've had enough of people who just want something casual. I want a relationship around which I can build a life and a future.'

The trouble is that when starting out on a relationship we're often reluctant to say what we want or think we want, perhaps for fear of driving the other person away. It often happens that people will settle for less than they want when they go into a new relationship. Perhaps they're lonely, perhaps they're just overwhelmingly attracted to the other person.

Yes it can be scary to lay one's soul bare early on in a relationship, and it can be pretty disconcerting when someone bares their soul to you, but fearless, compassionate communication really helps. Such things are almost always easier if one isn't too fearful of hearing 'Sorry, that doesn't work for me'.

- **I have the right to be a part of discussions about decisions that affect me, wherever possible and practical.**
  It is unfair to be told about changes in the form and rules of my relationships after the fact. While it is not reasonable for me to expect full decision-making partnership in all aspects of a couple's primary relationship, for example, I do expect to be part of negotiations about the form my own relationship takes.

Dating a couple or one half of a couple is a bit like being in a legislature of three lawmakers. There's a risk of an inbuilt majority. Things may get debated, but what's the point of debate if the outcome is a foregone conclusion?

Generally voters like to see their politicians working together and finding common ground. There's an element of that in CNM relationships. It's generally better to try to work together so everyone's wants and needs are met as far as is possible.

Take Zul and Anushka, the primaries in this example: If they expect a say in whether Anushka's boyfriend Ian moves away for a new job, then it seems logical that Ian should have a similar say on whether Anushka moves away to follow Zul to his new job. Reciprocity is always a good rule of thumb. But perhaps a better approach is to discuss ahead of time what areas of one another's' lives Zul, Anushka and Ian expect a say in and what they don't.

- **I have a right and responsibility to set clear limits on the obligations I am making.**
  My having no other partners does not mean all of my time and resources are available. Just as I, as a secondary, cannot expect to monopolise all of my partner's time, my partner cannot expect to monopolise all of mine. Sadly, people take advantage of others. The power dynamics in a two vs. one situation mean the one needs to be especially prepared to set good boundaries.
- **I have the right to ask my partners to compromise and seek to reach a middle ground when possible.**
  I should not be the only one to do all of the bending.

Again, this wouldn't need saying if people always took the honesty, integrity, compassion and sensitivity principles to heart. All too often we enter into complex personal arrangements with too little thought to the ramifications for ourselves and others. There needs to be plenty of room for everyone to deal with 'events, dear boy'. In relationships, a good deal is only a good deal when it's good for everyone.

- **I have the right to have relationships with people, not with relationships.**
  That is, I have the right to conduct my relationship with a living, thinking human being rather than with an established relationship or a set of rules. I have the right to time with each individual separately as well as in a group.
- **I have the right to expect that plans made with my partner will not be changed at the last minute just because a primary partner has had a bad day.**
  As a secondary, I deal with most of my bad days alone and have the right to expect last-minute changes in plans to happen only in rare and unavoidable situations.

And the primary partner(s) should also be able to expect a similarly reasonable degree of reliability. It definitely becomes an issue if one person pulls rank, or makes a fuss and expects the world to shift on its axis for them, but wouldn't countenance the same from their metamour.

If a new partner or a partner in an existing relationship needs a high degree of support it is important that everyone knows from the outset so they can ask themselves if they can be fair and/or understanding in those circumstances, though inevitably problems can arise if people find the reality harder than they expected.

- **I have the right to a balance between what I give to the relationship and what is given back to me.**
- **I have the right to be treated as an equal individual (which is different than being an equal partner).**
  I deserve to have my partner spend time in my world as well as visiting his/hers/theirs. My likes, dislikes, desires, and hang-ups should not be dismissed simply because I am secondary.

It's not unreasonable to expect reciprocation; a little of what you like, a little of what I like. Again this holds equally true in monogamous relationships.

- **I have the right to enjoy NRE (within reason), passion, and special moments with my partner without guilt or apologies.**

The 'within reason' is telling, as we'll see in the chapter on NRE—New Relationship Energy. It's exciting to be newly in love, and not to be allowed to enjoy that excitement is to be denied an important and fundamental human experience. However, as we all know, being in love doesn't give one carte blanche to be self-centred and inconsiderate. Indeed, managing the feelings of existing partners is a key aspect of enjoying NRE in a consensually non-monogamous setting.

- **I have the right to privacy.**
  The details of physical intimacy and emotionally intimate conversations should not be shared without my knowledge and ideally not without my consent. This does not mean I have the right to keep secrets from the other people involved; it merely means that whatever rights to basic privacy they may enjoy, I may enjoy as well.

Certainly if some people have all the information and others don't, if the privacy of one is respected and that of another is not, it makes it difficult to have a just and fair relationship.

- **I have the right to be told the truth at all times.**
  This includes a right to know about fears, doubts and concerns as they arise, not after they become insurmountable. Don't tell me what you think I want to hear; tell the truth—that is what I need to hear.

In the absence of the best available information, someone can't give informed consent.

- **I have the right to have and express all of my emotions.**
  I accept that being secondary may place limits on many things (such as sharing others" family holidays or vacations, or having them with me in my times of crisis or celebration). My acceptance of that possibility does not mean that I won't be disappointed or sad. Further, being secondary comes with some built-in challenges to security, and there may be times I need reassurance as to how and where I fit into my partner's world.

This is an age-old conundrum, and once again not specific to consensual non-monogamy. As one thoughtful writer, talking (as it happens) about the impact of childhood trauma on adult adoptees, put it (and I paraphrase): 'It may be completely understandable that you feel like this, and that you neither invited nor deserved the things that happened to you, but that doesn't mean anybody is going to want to put up with your shit.'

For me that's it in a nutshell. We're all dealt a hand in life and some people just get dealt a terrible hand. They're abused, they're traumatised and good people do their best to make the world a better, fairer and more just place and support those who need it. But... and here's the but... no one is obliged to put up with unreasonable, let alone abusive behaviour from someone else even though it may be understandable (as in comprehensible).

So on the one hand we all have the right to our feelings but at the same time we have a responsibility to be sufficiently emotionally continent that others can work with us to resolve problems.

The flip side of that is that we do need to respect displays of emotion equally from people regardless of their gender, skin colour, age, ability or orientation. We live in a world, in the West anyway, where it seems that the only acceptable anger is white male anger. The anger of women, people of Asian, African, Indigenous and Latin American origin, the anger of queer people and the disabled, is uncomfortable to the point of being unacceptable. It's hardly surprising it's uncomfortable. It's often righteous anger borne of injustice, and that's hard to deal with if you're benefitting in some way from that injustice, even unwittingly or unwillingly.

- **When I am in a relationship with one person, I am in some relationship with all the other people that person is involved with, especially the primary partner(s)—even if there is no romantic connection between us.**
  If I am resented in any way by them, that resentment serves to undermine my relationship with another and keep it from being "real." Resentment should not creep into rules and definitions that are set in place.

Yes, if you're not wanted by your partner's other partner, or by their friends or parents or whatever, that does have an effect on you. However it's a fact of life, whether you're celibate, single, monogamous or non-monogamous, that not everybody will always like you. Regardless, you deserve to be treated decently. Conversely, it's your responsibility to accept that if you and they don't get along, if only for the sake of the person you both love/adore/shag frantically, you do your best to get along.

- **I have the right to have a voice in the form my relationship takes.**
  Even when I am joining a pre-existing relationship, I have a right to have some say in the time I can spend with my lover and other things about the form and structure of that relationship. If my partners attempt to impose pre-existing agreements about the form, time, or circumstances under which I may spend time with my lover, I have a right to speak up if those agreements do not meet my needs.

A MORE UNIVERSAL FOUNDATION

The *Bill of Rights* from the More than Two website is a very personal document, but we're not short of more universal statements of rights to draw on.

As we know, the golden rule and its variants have shaped religions and philosophies in most corners of the world as Confucianism, Hinduism and Buddhism, and the great Abrahamic faiths; Judaism, Christianity and Islam, attest.

The development of our present understanding of human rights is usually traced through a series of events, largely in the West, that include the signing of Magna

Carta (1215) at Runnymede, the Putney Debates (1647) by the Thames in London, the adoption of The Bill of Rights (1689) by the English Parliament, the Declaration of Independence (1776) of the United States, The Declaration of the Rights of Man and the Citizen (1789) in Revolutionary France, and the publication of the first ten amendments to the US constitution that is also known as The Bill of Rights (1789).

In 1948 a United Nations Committee under the auspices of its chair Eleanor Roosevelt produced the Universal Declaration of Human Rights that gave many of the principles expressed in those earlier declarations new voice and new authority in a world still sober after the atrocities of the Second World War. It was drawn up by delegates from countries as diverse as China, Lebanon, France and Chile, with the Indian feminist Hansa Mehta prevailing upon the committee to make the declaration less gendered.

And for the last three quarters of a century it has remained the world's touchstone for its peoples' rights, freedoms and for what it means to respect a person.

So here are those of its principles that I think apply in relationships (with my comments).

Article 1. All human beings are born free and equal in dignity and rights. They are endowed with reason and conscience and should act towards one another in a spirit of brotherhood.

People are autonomous individuals. Respect that. No person's dignity and well-being are ever innately lesser than another's. Some people's needs (as opposed to wants) are sometimes greater than those of others. but even if you can't or won't meet those needs, there's no excuse for belittling or denigrating someone or for failing to respect their integrity as a human being.

Article 2. Everyone is entitled to all the rights and freedoms set forth in this Declaration, without distinction of any kind, such as race, colour, sex, language, religion, political or other opinion, national or social origin, property, birth or other status.

Simple really; you aren't a lesser person because your skin is brown or you have a vagina, or you use a wheelchair, or you love differently than someone else, or you hail from a 'shithole country'. People are to be judged by their actions, not by their origins or immutable characteristics. Please don't treat people otherwise.

Article 3. Everyone has the right to life, liberty and security of person.

Though 'security of person' in this context relates to habeas corpus and the right not to be subject to arbitrary arrest, we could equally apply it to the right to freedom from violence, fear, coercion and insecurity in the home and from those closest to you.

Article 4. No one shall be held in slavery or servitude; slavery and the slave trade shall be prohibited in all their forms.

Coercion doesn't always take such egregious forms. We shouldn't treat anyone as our servant.[60] Just because you're dating someone doesn't mean you can coerce them to look after you and your stuff and do your work because your mum did it for you and you somehow concluded it's your birth right. Such things require negotiation as equals and wholehearted consent.

Article 5. No one shall be subjected to torture or to cruel, inhuman or degrading treatment or punishment.

In the context of a relationship this absolutely means no physical or mental abuse or coercive control. It's repellent.

Article 7. All are equal before the law and are entitled without any discrimination to equal protection of the law.

Equal rights. Whatever is fundamentally reasonable for one is fundamentally reasonable for another.

Article 10. Everyone is entitled in full equality to a fair and public hearing by an independent and impartial tribunal.

Just a gentle reminder that you and your partner are not a fair and impartial judge, jury and executioner when it comes to making decisions about another partner or about each other's behaviour. It also establishes an important principle (as we'll see later) for how communities, like the swinging or CNM communities should handle disputes and accusations.

60　...and no this isn't the right place to say 'but what about my 'master/slave' relationship?'.

Article 12. No one shall be subjected to arbitrary interference with his privacy, family, home or correspondence, nor to attacks upon his honour and reputation.

Don't read your partner's email or your metamour's email without asking. Respect their space. Respect them. You should reasonably expect the same in return. There are apparently some in the poly community who insist on oversight of all communications between their partner(s) and metamour(s). This is not just intrusive and indicative of a lack of trust. It's controlling. It should be unacceptable.

Article 17. (1) Everyone has the right to own property alone as well as in association with others. (2) No one shall be arbitrarily deprived of his property.

Your partner's or metamour's stuff is theirs, not yours.

Article 18. Everyone has the right to freedom of thought, conscience and religion.

If someone disagrees with you, especially if their views don't threaten the fundamental rights of others, remember it's okay to disagree. If you find their views repellent you can challenge them (respectfully) or withdraw. Forcing someone to 'agree' with you is not cool.

Article 19. Everyone has the right to freedom of opinion and expression.

See 18. Plus people have a right to a voice and to be heard. Within wide bounds, people also have a right to be wrong. No one should be silenced by fear.

I do accept the limitations of taking a grand declaration of human rights and applying it to the microcosm of two, three, four people and their intimates—but working from principles that have been tried and tested gives you a firm foundation on which to base sound judgements.

AND MY OWN

FINALLY, TO CLOSE, here's my own three and a quarter groats' worth. These are less principles more notes in the margins of the above, if you like.[61]

   1. It all starts and ends with consent. If people aren't giving wholehearted and informed consent to something, you're skating on thin ice. If you're saying or hearing 'Well, I'd prefer...' or 'I'm not sure...' then best slow down and wait for that consent.
   2. Other people have all the rights you would ascribe to yourself. They are as real as you, even those you don't know yet. Life is not a video game (though there's an interesting philosophical point right there—and possibly a movie). As I mentioned at the outset of the book, 'Do as you would be done by' is an ethical foundation that has weathered the ages.
   3. Rules are problematic, agreements are inclusive. Dating someone(s) who makes, interprets, judges upon, and enforces rules is disempowering. Some people do seek out a relationship in which they play a wholly submissive role. This is at the heart of the D/s kink dynamic, and even then it is all based on the sub's consent. However plenty of people find themselves tolerating a relationship where they have very little say when this is not what they want. Talk, discuss, negotiate, seek compromise. Respect other people's agency—and require respect for your own.
   4. Be clear about boundaries and expectations, both yours and others'. If you have red lines (regarding yourself), make these clear at the outset, ideally at first meeting. Likewise, if you do intend to impose 'rules' on others—give them plenty of opportunity to run away screaming. Don't wait until someone is emotionally invested to spring it on them. Make sure the other party or parties have a clear and easy exit to leave with dignity if they don't like what's on offer.
   5. Don't stop communicating. In most CNM relationships, constant communication and negotiation are a given. You may have stated your needs, boundaries and expectations once. Once is not enough. Don't assume. Check in. Check often.
   6. Feelings change. People find themselves wanting more or less. Whatever you agree now is contingent. If circumstances change so may people's wants, needs, desires and dreams. In the realm of love and sex, no agreement is binding beyond the point where one or more people withdraw their consent to it. If you can be flexible and still be content, be flexible. If being asked to be flexible beyond a certain point makes you unhappy or uncomfortable, you're under no obligation.

---

61   Groats not goats. Goats are the ones that nibble a hole in your pocket, groats are what fall out of the now-nibbled pocket.

*7. **People change. Let them.*** Those you love evolve and grow. So do relationships. Give people and relationships the room to find their own expression and level.

*8. **Mutuality is a foundation stone*** for most successful relationships. If one of you wants something very different from another, such as levels of commitment or ways of living, then to have a successful, healthy relationship may require you both to step back. Just being friends is a great option in many circumstances.

*9. **It's okay to prioritise.*** Recognising *the equality of everyone's humanity* is essential but that doesn't mean everyone is equally important in your life. However it helps if you make your priorities clear from the beginning. Sometimes priorities change. If this happens, kindness, compassion, and clear communication can make a potentially difficult situation less so.

*10. **Be honest.*** Give people the information they need and the means to make well-informed decisions. They may not like what they hear, and you may not like what they decide, but it's important to ensure that everyone has agency. Without honesty how can there be true consent? Better to deal with some disappointment now than more disappointment and heartbreak later.

CHAPTER THIRTY-THREE

Metamours

Metamour. *n*. One's partner's other partner(s). Someone to whom you are linked by virtue of sharing a romantic or sexual partner but where no direct romantic and sexual relationship is implied.

Metasqueeze. *n*. As per metamour but rather more informal.

FOR SOME, METAMOURS are one of the great unexpected blessings of consensual non-monogamy. For others they're an inevitable but not necessarily welcome part of their partner's seeing other people.

What people new to consensual non-monogamy soon find is that their metamours, whether they're present or not, can play a significant part in their lives.

Sometimes a partner's choice comes as a welcome relief: 'Thank god he's found someone who likes musicals. I'm not sure I could take seeing Cats again.' Sometimes it's a drain: 'They're so needy. She seems to spend all her time on the phone with them.' Sometimes it's outright antipathy; 'Seriously, how could he date someone who voted for *him*?' But there's also the possibility of support you'd never anticipated, or a new friend.

Seb, for instance, feels that having a sympathetic and supportive metamour can enhance one's own relationship with a mutual partner.

Once you realise that someone can genuinely raise the collective happiness and quality of life for not just two of you, but all three of you, you realise that what would typically be seen as a negative is, if you're a bit lucky, a positive if the right people are involved.

Charlotte is one of those who thinks it's better to engage with metamours whenever possible.

> They're really important. Poly is so much easier when you get on with your metamours, possibly even become platonic life partners with them.

February 28th has even been designated Metamour Day (Feb 14 plus 14... - Double Valentine's, geddit?) in honour of 'polyamory's most distinctive relationships'. Dr. Elisabeth Sheff, who has studied poly families for more than two decades, thinks success or failure of poly relationships often rides on metamour relations:

> What has stood out to me about these families who remain together in long-term polycules is that the metamour relationships make or break the family over the long term. These emotionally intimate, non-sexual chosen family relationships are so important in polyamorous families that I made up the word *polyaffective* to describe them.

> Positive polyaffective relationships among metamours who become chosen family over time are the backbone of the poly family. Metamours who can't stand each other and are never able to establish comfort (much less delight) in each other's presence are not going to happily coexist over the long term. Metamours who add value to each other's lives, however, can not only support each other when life inevitably throws them a curve ball, but also support the polyamorous relationship with their mutual partner if it falls on hard times.

There's no doubt that a lot of poly people see a situation where metamours are close as an ideal worth pursuing. The Philadelphia-based author and educator Kevin Patterson, on the other hand, is not particularly fussed. For him a metamour is pretty much like anyone else he might meet. If he gels with them it's someone new to hang with, if he doesn't it's no big deal.

> I wouldn't say they're terribly important, but I do value the ones that I have. If I didn't have a relationship with my metamours, I'd be fine. I wouldn't cry myself to sleep over it. But I actually do have relationships with a couple of them and I like that. I like that I could watch football with one of my metamours. I like that I could just talk video games with another.

Sometimes metamours bring something into one another's lives that they both benefit from. For Nathan, his metamour Arty was a source of advice and wise words even if they didn't make a huge effort to seek out one another's company.

> To say my metamours are non-standard implies that there is a standard metamour: doesn't exist. We're all just people living our lives. Arty is a good person to have in my life in that position. I really enjoy the time that I spend with him, the encounters I have with him, all the group stuff, it's delightful. I don't have a super friendship relationship, but when we're in each other's presence, we're happy that the other is there or at least that's my impression. He's a very clever man, he could be planning on taking over the world. I do very much enjoy him in my life and when need be I talk to him about stuff. Things with our partner, things with his marriage, his relationships.

Sometimes relationships just get difficult and metamours exacerbate that. Sometimes it's the metamour that seems to be the problem. For Xena it was made more complicated by the fact that one of her friends became her metamour.

> [My partner] was seeing two [other] girls at the time. I feel I had more difficulties with my friend. I think it's got to do with because I have boundaries which I find they keep pushing at, and I feel like I was disrespected by them of my opinion and how I felt. But I felt okay with the other girl.
>
> Maybe it was me that encouraged them. My ex was new to this and he didn't know what it was. I told him many times it would have been more comfortable if, rather than dating another girl, it was my friend—because she already knew what it is like, how the rules work and that sort of thing. So I sort of encouraged it. And I also knew that my friend liked him. So I thought okay, I guess is better with you than with other girls. But after that I feel not so comfortable with things, and I couldn't talk anymore with her, and they continue to dismiss my feelings and that kind of hurt me, and that's when I fell out with everyone. The saddest thing was that they didn't seem to care that it matters to me. My friends are like my family to me, that's how I treat them, and then I feel like they both betrayed me. It's a strong word but that's how I feel.

That is probably a fairly extreme example of what can go wrong, but most of us understand the capacity for human relationships to end up in conflict when strong feelings are involved. Where people are already bringing out the worst in one another, adding the 'wrong' people to the mix can easily end up as a total clusterfuck.

It's equally possible for more people, if they interact in positive ways, to really calm things down. Just as with any other sort of relationship, it ultimately comes down to how those involved interact.

Joreth Innkeeper has seen a lot of metamour conflicts. She warns that rather than see the problem as inherently with the other, ultimately we have to ask ourselves what our reaction to them says about *us*.

> I get into this discussion in the forums online all the time. People have a problem with their metamour. 'What am I going to do about my metamour?' 'I don't like this other person, what are we going to do about it?' Ultimately, the problem is always between you and your partner.

> Your partner likes that person, your partner finds something valuable about that person. What they find valuable about them may be a reflection on your partner. And if that is somehow incompatible, is that an incompatibility between you and your partner? And almost always metamour problems really come down to 'Me and my partner are incompatible in this way'.

Franklin Veaux provides an example:

> If I was dating somebody and then she started dating some new person and that person was for example openly racist or openly homophobic or something like that, now, clearly I would not like that in that this new partner but if my partner thinks that's okay, that tells me something about my partner where, you know, she and I have a problem.

Your partner's choice of other partners can tell you quite a lot about them, some of which might come as a surprise. It's a good indication that you have things to talk about.

Incompatibility aside, it can also point to other issues; someone may feel they aren't getting enough attention or enough sex. It could highlight worries about money or a partner's contribution to keeping the household on the road. But Joreth's point is well made; these things generally relate to matters closer to home.

So are there any good rules of thumb for getting on with your metamours? One thing to bear in mind, says Kevin, is to remember that (presumably) you all have at heart the happiness of the person you date in common.

> Try to remember that you're on 'team shared partner'. My wife's name is Antoinette. Everybody that's connected to her, we're all teammates on 'team Antoinette'. Everyone that's dating me, they're all on 'team Kevin'. Just remember that you are part of the team and that you're a teammate. And if you can manage having, at a minimum, a polite relationship with this person, it benefits somebody that you both care about.

It should go without saying that if you both care about someone then you don't want to cause them unhappiness. So, if possible, address any conflict or issues you have with your metamours without forcing your partner to take sides—or to act as an intermediary. You may dislike a metamour, or perhaps you simply don't particularly warm to them, but you do have an interest in getting things to work as well as practicably possible. However, as Meg-John Barker says, while there's no one right approach, trying to find a pragmatic means of co-existence is sensible.

> I'm wary of anything that says you *must* or you *ought* to do anything. But there's a real practical element of if you're two people in another person's life and that person needs care, how are you going to manage that? If you're not in contact at all and if you can't say a pleasant word to each other that's going to be rather difficult. So I think there's something about needing to consider the wider system rather than just the dyad, with a sense of what are the connections while not trying to force people into anything. Again, that would be non-consensual. If you don't actually have a very good connection with that person, you shouldn't have to play board games with them every Saturday or have a threesome with them or anything else.

There are times, however, when it's not unreasonable to intervene. No one should stand by and say or do nothing while someone they know is subjected to abusive behaviour. It's a judgement one needs to make carefully. Franklin Veaux:

> If you feel like your partner is being abused, I think it is absolutely reasonable to sit down and say; 'Look, I see this happening, this is really destructive, are you aware

that this is going on?' You can't necessarily expect that they will do what you want them to do, of course. You can't necessarily say, 'Well I demand that you break up with this person'.

There is a fine line between intervening to protect a partner and just plain interfering. It's easy to get it wrong. If you can interrogate your motives that can help. If you're in any doubt about whether you're doing something for your own or your partner's wellbeing, take a moment to reflect. But you don't have to wait for them to come home with a black eye or in a state of terror, or to have their self-esteem wrecked, to speak up. If in doubt, think about checking in with mutual friends to get a slightly more dispassionate opinion.

RIPPLES IN THE POND

IF YOU'RE PART of a network of emotionally related people, things that affect your metamours, even your meta-metamours, can affect you.

All sorts of major life events—divorce, illness, bereavement, unemployment, financial and legal woes, crime and incarceration—can bring us low. Many of us have experience of supporting a partner through one or more of these situations.

When you're consensually non-monogamous the possibility, even the likelihood, arises that one of your partner's other partners will need support at some point. That may mean that your partner has less time and emotional bandwidth for you.

Many people already have the tools to cope with this. If you grew up with siblings, there may well have been moments when a brother or sister needed your parents' undivided attention or support and you had to be more self-sufficient for a while. Attention is not a direct correlate of love. Just because someone's focus is elsewhere it doesn't mean they love you less. It means they've had to prioritise.

There will also be situations when your partner experiences a breakup with another partner. There is no single right way of handling this, though sympathy and respect certainly help. It may be that you didn't like your metamour very much. It happens. Try to remember that your partner *did*. If you're glad that they split up there may come a moment when it's appropriate to say 'It was for the best' or 'I didn't think they were very good for you', but that moment will almost certainly not come until after they've finished grieving.

There are situations where you may sympathise with your metamour rather than your partner. The people we love are not necessarily any more reasonable than anyone else, ourselves included. Is it acceptable to stay friends with a former metamour even after your partner has broken off contact? This will be a judgement only you can make, but generally I'd expect to hear from CNM people that our partners should not dictate to us who our friends are—and that goes for all of us, whether we're monogamous or not.

As already noted, one of the interesting features of consensual non-monogamy is that your partners' choice of other partners will sometimes delight you, sometimes perplex you and sometimes appal you.

Alice was very unhappy with some of her partner's relationship choices because she felt that they were having a tangible impact on their own relationship, all the more so because her partner discouraged her from seeing other people.

> There was one incident where he picked a much younger girl and I basically went, 'She's going to scream rape and you are going to be fucked because this girl is incredibly insecure.' She was 19, I think there were huge daddy issues, very, very young, and he was like 'Yes, but she's hot' and I'm like, 'That's precisely the point'.

> And there was another girl who had emotional issues and he likes to be this knight in shining armour that tries to save women. And I say, 'You can't save everyone, start with yourself if you can'. So I had issues with these two particular women. It was just a threat that I felt would destabilise our relationship because we already had a lot of shit on our plate. I don't need more, more drama to rock the boat.

> Like he was speaking to women who were depressed and wanted to kill themselves and he was getting depressed, and I'm like, I'm already depressed. Why are you spending the time trying to save these women that can't be saved. I'm sorry but find someone else. To the extent where he was complaining to me about these sorts of partners, I don't want to hear about X, Y, Z's problems, I have enough of my own.

Thankfully, as often as not metamours are kindred spirits. People often have a type and it may be that they uncovered a pair (or more) of aces—of which you're one. Alan, who is based on the US East Coast, has attended numerous poly conventions.

> It's kind of a known thing that when you see groups of three or four roaming a convention together, two of them sometimes look noticeably alike. I mean, like two brothers or two sisters or at least cousins. People do have a type, and when two of the type meet as metamours they may find they have a lot in common.

I spent an afternoon down the pub with three of one of my interviewees' partners while she was at a nearby event with a fourth, and they all knew each other well and got on like a house on fire. There were even occasions when they would intervene (nicely) with their mutual partner because they were concerned about one of the others' wellbeing.

For some, metamours can be a source of mutual support. It may seem counter-intuitive to monogamous people who are, whether by inclination or socialisation, primed to see 'rivals' and 'threats' rather than allies when their partner shows an interest in someone else. Clearly it doesn't have to be that way.

CHAPTER THIRTY-FOUR

New Relationship Energy

NEW RELATIONSHIP ENERGY—that giddy sense of infinite possibility, obsession, adoration that we associate with falling in love—is such a common topic in consensual non-monogamy that it's often reduced to the initialism *NRE*. The American psychologist Dorothy Tennov coined the term limerence[62] in her 1979 book *Love and Limerence: The Experience Of Being In Love.* It has similar connotations albeit NRE can equally cover lighter feelings of new love than that sense of involuntary and obsessive attachment to the object of adoration that limerence seems to imply. As many of us know from experience, new relationship energy is the uplift, the excitement, and the enchantment that seems to colour our entire existence when we begin a promising new romance. For some of us it's like walking into a beautiful patisserie and knowing that all the cakes just want us and no one else. You're welcome to find your own metaphor.

For lots of people these early stages are the best bit: the thrill of discovery, of exploring a new person, a new body; all that oxytocin, the long online exchanges, the all-night conversations; the novel, exciting and energetic sex. It varies from person to person, but many of us experience a similar raft of these phenomena at the outset of a new relationship.

However, for the most part, when monogamous people experience this, they are single and entering one relationship. True, there are those whose relationships over-lap. They may meet someone as an existing relationship is coming to an end and they prefer to jump ship than be alone. Some are ostensibly monogamous but cheat, and have to manage the outward signs of their excitement so as not to arouse suspicion. For some people who are drawn to infidelity, in other words to *non*-consensual non-monogamy, this simply adds to the thrill and the appeal. Some people just love the

---

62 *Love and Limerence: The Experience Of Being In Love* (1979) 2nd Edition by Tennov, Dorothy (ISBN: 9780812862867) (1998) Pub: Scarborough House

vertiginous drop into the emotional unknown so much that it's the *sine qua non* of their (love) lives. And there are those for whom NRE is unexpected and uninvited and quite possibly unwanted, but life... Mostly, however, monogamous people get to enjoy new relationship energy without it much affecting anyone but the two. Friends might ask you where you've been for the last two months, or your parents want to know why you're like a ghost in the house or never call them. But mostly (Romeo and Juliet notwithstanding) it's something that has limited fallout.

Not so if you're consensually non-monogamous. When you have an existing partner or partners, the arrival on the scene of someone new can usher in a huge amount of uncertainty. It has the potential to throw into sharp relief other people's insecurities and if the new love/lust-birds don't know where things might lead, for those one remove away it's even more unfathomable.

It's especially important to be aware of one's own behaviour when in the throes of NRE. Some people will find that they are simply in a good mood and this lights up all their relationships. Others can find themselves losing interest in existing partners or obsessed with their new flame. It can make us our best selves, it can make us not ourselves, but very rarely does it leave us our normal selves. Roxy Music weren't wrong when they sang 'Love is the Drug', says Kevin Patterson.

> I find that new relationship energy is like alcohol or any other intoxicant. We all have that one friend where they're a lot more fun when they're a little bit up. Then you've got that other friend that is a complete wreck on alcohol and you try to steer them away from the drinks. Everybody has a different sort of reaction to it. My wife on NRE gets really impatient. She gets really impatient with everything that isn't the new shiny person that she's into. Meanwhile for me, NRE means a bunch of goofy smiles and random laughter.

That analogy is powerful not least because new love, the whole process of bonding with a new mate, does release powerful hormonal chemicals into our systems. Penny, in Jakarta, positively enjoys seeing her husband happy in the throes of a new relationship:

> We're in the house all the time and we usually sense it. For example, I can see him singing and look happier and much more energised. I mean it also gives a positive energy in the house too. So it's not something that we think of as an issue. We think it's a good thing. I feel we both think it's more on the positive way.

The internet is full of dubious surveys telling us how many times people fall in love during a lifetime. Scientific they're not, but there seems to be a broad consensus that most people only fall 'properly' in love (as opposed to being rather besotted) a handful of times. Given that each time can be quite different and that we're hardly objective about ourselves, most of us have limited data about how we behave when we start a new relationship. We should pay close attention, says Kevin.

> A part of it is understanding the effect that NRE has on you. The same as with alcohol. If you know that you're a violent drunk, you know that you shouldn't be having drinks. I know that my NRE doesn't really have a ton of impact on my other relationships, but my wife, she understands that it does have an impact on her other relationships. So knowing that, she's able to gauge what her reactions are, and actively counterbalance that.

We'll look at insecurity and jealousy in more detail in a later chapter. However it's not unusual for all but the most secure and self-contained people to find it disconcerting when their partner is experiencing NRE. If you're in the throes of NRE and have the presence of mind (as CNM people strongly recommend) you might do well to pay extra attention to your longer-standing partner(s) to pre-empt their concerns and channel some of your good feelings their way. As DK Green says, a lot of the time all that's needed is 'a shit ton of reassurance'.

> NRE is a thing, New Relationship Excitement, the shiny, the new that is drawing my attention, like shiny things to a magpie right now. It does settle, it does wear off so that it becomes a normal relationship instead of the sort of fireworks whizzbang beginning relationship. I have been in a position as a therapist to help people to navigate [a partner's experiencing NRE]. And it is perfectly possible to wait it out and realise that the acute state of discomfort is going to be temporary. And in three years' time it'll be tickety-boo. But for some people, the pain of that period of time is actually unbearable and they can't weather that storm. So, yes, absolutely a shit ton of reassurance. Sometimes it's enough and sometimes it's just not.

Three years? Good grief, you say. Can't they just get over all that stuff in three months or, better still, three weeks? If it's still going on after six months no one in the poly scene is going to think the worse of you for chucking a bucket of cold water over them. Seriously. (I am joking BTW—unless they consent to being drenched!) But, yes, it can be a slog as you wait to get your old lover back.

Seb first encountered NRE after he and his wife opened their relationship:

> I would say that with her, new relationship energy is particularly noticeable. Right
> at the beginning I didn't have a sophisticated understanding about what that was.
> And so I found that it was difficult and threatening to deal with, because it felt like
> a new partner was much more interesting than me and much more attractive than
> me simply based on the intensity of attention that that other person was getting.
> These days, having gained some knowledge and experience over the years, I'm a
> lot more relaxed about it because I'm a more familiar with how it works. I'm aware
> that she is particularly affected by new relationship energy and I know that, when
> it happens, the best thing to do is just let it play out.

When Mawar first dated Seb she had to make sure that her existing partner,
Adam, didn't feel he'd been forgotten.

> I'm actually quite good at handling new relationship energy. If it's my partner
> who's the one experiencing the energy I would usually encourage them to pursue
> the new relationship. But if I feel neglected I could just tell them that I feel ne-
> glected and we can arrange something. If I was the one who experienced the new
> relationship energy, I think I have always been very considerate of my partner's
> feeling and try to make up for them, if they are feeling left out.

> With any new relationship, it was usually very difficult for us, but then we ease into
> it. So when I first dated Seb, Adam was very anxious and restless and feeling inse-
> cure. But after a while Adam clearly can get along with Seb and every time I have a
> date with Seb and Adam felt jealous or something, I would make sure to have extra
> time to spend with him before I met Seb.

In truth you're unlikely to get them back in quite the same condition they were in
when you handed them over. But sometimes that's a good thing. It's worth remembering that every new relationship of significance can change us.

Again, if you're the one going through NRE, Kevin suggests making sure you
schedule things to do with your existing partners. Basically pre-empt your own shortcomings and plan around them.

If I'm the kind of person who neglects my other relationships and I know that about myself, I can anticipate that when I'm in NRE. I'm going to make it a point to have something on the calendar with each of my partners just so that I know that I'm not neglecting them. I would have a date prepared so that I'm not doing what I know I would normally do under the influence of NRE.

This might even be to have sex. Quite often a flagging libido revives when we're in a new relationship and other partners often appreciate it when some of that comes their way.

In short, new relationship energy can be lovely. Enjoy it. It's a rare rush. But do try to make sure that a special experience for you isn't a dispiriting one for your partners. They deserve the best of you too.

WHAT WE CAN ALL LEARN ABOUT HANDLING NEW RELATIONSHIP ENERGY

OKAY, YOU MIGHT not be juggling more than one romantic relationship, but you probably have other significant relationships aside from your new love: friends, family and even colleagues.

It's thrilling to be newly in love, but you don't want to burn others who will still be important to you when the initial flush of romance has subsided and you and your new partner are settling down to some sort of normality.

Take Kevin's advice: Put aside time for friends and family and make sure it's there in your calendar.

CHAPTER THIRTY-FIVE

Sex

PROBABLY THE MOST common assumption that people make about consensual non-monogamy is that it's all about sex. And if in a sense that's true, it's not necessarily in the way that people might think.

One of the fundamental issues with monogamy is that it only accommodates a fairly limited range of sexual and romantic needs. It assumes sexual compatibility not only at the start of a relationship but for the long term. It ignores the possibility that people's sexual capacities and even orientations can be fluid.

Interestingly this seems to affect women before it does men. According to Marta Meana of the University of Nevada at Las Vegas, 'Long-term relationships are tough on desire, and particularly on female desire.' She blames the 'institutionalisation of the relationship, overfamiliarity, and desexualisation of roles'.[63]

The same article refers to longitudinal studies from the UK and Germany that suggest that when women cohabit with a partner their desire flags more than if they don't. Whichever way you read the research, monogamy doesn't seem to be about long-term hotness.

And yet the monogamous ideal requires people to cleave to one another sexually until death. Some people find a formula that allows them to navigate these constraints, others don't. The same applies to an extent to people's needs for romance and emotional intimacy.

In contrast, one of the great strengths of CNM is the very wide range of sexualities and levels of desires that it makes space for.

For some, like Penny, consensual non-monogamy is very much about sex. At one point she'd slept with perhaps 200 men in 3 or 4 years. However she still needed other things from those connections.

---

63 'The Bored Sex', *The Atlantic*, 14 Feb 2019. https://www.theatlantic.com/ideas/archive/2019/02/women-get-bored-sex-long-term-relationships/582736/

[My partner and I] always discuss what we need from this, because we have kind of different needs of the intimacy, like sexual intimacy, emotional intimacy, intellectual intimacy. And for me it's more on the sexual, like physical intimacy, end and the intellectual intimacy. Because I like to meet not just for sex, but I'd like to have a talk and discussion and pick up some brains.

Dr. Liz Powell, who describes herself as a sex-positive psychologist, has a similar perspective. If anything, for her, sex is even more central to the way she relates to other people. However she's also the first to acknowledge that consensually non-monogamous people don't conform to any particular stereotype.

I identify as a megasexual. Megasexual is a term that myself and Rebecca Hiles came up with to describe someone who's kind of the flip side of a demisexual. So, whereas a demisexual needs romantic connection in order to experience sexual desire, a megasexual needs sexual connection in order to experience romantic desire. So, I am very much a fuck-first person.

I feel like I don't know a person and I can't figure out if we're going to be okay in a relationship until we've had some kind of sexual connection; because sex is a way through which I very much come to understand a person and get to know them and feel connection with them. I have a good friend who's asexual who's also polyamorous and for her she has several different partners, they're wonderful, she's very much in love with them, and she just doesn't have sex and that's fine for her and for her partners.

There are certainly many non-monogamous people, like Liz's friend, who are primarily emotionally or romantically non-monogamous. The sexual element can be limited or even wholly absent. A relationship or relationships absolutely don't have to be sexual for them to be polyamorous. Nor do they have to be romantic. Some people are aromantic in the way others are asexual.

Perhaps this goes to the heart of what consensual non-monogamy is: It's everything that monogamy isn't, insofar as those involved give their unreserved consent. As monogamy is quite narrow, by definition CNM is broad and inclusive and it includes pretty much all consensual extra-dyadic sex.

THREESOMES AND MORESOMES

I KNOW YOU might like to think that CNM is all threesomes, foursomes and sex parties, but a lot of consensually non-monogamous people don't engage in group sex at all. Rather it's Sunday walks, making a big casserole for all their lovelies, and keeping track of odd socks they may have left at different people's houses.

However, some people do engage in sex with multiple bodies. It's not something most people have a script for. Sex education at school often struggles to cope with the idea of sex being recreational full stop, let alone handing you a blueprint for what happens at your first swing party. So a few tips.

Most of what's worth thinking about is less the 'what goes where' than the 'who and how' and the million feels those engender. Threesomes are a very common fantasy and something that many couples decide they want to make happen.

It should be simple, right? Two people who like having sex with one another invite a third. Exit, pursued by a bear. Grizzly end off-stage.

There's no definitive how-to-do-it any more than there is for any other aspect of consensual non-monogamy, but here are a few things you might want to bear in mind.

Consent! Everything starts from consent. Everybody has to be actively and enthusiastically opting in. They need to know what they're opting in to, so...

Find out what everyone wants from it. You're going to have to be honest.

Make any ground rules clear. Some people prefer never to repeat the experience with the same third. Make sure that anyone you invite to the party knows that and be prepared for people to have unexpected feelings. (For this reason some people suggest that for a couple's first experiment it makes sense to hire a sex worker. Everyone knows that feelings aren't part of the plan).

Choose your third (or the couple you're joining) carefully. The complexity of three-way chemistry compared to two-way increases the likelihood of the experiment going up in a poof of acrid smoke.

Negotiate before you get it on. The sex educator Midori is queen of artful negotiation. Her advice is to work it into the flow of play. You can swing a lamp, don a long leather coat and a monocle and interrogate your play partners Stasi style if that's the theme, otherwise just ask 'Hey, if we were to do this, what then? How would it go next?' People will often pick up on your story and write the next chapter for it.

Make sure everyone gets the attention they need. Focus on making the other people feel like a million dollars. Novelty is beguiling.

The most common way that things do end up going *poof* is if someone ends up feeling neglected. It's quite normal when having an encounter with someone new to become very focused on that person. It's wholly understandable. There can also be a tendency to assume that an existing partner is fine 'because they're always fine'. Unfamiliar and/or potentially tricky situations are often the times when you find out the limits of fine and, in any case, checking in regularly is rarely a bad thing. It's good to ask how they are and to make eye contact. Some people recommend maintaining some physical contact with everyone else for most of the time (assuming everyone is okay with this), even if it's just a squeeze of the hand or a hand on the shoulder. It can help to keep you more attuned to others' body language so you know sooner rather than later if someone you care about is getting wibbly.

Many of those who participate in group sex see it as a powerful mental and social skill-builder. It's good to check in with oneself too. Self-respect will stand you in good stead, unbridled ego probably less so. If you're having an "I am a golden god" moment à la *Almost Famous*, take a quick reality check. That goes for goddesses too.

Make sure you're tested regularly for STIs (it's not just a courtesy, it's essential) and practice safe sex at all times. We'll look at sexual health in a separate chapter.

Be prepared to use multiple condoms: for toys, for penises, and surgical gloves for fingers that will encounter fluids (and new gloves for new fluids). You're not just protecting yourself and one other person, but the three or more of you and everyone's other loves as well.

PLAY PARTIES AND GROUP SEX

REMEMBER WHAT YOUR mother told you about wearing clean underwear in case you get run over—make sure you're reasonably freshly scrubbed and groomed.

Just because someone's at an orgy it absolutely doesn't mean they want to have sex with everyone there, so don't assume you can join in with someone else's scene. Watching is fine (but do your best to be very aware of personal space), being Sherlock Holmes with a magnifying glass or an amateur gynae/proctologist ain't. Keep a respectful distance. If someone wants you to join in they will invite you, otherwise don't.

Don't get dragged into scenes you don't enjoy. You have an absolute right to say no. If you're not really enjoying yourself, leave.

Don't be that creepy guy (or non-guy). Be chilled, comfortable in your own skin, and content just to hang until things unfold naturally.

Keep checking in on the consent front. Make sure you know the safewords agreed for the party if there are any. As a minimum ask 'Is this okay/good for you?' Don't forget: Consent for *x* does not equal consent for *y, or for x* later.

If it's your first time there's no need to rush. If it suits you there will be a second time. It's fine to be keeper of the lube and condoms or, even better, to make the tea. (That's an actual thing at some orgies. A number of my British interviewees were very clear about the importance of a good cup of tea at an orgy).[64]

---

64   Quite right frankly. No point letting standards slip just because you're stark naked in a room full of people all having sex with one another. A word to the wise though, don't get biscuit crumbs on the sheets. It won't win you friends.

CHAPTER THIRTY-SIX

Do Consensually Non-Monogamous People Have Better Sex?

I SUPPOSE THE brief answer would be 'Duh! Yah! Okay?!' on the basis that a) lots of people seem to suspect that everyone *else* is having more/better sex than they are, b) that seems like a suspicion worth encouraging, and c) there's a long tradition of giving other people the impression that *we're* having more/better sex than we actually are. I'm all for tradition.

However, slightly more seriously, things are a tad more nuanced than that. Some of the best data we have comes from academic research.

In their 2018 study,[65] Terri Conley, Jennifer Piemonte, Staci Gusakova and Jennifer Rubin of the University of Michigan brought together the results of two different studies and compared sexual and relationship satisfaction between monogamous and CNM people, breaking the CNM cohort down into swingers, people in open relationships, and people who consider themselves polyamorous.

The good news for everyone is that regardless of what group they fell into, people reported high levels of sexual and relationship satisfaction across the board. However there were variations from group to group.

The ones that fared slightly less well were those in open relationships, i.e. where both halves of a couple had other sexual relationships independently of one another. Levels of sexual satisfaction were comparable to monogamous people. Those in both groups were equally likely to have had sex recently and had an orgasm during their last sexual encounter. But *relationship* satisfaction was lower amongst people in open relationships than in monogamous ones.

65　'Sexual satisfaction among individuals in monogamous and consensually non-monogamous relationships', Terri D. Conley, Jennifer L. Piemonte, Staci Gusakova, Jennifer D. Rubin, University of Michigan, *Journal of Social and Personal Relationships* (2018), Vol. 35(4) pp 509–531.

Polyamorous people, meanwhile, reported higher levels of both relationship and sexual satisfaction than monogamous people (although satisfaction with a 'primary partner was fairly similar'). They were very slightly more likely to have had an orgasm during their most recent encounter (82% vs 78%, not statistically noteworthy in this context) but rather more likely to have had sex recently (48% vs 37%).

Lastly, swingers' relationship satisfaction was on a par with that of monogamists but their sexual satisfaction was higher: 79% reported frequent sex (vs 37%) and 92% had had an orgasm last time they'd had sex (vs 78%). Lucky bloody swingers.

Why did the study's authors think this was?

> The most straightforward possibility is that CNM people are less subject to normal habituation processes that occur in the sexual relationships of monogamous people. Perhaps the introduction of additional partners provides enough variety to effect higher levels of satisfaction in the primary relationship.

Basically boredom, or perhaps, put more kindly, familiarity. Another possibility the authors consider is that people enjoy relationships and sex more when they don't feel they're under pressure to do so in a particular way.

> A second, related, possibility is that CNM participants experienced more sexual satisfaction than monogamous participants simply because they feel less reactance (Brehm, 1966). Psychological reactance occurs when people perceive that their free will is threatened—when someone else is making choices for them or trying to induce them into a particular course of action.

Lastly, they speculate that the high levels of sexual satisfaction that swingers reported was down to the fact that a lot of swingers build their social lives around 'the lifestyle'.

The study doesn't seem to consider why those in open relationships have lower relationship satisfaction than the other groups. One of the features of swinging is that couples tend to swing together, while many people practicing polyamory place a high value on communication and openness.

It's certainly worth considering that one of the things that makes certain non-monogamous relationships work is an increased level of intimacy brought about by sharing experiences or feelings (either be doing things together or through honest communication). In open relationships, though, it's more usual for couples to maintain very separate outside romantic and sexual relationships, often within a 'don't ask, don't tell' agreement. Perhaps this can lead those involved to feel more separate and even alone. If that's the case, it would be further evidence for the argument that the closeness of our human connections is a major factor in determining our health and happiness.

CHAPTER THIRTY-SEVEN

Asexuality and Demisexuality

THERE'S A CERTAIN irony that despite the popular perception of consensual non-monogamy being all about sex the reality is that by being 'everything that is consensual but isn't monogamy' CNM's greatest strength is arguably its ability to accommodate a greater range of physical and emotional needs.

That means it reflects both the variety that some people crave both emotionally and sexually, but also the fact that it makes space for a vast array of different sexualities.

Asexuality, alosexuality, and demisexuality are simply not discussed as much as they should be. Society is not much more forgiving of people with low levels of sexual desire than it is of those with high levels of sexual desire. The script from which we're expected to work says, in effect, 'This is how horny you're supposed to feel, when and with whom—not too much, not too little, not too hot, not too cold, but just right'. It's like Goldilocks and her three partners.

Asexuality (often abbreviated to *ace*) shouldn't be understood as a choice (the way celibacy might be) so much as a disposition or orientation. While it covers a spectrum of experiences, the common point is a low level of sexual desire, whether that be 'not very much' or 'none at all'. People can absolutely be asexual without being aromantic. If you're asexual you are perfectly capable of craving connection, affection, love and touch; you simply don't desire sex as much as most others, if at all.

Sometimes people with low levels of sexual desire but who nevertheless experience it to a degree use the term 'gray', as in *graysexual*.

Alosexuality is quite poorly defined. The best I can offer is along the lines of someone who experiences sexual pleasure without experiencing attraction to or desire for anything or anyone.

The 'demi' in *Demisexuality* might seem to imply 'half' or 'lesser' but that would be inaccurate. Demisexuality is about context. A demisexual needs a strong emotional bond to another person before they want to engage in sex with them. This is quite separate from someone who requires a romantic relationship first in order to conform to social expectations or to assuage inner sexual guilt. Many people feel strongly sexually attracted to people they're not emotionally involved with but choose not to have sex until they're in a relationship. Demisexual people simply don't experience strong sexual feelings without that connection; it's not a matter of choice.

So, how does that relate to consensual non-monogamy? CNM *makes more room for all these variations.* Meg-John Barker says that it helps people with differing sexual needs and capacities to find ways of parlaying those differences. In a monogamous relationship, asexuality would usually mean that either one party's needs won't be met or the other has to endure sex when they don't want to. CNM can remove such pressures.

> In any relationship you're going to have different types of desire and different levels of desire. Even if you're perfectly matched initially it's going to change over time. Non-monogamy opens up the possibility for people to get their desires met from other people and also enables them to pursue the possibility of having ace people in relationships who don't then have sex that they maybe don't want to have. Some ace people do have sex with partners for other reasons than sexual attraction, but a lot of ace people don't want to have any sex. That can make it easier rather than creating a sense of pressure. Also, I think that asexuality has a lot to offer polyamory in terms of reminding people that sex isn't the be all and end all.

These incompatibilities are often thought of in very loaded terms. We have pejorative words like 'frigid' (disproportionately used about women) for people who don't enjoy sex or who simply don't experience arousal. As Magick says, couples have historically arrived at a variety of ways of dealing with sexual incompatibility.

> In the old days I've seen asexual people have relationships with people where they've considered sex work to be okay; where it's said 'I know you're in a relationship with me but I realise you want to have sex, so it's okay going to see prostitutes.' And so I guess that was the safety valve.

We tend to think less about how asexual or graysexual people feel in the context of a loving relationship when they are unable to give their partner what they desire. Luciano, a computer software engineer from Brazil, has a number of relationships, one with an ace woman.

She's actually in a poly relationship where she doesn't have to get involved with sexual activity. It's something that makes her a lot more at ease because if she's in a monogamous relationship but they're not having sex, the fact that her partner is making that sacrifice for her doesn't make her feel comfortable. So it is something that is better for her.

Once again we're back to a point that is cropping up regularly: that consensual non-monogamy is a toolkit or a construction set for relationships, not a ready-made product. And because it's a way of designing and building relationships to suit individual circumstances, it opens the way to multiple ways of loving and relating that are less available or even effectively unavailable in monogamy. It's certainly been that for Maxine.

I often like to say that to me polyamory isn't about many loves, it's about many kinds of love. Because in my experience it's opened up possibilities to be a small but good thing in the lives of a lot of people who I could never have had a major relationship with. I have an interesting situation within my relationship network. I'm not asexual. I think the term is allosexual[66]. So, I like sex, I have sexual relationships. But within my network, I have some relationships that are romantic but not sexual. And some of those are with people who are sexual, with others we're not sexual with each other because that's the way that relationship works. So, we're not asexual people but the relationship is asexual. It wouldn't be possible for us to have these relationships if we were trying to be monogamous.

I have a boyfriend who is gay with whom I have the asexual romantic relationship I referred to. I've got all sorts of little long-distance relationships. None of those would work if I was trying to be monogamous with any of them.

The judgemental stance that society has traditionally been taken toward different sexualities could be said to be a by-product of monogamy. Monogamy is, in relationship terms, a black Model-T Ford in a world where the only affordable car is the black Model-T Ford. You either drive a black Model-T or you don't drive. If you're too short, too tall, too round, not strong enough to turn the wheel, if you have a family of ten, if you can't afford the fuel let alone a car, if black cars scare you... you walk.

66   Allosexual (as opposed to alosexual with a single *l*) means attracted sexually to other people. It's essentially the opposite of asexual.

Like the Model-T in the 1910s, monogamy needs widespread buy-in. It needs people to think that any faults are with themselves and not with the restrictive nature of the model on offer. Just think of the words for people who don't fit into a monogamous mould; frigid, slutty, nymphomaniacal, skittish, immoral, filthy, etc. etc. Mononormativity needs people to question themselves and not the system because, in many respects, the system doesn't bear much scrutiny. I like this observation from Morgan:

> I tend to find that emotionally intense relationships are very satisfying and I have some of those with people who are asexual, demi, grey ... Everyone deserves love.

Everyone deserves love! Stop thinking of all the really terrible people who you want to say *don't* deserve love—the dictators, mass murderers, the unkind, the selfish and the greedy. Just stop to consider all the people you know who don't quite conform to the cookie-cutter roles that society has handed out to us. Some, most, maybe all of those people have something lovable about them. Changing the rules of love expands the franchise. What kind, generous, decent human would deny another love? That, in short, is what the consensually non-monogamous people I've interviewed see in what they do—an opening up rather than a walling off of love.

CHAPTER THIRTY-EIGHT

Overlaps with Kink/Fetish/BDSM Communities

FOR A NOT insignificant group of people, the route into consensual non-monogamy is through kink, in the broadest sense. For others, consensual non-monogamy has brought them into contact with the kink scene for the first time. In many places there is a notable degree of overlap between the two scenes.

With apologies to those of you for whom this will be teaching grandma to suck eggs[67], 'kink' is an umbrella term for sexual or quasi-sexual inclinations or practices, including BDSM (a portmanteau initialism for bondage & discipline, dominance & submission, and sadism & masochism) and fetishes that fall outside the mainstream. A kink is a deviation from the norm, and as such is often applied as a value judgement by people whose sexuality is more conventional (or 'vanilla') and as a badge of honour by people who identify as kinky.

As Kevin Patterson observes, the degree of crossover between kink and CNM varies from place to place.

> I know that kink and swinging and polyamory have a lot of overlap in the Philadelphia area. I was in places like Atlanta with a similar amount of overlap, and places like Denver or New Mexico where there's not nearly as much overlap.

There are other reasons the two intersect. Just as with the goth, nerd, geek, queer, counter-cultural, environmental and radical political spheres, the convergence is partly built around the acceptance of difference. Both also share values that underpin the idea of creating safe spaces for everyone, something that Charlotte appreciates.

---

67   Egg sucking is indeed a kink in its own right, albeit a rather obscure one...

Probably part of the reason why there is such a big overlap between kink and poly is because both of them require discussion and consent forward. Because I do find it really weird sometimes; I go out to vanilla clubs and I have occasionally skirted swingers' events and they are both far less consent focused than the communities I am used to inhabiting. And it can be really confronting, that some people will suddenly touch your bottom without asking first.

Though kink and CNM communities are for the most part very tolerant and welcoming, there are certainly things that are generally agreed to be unwelcome, such as grabbing people without their consent. Having mutually understood ground rules makes the two scenes broadly compatible.

I was once asked to define kink and my answer was, 'The exploration of our psychology through our sexuality and of our sexuality through our psychology.' That still works for me.

Our sexuality can be immensely complex. It's hard to see how it can be disentangled from our psychology. We sexualise many of our experiences, some happy, some formative, some traumatic. Some turn to sex in order to work through some of the seemingly intractable problems they face. The kink community is, I would suggest, a manifestation of that, albeit one that rather than suppressing its complex sexuality, engages with it, and plays with it—often positively and mindfully, occasionally imperfectly.

Kink also highlights the wide differences in people's needs and predilections, generally in an accepting and forgiving way. There's even an initialism common in the kink community, YKINMKBYKIOK: 'your kink is not my kink but your kink is okay'. The main qualifying condition being, of course, consent. This is a neatly stated acceptance of the fact that on a planet of seven-billion-and-counting people there will be seven billion different sexualities, many of them fairly similar but every one of them as unique as that individual.

Many things draw two people into a relationship with one another. There are, of course, physical attraction, emotional and intellectual compatibility, shared experiences, aspirations and needs. There is simple pragmatism, and there is the exquisite irrationality of human beings, drenched in hormones, that leads to decisions that make for a good story, if nothing else. Kink is rarely top of that list, especially in monogamous cultures. To adapt that Alain de Botton observation, we rarely ask on a first date 'And how are you kinky?'

Many people are at best guarded and at worst ashamed or in denial about their kinks. Most of us only reveal those parts of our psyche to another when we have reached a point when we feel secure in a relationship. But what are the odds that you and your new-found lover will both share a thing, for instance, for latex? People who are into rubber are generally *really* into rubber. As in head-to-toe, eye-popping, Popeye the Sailor or French maid rubber outfits. For most other people rubber is at best meh and quite possibly WTAF?

It can seem hard enough finding someone who is compatible with you in things that shape your day-to-day existence without adding particular kinks to that list. The more criteria you add the more you shrink your pool of potential partners, and kink is often *quite* specific; niche even.

Of course those whose kink is a defining aspect of their personality and way of life often start by looking for partners in that scene and then select on the basis of other compatibilities. However not everyone is aware of their kinks at the outset. One's identity often emerges with time. Things we deny or suppress or develop later in life finally find voice, and when that happens we may seek an outlet.

One consequence of this is that people who feel a strong desire to explore their kink but find themselves in a committed monogamous relationship often struggle. They either suppress their desires or they seek an outlet. For some it's their route into non-monogamy. Laura for example:

> To me sex is just sex. I've never thought that you need to be in love with someone to commit the sex act, but for me to want to have sex with somebody I need to connect on a particular mental or emotional level. I need to like the person. But I can have sex acts with a number of people aside from my significant other. So right from the start we knew that we enjoyed having other people in the bedroom. We really liked attending play parties together, BDSM play parties together, and we liked engaging with other couples so that was how we started.

Mawar in Jakarta also came to consensual non-monogamy through kink partly to maintain an existing vanilla relationship while meeting her sexual needs.

> Initially I thought it was a good sort of combination because I was with Adam who is vanilla and then I was with Seb who is kinky. So I thought mix-match would suit me very well. But along the way, I realised that kink is quite important for me. Vanilla sex is okay, but only if it happens like once or twice in three months or something. So eventually I realised that kink is what I identify with. So now I'm only looking to be in a relationship with someone who is also kinky. And I think more than being in a poly relationship, I think kink is more liberating for me. And in terms of being a feminist I think it's more relevant for me than poly itself.

Or take Kerilyn. Kerilyn was born in Zimbabwe but moved to the UK as a child and is now in her mid to late twenties. She works in the voluntary sector supporting people in crisis.

> I was in a monogamous relationship with a non-kinky person but the more I delved into [the BDSM/kink social network] Fetlife, the more I realised at least that that particular relationship was not working. Emotionally we were very good friends but on that physical level, we wanted different things, we literally wanted polar opposites of each other and while we tried, when it's not there, you can feel that it's not there.

> I encountered kink first. I think if I hadn't I probably wouldn't have then come to non-monogamy. I was on a very stereotypical path prior to that. The first person I actually started talking to when I discovered Fetlife was non-monogamous, but had a harem-y type non-monogamy that I couldn't relate to; a male dominant with, I believe, three female submissives with a hierarchical sort of structure with an alpha sub and beta subs underneath that. Being that it was my first introduction to non-monogamy, I assumed that it would not be something for me.

After she separated from her long-term partner, Kerilyn entered into her first BDSM relationship. It wasn't without its problems. As mentioned earlier her partner was married and his wife imposed numerous restrictions on their relationship. But she found other relationships and wouldn't go back.

> I can't see myself being monogamous again for a number of reasons. It wasn't just not being able to get from each other what we wanted, but also feeling as though you're responsible for providing that for someone else, and that someone else is responsible for providing everything that you need.

This is a recurring theme amongst people who've chosen non-monogamy: a sense that no one person can be their everything. Kink is one of those areas where desires can be both strong and quite specific, forcing people experiencing them to make a choice. Quite a lot choose CNM, as Charlotte explains.

> There is a big overlap between kink and CNM, something like a Venn diagram where the overlap is quite large. It's not complete. There are certainly poly people

who aren't kinky and plenty of kinky people who are so ridiculously monogamous it's insane. I mean kink is somewhere where you can literally own another person.

Indeed it is. It's one of those areas of CNM that verges on cognitive dissonance that, despite the emphasis on autonomy and consent, some people choose to give up their autonomy in the context of a 24/7 master/slave or D/s relationship *and* do it while being polyamorous at the same time *and* being into egalitarian poly, such as solo poly/ non-hierarchical/ RA.

It seems contradictory, and sometimes, for those involved it is contradictory. It's a matter of embracing one's inner contradictions. Some people who are assertive and consciously egalitarian in most of their lives crave a space where they can shuffle off any semblance of personal autonomy and responsibility because it offers an escape from those things. There are also plenty of people in D/s relationships who will tell you that it's the sub or slave who is ultimately in charge and point out that they can end the relationship at any time. In principle, at least, the sub/slave is far from powerless. In principle....

However it's also common for people who feel this need to compartmentalise it, either by seeing a professional dominant/dominatrix or by choosing to keep it within a specific BDSM relationship that doesn't intersect with the rest of their life. Again this leads into non-monogamy.

Consensual non-monogamy's capacity to accommodate a wide variety of tastes and needs is important. For instance, the ability to compartmentalise different parts of one's life and explore those with different people allows those with a need for the familiar and the stable to have a committed vanilla relationship with one partner where it gets no more kinky than barbecuing of a weekend, while having another, perhaps occasional relationship undiluted by domesticity or over-familiarity where the focus is shared sexual interests. It's far from universal within either kink or consensual non-monogamy but nor is it at all uncommon.

LESSONS FROM BDSM AND KINK

THIS ISN'T A book about BDSM, and covering the topic comprehensively will require another volume (watch this space, as they say...). Plenty of books and resources on the internet will serve as an introduction. However, as a minimum, if you're interested in exploring kink, even casually, there are a number of things it's essential to pay attention to. A good BDSM book or website will stress consent, safety, and wellbeing.

If it doesn't then try another. Likewise, if a play partner doesn't seem to be genuinely *au fait* with consent, exercise caution. There's plenty of harm that can result from ignorance, inexperience, or insensitivity.

Consent

Everything starts from consent. It's a mantra. I set out the principles at the beginning of this book. Given that people use BDSM and kink for reasons including exploring their own psyche and traumas, it's important to pay attention to the mental well-being of all involved. Someone can *apparently* give consent to something that doesn't serve their best interests. You may also be concerned that someone isn't in a state of mind that allows them to give informed consent. That may include intoxication or being deep in *sub space*, a trance-like, or even out-of-body state that submissives sometimes enter as a result of intense BDSM experiences. If in doubt, stop. You don't owe it to anyone to be kinky with them. You don't have to be the person who goes along with something you're not sure about.

Safewords

We live in a society that continues to shame people about their sexuality, all the more so if it falls outside certain restrictive bounds. For this reason it's not unusual that people want to act out resistance during sex. That can include struggling, fighting back or saying 'no'. For some people being able to do this is an integral part of their enjoying sex. It may be a way that they can shrug off the internalised feelings of disapproval and disgust that are foisted on us.

Clearly this needs to happen in a consensual, pre-negotiated setting. If someone says no to you or pushes you away without there being an explicit agreement to the contrary, then *no* means stop, back off, go away.

But it also means that in consenting situations, where 'no' has been agreed not to mean no, there needs to be another word or signal in place that does mean no. For this reason we have safewords and signals.

A common solution is the traffic light system where people will say 'green' for go ahead and 'amber' or 'yellow' if they are starting to get uncomfortable. That's a signal that they would like things dialled down but not stopped. If you're touching someone in a place or in a way that is getting too intense for them they may say 'amber'. Likewise, 'red' means stop. It means 'Stop now!' It does not mean stop in thirty seconds or in five minutes or after you've reached orgasm.

People will often choose their own safewords. It's *de rigueur* to agree these before a play session, especially if you haven't played with someone before. Likewise there are visual signals, such as slapping the mattress or one's chest three times — these can be essential if someone cannot speak or the environment is loud.

Sadly, consent violations happen in the BDSM/kink scene way more often than those in the community might hope given that kinksters generally pride themselves on greater awareness of consent and safety and on prioritising it rather more than the average Jo(e). Consent violations, even between people who are already intimate and even in a relationship, can be extremely damaging.

Even a cursory survey of Fetlife, the main kink/BDSM social network, will reveal a site that's bedeviled by misogyny, white supremacy, and the many ills of the Internet. It's also periodically convulsed by allegations or cases of rape and sexual assault. Just as the venal and malicious cloak themselves in the language of CNM so too they use the trappings of the kink/BDSM scene. They're often aided by an understandable unwillingness to go to the police. 'So Miss, you were wearing a corset and thigh high boots when you were attacked..?' Yup. Same old, same old.

Sadly the best advice is to apply the standard safe-dating rules and add knobs to them. Don't go to a new person's place alone, tell someone where you'll be and with whom, be seen to call friends and tell them your location. Many veterans of the scene advise newcomers to put aside shyness and only play in public group environments, such as well-supervised kink clubs or 'dungeons.' The more community members you have around you when you're getting tied up, whipped, or whatever, the more you will reduce the risk. That said I'm aware of cases of abuse happening in plain sight at some venues. You might consider buddying up and operating in a pair so you can check in with one another until you know people well enough to be able to make better-informed choices.

CHAPTER THIRTY-NINE

Sexual Health

LET'S TALK ABOUT STIs—sexually transmitted infections. Uncomfortable? Many people are. Sex is often portrayed as much as a way of sharing infections as it is of sharing chromosomes, let alone connection, love, intimacy and fun. Indeed, as I've said, some cultures approach sex more in terms of avoiding disease than as positive, pleasurable experiences. They push the message that sex is only safe if it takes place within the hermetically sealed and bacteriologically sterile bounds of holy matrimony, with prayer and abstinence the only proper prophylactics.

Oddly, however, sexual health risks amongst monogamous people are often handled less effectively than among the openly non-monogamous and with worse results. One fundamental issue with sexual health and monogamy is infidelity. Terri Conley, Jes Matsick, Amy Moors, Ali Ziegler and Jennifer Rubin's 2015 paper 'Re-examining the effectiveness of monogamy as an STI-preventive strategy'[68] puts it neatly if somewhat academically.

> If established couples do not use barrier methods of protection in their relationship because of existing monogamy agreements, it is highly unlikely that an individual who has committed infidelity will reintroduce barriers after infidelity occurred—doing so would likely raise suspicion about that person's fidelity (Misovich et al., 1997; Conley and Rabinowitz, 2004). Therefore, after infidelity has occurred, risk of STI acquisition for the non-cheating partner increases because of the assumption of mutual monogamy.

---

68 Conley TD, Matsick JL, Moors AC, Ziegler A, Rubin JD. Re-examining the effectiveness of monogamy as an STI-preventive strategy. Prev Med. 2015 Sep;78:23-8. doi: 10.1016/j. ypmed.2015.06.006. Epub 2015 Jun 24. PMID: 26116890.

And the key finding?

> Given idiosyncratic interpretations of monogamy, compliance issues, and posi-
> tive relationships between consensual non-monogamy and safer sex behaviors,
> monogamy directives may not be the best way to curb STIs. Researchers and prac-
> titioners should address the utility of promoting monogamy as a safer sex strategy
> relative to other STI-prevention methods, such as consistent condom use, STI test-
> ing, and partner communication.

I love that use of 'idiosyncratic'. Academics have all the best put downs. In plain
English, some people interpret 'monogamous' to mean 'I can do what the hell I please
so long as no one finds out' and so promoting monogamy as an STI-prevention strategy is rather less effective than promoting condom use and better communication—
two foundational tenets of most CNM.

After all, if you're an established couple, you don't use condoms and one of you
cheats without using a condom, what are they going to do? If you suddenly turn to
your partner and say 'Hey, I think we should use condoms now,' it invites the obvious
question 'Why?' So, people don't say that. They just cross their fingers and hope for
the best. At most they quietly go and get tested and, if they test positive for an STI, take
a course of antibiotics. That could mean weeks of 'Sorry darling, I have a headache'.

You can see why prescribing monogamy as a means of preventing STIs, as opposed to say, condom use, can be less reliable. People cheat—and people who cheat
are less likely to use condoms perhaps because it would make their cheating seem pre-
meditated. People don't want to get caught. They do stupid things. Often they don't
want to admit to themselves what they're doing.

It's not that such things can't happen in non-monogamous relationships. People
do cheat. They break agreements. One member of a couple or group that is fluid
bonded (i.e. not using barrier protection within the couple or group) might have unprotected sex outside that group and fail to tell the others because they were supposed
to be polyfidelitous. However, telling your poly pod 'Sorry, I slipped up and didn't
wear a condom, so I'll need to use barrier protection until I've tested negative' if it's
communicated quickly before anyone else is put at risk, is much less of a relationship
destroyer than 'Darling, I broke our wedding vows'.

And, hell, condoms break. They slip off. You can have a perfectly understandable
accident in a non-monogamous context and simply be upfront about it.

The problem is that we're socialised to see monogamous sex as safe (and therefore
good) and non-monogamous sex as risky (and therefore bad). And yet if we look more
closely at the issue we might question that. As the CNM community is generally very

aware, safer sex means following safe sex practices *all the time*! As Dr Liz Powell argues it all reflects the problems we have quantifying risk.

> I think that there is this fascinating filter through which we view sexual risk. It's [that] there's a lot of overlap between emotional and sexual risk. The thing is, humans in general are terrible at perceiving what the actual risks of a thing are and it's largely dependent upon the messages we've been told. So, for instance, driving a car is an immensely risky activity but we all engage in it on a regular basis.

Indeed people are far more afraid of being blown up by terrorists than they are of being killed in a car accident, even though the risk of the latter is far higher. Nassim Nicholas Taleb eviscerated our risk assessment abilities in his book *Black Swan*, published in April 2007. His particular focus is our propensity to mis-quantify outlier events. Taleb's timing was impeccable. August and September 2007 saw the pre-shocks that heralded the financial crisis. The financial system unravelled the following year and we spent more than a decade living with the consequences.

Then in January 2020 another shock, this time from the coronavirus pandemic. Governments were slow to respond and many people were remarkably complacent even after being ordered into lockdown, and even though thousands were dying every day.[69] We were unprepared even though 'the next pandemic' had been expected for decades. The consequence was the worst public health crisis in a century.

As Liz Powell points out, with sexual risks we're less driven by facts and rationality and more by the fear and shame we carry.

> Anything related to sex we view as a much bigger risk and a much bigger deal. In the United States there are huge movements against vaccinations for children. It is huge in the amount of risk, and it's riskier than engaging in a ton of un-barriered sex particularly among populations that do regular STI testing. I think that the way we talk about risk is driven from this moralistic problematising-of-sex perspective, where we view sex necessarily as something that is dirty and wrong and shameful— so it must have dirty, wrong, shameful [health] implications as well.

Back in the 80s the Scottish comedian Billie Connolly used to tell a gag, albeit one that hasn't aged well, that went along the lines of: 'One thing about AIDS, it's

---

69 Ironically, many of the people refusing to wear masks were the same ones preaching that sex outside marriage would see you die in a plague pit.

made people a lot less worried about herpes. ' Before the panic surrounding the AIDS crisis erupted there was a similar panic about herpes. In retrospect the herpes panic was unwarranted. The herpes virus is incredibly common; the World Health Organization estimates (2020) that two-thirds of the world's population carries HSV-1 and 11% carry HSV-2.[70] The former used to be called oral herpes and the latter genital, but now both are recognized as infecting both places. Most people are asymptomatic. Symptoms can be treated and prevented with cheap, safe medication. The panic about AIDS, on the other hand, reflected a serious risk of death. But fear and prejudice and moralising may have cost the lives of countless millions by delaying the development of effective AIDS prevention programmes and treatments, especially in the 1980s, and by stigmatizing testing even now. Liz Powell says it's important that we keep a sense of perspective.

> These days the majority of STIs, particularly in developed nations, are not usually that big a deal. If you get herpes it's [occasionally] unsightly and it's painful and it's probably not going to affect the rest of your life very much. If you have HIV, the medications these days are effective enough that they can take you below a detectable viral load at which point you are non-transmissible. If you have gonorrhoea or syphilis or chlamydia the majority of them are easily treatable with antibiotics. There are some strains that are becoming antibiotic resistant but there are also strains of streptococcus that are becoming antibiotic resistant. We don't say you should never go to the gym because there might be MRSA there. The way that we think about sexual risk is completely out of step with the actual risk involved.

In the sex-positive community, one that encompasses many consensually non-monogamous people, there's a great deal of awareness about managing risk. That's not to say that there aren't people who are reckless. Nor should HIV be treated as minor just because it can be managed. Having lived through the coronavirus pandemic, no one should need reminding of that.

Therefore the decision to be fluid-bonded with someone is, as Eunice explains, a serious one.

> Even if you're not fluid-bonded you need to have the trust and knowledge and regular testing and all of that stuff. With fluid bonding specifically, you have to be much more aware of who it is that your partner is also fluid-bonded to. And some things

70 'How many people have herpes? What to know. Medical News Today, updated Sept. 2020. https://www.medicalnewstoday.com/articles/how-many-people-have-herpes

do pass between partners even when you are wearing barrier protection. That's just a fact of life.

However there are certain things that you can do to make sure that you're safe. Saying 'Here are my boundaries' is not saying 'Here is a rule I'm putting in place over you, so that you cannot have sex with X, Y, Z.' This is a boundary that's 'I cannot be fluid-bonded to you if you are doing X, Y, Z things, for my own wellbeing.'

That means that decisions to be fluid-bonded need to be negotiated with everyone you are or planning to be fluid-bonded with. Mawar, the arts administrator from Jakarta, and her partner Adam did just that when she wanted to fluid-bond with a new partner.

> Adam and I sort of had this arrangement that we are in the relationship so we can have sex without condoms. But whenever we are having sex with someone else, we need to have condoms and we need to make sure that the other person is clear on sexual transmitted diseases. And when my relationship with Seb was getting serious and we decided not to use condom, I told Adam beforehand. He was fine.

As Eunice says, trust is critical but trust needs to be reciprocal and honoured. Surely most people wouldn't want to be fluid bonded with someone they don't trust.

And you have to be able to stand your ground. The writer Anita Cassidy had a breakdown in communication with her partner, and when she learned that he had been having unprotected sex with another partner, she didn't feel able to set a boundary.

> We are the only people that each other is fluid-bonded with right now, but he certainly was having a relationship of that type with his other girlfriend last year. And at that point in time he never explicitly told me that they weren't using protection, and that's something that was problematic, but it's also something I didn't have the confidence or the skills to challenge him on, and that's something that he and I have had to kind of navigate and learn together.

Many people in the CNM community would see Anita's partner's behaviour as a breach of trust. By not giving her the information she needed, he denied her the opportunity to take adequate precautions.

One of Penny's regular partners had unprotected sex with a sex worker in Papua—an exceptionally bad idea—didn't tell her, and gave her gonorrhoea. Worse, when she then told her other regular partners they slut-shamed her, even though she hadn't at that point put them at risk.

> I used to have multiple partner at the same time and I would like to have this understanding and agreement that if I do risky, unprotected sex, then I wouldn't do it with another person, and I give full trust to that person to do the same. But from my experience you cannot always trust them a hundred percent. So that experience taught me that you have to be very, very selective. And I would say that doing it unprotected, still have to test it like maybe three months or every two months.

These situations *do* occur, particularly when those involved are relatively new to CNM. If you know the usual protocols for a given situation it's easier to say, 'This is how people in our situation normally handle things. That's what I want to do'.

It reminds me of the problems described by too many women during the sixties and seventies in the wake of the pill and the second wave of feminism. Far too often it was; 'Well, you have the pill and you're supposed to be liberated, so why won't you fuck me?'. Women were often left vulnerable because of a desire not to be seen as uncool or hung up, and that same problem can occur within CNM if people are inexperienced.

Consensually non-monogamous people are all supposed to be very chilled and free, right? Well, here's news (actually I already told you this but it can't be repeated too often); there are plenty of people being manipulative and abusive under the guise of consensual non-monogamy. Good information is part of the answer. That makes it easier, if not easy, to challenge questionable behaviour or outright abuse. By the same token, people are also often loath to negotiate or impose boundaries if they feel it might jeopardise a relationship or are unsure whether it's a reasonable request. A relationship where one party is unable to walk away isn't a healthy relationship.

So, what are the norms? McFadden is part of the CNM scene in San Francisco.

> It has become de rigueur to have what we refer to as a safer-sex conversation with new partners or with recently renewed partners. I think it's both become an expectation and standard practice to be able to report that one has had an STI test within the last three to six months. It's also expected that one will be honest about the results of that test and that one will disclose to one's partners, one's community, a positive STI result basically immediately and that it's one's duty to do so.

Barrier protection is also regarded as de rigueur in the sex positive communities of which I'm a part, bearing in mind that my experiences are primarily with more structured forms of non-monogamy. I would say that fluid-bonding is typically a thing shared by one or two other people, that's my experience, and again I think it's mostly concern for safety and for a sense of not having to be anxious about other people's activity.

McFadden's is a more-or-less consensus summary of the essentials of safer sex:

- *Use barrier protection for all casual encounters.*
- *Don't treat barrier protection as infallible.*
- *Get tested regularly for a full spectrum of possible infections.*
- *Have conversations about safer sex with everyone you have sex with, before you have sex. Disclose any conditions.*
- *If you test positive do your own contact tracing. Tell everyone you've had sex with since your previous test.*
- *Don't worry about the wellbeing of pubic lice. You don't owe them a habitat.*
- *In a pandemic just stay at home as much as possible and take sensible precautions. Loving many shouldn't equate to infecting many.*

To that one might add, assess a potential partner's level of risk tolerance in any context. If it's markedly higher than your own, be doubly cautious about protection or pass them by.

Above all, communicate. The CNM community is overwhelmingly sex-positive. Very few people shame others for their sexuality. If you find yourself being shamed that should be a red flag. Being able to talk frankly about sex and sexual health is liberating and a positive indicator.

However, it's important to recognise that until recently this wasn't particularly easy in the West, and there are cultures where it remains very difficult for people to talk about intimate desires or health issues. If you live in a culture where you feel unable to talk frankly and freely about your sexual activity and risk you will need to decide what level of risk you're prepared to tolerate.

Create safe spaces for people to talk about things that make them feel awkward. If a partner or lover has contracted an STI keep a level head. Get tested. Get treated. Don't apportion blame. It needs all parties to actively ensure everyone's sexual health.

WHAT WE CAN ALL LEARN

IF YOU DO happen to have unprotected or maybe even protected sex with someone other than your regular partner(s), don't compound the situation by taking a risk, let alone passing on an STI. Get tested and don't have unprotected sex with your partner until you're in the clear. That may be awkward but a good deal less awkward than their finding that they have contracted an STI and you're the only possible donor.

It's normal in many countries to wait four weeks after unprotected sex before being tested. Four weeks is now the period after which modern blood tests can detect HIV. Where the older ELISA test is used you need to wait three months before it'll identify an HIV infection. Results in many countries are now delivered in days or even hours.

CHAPTER FORTY

Mental Health

FOR AS LONG as people's sexuality has strayed outside the norms of their society, others have sought to demonise them as mad. As we enter the third decade of the 21st century, there are still people peddling conversion therapy as a 'cure' for homosexuality. Equally extraordinary are attempts to control the minutiae of people's sex lives, such as their desire to masturbate. This is from the abstract of a research paper published by four Iranian academics.

> Studies showed that Iranian men and women, 92 and 62 percent respectively, have masturbated during their life and no sexual activity is as controversial but common as masturbation. This study attempts to investigate the most important and the commonest sexual threat, masturbation, to teenagers and the youth, especially among the university students and to provide some information about physical, mental, spiritual, moral and ethical damages of masturbating.[71]

This paper was actually published in 2011, though one might be forgiven for thinking it comes straight from 1911. It makes one worry for the 8% of men and 38% of women who, it appears, have missed out.

If sex is happening that doesn't involve a man and a woman, the missionary position, and the intention to procreate, especially if there is pleasure involved, there will be a group somewhere dedicated to shaming those involved. Often the shaming involves labelling people as mentally ill.

---

71 'Masturbation: Prevention & Treatment', A. Shekarey, M. Sedaghat Rostami, Kh. Mazdai, A. Mohammadi, 2011.

However there seems to be no evidence that poor mental health is any more prevalent amongst consensually non-monogamous people than in the general population. Nevertheless it seems legitimate to ask whether CNM attracts people with certain issues or exacerbates those.

DK Green is a member of the Pink Therapy network based in the UK, which brings together mental health professionals who work with a wide range of sexual minorities.

> I don't believe [CNM] causes any kind of mental health issues. However where insecurity is concerned, it can absolutely exacerbate any existing or underlying depression or anxiety. If you have a person who happens to be at a point in their development where they seem to be [particularly] insecure, that is going to be ramped up by poly relationships.

Ruby Bouie Johnson, a CNM activist and therapist based in Texas, often encounters similar issues amongst her clients.

> Anxiety is a big one, anxiety is because of the level of insecurity. Some people want variety, and so that can become very compulsive. Also depression; there's all this untreated anxiety, untreated depression.

None of these things is peculiar to consensual non-monogamy. However, anecdotally it seems likely that CNM people have to deal with situations within their relationships that have the potential to provoke such responses far more often than monogamous people.

That raises the question whether consensual non-monogamy draws in people with particular mental health issues. Again there appears to be no reliable research, but DK Green does suspect that it might.

> If you asked me this 10 years ago, I probably would have said no. But I have had an awful lot of cases where certain mental health issues, for example Borderline Personality Disorder [BPD], are drawn to it, probably because it offers, or it seems to offer, lots of love and attention, which is something that is desperately needed. But the flip side of that is, for example, that one of the core 'ouches' of BPD is the fear of rejection and criticism.

> So basically someone with Borderline Personality Disorder essentially feels things far deeper and stronger and for longer than your average Joe [or Jo]. So that means

all the emotional complexities of poly are going to be magnified for them and therefore more difficult. But it does seem to offer all the love and attention, which is often what that person needs to feel secure. However, the flip side is because they are poly, [a partner] might see somebody else and that might be felt as a rejection, which is the keenest fear hotspot for a BPD person: rejection or abandonment. Poly might look to offer a wonderful panacea but actually it tends to cause a lot of complex difficulty. Does that mean someone with BPD can't have a poly relationship? Absolutely not. But they're going to need a lot of support to be able to manage it.

BPD is commonly associated with things like eating disorders, substance abuse, and depression. Rates of suicide amongst people coping with BPD are high.[72] Someone who feels emotions, both positive and negative, with greater intensity than most may be attracted to having the highs of beginning a new relationship without the lows of needing to end another first. Being part of a network can also seem attractive. Perhaps the idea of having more than one partner so there is a buffer should a relationship end seems attractive. If one has unusual emotional needs, being able to turn to several people to meet those, rather than one, has considerable appeal.

However if you're someone who needs support with mental health issues it helps if people in your network have a minimum of skills and the capacity and willingness to help. It's wholly possible that one person within the network may end up doing a disproportionate amount of the emotional labour required, and that's assuming that anyone at all is prepared to provide that support.

Ruby Bouie Johnson, who is also a licensed chemical dependency counsellor with a focus on addiction and obsessive-compulsive behaviour, sees an addiction-aware approach as useful in a wide variety of contexts including relationships.

> It's applicable literally from people using substances to people using people. And so there are certain individuals predisposed to find polyamory attractive. That's the first thing; what we used to call co-dependency. So in looking at addiction, people cope with anxiety in a cluster of ways. For instance someone may increase their use when they're starting out in a new relationship.

In other words, if people have coping strategies that involve substances or a high level of reliance on certain behaviours, those may come to the fore at moments of

---

72   BPD is generally diagnosed in >2% of the population at a given point in time, though some estimates are higher, and women are typically over-represented amongst those diagnosed.

emotional stress. And while the start of a new relationship is generally seen as a happy and uplifting phase, that doesn't mean that everyone will experience it that way. For some it may provoke anxiety or insecurity, especially if they have had difficult past experiences.

In many ways the CNM 'community' (if we can describe it as that) should ideally be equipped to provide support for people who struggle with such problems. However, its image of itself doesn't always square with the reality. That image is generally one of inclusion, warmth and welcome, of making space for difference, of tolerance and compassion. It can indeed be, and often is, all of those things. However, in Ruby Johnson's experience the community doesn't always live up to its ideals.

> What we don't actually consider a lot within the polyamorous community is how we isolate people who have addictions or who are in recovery. And number one, whether we want to believe it or not, we're a small community and any group that is stigmatised typically tends to 'other' another group within it. We're a community that lives on consent, we live on autonomy and agency. And so folks with addiction... we can easily disenfranchise them and anyone within our family who is struggling with addiction. We live in denial a lot but it is something we need to actually address.

In short, what Johnson is saying is that the 'take responsibility for yourself' attitude of some of the CNM scene is actually part of the problem for people who struggle with dependence or addictions, whether emotional or to substances. 'Take responsibility for yourself' can also be shorthand for 'I don't care, you're not my problem.' At some point this dynamic has the potential to be abusive, as Johnson found when counselling a triad.

> One of them had alcohol issues and when she got into the relationship, she was five years post having elective surgery to lose weight. She identified as having a food addiction and then she had the surgery. But she did not get the therapy that she needed afterwards to deal with self-worth and she simply substituted addictions. After she got married she started drinking because she struggled with dealing with her husband spending time with this other woman. And so she started self-medicating. And what ended up happening is that her husband and the other partner started creating an alliance and she became 'the other'. He stopped supporting her and they started talking negatively about her and it created a whole lot of mess, and she did not have the support she needed.

There's a duality to the culture of consensual non-monogamy that owes much to the fact that it has emerged from the United States in the late twentieth century. On the one hand it reflects its roots in the very liberal counterculture of San Francisco in the 1960s, with its communal, collectivist outlook. On the other hand it's also influenced by a strong libertarian tradition that often boils down to a very Darwinian 'my life, my rules, you look after yours, I'll look after mine.'

This is the ideal of 'rugged individualism' that Martin Luther King Jr. tore into when he said, 'This country has socialism for the rich, rugged individualism for the poor.' It has been fetishized in America to the extent that interdependence (as opposed to co-dependency) is often denigrated. This, after all, is a culture that has canonised the cowboy, the entrepreneur, the frontiersman, the biker and the trucker. Many Americans are surprised to find that other cultures don't share their tendency to elevate individualism above collective well-being.[73]

This has coloured a lot of the messages about consensual non-monogamy that have come out of the US, which is still, as of the 2020s, its centre of gravity. If that centre of gravity were in Africa or Asia, places with very different notions of individuals' relationships with one another and with their community and society, we might have a very different consensual non-monogamy. We should be aware of this if we want to produce better mental health outcomes. Sadly, the United States has some of the worst mental health outcomes in the world.[74] By contrast both Africa and East Asia, regions of the world with high, culturally underpinned levels of interdependency, fare well for mental health.

So it's strange and at the same time understandable that the language of self-reliance has shaped that of consensual non-monogamy. I'm reminded of a polyamory talk I attended in Leipzig where the presenter asserted, quite irresponsibly, that 'No one can *make* you feel anything'— immediately negating the experiences of anyone who has been emotionally manipulated or abused.

The truth is that we do depend on one another and that, looking broadly at mental health outcomes, more interdependent cultures seem to fare better. Consensual non-monogamy could learn from this. Its more collective leanings can be a strength.

---

73 As an illustration, consider the Americanism 'gung ho'. In American English to be gung ho is to be enthusiastically 'can do', perhaps to a fault, as in; 'He's very gung ho about it. He doesn't see risks, only opportunities.' Yet gung ho is actually a corruption of the Chinese gōng hé,, the short form of Gōngyè Hézuòshè [工業合作社] meaning 'work together', the name given to Chinese Industrial Cooperatives that were a bridgehead for industrialisation in China in the 1930s and 40s. To non-Chinese eyes these cooperatives were full of vigour and can-do spirit, but the cultural translation is telling; what is born out of Chinese people working together to achieve a collective goal becomes something that's often more individualistic in US culture.

74 Based on IHME figures. https://ourworldindata.org/mental-health

They can make supporting someone easier. Equally they can be used to exclude and abuse (as we'll see in a later chapter).

The value of our interdependence and interconnectedness as human beings, Johnson argues, can also be seen at work in the healing process.

> The type of clients that I work with do not have a lot of confidence within systems, with institutions, with mental health [organizations], so therapy is already a Herculean task to get folks to. And so experiencing insecurity, being very avoidant of institutions and additionally not having the support within the polyamorous community, can be very challenging—and the role of the community can be so important. That's why with face-to-face support groups, meeting physically is so important because [you] can't find the answers you need in a silo.

Alice's Experience

Alice, a professional in the musical arts, had struggled with anxiety and depression before her last relationship, and her mental wellbeing crashed after the relationship ended in a particularly brutal breakup. She sought help from a psychiatrist who put her on medication. Nine months later she'd started to get a handle on the experience.

> I was already in and out of depression. I called it the creative cycle. My psychiatrist said it's just depression. So I had it for a very long time without knowing that I had it because I was high functioning. So it made things worse at one point. I wanted to self-harm, which wasn't very good. So I wasn't the most stable person to date in that sense.

> *Jonathan:* Do you think you need reasonably good mental health to be non-monogamous?

> *Alice:* I think you just need a high level of self-awareness. For example, like when I was incredibly depressed, I had an awareness that something is not right and that I should seek help. And that was what stopped me from self-harming. I wanted it to cut myself very, very badly. And I said, well I'm not going to take a kitchen knife and run it across my thigh because that would give me an infection. I need alcohol, swabs, I need medical scalpels, I need needles and things like that. And that stopped me. So even at my most depressed, when music didn't even make sense to me, I had that level of self-awareness that something is not right, go seek help, go talk to someone.

Jonathan: And how important was it seeking help, talking to someone?

Alice: It was incredibly, incredibly important for me because that helped talk me out of that suicidal tendency. When I'm in my 'creative cycle', when I'm depressed, I am not the best person to be with. I have thoughts that come into my head that says I am completely useless and fucked and that nobody should love me. But being aware of those thoughts was very important because I could stop myself and say, okay, I'm having these thoughts again. Let's go do something else or let's talk to someone about it or let's look at some of the past projects that you've done to know that you're not all that fucked.

So I wouldn't say that, you know, you have to be in reasonably good mental health to do polyamory. Anyone can do polyamory, but you just have to have a high level of self-awareness of what's happening to you and have empathy for your partner as well.

Just as there's never a perfect time to open a relationship, there's never a perfect mental state to explore consensual non-monogamy. Indeed the idea of there being a perfect time or place or situation or state of mind is difficult in itself, because it quickly runs up against the fact that humans don't do perfection.

Equally, it's useful to be as aware as possible of the state of one's own mental health. Being realistic about whether you are in a better or worse place allows you to communicate that to others. It's also helpful to be able to unpick the sense of 'I'm not feeling great in myself right now' from a fundamental feeling of 'consensual non-monogamy isn't for me'. If your actual sense is indeed that 'I will never be in the right place for this', it also helps others to know that.

IN THE CHAPTERS that follow, I'll consider some of the emotional challenges that people exploring consensual non-monogamy often say they face. CNM often provokes envy, anger, insecurity, anxiety, and jealousy amongst other feelings. I'll look at the last three of these in particular.

Any of the emotions we are capable of probably evolved for a reason. They're not of themselves problematic and don't necessarily fall within the bounds of mental health issues. However, when our emotional reactions are inappropriate or miscalibrated to the extent that we cause ourselves or others harm, then they bear closer scrutiny and we may need to seek help.

I've included thoughts in these sections about coping with difficult emotions and about seeking help.

It's Illogical, Captain!

CHAPTER FORTY-ONE

Jealousy

Oh, beware, my lord, of jealousy!
It is the green-eyed monster which doth mock
The meat it feeds on. That cuckold lives in bliss
Who, certain of his fate, loves not his wronger,
But, oh, what damnèd minutes tells he o'er
Who dotes, yet doubts— suspects, yet soundly loves!

Othello, Act 3, Scene 3

It usually feels like I'm almost sick to my stomach; it feels more like almost like an anxiety attack with a little bit of anger behind it... Jealousy is something that the more I see it the less I like myself for it.

— Debbie

IF THERE IS a single topic in consensual non-monogamy that's more endlessly discussed and picked to pieces than any other, jealousy is surely it. These days there are plenty of advice columns for poly and open people online, and CNM questions increasingly find their way into the mailboxes of traditional newspaper agony aunts. Poly advice returns to the subject of jealousy with the same inevitability with which summer follows spring and with which Cosmo writes about 'keeping it fresh in the bedroom' for monogamous people.

So, what is jealousy? Well, I'm going to argue four things.

1. Jealousy evolved because, at least at some point, it conferred a reproductive advantage. Did it have a role that went beyond simple 'hands off my mate' behaviour? We don't know.

2. Jealousy is shaped by the social environment.

3. When most people talk about jealousy they're using it as an umbrella term for a complex set of emotions that includes anxiety and insecurity, envy and anger. There's also a narrower definition that possibly harks back to 1.

4. There's a proper role for jealousy as a signal that perhaps we're not being treated with proper consideration. However, the fact that we're experiencing jealousy doesn't necessarily mean this is indeed the case.

PRETTY MUCH EVERYTHING about us, including our emotions, evolved for a reason. As Prof. David Barash says; 'The idea is that evolution works to maximise the fitness of individuals and/or his or her genes.' Our emotions are part of the toolkit we inherit that help us survive as individuals. Genes don't do survival of the species. The traits we share are common because our most distant ancestors who had them survived long enough to pass them on, and their descendants survived and passed them on.

That doesn't mean that everything we've inherited still has a role. But many of the things we thought of as redundant have been found to remain useful in some way, like the appendix.

Take shame, for instance. Shame alerts individuals to behaviour that risks exclusion from the group, vital for our ancestors for whom exclusion meant death. We still experience shame, but things change. Exclusion is not life or death in the way it was for tribes of hunter-gatherers (albeit isolation and exclusion are still very bad for our wellbeing). And the triggers change. In the course of a generation the shame heaped on queer people has been replaced (in many places) by pride. Similarly I'll argue that the things that provoke jealousy shift with both time and culture. That may suggest that a jealous response is learned and thus can, to a great extent, be unlearned.

Jealousy, like anger, insecurity, anxiety, envy, etc., can become miscalibrated. As we'll see when we look at anxiety, that miscalibration can be the result of trauma resulting in chronic heightened feelings. Feelings that have evolved to keep us safe can end up doing us, and others, harm—jealousy included.

WHAT I'M TALKING ABOUT WHEN I TALK ABOUT JEALOUSY

Do we actually know what we mean when we talk about jealousy? We certainly think we do. Dictionaries are a snapshot of the way people use a word. To be jealous, according to the *Shorter Oxford*, is to be 'vehement in wrath, desire or devotion'; 'ardently amorous, fond, lustful'; 'vigilant in guarding, suspiciously careful or watchful'; 'troubled by the belief, suspicion or fear that the good one desires to gain or keep for oneself has been or may be diverted to another'; 'resentful towards another on account of a known or a suspected rival—in love or affection esp. sexual love'; 'suspiciously vigilant'.

Even god gets to be jealous. 'For thou shalt worship no other god: for the LORD, whose name is Jealous, is a jealous God.' (Exodus 34:14). According to the *Oxford English Dictionary*, God's jealousy in this context amounts to 'having a love which will tolerate no unfaithfulness in the beloved object'. How many of us will think; 'That sounds just like every controlling partner ever'?

But wait. A whole host of different emotions are wrapped up in those definitions: anger, lust, anxiety, insecurity, paranoia, resentment, affection, desire, love. What's not included? If you sit a group of people down, as Meg-John Barker did, and ask them to describe what they mean by jealousy, you'll probably get as many different answers as there are participants.

> I did some research on this, it was at an early Polyday I think, and we got people to draw or collage their kind of experience of jealousy. And what was really striking was that pretty much everyone in that room had a really different understanding. Some of the jealousies felt very angry and hot. Others spoke very small and cool. Some of them felt much more like on the insecurity end of the spectrum versus the wrathful end of the spectrum, or the scared. Again, it's really clear that there were so many shades of jealousy and it meant very different things to different people depending on the situation.

And this is part of the problem when we talk about jealousy. As Joreth Innkeeper says, using the word can be unhelpful because it's woolly. We go looking for this nebulous thing, 'jealousy', when there's something we need to deal with right under our noses.

> I don't find jealousy to be a particularly useful term; because jealousy is an umbrella term and you can't fix the jealousy until you root down and find the actual root of

the problem anyway. So, I prefer not to talk about jealousy and just go straight for what is the actual problem. Insecurities can cause jealousy so it's more like the insecurity falls under the jealousy umbrella; it's not the only thing that can cause jealousy but it's one of the things. And so, if the problem is insecurity then just skip over the word jealousy, go straight to what the insecurity is.

Some argue that jealousy is not a *primary* emotion, in the way that love, hate, attraction, fear, happiness, sadness, etc. are, but a *compound* or *complex* emotion, one made up of several primary emotions in various proportions. So when people talk about jealousy they often mean a whole range of emotions that can encompass envy, insecurity, anxiety, anger, resentment and more.

Jealousy has also been framed as 'fear of loss' of a valued something or someone, as opposed to *envy*, which is resentment over something one wants that someone else has; a desire for gain rather than fear of loss. Then there's jealousy in a very narrow sense of a reaction when we're being treated unjustly. That's jealousy understood more philosophically.

Separately we'll also look at jealousy as a neurobiological phenomenon, a neurochemical reaction in the brain, for instance, when something happens to threaten a pair bond.

But before I go through these let's take stock. As a starting point, let's simply accept that 'jealousy' is hardly uncommon. It's within the normal spectrum of human experience, and it can and does crop up frequently both in monogamous and non-monogamous settings. Some people barely experience it. Others experience it so strongly that it becomes debilitating, making it difficult or even impossible to have relationships to the point that it becomes a threat to their own and other people's mental, emotional and even physical wellbeing.

When people talk about jealousy it is often in the context of perceived threats to their relationships. Even within monogamous relationships there are often plenty of triggers. Once you abandon monogamy you have to face up to the likelihood of your partners having romantic and sexual relationships with other people, something we've been socialised to see as a threat. Not for nothing did Shakespeare describe jealousy as a 'green-eyed monster'. These are not pretty emotions. They can become all-consuming, the stuff of obsession, and can feel very restrictive for those around someone dealing with these feelings.

And yet our reaction to another's jealousy is often rather conflicted. In some cultures and settings jealousy is considered normal, even desirable, and people are encouraged to react jealously when their partners attract attention or give attention to others. It's sometimes romanticised, with jealousy being depicted as a worthy expression of love or desire or even expected from a partner as a sign of devotion. There's also often shame and shaming around jealousy. There are those in the CNM community who will say, quite explicitly, that experiencing jealousy, in the wider sense, is tantamount to failure. To have 'transcended' jealousy has become almost fetishized. But let's not point the finger or belittle people for feeling jealous. It's far more helpful first to understand what we mean by it and what it stems from, and then to find ways of mitigating or disarming it.

So, in the following chapters I'm going to look at jealousy from various angles and ask what it is. I'll start with the neurobiology of jealousy, its narrower meaning and role as a defence mechanism, and its place in our culture. Then I'll pull apart those feelings that most of us are actually talking about when we talk about jealousy—insecurity, anxiety, envy, and anger—and ask what we can do to listen to them, respond to them, manage them and overcome them.

CHAPTER FORTY-TWO

What Titi Monkeys Know...

As MENTIONED ABOVE, some psychologists define envy as wanting what someone else has, and jealousy as protecting something *you* have. As with all emotional definitions this has its limits. What it does do, however, is associate jealousy squarely with mate-guarding behaviour. It's a threat response.

We know surprisingly little about how jealousy in this sense works in the brain. It's not the easiest condition to study in humans because, for reasons that have never been entirely clear, people experiencing jealousy rarely run to the nearest neurobiologist demanding 'Put me in your MRI machine now!' Instead they're more likely to yell things like "gerrorf 'im yer slapper," or "You looking for trouble mate?" The mysteries of science, eh?[75]

Titi monkeys, however, are far easier to study. For a start they'll do pretty much anything for a banana, or more specifically for a diet of 'New World monkey chow, rice cereal, banana, apples, raisins, and baby carrots and water.' Sounds pretty good.

Karen Bales and a team at the University of California, Davis set up an experiment to study eight male titi monkeys and their mates. They chose titi monkeys because this species pair bonds and is one of the few that is socially monogamous.

> What we've tried to do is both look at changes in the brain associated with forming a pair bond, and changes with what's going on in the brain when maintaining the bond.

> So, a pair bond is the adult version of what we would call an attachment relationship. So, if you look back at John Bowlby's work and Mary Ainsworth's work, it's,

---

75 Okay, there have been some studies, but it's much harder recreating the complex social dynamics that lead to jealousy in a lab than down the pub.

a relationship that's defined by three things. One is a preference for that specific partner. It's distress upon being separated from the partner. And it's the ability of that partner to buffer you against stressful situations. So that's the same definition as we used towards infants' attachments towards their moms.

We have a lot of behavioural mechanisms to maintain pair bonds, and jealousy is just one of them. So we feel pain, essentially feel social rejection, if there's a threat to one of our close relationships. And that's really what jealousy is. This is the feeling you get when your relationship is threatened.

The researchers built a funky monkey pad, divided in two by a wire mesh, and a short distance away they set up a viewing cage. The subject, one of the male titi monkeys, was put in the viewing cage. Into the monkey pad they introduced the male monkey's mate and, separated by that wire mesh just in case they didn't get on, a male stranger. As a control they did a similar experiment a few weeks before or after the main experiment but using a female and male who were strangers to the male subject.

Each subject was injected with fluorodeoxyglucose (FDG), a substance that acted as a marker when the team subsequently gave the monkeys a PET scan. It showed which areas of the monkey's brain had been activated when he'd watched his mate in close proximity to another male, and on the other occasion when he'd watched two strange monkeys near each other. As the study reported,

> After seeing his female pair mate next to a stranger male, male titi monkeys showed increased FDG uptake in the right lateral septum (LS), left posterior cingulate cortex (PCC) and left anterior cingulate (AC), and decreased uptake in the right medial amygdala (MeA) compared to the control condition.[76]

The cingulate cortex is associated with the processing of emotions and pain in humans. Bales says the correlation in humans isn't exact but it is interesting.

> One of the areas of the brain that we saw the most unambiguous response was the cingulate cortex. I don't know that it's been studied explicitly with regards to

---

76 'Imaging, Behavior and Endocrine Analysis of "Jealousy" in a Monogamous Primate', Nicole Maninger, Sally P. Mendoza, Donald R. Williams, William A. Mason, Simon R. Cherry, Douglas J. Rowland, Thomas Schaefer, and Karen L. Bales; University of California, Davis; *Frontiers in Ecology & Evolution*, 19 Oct 2017.

jealousy, but it's been studied really, really often with regards to any type of social exclusion. [In her research] Naomi Eisenberger uses a kind of a computer game; the game is just little computer figures throwing a ball back and forth. Then at some point the subject quits getting thrown the ball, and this really affects people emotionally. There's a video from her lab where subjects come out and talk about how upset they were because all of a sudden they weren't being included. And so it's that feeling of 'I'm on the outside', of a social relationship that very robustly activates the anterior cingulate.

The other area of the monkeys' brains that was very active was the lateral septum, which is associated with social behaviour, including cooperation, pair bonding, and the expression of fear.

You can get a response to oxytocin [from the lateral septum] both in positive and negative social situations. We know that titi monkeys have oxytocin receptors there and so do humans.

Oxytocin, of course, is a hormone released when we cuddle or have sex (among other things) and is strongly associated with bonding. The researchers also recorded higher levels of testosterone and cortisol in the male titi monkeys when watching their mates near an unknown male. The more time they spent focusing on their mate, the higher the cortisol level. Cortisol is our main stress hormone, and levels go up when we enter fight/flight/freeze mode. Testosterone is linked to mating-related aggression.

So, what can we deduce from this? Well, in a species not a million miles removed from ours, when there's a perceived threat to a pair bond we can see biochemical and behavioural responses that have parallels with our own.

If we feel our pair bond is threatened, we might worry about being socially excluded—the part of the brain that we know is linked to social exclusion lights up (and in evolutionary terms social exclusion is potentially life threatening). We can feel our wellbeing or survival is at stake—pair bonds seem to exist as both a mating and survival strategy—so we experience a rush of testosterone and cortisol, apparently 'designed' to get us to fight back.

So what we tend to call jealousy is an animal response in creatures that form pair bonds. However humans, most of them anyway, are different from titi monkeys and in more ways than simply lacking a tail. Karen Bales again:

If you look at humans, we can have very close selective relationships with more than one individual. So we can have a partner that we're in a very close relationship with, but we also maintain often very close relationships with our parents or children or some people with multiple partners. And so I think that humans have the capacity to have more than one close selective relationship at a time that all of our [animal] models don't have.

So while we're wired neurologically and biochemically to experience something that we label jealousy when we see a close relationship threatened by an intruder, we're not helpless in the face of that chemistry.

Critically, we're able to assess the supposed threat and tell ourselves that it is not in fact a threat—if it isn't. And as Professor Bales points out, our partners have a role in regulating our emotions and we theirs. That can include reassurance, as we'll see, a major tool in dealing with jealousy and many other emotions.

CHAPTER FORTY-THREE

Does Jealousy Have a Purpose?

People came up with lots of different words for different kinds of jealousy. A bit like, and I don't know if it's true, but the idea of Inuit words for snow that, if you're in the snow all the time, you need multiple ways of describing different kinds of snow. Maybe this is true for jealousy—that if you're non-monogamous, it's useful to have words for smaller jealousies and bigger ones: ones that you want something done about versus ones you don't.

— Meg-John Barker

LANGUAGE SHAPES THE way we think. Famously it's been claimed (wrongly as it happens) that the ancients Greeks didn't see blue because they had no word for it. But equally this is evidence that they thought about colours differently. For instance Homer's sea was 'wine dark' and to modern sensibilities that probably seems odd because we think of wine as a dark red with purple tones. But the Greek word κυάνεος (kyaneos), while meaning dark blue, equally described dark green, violet, black or brown, while γλαυκός (glaukos), covers light blue, light green, grey, or yellow. So the Greeks classified colours tonally, rather than by segmenting the spectrum of light as it refracts through a prism (as we moderns tend to do) or by how pigments combine to make other colours (as artists have done for centuries).

Frankly who is to say where the idea of blue ends and that of purple begins, or what is a greenish yellow and what is a yellowish green? At some level the way we group objects or ideas or phenomena is arbitrary because of perceived similarities and differences, and these are often cultural. People have simply agreed that zebras are more than stripy horses and are a distinct thing, whilst ponies are not.

So what happens if an emotion-label we create becomes a shorthand for a range of feelings that aren't necessarily homogenous?

The philosopher Kristján Kristjánsson illustrates this in his book *Justifying Emotions—Pride and Jealousy*.[77] He argues that jealousy, like pride, is—when felt about the right things at the right moment to the right degree—a proper and even necessary part of a well-rounded life, the goal of a flourishing human existence that Aristotle terms εὐδαιμονία (eudaemonia).

I'm going to go into some detail here, because if you're hoping to navigate CNM well, self-examination and analyses of emotions and values will quite probably become a more salient part of your life. And these are good skills for understanding your place in any relationship at all.

First, Kristjánsson has the challenge of nailing down just what he means by jealousy, so he stages a thought experiment.

Imagine, says the Professor, a scenario during a gold rush in the 19th century. A mine owner (C) gives a portion of his claim to each of his two sons (A & B), each portion being unexplored and, on the surface of things, appearing to have equal prospects. However, once they begin digging son B strikes it rich while son A's portion turns out to be a dud. A resents B's success. B has something A doesn't. A would like to have B's gold. A wishes B wasn't better off than him. This, says Kristjánsson is *envy*!

He then posits four variations. In the first A has spent most of his time drinking while B worked hard and yet A still resents his brother simply because of his success vis-à-vis his own. This he labels *invidious envy*.

In scenario two, A believes B went into A's mine at night, found a rich seam that A hadn't yet spotted, and carried off the ore to his own mine. A's resentment of B rests on his belief in B's dishonesty. Kristjánsson terms this *angry envy*.

Next we have kindly, hard-working A slogging his guts out for weeks while lazy loser B pisses it up; A still finds no gold, but on the first day that B sobers up and gets digging he strikes lucky. A resents B's undeserved good luck. This is termed *indignant envy*.

Lastly we have a situation where A believes, with reason, that their father C suspected or knew that A's mine would prove barren while B's would yield rich returns. Believing himself to be an equally good son and equally deserving of a fair chance, A resents B for being handed good fortune knowingly denied to himself and is also angry with his father. This is, Kristjánsson says, *jealous envy* or *jealousy*.

However Kristjánsson points to another subtle distinction between *angry envy* and *jealousy;* in the angry case, where A believes B has stolen gold-bearing ore from A's

77   Kristjánsson K, *Justifying Emotions* Published by Routledge, London and New York (2002) ISBN 0415408474

mine, A believes B has violated his moral rights. In the jealousy case, A feels that his treatment by his father is undeserved given that he's been a good son. There doesn't have to be an element of anger, argues the philosopher, but what he has put his finger on is a sense of injustice. This can then often be blended with anger and indignation depending on the circumstances.

Kristjánsson's point is that the standard modern distinction between envy and jealousy, which holds that envy pertains to things you don't have but would like, while jealousy is about what you have and don't want to lose—a formula occasionally repeated in some CNM and poly circles—is flawed. Instead he has zeroed in on the element of perceived injustice.

This is interesting.

Firstly, the examples of jealousy involve a triangular relationship, a dynamic that seems to be an essential element of jealousy proper. One person is jealous of another for having received preferential treatment, over themselves, from a third. Envy typically involves just two parties.

Secondly, for something to be 'jealousy proper', as opposed to anger or insecurity or whatever, there needs to be an element of injustice, actual or perceived.

Thirdly, I would argue that the situation needs to be personal. The fact that film star P and film star Q fall in love and get married may make some fans envious, but unless someone was personally spurned by P or Q it's not jealousy. Yes, in the great scheme of things, it may be unjust that one's talents were ignored and one didn't become a film star and meet and fall in love with another attractive film star, but there are doubtless a million others who feel the same way. The world is unjust. That's different from being treated unjustly *by someone*.

If these three conditions aren't met then what we have, surely, might be something that people might label jealousy but is more correctly thought of as envy.

Let's consider another example. Suppose that a couple have three children: Anthony has made millions in finance, Beatrice is a teacher who struggles with an addiction to gambling, and Charlie is unable to work because of an accident and lives on meagre state benefits. All three have been dutiful and have cared for their parents over the years; Anthony provides his parents occasional financial support, Beatrice does occasional cleaning and chores, but Charlie will always share what money he has, provides a listening ear, and even visits regularly to keep his parents company, even though the journey is a struggle for him. The parents make out a will dividing their estate between the three. They consider a number of options, mostly reflecting social norms.

> Option one: Treat all three equally regardless of circumstance.
> Option two: Allocate resources on the basis of need (i.e. Anthony would get

mementos only as he's already rich, Charlie would get the most).

Option three: Allocate inheritances on the basis of how well the parents think the money will be used, and either give Beatrice less or get Anthony to manage Beatrice's share so she doesn't gamble it all away.

In the end the parents opt for sheer favouritism; they never much liked Charlie, they think Beatrice is a wastrel, while Anthony was always the golden child. So Anthony, despite being wealthy, gets most of the money while Charlie's share is paltry.

Charlie is angry and upset. He's resentful of his parents and jealous of Anthony.

My question would be, 'Does C have a reasonable expectation of better, or is his jealousy and resentment the result of an unjustified sense of entitlement?' Doubtless some would respond 'It was the parents' money to do with as they liked' and others would say 'C was poorly treated.'

Ultimately Kristjánsson argues that jealousy is a proper response in such situations because it's vital for self-respect not to take an injustice lying down, and without self-respect there can be no εὐδαιμονία—eudaemonia, a flourishing or well-lived life.

In this respect one can see why jealousy might have evolved—as an emotional warning flare that one is being treated unjustly and that one's rights and needs are being unfairly undervalued compared with others'.

However reasonable this might conceivably be, we often get into a muddle because, especially when we get into the field of romantic relationships, distinguishing proper jealousy from entitlement and mate-guarding behaviour is difficult and often quite subjective. It's also possible to feel righteous indignation at personal mistreatment or injustice without being jealous of someone else for getting better treatment

ENTITLEMENT

HAVING DISCUSSED THIS issue with various people, it's hardly surprising that there's pushback. 'Feeling jealous about someone giving x to someone else when it should have been given to you is just entitlement,' they've said.

Well is it, and is feeling entitled to something always wrong? Let's start with a definition: entitlement is a sense of something being due to you by virtue of it being a right. So let's look at two ends of the entitlement scale.

First there's entitlement as it's often used these days to mean a sense of *social* entitlement, where someone simply feels that they're due something by virtue of who or what they are, or because it is just what they are used to getting.

We might imagine a wealthy white guy with a busy schedule reacting with outrage that he's made to wait his turn in a queue behind a poorer, brown woman whose own battles he doesn't know or care about. This is the entitlement of privilege, the kind that leads certain privately educated white, or indeed orange, men to speak with authority about things they know nothing about; the Dunning-Kruger effect in living Technicolor. It's the wellspring of that feminist prayer; 'Dear Lord, grant me the confidence of a mediocre white man.' It's entitlement such as used to be enshrined in law, as in apartheid South Africa and the Jim Crow-era southern United States. Not for nothing are such sentiments these days met with a cry of 'Check your privilege.'

But there's another sort of entitlement, one that we need in order to make society work. For example: if X makes a contract with Y whereby X pays \$500,000 to Y in exchange for 200 tonnes of coffee, then if X pays the money they're entitled to their goods, end of discussion.

These two types of entitlement are quite distinct. The second is explicit and based on an agreement. The first is often implicit, meaning unstated and maybe not even thought about, and based on social conventions or power rather than agreement between the parties (though sometimes this sort of entitlement does have the force of law behind it).

Obviously there are disputes about contracts. It's what keeps lawyers in biscuits and Savile Row suits. However whether we're monogamous or non-monogamous we've typically developed expectations (that some might characterise as entitlement) from the world we grew up in. We take these into our relationships unspoken and unquestioned and then we find that we're in a relationship with someone who has a different set of expectations. How many disagreements in relationships come down to 'I never signed up for that?'

But where does that leave us if an expectation, though unspoken, might be widely agreed to be reasonable, indeed sufficiently reasonable that no one thought it needed explicitly agreeing?

Let's take another example. HuangYi is married to Peter and they have children together. They are consensually non-monogamous and are both free to date who they please. They both work because one income won't pay the bills, but they each manage their own finances. HuangYi, like many women, does the lion's share of the childcare and running the home as well as working, and Peter often works late. Recently Peter has started seeing a new girlfriend, Sophia. Peter, in the throes of new relationship energy, showers Sophia with time, affection and presents.

HuangYi feels neglected. She doesn't have much time to date because she's got too much to do with her job and running the home. It's been a long time since Peter showered *her* with presents and, in any case, that money would be better spent on the house and children as they already struggle to make ends meet.

No one has broken explicit agreements, but HuangYi feels under-appreciated and neglected. Consequently HuangYi feels resentful of Peter and jealous of Sophia even though Sophia doesn't 'owe' HuangYi anything.

Kristjánsson would presumably argue that the jealousy here is to alert HuangYi to the fact that she may be being treated unjustly. It's a flag that boundaries may have been crossed. That doesn't mean that she *has* been treated unjustly, simply that she feels that way.

Jealousy is not right or wrong *per se* but it is an invitation to examine what is prompting it. This could lead us to dealing with insecurity or anxiety; it could also prompt us to re-examine our boundaries or even our relationships.

So, in summary:

Firstly, jealousy is triangular—it involves A, B and C. These can be individuals or even groups. The dynamic is that A, the jealous one, has a relationship with B whereby, when B gives something to C, A is jealous of C and resentful of B.

Secondly, jealousy is personal. You can't be jealous of people with whom you are not personally linked. That would be envy.

Thirdly, A feels a sense of injustice at C receiving something from B.

Fourthly, jealousy doesn't travel alone. It's accompanied by a whole train of other emotions. But because jealousy can be such a dominant emotion, obsessive and all-consuming, and because it is so uncomfortable, it's the feeling that we're most conscious of.

Jealousy 'proper' arises when someone feels that someone else is benefitting to their detriment, while their own reasonable expectations and needs are not being met. However—and this is critical—in many cases what we think of as jealousy proper isn't. It's anger or insecurity or anxiety or a combination of such things. And, as such, it is something that we can choose to address. Whether the jealous person's expectations or feelings are reasonable and proportionate or are misplaced—whether they arise from genuine insecurity, a mere perception of insecurity, or prejudice or entitlement—is something that needs close examination.

At best the role of jealousy is to keep us safe by dissuading us from tolerating an injustice that we should not tolerate, where to do so would compromise our self-respect and wellbeing. What we can do in response is communicate, state our needs, if needs be reassess our situation, decide whether our treatment is acceptable, and if we feel it's not and we can't bring about change, then consider our options including that of leaving.

CHAPTER FORTY-FOUR

What Attachment Theory Can Tell Us

BEFORE WE GO on to look at anxiety and insecurity, it's worth doing a quick survey of *attachment theory*. As paradigms in psychology go, attachment theory is one of the most thoroughly researched and, as a result, is supported by a large body of evidence. It is widely, if not universally, accepted. It draws a link between how we form relationships in early childhood and how that plays out in our adult interactions.

Attachment theory has its origins in the work of the British psychologist, psychiatrist and psychoanalyst John Bowlby, who was commissioned by the World Health Organization to write a report on the mental health of homeless children in Europe in the wake of the Second World War. His report appeared as 'Maternal Care and Mental Health' in 1951.

Over the years, under the influence of other researchers, notably Mary Ainsworth, Bowlby's thinking evolved. He came to see children's development as shaped primarily by their experiences of external realities, as opposed to the prevailing thought at the time that children developed through internal fantasy.

Bowlby and Ainsworth were both particularly interested in how children form attachments in early life with their primary caregivers (typically the child's mother). Ainsworth designed a scenario to study the way children reacted to being brought into an unfamiliar situation by their caregiver. The caregiver would withdraw, leaving the child to cope with the situation alone, before returning. The researchers were particularly interested in the way the child reacted to their caregiver's return.

They described the various reactions by placing them in three broad categories. 'Securely attached' children, just over half of those studied, were aware of their caregiver's absence but needed little reassurance upon their return. Insecurely attached children were initially placed into the two other categories: 'anxious-avoidant' and 'anxious-resistant' (often labelled as simply 'avoidant' and 'anxious' by other researchers in the field). A colleague of Ainsworth subsequently added a fourth category, 'disorganised/disorientated'.

In crude terms 'avoidant' children appeared unruffled by their carer's departure, absence or return, tending to ignore them or keep them at arm's length. The researchers suspected this behaviour was masking anxiety, and subsequent monitoring of their vital signs tended to support this hypothesis.

'Anxious' children displayed anxiety even before their caregiver's departure and were 'clingy' both before they left and after they returned, and they were hard to soothe.

Those in the final category, 'disorganised/disorientated' variously exhibited distancing and clingy behaviour patterns but showed no coherent coping strategy, and their levels of cortisol—a stress hormone associated with 'fight or flight' responses—were higher than those of children in any of the other three categories.

Towards the end of the 1980s, Cindy Hazan, of the Department of Human Development and Family Studies at Cornell University, and Phillip Shaver, of the State University of New York, started to use attachment theory as a framework for understanding adult relationships. Various researchers have suggested that patterns of behaviour learned in early childhood carry over into adult experiences of work and intimate relationships.

Adult categories broadly correspond to childhood ones, though in adults 'anxious' attachment is often referred to as 'anxious/preoccupied' and 'avoidant' as 'avoidant/dismissive'. A fourth category, 'fearful', is sometimes seen as a subset of 'avoidant' behaviours, sometimes as an amalgam of anxious and avoidant types, and is characterised by people worrying about being both too close and too distant from others.

A person is generally classified into one of these four groups according to their self-esteem and sociability (i.e. regard for others).

Those with *secure* styles have both high self-esteem and high sociability. Broadly speaking they're more empathic, their emotions are better regulated, they're more likely to share intimate feelings, maintain long-term relationships, have strong boundaries and respect those of others, and they're less likely to experience jealousy in the broad sense.

Avoidant types have high self-esteem but low sociability: 'I'm awesome but everyone else is disappointing'. They have an internal conflict between their genuine need for connection and their reluctance to become vulnerable. The result is that avoidant people often tell themselves that they don't need relationships and prefer independence over interdependence. Typically relationships remain emotionally superficial even if they're sexually charged, and there can also be a tendency to sabotage them when partners threaten to get too close.

Those with the *anxious/preoccupied* style combine low self-esteem with high socia-bility: 'I really want to be close to people, I just wish they'd like me back.' They have a tendency towards hyper-vigilance. They're often highly attuned to their partners' every change in mood to the point of over-interpreting every signal. Preoccupation is a good description of their state of mind because of the sheer amount of brain power they devote to 'solving the problem' of their relationship(s). Whereas someone who is securely attached will, by default, tend to assume that their partner(s) will stay, the anxiously attached assume they will leave. The anxiously attached both fear and ex-pect abandonment and need constant reassurance.

The *fearful* attachment style is characterised by both low self-esteem and low re-gard for others. It is often linked to early trauma and abuse.

Despite some people's scepticism about psychology being a soft science where it's harder to match inputs to outputs in the way that, say, physics can, attachment theory is one of the areas of psychology where the research results are consistent, and where the findings actually seem to be useful. They give us a starting point for looking at the characteristics of the relationships that people typically form, or don't. And that allows us to ask whether people within CNM relationships are typical of the wider population, given the greater opportunities in CNM relationships for triggering what we tend to label as jealousy.

So are the insecurely attached (the anxious, avoidant and fearful) more or less likely to be drawn to consensual non-monogamy? Robin Edelstein and Amy Moors carried out two studies. The first focused on the attitudes towards consensual non-monogamy of heterosexual people who had never been in a CNM relationship (and were thus monogamous).

> Consistent with our hypotheses, Study 1 revealed that avoidant individuals hold positive attitudes toward CNM and report greater willingness to engage in vari-ous forms of CNM. Additionally, those higher in anxiety held negative attitudes toward CNM; however, anxiety was unrelated to willingness to engage in CNM.[78]

These results begged for more research: specifically how people who are *actually engaged* in consensual non-monogamy measure in terms of attachment. Edelstein, Moors and colleagues had a hunch what they were going to find.

---

78 'Attached to monogamy? Avoidance predicts willingness to engage (but not actual engagement) in consensual non-monogamy', Amy C. Moors, Terri D. Conley, Robin S. Edelstein, William J. Chopik; University of Michigan. Published online 1 April 2014 in *Journal of Social and Personal Relationships*.

Given that individuals in CNM relationships and secure individuals report similar relationship qualities, including high levels of trust, honesty, intimacy, and relationship satisfaction as well as low levels of jealousy (e.g., de Visser & McDonald, 2007; Jenks, 1985; Ritchie & Barker, 2006), we expected that individuals lower in avoidance and anxiety would be more likely to be in a CNM relationship.

So that was the hypothesis. It's worth pointing out that the CNM people surveyed were not segmented into swingers, poly folks and those in open relationships, which would have been really interesting (though given how hard it is to get funding for this sort of research we're pretty lucky to have what we have). So, what were the results?

> Consistent with our predictions, individuals lower in avoidance were more likely to be in a CNM relationship over a monogamous relationship. However, inconsistent with our predictions, anxiety was unrelated to current relationship status.

This, I'd suggest, is fascinating. Let's first put this into a plainer form. If you take 1000 broadly representative monogamous people and 1000 broadly representative consensually non-monogamous people, you'll find that avoidant/dismissive people—the ones who prefer to be independent and keep their partners at an emotional arm's length—make up a bigger proportion of the monogamous group than the CNM group. This despite them being *more* interested on average in the possibility of CNM relationships. Basically, by inference, they like the idea but not the reality.

Meanwhile the anxious/preoccupied types, although they are more inclined to see, from the outside, CNM as a bad idea, are not discouraged from exploring it. The unspoken finding here is that securely attached people are over-represented in CNM groups. Wow!

That begs a big 'Why?' Well here is the Michigan team's take.

> These results support previous work that has shown that people in CNM report relatively high levels of trust and intimacy as well as low levels of jealousy in their romantic relationship (e.g., Barker, 2005; Bonello & Cross, 2010; Jenks, 1985). Moreover, couples with insecure orientations report more negative communication patterns (e.g., demand withdraw and mutual avoidance) than couples with secure orientations (Domingue & Mollen, 2009). CNM relationship[s] may require more open and honest communication among partners and [this] is also congruent with

the finding that people engaged in CNM are lower in avoidance than individuals engaged in monogamy. In sum, our findings provide important new evidence that people can exhibit aspects of security (i.e., low levels of avoidance) without sexual exclusivity.

So, let me do that journalistic thing again where I take the carefully phrased findings of a group of diligent social scientists, toss them out the window and instead use the sort of broad-brush language that makes researchers go 'Eeeek'. Don't you just love it when they go 'Eeeek'?

Consensual non-monogamy, especially the most prevalent forms of polyamory, demands a higher level of honesty, openness and communication to make it work. From the outside, avoidant people take a superficial look and go 'Yay! I get to shag around and have lots of ongoing superficial relationships with great sex and low levels of commitment and engagement. It's like dial-a-slut.' But when they actually investigate and meet poly people, or someone who is into swinging, they find that actually there's lots of talking and checking in to find out how they're feeling, and negotiation. In fact there's way more than in a comfortably dysfunctional monogamous relationship, where you can find an anxious-preoccupied person who'll cling onto you for dear life while you hide out at the office, watch TV with them in silence, and have meaningless affairs on the side. So faced with the reality of all that talking about feelings and stuff, such as the need to negotiate regularly, they go 'No thanks' and stick with serial monogamy, serial infidelity, or the emotional void that makes them happy.

Anxious/preoccupied people, meanwhile, go 'Yikes! That looks awful. I'd have to deal with my partner sleeping with someone else and, you know what, they'd find lots of people who are smarter and better looking than me and they'd probably leave me in a flash. Definitely can't deal with that.' But when they explore CNM they find that there's lots of talking and checking in and reassurance and, because they have more than one relationship, when partner A is off with someone else they talk to partner B or C and get reassurance and love from them too. They've effectively hedged their bets so if A does indeed abandon them there's still B and C, and the possibility of a D on the horizon, so their chances of being left all alone are lower. It's not that CNM is intrinsically more attractive to the anxiously attached than monogamy; it's more that it offers ways to manage their anxiety.

Then there are those annoyingly securely attached types who seem to breeze through the travails of CNM because, you know what, they have the tools to make it work. They're at ease with their feelings. They expect people to stick around just as they expected their parents to stick around. They have high self-esteem combined with high sociability and don't see metamours as a threat. They're overrepresented not so much by virtue of a positive choice, but more by the fact that avoidant types absent themselves, and if one group is underrepresented, another is inevitably over-represented.

I should also let Dr. Dylan Selterman from the University of Maryland's psychology department get a word in edgeways at this point with this observation, because it's important.

> In my research, for example with Jon Mohr and Ruth Fassinger, we found that there was no association between monogamy status and relationship outcomes, like satisfaction or commitments, for those people who are more secure. For those who are insecure, they tend to have more trouble in all kinds of relationships. And so it might make things even more difficult if you're trying to have an open relationship. If you're trying to make it work with multiple partners, it might be even more difficult to do that kind of thing if you're feeling more insecure.

If you have attachment issues, you don't get to escape them simply by picking monogamy over non-monogamy or vice versa. They travel with you. Neither way of relating is, of itself, an answer to being avoidant or anxious or fearful.

However, and this is the silver lining on the cloud of insecure attachment, it's possible to 'learn' a secure attachment style. It takes time, and it helps to have a relationship or relationships where someone, typically a secure someone, provides a secure attachment that allows the insecure person to feel that they're safe and to come to expect and rely on that connection in a way that had eluded them previously.

By the same token, traumatic events such as the loss of a partner, especially if there was betrayal involved or, sadly, the loss of a child, can shake securely attached people. Life can pull us up or knock us down.

Another thing that can help is sufficient self-awareness to enable us to watch our own behaviour from a distance and acknowledge what's going on. Before we can take steps to address the issue, we must first know it exists.

ABUNDANCE / SCARCITY MINDSET

THOUGH NOT FORMALLY related to attachment theory, this seems an appropriate place to mention the discussion about abundance and scarcity. If attachment theory is heavily researched and evidenced, abundance/scarcity is more a feeling. You could say it's a philosophical or spiritual way of thinking about relationships.

Those who subscribe to it broadly argue that if you see love and the opportunity to love and form relationships as *abundant,* you'll actually find more opportunities. You'll be less likely to settle for relationships that don't meet your needs, because you assume there will be a better someone or several someones out there.

Conversely if you see love as *scarce,* you may give up looking before you start, settle for second best, or cling for dear life to whatever you have for fear that nothing else is on offer.

In CNM circles the abundance-vs.-scarcity theme often comes up because people (understandably) may say, 'It's hard enough finding someone without needing to find someone open to CNM or kink or whatever'. And a common answer to that encourages us to see love as abundant and to remember that there are seven billion people out there offering countless thousands of opportunities even if you have special requirements.

And yet I hear people, often the same ones, do the maths for a couple looking for a unicorn and say 'That is really, really difficult'.

As I said, it's more a feeling than an analysis.

It's something of a truism that if you're depressed or feeling bad about yourself, it will get in the way of finding potential partners—just as feeling like a million dollars because you're feeling good in yourself and your life is going well contributes to your feeling and being attractive.

However, it's quite possible to have a scarcity attitude because you simply don't find many people interesting and attractive or because your opportunities to meet like-minded people are highly restricted by your circumstances (which might look and feel like much the same thing). That's not necessarily self-esteem but more being particular. Being non-monogamous doesn't necessarily equate to being undiscriminating, any more than being monogamous necessarily makes you picky.

CHAPTER FORTY-FIVE

Anxiety, Fear and Guilt

ANXIETY IS HORRIBLE, sickening, and debilitating, but like many of our emotions it's a natural response that evolved to keep our ancestors safe. It's closely related to fear. If fear is a response to actual danger, then anxiety is our being primed for potential danger. It keeps us alert. It keeps us vigilant. It was pretty handy when there were sabre-toothed tigers living in the downstairs cave, and it's still useful when you're driving in a strange country and the other drivers aren't behaving as they would back home.

Anxiety has chemical and physiological effects. Among these are low levels of serotonin, high levels of thyroid hormone (possibly the result of hyperthyroidism, an overactive thyroid), the malfunctioning of GABA transmitters, and high levels of the hormone norepinephrine. Likewise, in people with a history of childhood trauma and stress, the area of the brain known as the *basolateral amygdala* is typically enlarged. The amygdala plays a role in activating our fight/flight/freeze/fawn mechanism. Its size and its density of connections to other parts of the brain are key predictors of whether someone will suffer from increased anxiety.

It seems that exposure to maternal stress hormones in utero and anxiety-provoking situations early in life leaves us more predisposed to feel anxious because those parts of the body responsible for regulating our stress response become overdeveloped and keep us constantly on edge. If you were growing up on the Asian steppe in an era when nomadic raiders regularly attacked your village, or if you lived in Europe when warfare was a near constant, then your body was arguably doing you a favour. It was priming you to fight or flee when the next attack inevitably came.

If you're stressed to f**k because you had a dad who got drunk and hit you, or a mother who was emotionally unpredictable, hypercritical or shaming, or you were bullied at school, or abandoned when tiny, your body doesn't necessarily stop priming you for craziness close to home just because the original threat to your wellbeing has gone. You can end up living your whole life constantly alert to potential dangers, real or imaginary. You may overreact to threats that do appear, because your fight/flight/freeze/fawn response is poorly calibrated. You can find yourself worrying excessively about the things that might happen.

Ruby Bouie Johnson regularly finds herself supporting clients who turn up at her practice suffering from anxiety.

> When they come into my office, you know, their family or their partners often don't understand why they are so volatile, or why they are so irritable or why they sleep a lot, things that they can't make sense of. And primarily it's the mood swings that people have because they are frustrated and they're very anxious. They have separation anxiety and they don't know how to manage it because that response is felt in the body. And so when someone's experiencing this it impacts communication, because maybe they want to talk to their other partners and it just creates a triangle of bad feedback. Also, people may act out in other ways. Maybe they'll get three new partners to distract themselves. [Anxiety] highly impacts how people attach and also the reason why they attach, which is what are they trying to fix in some way.

That experience of anxiety as a very physical sensation is not uncommon. For instance Debbie experiences jealousy as anxiety, and there's a very strong physical component.

> It's usually like I'm sick to my stomach, it feels almost like an anxiety attack with a little bit of anger behind it.

To some extent we're going to be splitting hairs over language here, because just as jealousy is a rather nebulous term, so too at times is anxiety. It's often conflated with other things such as fear and insecurity. However I think it might be more useful to think of anxiety primarily as a biochemical and physical reaction rather than as an emotion. As such it accounts for the threat response that can accompany emotions like jealousy or anger or fear or insecurity.

Take McFadden's experience of jealousy:

> To my mind jealousy is a response to perceived scarcity. I try to bear in mind that the perception of scarcity is much like the perception of security; it's illusory and

a projection that we impose upon the world or upon ourselves from a place of anxiety.

It's an interesting observation. We often use the label 'jealousy' to describe this feeling that someone else is getting something that we feel is due to us or at least isn't due to them. It can feel like a threat to our wellbeing. There is often a sense of unfairness or injustice (what I suggest could be considered 'jealousy proper'), but it's often complicated by a fear of loss and the anxiety that that provokes.

McFadden also points to a social taboo: The model of masculinity we're typically presented with is very narrow and anxiety in men is treated as a unmanly. That makes it harder for some men to acknowledge and deal with it.

> In general I think that it's taboo for a man to outwardly experience anxiety and to have emotional needs that are consequent. That's basically it in a nutshell. I think, across the board, men who evince anxiety are perceived to be cowardly, unattractive and so on.

However anxiety is absolutely something that can be managed. McFadden, finds it helpful to have reassurance, confirmation that he won't lose out, and knowledge that there is no threat.

> I have a very clear coping strategy for dealing with jealousy, which is when I have jealous feelings, to speak those feelings aloud to my partner and to ask them for reassurance around the sense of scarcity or anxiety that I have. It's hard, as a man, to own that emotional need and to be able to say what I am actually insecure about. I have feelings of insecurity or anxiety around your affection for me or your attraction to me or, you know, some aspect of the relationship that we share. And I want to be told aloud explicitly that affection, or that support, or whatever is actually dependable.

I've included some general advice on dealing with anxiety in the next chapter. There's a lot we can do for ourselves. It's hard unlearning anxious responses and resetting those parts of our limbic systems that manage anxiety, but not impossible. With application, and ideally with support from those around us, we can let go of some of those feelings.

GUILT

IT MIGHT SEEM odd to talk about guilt in a book about consensual non-monogamy, where the presumption is that you have negotiated your relationships and that your partners have freely consented to the relationships being non-monogamous.

And yet, for some CNM people, some things can still feel like cheating even if they're not. It's what Dr Lori Beth Bisbey and Anita Cassidy have dubbed the 'monogamy hangover'. Eunice believes the root of the problem lies in the idea that our capacity to love is limited.

> A big part of it feeling like it's cheating is that you are somehow not giving the full amount to each partner, because love, in a monogamous society, is considered to be a finite resource. If you give some of it to people who society tells you do not 'deserve' it then you are giving less of it to a partner who does [deserve it]; perhaps the person who you were originally in a monogamous relationship with or who feels like a 'primary' partner.

Seb struggled when he and his wife opened up their relationship, and after almost eight years still has moments when he feels guilty.

> Even if you're comfortable with poly you can still feel guilty about somehow letting your partner down and not being fully faithful to them when you're with somebody else. And I think that's partly because we are just conditioned so much in both express and implicit ways and with hundreds and hundreds of cues right from the beginning, from different parts of our lives, that the only acceptable romantic relationship is a completely faithful monogamous relationship. It's also predicated on the idea that there is one person for you out there and once you find them there's something wrong with you if you're not completely 100% satisfied in every aspect with that other person

The pervasive presence of the romantic ideal and the sense that consensual non-monogamy is not just failing to embrace that idea, but consciously violating it, brings our realities into conflict with our conditioning. Guilt is a common by-product. Conflicted feelings and a sense of guilt can also arise if someone senses that a partner or partners are not getting as much from the arrangement as oneself (the flipside of the jealousy that some experience when a partner appears to be getting more from it). For instance Seb's wife has been unable to see her other partner because of the pandemic.

I definitely feel guilty that I feel right now I'm benefiting from the polyamorous setup much, much more than [she] is. We talked about it. She says she sometimes wonders if she should try to go on a date but basically no, she doesn't want to. And I think I do feel guilty about that. It would be better if her other partner was able to visit. It would feel much more balanced at that point.

Of course, within CNM, when any given emotion is expressed there's almost always a chorus of people saying that it's wrong or unnecessary or that, as beings from a higher plane, they have transcended it. However, as Eunice says, don't beat yourself up.

Societal conditioning is extremely powerful. It is not *all*-powerful. But if you are aware that the conditioning exists you can work towards lessening it. You may or may not be able to get rid of the conditioning entirely, and some people don't.

As with most feelings that humans experience, guilt evolved for a reason[79]. Sometimes feelings of guilt are warranted because someone has transgressed and sometimes they're misplaced. That doesn't necessarily make those feelings any easier to escape. Awareness helps. So does self-compassion. By treating yourself with the same kindness you would extend to others you can free up a great deal of energy that would otherwise be wasted in self-recrimination to bring about change.

---

79   Guilt is often contrasted with shame. Both seem to have evolved from a need to promote social cohesion. It's sometimes argued that shame is social disapproval imposed from without while guilt is internal, resulting from a violation of personal ethics. In either case the effect may have been to reduce the likelihood of harm being done to others and to allow the wrongdoer to display contrition making forgiveness easier.

CHAPTER FORTY-SIX

Coping with Anxiety and Other Mental Health Issues

ANXIETY FEEDS INTO and exacerbates many of the other feelings we may deal with in consensual non-monogamy: anger, fear, insecurity, envy, jealousy. For that reason, managing anxiety helps us to manage everything else that much better.

THREAT ASSESSMENT

ANXIETY IS NOT so much a threat response as threat readiness.

Let's try an analogy, the states of alert used by governments. The United States has five 'defcon' levels to determine its state of readiness for nuclear conflict, from Defcon 5—'Fade Out'—its lowest level of readiness, to Defcon 1—'Cocked Pistol', when war is imminent or under way. In the UK the threat levels are termed 'low', 'moderate', 'substantial', 'severe', and 'critical'.

So why not keep your security services at 'Defcon-1' or 'critical' all the time? Because it's bloody exhausting, that's why. Plus, with time, people's levels of alertness naturally fall. We're not built to be on constant guard. It's not good for us. As a result governments tend to look for opportunities to stand their people down, both so that they're rested and also so that when there is a threat they're able to shift to a higher gear.

But if you suffer from high levels of anxiety you can be constantly at 'substantial' or 'severe'. Trying to be realistic about the actual level of threat can help. However, anxiety is like a subroutine running in the background. It's not always possible to 'outthink' it. Indeed the problem can be exacerbated by overthinking. One tool that has been shown to reduce anxiety seems to work by interrupting that process.

MINDFULNESS

BEHIND TODAY'S MINDFULNESS hype is an increasing body of science. Even the University of Oxford has a centre for mindfulness within its psychiatry department.

Mindfulness techniques, like focusing on one's breathing, engages the pre-frontal cortex and gives the anxiety centres of the brain, notably the amygdala, a break. It also means that we can persuade that part of our system to mimic a state of relaxation. Short shallow breathing is associated with stress and anxiety. If you pant quickly you can raise your stress levels. Slow deep breathing calms us. Consciously controlling one's breathing is a very common mindfulness/meditation technique. As Tom Ireland put it in a piece for *Scientific American* research suggests that this and other mind-calming techniques can permanently alter the way the mind functions, reduce activity between certain areas of the brain, and even reshape it.

> MRI scans show that after an eight-week course of mindfulness practice, the brain's "fight or flight" centre, the amygdala, appears to shrink. This primal region of the brain, associated with fear and emotion, is involved in the initiation of the body's response to stress.
>
> As the amygdala shrinks, the pre-frontal cortex—associated with higher-order brain functions such as awareness, concentration and decision-making—becomes thicker.
>
> The "functional connectivity" between these regions—i.e. how often they are activated together—also changes. The connection between the amygdala and the rest of the brain gets weaker, while the connections between areas associated with attention and concentration get stronger.[80]

Meditation does need a degree of commitment. But some free apps use gamification to encourage you to stick with your mindfulness practice. Over a period of time the effects accumulate, and people whose anxiety is easily triggered find that they react less strongly to common events.

EXERCISE

EXERCISE APPEARS CONSISTENTLY on lists of things that provide a measurable boost to

---

80 'What Does Mindfulness Meditation Do to Your Brain?', Tom Ireland, *Scientific American,* 12 June 2014.

physical and mental wellbeing. It seems that we're not cut out to loll about all day like lions who've overdone the wildebeest tartare and antelope carpaccio. A study carried out in 2008 found really quite dramatic reductions in anxiety levels resulting from modest amounts of regular exercise.

> A 2-week protocol consisting of six brief sessions that involved 20min of exercise at 70% of HRmax [age-adjusted maximum heart rate] yielded large reductions in anxiety sensitivity. Our results also provided support for the hypothesis that reducing anxiety sensitivity with exercise leads to significant improvements in levels of anxiety and depressed mood.[81]

The researchers measured the results using the Anxiety Sensitivity Index. The ASI is an assessment tool consisting of 16 questions where the respondent rates from 0 to 4 how distressing their anxiety symptoms are and how serious their worries are about the effects those might have. Scores above 25 are seen as potentially indicating clinical issues, and scores over 30 could point to panic disorder or PTSD.

Among the study's participants, anxiety scores started in the range of 32 to 34, all at possible panic/PTSD levels. They dropped to around 14 to 15 after the course and further dropped to around 11 and 12 at the follow-up stage (presumably with the exercise being maintained). Among those who followed through on the course, the percentage who saw clinically significant changes was over 79% after the two weeks and over 93% when followed up.

That, from a lay perspective, seems pretty remarkable and a huge endorsement for the idea that physical and mental wellbeing are intimately linked.

Of course 'moderate' exercise means different things to different people, and their opportunities to exercise can be affected by health, income, accessibility and disability.

SLEEP AND DIET

SLEEP DEPRIVATION CAN have a very serious impact on our mental health. Around half of those who experience high levels of anxiety and have been diagnosed with generalised anxiety disorder have problems sleeping. These two problems can create a negative

---

81   'Reducing Anxiety Sensitivity with Exercise', Jasper Smits (Southern Methodist Univ., Texas.), Angela Berry (SMU), David Rosenfield (SMU), Vincent B. Powers (Univ. of Amsterdam), Evelyn Beharand (Boston Univ., Massachusetts), Michael Otto (Boston Univ.); *Depression and Anxiety*, 26 Aug 2008. https://onlinelibrary.wiley.com/doi/abs/10.1002/da.20411

feedback loop. But a study of teenagers in the US found that sleep problems *preceded* around 27% of cases of anxiety.

Taking steps to sleep better, such as reducing or eliminating caffeine after a certain point in the day (typically after lunch), not staring at screens before bed, keeping screens entirely out of the bedroom, setting the room temperature to your optimum for sleep (often that's lower than you might think), keeping the bedroom properly dark, getting the best mattress you can afford, etc., are all practical steps you might consider. Exercise during the day also promotes sleep at night.

Likewise diet. We know that poor diet diminishes wellbeing and that a healthy diet improves it, but there is growing evidence that eating the way our forebears ate (something that's still in evidence in traditional Mediterranean and Japanese diets) is associated with a depression risk 25% to 35% lower than with a modern western diet. According to Eva Selhub, writing in Harvard Health:

> Multiple studies have found a correlation between a diet high in refined sugars and impaired brain function—and even a worsening of symptoms of mood disorders, such as depression.[82]

It may sound boring, but a diet rich in raw and whole foods, vegetables, poultry and fish is good for you, and not just for its effects on your body. The food industry has become very adept at delivering a 'perfect' mix of sugar, fat and salt to reach what it rather cynically calls a 'bliss point' that lights up the nucleus accumbens, the same part of our brains that's stimulated by cocaine, nicotine, and morphine. Chasing that high becomes addictive in the way that it does for drug addicts. As with most highs there's also a crash.

A simple rule of thumb is to avoid highly processed food. Beware food-industry attempts to create a false equivalence between the processing that happens in your home (cooking, blending, etc.) and what happens in their labs and factories. The latter is for their benefit, not yours. Avoiding sugars and simple carbs (white rice, potatoes, bread, especially white bread, etc.) will all help. Eating healthily on a low income can be hard and lack of time, lack of access to fresh ingredients and disability can all make it harder. But the wonderful food writer Jack Monroe has faced all of those and is an excellent source of advice and recipes that at least make a little money go much further. (Just Googling 'Jack Monroe recipes' will bring up loads of links to tasty, healthy meals you can make with good but low-cost ingredients.)

---

82 'Your brain on food', Eva Selhub, Harvard Health; *Nutritional Psychiatry*, 16 Nov 2015.

REASSURANCE

IN A RELATIONSHIP we can do a great deal to help one another regulate our emotions. Reassurance is one of the tools. However there's a big difference between looking to a partner for reassurance and blaming them for the anxiety. It's possible to accept that one's partner is doing something simultaneously anxious-making *and* entirely reasonable. From the other side, it's equally possible to accept that your partner being anxious doesn't have to mean they want you to do things differently. Reassurance helps people overcome their fears.

Listening to someone, acknowledging and understanding their feelings, communicating that you understand, and offering them a safe place to discuss things, all help. You can, *sensitively*, encourage them to question thoughts that are based on imagined rather than real threats, and you can encourage them to consider evidence. Above all, if they're anxious about the relationship you can tell them what they don't need to worry about. If there are things that put the relationship under pressure try to discuss those honestly and compassionately.

It's hard to get a grip on things if what your instincts tell you don't match what you're hearing. But if there are practical things you can both do to address the thoughts that are provoking anxiety, you can take steps together. Remember, anxiety is primarily about all the unwanted things that *might* happen. Healthy control of anxiety is being alert to real potential dangers and downgrading worries about the highly unlikely and the fantastical.

SEVERE ANXIETY, THERAPY AND TREATMENT

SOME PEOPLE EXPERIENCE anxiety at levels that are debilitating. The first thing to say is that it's important to avoid self-blame. We're all somewhere on the physical/mental health spectrums, and I struggle to think of a scenario in which we're culpable for having a poorly calibrated limbic system. At some point anxiety can become sufficiently serious that it harms your wellbeing, both mental and physical, and you may decide to seek professional help.

One thing to bear in mind is that therapists tend to turn to the tools in their box. A clinical psychiatrist is far more likely to favour medication than a psychotherapist, who will most likely favour a form of talking therapy. To borrow from the psychologist Abraham Maslow 'I suppose it is tempting, if the only tool you have is a hammer, to treat everything as if it were a nail.'

Choosing the right therapist for you is critically important. There's a longer discussion about how to find a therapist in the next section.

Many people are suspicious of medication. There's considerable evidence that much or most of the impact of drugs such as SSRIs is due to the placebo effect, while people do complain about side effects.[83] However there are caveats. Firstly the placebo effect is a powerful therapeutic tool in its own right, secondly there does appear to be an additional benefit from antidepressants over and above the placebo effect and, thirdly, that benefit increases and the placebo effect decreases with the seriousness of the depression.[84]

There are people who've succeeded in improving their mental health without drugs and others who are still alive because of them.

Meanwhile there is quite a range of talking therapies available, from psychoanalysis to CBT and much more. The most important factor that seems to determine the success or not of therapy, regardless of the form it takes, is the relationship with the therapist. Therefore it's very important to find a therapeutic relationship that works for you.

GETTING THE HELP YOU NEED

THERE ARE RESOURCES in some countries for people who are members of sexual minorities, but often resources are least available where they're needed most—i.e. in places where GSRD people face most discrimination. In the United States there are places to turn to like The Trevor Project for LGBTIQA people and Trans Lifeline for trans people. There's also the Kink Aware Professionals, Open List, Poly Friendly Professionals and Loving More's Member Professionals. In the UK there's Pink Therapy, in Brazil Rainbow Psicologia, Rosa Strippe and others in Germany. Singapore has a smattering of gay-allied therapists. In Indonesia some resources can be found through atheist groups on Facebook, albeit because of the growing influence of conservative Islam in Indonesia these groups are often private.

Although many therapists try to provide what's called 'unconditional positive regard', in other words a completely accepting and non-judgemental environment for their clients, this is far from universal. Some therapists bring their own strong moral or religious convictions into the consulting room, and those may well clash with the values and lifestyles of their clients.

It's often useful to have an exploratory meeting. Many therapists won't charge for this first session. Use this time to establish whether or not you can work with them.

83   Do antidepressants work? Jacob Stegenga, Aeon, 5 March 2019 https://aeon.co/essays/the-evidence-in-favour-of-antidepressants-is-terribly-flawed
84   In defence of antidepressants, Vasco M Barreto, Aeon, 11 July 2019 https://aeon.co/essays/why-the-constant-trashing-of-antidepressants-is-absurd

A good therapist will be frank if they think that they're unable to help a client. There are always those, however, who either can't or won't distinguish between religious counselling and mental health counselling. Some believe that their own value system will help the client and that through therapy a substitution can take place. Meg-John Barker says it's important to find a therapist who is right for you, especially if you are queer or poly or kinky.

> It's really concerning for me, the number of therapists I've met, who have all kinds of stereotypical and problematic notions around these things. And yet again, this is to be expected because therapists are in the culture, so they're going to be mono-normative, they're going to be heteronormative, unless they've really interrogated that stuff. And even then it will probably slip out sometimes. So, finding a therapist who is within these communities or at least really affirmative around them, a poly-friendly therapist—and there are good lists of those online these days luckily—and finding somebody with expertise around trauma, working with them, that would probably be the best bet.

Some people in crisis or in urgent need of counselling do not feel able to interview a therapist thoroughly or challenge them to be honest about their compatibility. Recommendations from within the community can help, though therapists generally prefer not to treat people who are closely linked to one another. People are often advised to evaluate three or even more therapists before choosing one. It's not unreasonable to ask for a free initial interview to explore if one can work with a particular professional.

Alice's experience is informative. She lives in Singapore, where some therapists reportedly find it hard not to bring their own moral or religious beliefs into the therapy room. Despite that, Alice found people she could work with

> I was incredibly lucky to have found my current therapist. I've been seeing her for almost a year now and together with the help of friends and my partner, I've learnt how to ask for help.

> In the beginning, I was put on two different types of anti-depressant, I hated it as some days I didn't even feel human. The medication affected my creativity and my art but now that I am off it, I can finally see what a mess I was and how the medication actually helped me with simple things like regulating my sleep cycle, which reduced my irrationality.

Before I got off the medication, I had to see another psychiatrist for evaluation and to see if I can start to taper off my medication. A question that struck me was when he asked if I still had the desire to self-harm, especially so since I told him that I am occasionally using needle play as a cathartic release. I told him that, yes I still enjoy needle play but the difference being I want to have a partner in the room that pierces me and that makes a huge difference as oppose to piercing alone. When those words left my mouth, that's when I thought that I was going to be okay even without the medication.

CHAPTER FORTY-SEVEN

Insecurity

If ANXIETY IS about being alert to potential dangers, then our insecurities are a source of fears for our anxiety to get to work on.

Anita Cassidy gives a good illustration of the fact that sometimes when we use the word jealousy what we're actually talking about is *insecurity*.

> I always describe jealousy as green-coloured fear. It's all about the fear that deep down I'm not good enough, and deep down I'm scared of change. So jealousy is, for me, the sense that there is someone else that will replace me, always better than me—and what that means about me and about the relationship I currently share with the person.

Although we often think about insecurity in terms of a relationship with another person, the key issue is often our relationship with ourselves. Jealousy proper is about the sense that one is being undervalued by someone else. Insecurity is about perceptions of self-worth and self-esteem. Thus, as the therapist DK Green says, when we're insecure we're questioning our value, either our intrinsic value or our value to another person.

> It's a fear of being 'less than.' It's very common. If your beloved finds a relationship with another person, it's very common to feel feelings of fear around 'what if they are better or more interesting, or can do this better, or can give that better'. You know, it's often a fear of being less than the new and shiny.

It's easy to see how jealousy and insecurity can be conflated—both are about questions of our worth, and they often go together. For Alice, as for so many people, her expectations of relationships were shaped by her early experiences.

> I've been abandoned all my life. I've always been abandoned. First of all, my father, [then] a series of men who abandoned me as well—that just upped and left. That became a huge issue with me, so I would do anything and everything to keep the peace in that sense. I have an attraction more to older men because of it. At the end of the day, I really just want to go back and be owned and all that stuff, to have a place that I can call home; that's very important to me.

It's not just early experiences either. If we've had relationships where we've been treated badly, we've been dumped suddenly or unceremoniously, or where a partner has deceived us, it has an impact on our self-esteem and that in turn can shape our choice of relationships in the future, as it did Debbie's case.

> The insecurity I've got to figure out might stem from something else, probably past relationships that failed miserably. The jealousy is... I've never actually had to put this into words before... the jealousy is something that the more I see it the less I like myself for it.

But insecurity isn't the sole province of those with low self-esteem. Seb is someone who is successful, good looking, comfortable in his own skin. He has no trouble finding attractive partners. But when he and his wife opened up their relationship he was completely unprepared for the wave of emotions that confronted him.

> Initially I was completely knocked over by how strong the feelings were of— "jealousy" is probably the obvious word, but I would say more "vulnerability", that I was feeling at the beginning. I think for every guy, when you come to open up a relationship, you experience a bit of a wake-up call. This is one of the very few times where the gender scales are well and truly balanced.

Seb's observation was that men and women reacted differently on dating sites to people declaring that they were in an open relationship. Guys encountering non-monogamous women were much more likely to be 'yes, why not?' while women would interrogate the whole situation and their own feelings about it far more closely. They were far more concerned about and alert to, for instance, the possibility that a man might be cheating. The consequence was, in his view, that men were much less given to questioning the non-monogamous women about aspects of women's lives and far readier to suggest a meeting or simply sex.

> When I first started venturing into online dating I would definitely get a level of interaction with people, but at the same time, my wife was getting at least a couple of hundred unprompted messages per day. She didn't have time to even read them all. And even though you know intellectually that this is fine and normal and a welcome rebalancing in at least one area of life, you still need to check you are emotionally okay with that.

Seb's case is a good reminder that however sorted you are, you're still vulnerable. It's simply human. We absorb all sorts of messages from the world around us about what it is to be likeable, attractive, and loveable, and our culture trades in unattainable standards of beauty and success. It sets out to hollow us out.

> I realised that I had an absolute basket of issues to deal with around sex and re-lationships. None of them came from any specific trauma or anything but I had something very good and very positive that I didn't think I would ever experience with anyone who was not my wife. I think there was a huge fear that polyamory would be the end of that, and I wouldn't have anything in its place either. So I kind of froze at the beginning, while I was struggling to deal with the feelings of jealousy and vulnerability. The way I got over the initial hurdle was I broke it down, in as intellectual a fashion as I could, into three components that represented what was making me so nervous and so panicky about it.

> The first component was having to get over what society teaches you—namely that the greatest sin in the world is to desire anybody else if you're in a relationship and to act on that. It felt hugely transgressive to be even having these interactions. It went away quite quickly, once I understood that it was just societal conditioning.

> The second has to do with what terribly poor specimens our male egos are. You start to worry about comparisons when the person you love is now sleeping with somebody else. What if they're better in bed than me? What if they make her happier than I do? What if they are better physically equipped than I am? All of those things.

And the reality is that there's always going to be a lot of people in the world who are better looking than you, who are better physically equipped and who are better equipped in certain ways to satisfy your partner in bed. You can get over that by making your peace with this concept. And if you can, I think it leaves you in a stronger place with regards to relationships generally. And particularly once you start to get some positive feedback about how another partner can make your partner happier, or complement her either physically or mentally or emotionally, then it becomes much easier to deal with. Getting comfortable with this second component of vulnerability took longer, but once I started to understand what I was working with, it became easier.

And then the third component was the fundamental one: that this is the person I love and I am terrified that she will no longer be in my life, because she makes me very happy and I'm terrified of losing her. And that is definitely a risk that you run by being involved in a non-monogamous setup. It's a much lower risk than people might think, but it's still there. Part of accepting a poly setup is accepting that risk exists but also remembering that risk absolutely exists in monogamous relationships as well.

Insecurity is bound up with fear of loss, and our fears generally stem from worrying that we're not good enough. It's not just romantic relationships. People worry in similar ways about friendships or their job.

Some of us cope by avoiding close connections so we never have anything to lose. This is the strategy broadly employed by those whom attachment theory would classify as dismissive/avoidant. We deny ourselves something to protect ourselves from losing it.

Shelly, the Israeli academic working in London, points out that the flip side is to cling onto the thing we fear losing even more tightly.

Possessiveness means 'I need this because it's mine' in which there's the hidden question 'What will happen to me if I don't have that?' That in turn goes back to a self-esteem question and simple questions of self-worth and simple questions of fear of abandonment and fear of replacement, and all of those things that are very classically associated with non-monogamy-related jealousy and with monogamy-related jealousy, of course.

As the writer and relationship therapist Esther Perel has observed, in relationships it's normal to want to feel unique, irreplaceable. That's as true of non-monogamous relationships as monogamous ones. In monogamous relationships people can still feel challenged by a partner's other relationships; with friends, colleagues, parents, children. But with non-monogamy there are even more opportunities to feel insecure if you're predisposed to do so.

Dr Liz Powell suggests we learn from the way we manage our friendships.

> We handle our feelings of insecurity, or our desire to feel securely supported by someone, so differently in romantic relationships than in other relationships. When you have a friend you don't ask your friend to guarantee that they will never be anyone else's best friend. You trust that they're going to still be your friend, they're still going to be there for you, and you recognise that maybe they're not going to be at some point and that's the nature of friendship.

Let's accept that if people can suffer from insecurity in a monogamous setting, consensual non-monogamy multiplies the opportunities to feel insecure. But at least in CNM one can talk about it honestly. There's less pressure to deny other attractions and feelings than there generally is in a monogamous relationship, and so there's less of a gap between what one intuits and what one hears. Too often that gap creates a space into which insecurity can creep.

FEELING MORE SECURE

So WHAT CAN we do to raise our self-esteem, and what can we do to support our partners if they're feeling insecure?

Most of us, by the time we've reached our mid-teens, have had to deal with a Pandora's box of formative experiences. Some of us emerge thinking we're just fab, others that we're irredeemably awful and unlovable. Most of us are somewhere in-between and struggle in one respect or another.

People tend to remember criticism far more readily than they do praise. The brain processes criticism more thoroughly. Criticism often invites change; praise does not. There are good evolutionary reasons for this—the things we learn from criticism may keep us alive.[85]

---

85   'Praise Is Fleeting, but Brickbats We Recall', Alina Tugend, *New York Times,* 23 March 2012.

The social psychologist Prof. Roy Baumneister reckons, broadly, that it takes five instances of something positive happening to balance out one bad thing. The psychological researcher John Gottman reckons there's a similar ratio needed in relationships: five positive interactions to each negative one to keep the relationship viable.

So what can we do to challenge low self-worth and set aside a lifetime of negative messages about ourselves?

1. Identify all your negative thoughts. Write them down. It'll be very hard with some, others will just seem silly. Do it anyway. Writing down our feelings can help turn them from feelings into statements and ideas, and we can challenge those differently.

What's on the list? Not successful? Not good looking? Not thin? Not clever? Not fit? Not lovable? If you were to sit your friends down and show them the list they'd probably be shocked. That wouldn't be how they see you at all. Our friends see the good in us. If we have low self-esteem we tend to see the bad, and we tell ourselves that's the real us. But is it?

2. Now write down some positives. Most of us have to work hard at this. In a culture like the one I grew up in we're taught to avoid self-praise. All the same, write down everything—whether it be skills at sports, in the kitchen, at work, hobbies, kindness to strangers, raising children. If you're stuck ask friends and family. Actually, just ask them anyway. You may be really pleasantly surprised at the positives you come up with. Focus on those every time you're overwhelmed by negative self-perception.

Also bear in mind that just as being too negative is bad for your mental health, so too is being too positive. People who have overwhelmingly positive views about themselves are prone to narcissism. A healthy ratio of positivity about yourself is two or three positive thoughts to one negative.

3. Maintain good boundaries. Distinguish compassionate criticism that genuinely has your wellbeing at its heart from gratuitous negativity. Try to reduce the time you spend with people who are thoughtless and just generally down on you.

Learn to say no to things. It's easy to get steamrollered into doing things we don't want to do and end up feeling overburdened. Downplaying our own needs simply invites others to ignore them or to exploit our good nature. People start to treat us with less respect when we don't maintain good boundaries , but standing up for yourself garners respect, including your own.

As Shelly says, being able to assert our own needs means learning to listen to ourselves.

Having a good sense of yourself and a good relationship with yourself is important. And if you don't have good self-worth, then probably having a high level of dialogue with yourself and being able to acknowledge and map and identify the issues and to create, kind of, the ability to diagnose yourself with, 'what do I need right now?' Do I just need a hug? Do I need to talk through this with someone? Do I need to be angry right now? Do I need to, like, *x*, is that useful for me?

Asserting your own needs doesn't necessarily require action from others. There's plenty we can do for ourselves given the time and resources. Sometimes all we need is to be left to get on with it.

4. *Stop comparing yourself.* This is a road to hell, especially in the social media age. A lot of time and effort goes into creating the impression that celebrities great and small lead perfect lives. Their currency is envy. Their own pain and insecurity are airbrushed out.

It's fine to model yourself after other people to improve qualities you'd like—we could all be kinder, calmer, more patient—but ultimately, as Anita says, you can only do you, albeit a better version of you.

> I tend to see any feelings of jealousy and insecurity as an opportunity to look at myself and how I'm feeling right now about myself, and about reminding myself that actually in this particular dimension there is only one me and there is only one him.

5. *Self-forgiveness and self-compassion.* When we forgive, it is the forgiver who is truly released. When we forgive someone else, remembering that to forgive someone is not the same as to pardon or absolve them, we can move on. That gets more complex where there's self-recrimination because we're on both sides of the equation, both accuser and accused. So when we have been blaming ourselves forgiveness lets us win both ways. Guilt, shame, failure—it's okay. It's the past. Give yourself a hug, picture yourself, and try telling *yourself* 'It's okay. I forgive you.' Forgiveness is about letting go—which doesn't mean we can't learn from it—we simply stop repeating what can amount to internal bullying. It took Yana a while but eventually she was able to go easy on herself.

> I was jealous and insecure when Ivan had just started seeing Alexandra. I was probably upset that we were not spending that much time together any more or maybe

I was thinking that I'm not good enough for Ivan... I am always very self-critical and I am always full of doubts and this sort of arrangement brought everything up and I was struggling with that. Ivan and Alexandra decided to slow down just a little bit and it helped me a lot with my own issues.

6. Self-approval and self-acceptance. Aristotle didn't exactly say 'The whole is greater than the sum of its parts', he said it a little more elaborately as something like 'The whole is a thing beyond a mere totalling up of its various components'[86]. Most of us are more than simply a collection of attributes, positive and negative; all these things and more combine to make something unique. And people who like us usually just like 'us', not the checklist from which we think we're constructed—something Mawar keeps in mind when she's feeling wibbly.

I keep reminding myself that despite me feeling I'm not smart and not pretty he still comes back to me, not just because he was my boyfriend, but because he *wants* to come back with me and he appreciates me.

Let's not minimise the challenges involved in rewriting a lifetime of messages, both absorbed from the world around us and repeated back by us to ourselves. Change is hard. It's not impossible. We need to be an active participant in addressing our issues.

However, it's also incredibly useful to have help and support.

WHAT WE CAN DO TO HELP SOMEONE OVERCOME INSECURITY

As with anxiety, perhaps the most valuable thing we can do for a partner suffering from insecurity is to offer reassurance.

Reassurance cropped up numerous times in conversations with consensually non-monogamous people. Many were either dealing with insecurity themselves or helping partners through it. Xena, from Indonesia, supported her husband after she'd started a new relationship.

It was a little bit rocky last year. He felt a little bit insecure when I was very much in love with my boyfriend. I gave him more attention, more love in a sense with

---

86   To be even more accurate; "...many things have a plurality of parts and are not merely a complete aggregate but instead some kind of a whole beyond its parts..." Aristotle, *Metaphysics* 8.6—except all in Greek, obvs.

compassion, and I always try to be there and ask him 'How are you doing?' 'How do you feel?' I try to spend more time with him because I know this is what he needs. When you're together for 19 years you sort of know that you are solid. I think everything can be solved with an understanding, compassion, and trying to listen and read between the lines of what your partner really needs.

When Alexandra started dating Ivan she was new to consensual non-monogamy, and she struggled to deal with worries about abandonment.

> There was always this nagging thought that if he's seeing other girls again, then what if he abandons me? But I think Ivan helped me deal with that very early on because he said I only wish to see Yana and one other person, that being me, because he didn't have time for another relationship. So, that was kind of reassuring for me.

For Debbie there was the feeling that if she allowed herself to act on her insecurity it would damage her relationship and provoke even more insecurity.

> I don't have a lot of time that I get to spend with my partner sometimes, and it feels like it's something that's going to throw that off even more, so there'll be even less time spent [together]. I'm learning that's a silly reaction to have because, even when we're not spending time together, every now and then he'll send me a stupid little text or some other message that lets me know 'Hey, I'm still thinking about you'.

It's hard to ignore Yana's self-recrimination 'I am always very self-critical and I am always full of doubts' or Debbie's 'Insecurity is something I need to deal with and jealousy is something that shouldn't be there at all'. Both are unnecessary but illuminating. No one likes to feel jealous. It's a cancerous 'emotion'. It eats away at us. It consumes us. But self-recrimination gets in the way, stops us pulling apart the layers of feelings that add up to what we label jealousy, and stops us analysing what is there and dealing with the things one by one. It's even less helpful when people shame us for our feelings, be they what we call jealousy or insecurity, anxiety or anything else. Let's not lose sight of the fact that anxiety and insecurity are mental wellbeing issues. DK Green again:

> For some people, their history, their life may have framed it so that they are secure with one person in a relationship and any other form of multiple relationships

will make them feel insecure. And that is a valid place. I don't want to undermine that. Insecurity is tossed about as a way of [criticising or denigrating someone]; "Oh, you're just being insecure." It's an insulting, derogatory thing. But actually we all need security and to feel secure in a relationship, whether that be with one, two, or many.

There is a bit of a cult of self-reliance, a bordering-on-the-brutal 'this is your stuff, deal with it' attitude, in parts of the CNM community. This may reflect modern CNM's origins in the US, where individualism and personal responsibility are prized and collectivism[87] tends to be denigrated. The importance of offering reassurance, for instance, was referenced less often by the North Americans I interviewed than people elsewhere. Those from Europe and Asia were more likely to emphasise collective or communal support.

The value of interdependence is recognised in attachment theory research and in its findings that it's possible to earn security. Reassurance is an important part of that. Through having a partner who is a rock, who acts securely and whose approach to the relationship is secure, we can absorb and internalise secure traits.

So let's have a brief look at some things to bear in mind when looking for help from partners or trying to provide a partner help.

Firstly, ascribing intent or motives to someone's actions can sound like blame. 'You're making me feel...' or 'You're being...' may put the other person on the defensive. That will divert time and energy into fault finding that could otherwise be poured into finding a solution.

Secondly, it's fine to talk about your fears. 'I worry that you'll forget me, won't love me as much, fancy her more....' Yes that's making yourself vulnerable, but vulnerability is a part of loving relationships. All you need to know is that your partner will respect that.

Thirdly, it's good to be clear about one's needs. You could say 'When you get excited when you're seeing someone new, I feel *x*,' but that is offering a problem rather than a solution. If you've worked through your feelings to the extent that you know, for instance that you're feeling neglected or forgotten, you might want to start asking yourself what you would *like* to have happen. 'When you're excited about a new

87 The American Psycological Association contrasts collectivism "a social or cultural tradition, ideology, or personal outlook that emphasizes the unity of the group or community rather than each person's individuality. Most Asian, African, and South American societies tend to put more value on collectivism than do western societies, insofar as they stress cooperation, communalism, constructive interdependence, and conformity to cultural roles and mores," with individualism.

relationship I'd like you to remember us too and make time for us to go out for dinner/ have more sex/go for walks together/say how much we mean to each other.'

Likewise if you're supporting someone who is struggling with insecurity, you can encourage them to talk about their needs and worries and listen without judgement. Once you know what they're dealing with you will know better how to reassure them. 'Of course I don't want to run off,' or 'No one is going to replace you.' Or, 'Akinyi, no one in the whole world is better than you at being Akinyi.'

The more you can demonstrate that someone has been heard and understood, the more specifically you can respond to someone's fears and needs. And the more you support your words with action, the more effective the reassurance will be. Above all, if you're fundamentally secure in your relationships (acknowledging that securely attached people have their own moments of insecurity), mirroring that back to an insecure loved one can help bring about change.

CHAPTER FORTY-EIGHT

Compersion

THE WORD *COMPERSION* was apparently coined in the San-Francisco-based Kerista community in the 1970s.[88] According to one account the word was the result of a session with Kerista's alphabet board, similar to a Ouija board, where two or more members would each place a finger inside a cup that would then be steered around 'via subconscious ideomotor activity'. They were apparently trying to come up with a word for the feeling of happiness or joy they experienced at a lover's happiness from loving or making love with others.

Another note on the Kerista website traces the word to a French term "*comperage* to denote the 'brother-in-law' relationship among South American Indians - including sexual sharing of wives" noted by the anthropologist Claude Levi Strauss "quoting a 17th century French Capuchin missionary who worked with Brazilian Indians, Yves d'Evreux".[89]

The word stuck; apparently there was a gap in the linguistic market as *jealousy* was one of the few emotion-describing words in English that didn't have an antonym or opposite. Today 'compersion' is standard argot in the CNM world.

If compersion sounds a bit sententious to some ears, that probably explains why the British poly community borrowed or came up with its own word: frubble (*n.*), or frubbly (*a.*) or to frubble (*v.*) or even frub (*n.*). If that sounds a bit silly it's because the Brit poly scene is rather less Deepak Chopra and rather more Monty Python, Douglas Adams, and Terry Pratchett.

---

88 Before you decry compersion as a neologism, the word 'empathy' has only been with us since 1908 when it was coined as a translation for the German *Einfühlung* (feeling into), which was itself only minted in 1858 by the German philosopher Rudolf Lotze. (Hat tip to Shantigarbha!)

89 http://kerista.com/compersion.html

Dr Meg-John Barker:

Well, I liked the story of the UK version of compersion. Because the British folks were kind of hearing about compersion from the US and thinking this sounded like a very silly pseudo-scientific name. So they wanted to come up with something more British and a person I knew came up with the word frubbly as a joke, like we could call it that and it sounds like a kind of Blackadder reference or something.

But, piss-taking aside, the concept of compersion is genuinely interesting on a number of levels. When I interviewed Dr. Dylan Selterman about his research into consensual non-monogamy I asked him what single thing had really made him sit up and think. His answer was something he hadn't formally researched but that he had often encountered anecdotally:

This idea of compersion is really fascinating to me. I remember one of my friends described this years ago, he said, 'When I see my wife and she's hooking up with someone, it fills me with such pleasure to see that and to know that'. And that was not something that I had even imagined was possible before, that this could be a real thing. And we see it all over the world, cross culturally. We see it in all types of demographics. So it strikes me that there's a lot of potential here for people to move toward relationship arrangements that make them really, really happy, and that the negative things we would normally associate with this type of relationship arrangement, not only are they not as bad as we thought, but it could go in exactly the opposite direction.

And at first when I heard that, I thought probably I'll never experience this, you know, this is not something that I'm capable of. But I've since changed my mind. I've since believed that any of us and all of us are capable of feeling this type of thing. And the idea of compersion, by the way, is something that also hasn't really been studied very well in the scientific literature. There's a much stronger focus on jealousy. And the idea is that if you have low amounts of jealousy, then you are more comfortable. But I don't think that fully captures the nuance of that particular emotional experience.

He's right, both in that compersion is fascinating and in that it's more than simply not experiencing jealousy. But is it all that amazing? Well yes and no. The core idea of feeling joy at someone else's joy, and happiness at their happiness, is hardly new.

Buddhists also have an term for it: *mudita*. If your friend who has been single and lonely for many years and had resigned themselves to a solitary life meets someone wonderful, what do you feel for them? Most of us would find ourselves being lifted by their happiness. It's the opposite, if you like, not necessarily of jealousy but of *schadenfreude* (taking pleasure, joy, or satisfaction from someone else's humiliation or misfortune)—a terrible (though occasionally delicious) feeling but a great, great word.

So compersion in that sense is not new. What is socially novel is that it's applied to our partner's enjoyment of romance and sex with another.

If jealousy is, in some sense, a threat response and even 'mate-guarding' behaviour, compersion first and foremost shows that it's not the only response. We may be wired to respond to threats, but could it be that what we do or don't perceive as a social threat is shaped primarily by society and socialisation, not biology?

Take the concept of family honour. It's not static in space and time. These days it's alien in most of the West, but two hundred-odd years ago it was very much a feature of respectable society. In Jane Austen's *Pride and Prejudice* the Bennett sisters worry that their youngest sibling Lydia's elopement with the disreputable Mr Wickham will ruin their family name and make them all unmarriable. An extreme form of 'family honour' results in the gruesome practice of honour killing associated with societies from Syria to the Indian subcontinent and with their expatriate communities.[90] If you lose face and status in your society for not acting a certain way, the pressure to conform is great.

By the same token, social attitudes towards jealousy differ from place to place and from time to time. In some societies tolerating your partner being hit on by another might be perceived not just as a threat to your relationship, but to your own reputation. Doing nothing could be seen as weak and unattractive, and your partner might actually expect you to act jealous and do the whole chest-thumping, mate-guarding thang.

So if the rules of society change so that a partner taking another lover is neither a threat to the relationship nor to one's social standing, is a threat response still needed? Arguably not. In short, change the social rules and it would seem you can change when jealousy comes out to play.

What's more, as Dylan Selterman has observed, people find strategies to deal with jealousy. Finding a path to, and experiencing, compersion can form part of that.

> There's an association between the closeness and intimacy that people have with their partners' 'others' and feeling less jealousy. So in other words, if my partner has other partners and I feel very close and intimate with them, then I feel less

---

90   It's worth pointing out that though it's mostly recorded in the Muslim community it's not exclusive to it, with instances of Sikh families also carrying out honour killings, while in Muslim-majority Malaysia and Indonesia and in the Mahgreb it's extremely rare.

jealousy. And that seems to be one of the big strategies, especially in a polyamorous context where you've multiple loves—like you love your partner but you also love these other people, and they love their other partners, and it is effective I guess in reducing jealousy in the sense that you're not seeing them as competition. You're not seeing them as A. N. Other, you're seeing them as part of your own self, your own self-concept.

Why would people feel like this? Is it a strategy of self-delusion to trick the brain into not experiencing jealousy or the raft of negative feelings that gets bundled up with it? Are we really to believe that people go around, metaphorically speaking, with their fingers in their ears going 'la la la, everything's fine,' maintaining a fragile illusion of happiness?

I suspect not. It's more likely, surely, that people who feel compersion actually get an emotional payoff from it and that goes beyond shuffling off the stress and negative feelings (though it's worth noting that it's perfectly possible to feel both compersion and anxiety and/or insecurity simultaneously). And, don't forget, compersion can be returned with partners taking pleasure in *your* happy relationships with others. Obviously not everyone's relationship with their metamours is such that they'll feel respected and supported by the people with whom they share lovers. However, as I've said elsewhere, for some people the feeling that one is part of something bigger than oneself, that sense of belonging, that a web of intimate relationships is stronger than the line joining two points, is a powerful one.

~~Loves Kills~~ Love Skills

CHAPTER FORTY-NINE

Healthy Relationships

THERE'S A LOT of advice out there about how to build and maintain healthy relationships, and plenty of it applies to both monogamous and non-monogamous situations. Indeed a lot of the advice applies to our non-romantic/-sexual connections as much as to the intimate. It steers us towards the skills we need for being good people and getting on with others.

To quote the philosopher and keen student of the human condition, RuPaul, "If you can't love yourself how in the hell are you gonna love somebody else?", but having a healthy relationship with oneself is definitely a good starting point if you want to have *healthy* relationships with others.

But as well as asking 'Do I love myself?', an important but distinct question is 'Do I like myself?'

'Do I love myself?' challenges us to ask whether we value ourselves, whether we have self-respect, good boundaries, a willingness to make sure our needs are met and to care about ourselves.

'Do I like myself?' is really a question about self-approval. Do we treat others well, are we kind, generous, trustworthy, do we contribute something, do we have abilities that we would admire in others, have we achieved something, are we nice?

So, once again, ask 'Do I like myself?' and whether the answer is 'yes,' 'no' or 'I'm the bleedin' curate's egg, me,' the next question is 'why?'

These are hard questions. What I'm getting at is that as humans we have a tendency to externalise internal conflicts. Criticism, for instance, is more painful if we have an inner critic that has already left parts of us bruised and tender (perhaps it's an internalised parent or teacher—Freud might have called it the superego, astrologers will tell you it's the planet Saturn!). If we feel lacking it's harder to be generous. If we're at war with ourselves we're that much more likely to go to war with others. If we've suffered trauma, those unresolved traumatised parts of ourselves may emerge during the conflicts that to some degree characterise almost every relationship, and those traumatised parts may decide to fight, flee, freeze or fawn even when our conscious, rational, everyday self doesn't want to.

In the next few chapters we'll have a look at some of the skills and practices (listed below) that can help to nurture and sustain healthy relationships. They're useful in monogamous relationships too, but consensually non-monogamous people typically either make more use of them or assume they do.

Some of these are pretty much baked into CNM and can offer food for thought for everyone. Others are skills we can all develop with practice and a little help from those who have gone before us.

Here are a few.

1. *Communication*. Most of us think we know how to communicate and that we communicate well, but it's amazing, isn't it, how often communication misfires or completely breaks down.

There's a lot more to communicating than simply talking to someone or firing off an email. Our words often paint us, or someone else, into a corner, and then communication ceases to be effective. Moreover, expressing ourselves effectively is only one half of communicating. The other half is *listening* effectively, and one could argue that this is the half that most people are worse at. We'll look at communications skills at some length and, in particular, at the approach known as non-violent communication.

2. *Acceptance*. Learn to accept and deal with change. Change can be great if you want novelty and variety but pretty damn scary if you're someone who craves routine and stability. However change, like death and taxes, is one of those things you can treat as a certainty. We can't avoid it. One of the most important lessons we learn is when we can resist change, when we can try to influence it, and when we simply have to surrender to it. It's worthwhile, as Shelly says, to recognise from the outset that the relationship you have now is not the same relationship that you're going to have in five years' time.

> [There needs to be] flexibility in everything. So you need the willingness and the ability to meet changing needs and circumstances and not be thrown back by the need to change a predesignated rule. I think that's important; the ability to recognise that reality is changing, you're changing, your partners are changing, and what you agreed on day one isn't going to be what's needed on day two or three or day seven hundred and thirty.

3. *Realism.* Don't expect someone to be your everything. This is one of those things that most non-monogamous people have realised (as discussed already) and that some monogamous people, who wonder why their partners aren't perfect, might take note of.

How many relationships do we begin where we see 'the potential' in someone—or someone sees 'the potential' in us? How often does that mean trying to shape a beloved into what someone else wants them to be rather than what they themselves want, or are? We don't have to play that game. Of course we should address those unwelcome parts of ourselves that cause us and others pain and unhappiness, but we don't need to turn someone, or be turned ourselves, into a 'walkin', talkin', livin' doll.' Kevin Patterson:

> I think the willingness to let go of the parts of our relationship that don't work is a good way to build healthy relationships: just understanding what it is that you need and what it is you have to offer, and being forthright about that, so that you're on the same page with the person you're with.

4. *Balance.* Make sure everyone's needs are being met. That includes your own. Self-care is important and it doesn't have to be selfish. Unfortunately, the concept of 'self-care' has been hijacked by marketeers who sell people 'self-care' in the form of shopping, or expensive spa treatments. 'Unfortunately' both because it trivialises the idea and because there is evidence that buying into the values of the cult(ure) of consumerism is linked to depression and other symptoms of poor mental health.[91]

What self-care means, as broadly set out in the chapter on mental health, will be different for different people depending on their tastes, abilities and means. It includes avoiding doing things that make you feel worse (perhaps staring at your screens pointlessly or spending time socially with people whose company you don't enjoy). It can mean eating healthily, sleeping well, and exercising. It can mean getting regular doctor's checkups and the medical attention you need. It can mean time with loved ones, time to relax, time to enjoy yourself, time on your own. It can mean laughing and creating happy memories! It can even mean, for those that can afford such things, shopping and a day at the spa. Just make sure that it's *your* idea of treating yourself and not the idea of some marketing spod, and that you actually feel better as a result—and not just for a couple of hours.

---

91   'Cuing Consumerism: Situational Materialism Undermines Personal and Social Well-Being', Monika A. Bauer, James E. B. Wilkie, Jung K. Kim, Galen V. Bodenhausen, Northwestern University, *Psychological Science*, 16 Mar 2012. https://journals.sagepub.com/doi/abs/10.1177/0956797611429579

Being fair to, caring for, and meeting the needs of the important people in your life is equally critical. Relationships are best when they're a two-way street.

5. Speak your partners' love languages. Gary Chapman's idea that people are predisposed to receive love and affection through their own particular 'love languages'—which he listed as *words of affirmation, acts of service, gifts, quality time,* and *touch*—still offers a useful framework thirty years after he first articulated it.[92] Whatever your partner's preferred love language, try to show them affection regularly. And make sure your positive interactions outweigh your negative ones several times over.

6. Trust. Build it. Do what you say you're going to do. Keep appointments. Be on time. Be honest. Understand that trust develops slowly and evaporates fast.

7. Fight nicely. There's no point pretending that you'll never have disagreements. Avoiding the work of resolving them doesn't make for good relationships any more than repeatedly warring over them. Fighting nicely is an art, like communicating well. You know you've fought well when the issue is settled and everyone genuinely feels better for it.

8. Get a life. It's pretty daunting when the most important thing in a partner's life is you. In contrast it's almost always inspiring to be in the company of a person on a mission. Strong interests outside of your relationships and an equally strong sense of purpose are very attractive. Just make sure you can change course if you or your partners' needs require it.

9. Authenticity. Ask the real you to show up. This goes back to the question about liking yourself. People who like themselves are generally easy to like, and they are always ready to bring their real selves to the party. Yes, most of us have something *about* ourselves that we don't like. We can always treat that as an invitation to change.

---

92   Queer activists have proposed additional love languages including *acts of solidarity and belief, acts of emotional labour* and *Commitment to Personal Healing and Growth*

CHAPTER FIFTY

Being 'Fair'

The notion of fairness is frequently invoked in families, at the workplace, and in people's interactions with neighbours, friends and even strangers. For instance, our spouse becomes sour if we do not bear a fair share of family responsibilities. Our children are extremely unhappy and envious if they receive less attention and gifts than their brothers and sisters. We do not like those among our colleagues who persistently escape doing their share of important yet inconvenient departmental activities.[93]

—Ernst Fehr & Klaus M. Schmidt, *'Theories of Fairness and Reciprocity'*

AFTER 'I COULDN'T be non-monogamous, I'd get jealous,' one of the most common reservations people express is about fairness. It's often framed as 'I'm not sure I could be fair to everyone,' though I do wonder whether that's another way of expressing worries about 'I'm not sure I'd get all my needs met,' or 'What if they're so busy with other people they're not fair to me?'

It's a problem most of us have to deal with in other contexts. If you have children, if you care for parents, if you have a wide circle of friends some of whom are struggling with illness or divorce (or just the crushing despair of living in a terrible world hurtling towards its doom in an ecological apocalypse/economic meltdown/morass

---

93 'Theories of Fairness and Reciprocity -- Evidence and Economic Applications', Ernst Fehr, University of Zurich and CEPR; Klaus M. Schmidt, University of Munich and CEPR.Published in *Advances in Economics and Econometrics, Econometric Society Monographs, Eighth World Congress*, Mathias Dewatripont, Lars Peter Hansen, and Stephen J Turnovsky (2003), , Vol. 1 pp 208-257.

of mutual cultural incomprehension), you'll know what it's like trying to juggle everyone's needs.

Our experience teaches us that there are times when that's easy and times when we run out of energy and hours in the day. However, few of us, on those wonderful but all too rare occasions when we meet a potential new best friend, go 'Hey, you seem great but I'm afraid I have too many friends already.' Most of us manage to make room. As Seb says:

> You're not dealing with a cake of a certain size that has to be cut a certain number of ways, that if you have three people, then they can each get a third and if you have four people, they can each get a quarter. That's not how it works. The idea is that the cake expands.

Those who know me know just how much I like a good cake metaphor, almost as much, indeed, as I like non-metaphorical cake. Seb is right. The cake can expand. However, to extend the metaphor if not the cake, cakes can rise too much and collapse in on themselves too.

> I know people who are very uncomfortable if you propose anything like a monogamous setup. More likely there are people whose bandwidth for extra partners is limited or who need a certain minimum of time and affection and availability for them to consider being in a poly relationship. It's just a case of lots and lots of communication and being very clear about what you want and don't want out of the relationship. So, honest communication—and trying to not slice up something finite so that everybody gets a little bit less than what they want, but to effectively grow these relationships so that they're able to meet the needs of multiple people.

That brings me back to my earlier point that while love may be infinite time is not, nor are energy and resources. One's emotional capacity can also ebb and flow. To this extent the foundation of fairness is knowing one's own capacity to give of oneself to other people—all the people that one loves and has responsibilities to.

Emotional responsibilities are like any others, in that it is better to be upfront and set one's limits than take on too much and let people down. This is one of the challenges of honest communication.

This need for communication is a point echoed by Nathan. Indeed Nathan is the first to acknowledge that he sounds a bit like a broken record when it comes to polyamory and communication. It's almost always the tool of first resort, not least because in managing multiple relationships, romantic or non-romantic, you need the best possible information to decide how to respond and how to allot your time and energy.

> It's such a dynamic situation—you have to check in with each person over and over and over. You just pop in and you go 'hey, you doing alright?' and they'll say 'yeah' and you kind of have to take their word for it. Sometimes it's appropriate to badger it out of them, and sometimes it's appropriate to just leave it because you know they just need some time to work it through.

> There is no prescription, there's no formula. The only thing you can do is check in and if you feel that something's changed or something needs to change, communicate it. I'm getting really tired of saying it, but it all comes back to communication and getting to it way early on. I know it's the truth and I'm not always the best at it, but it's the thing that solved the most problems for me.

There are different models for fairness. As the economists I quoted at the beginning of this chapter say, economic arguments about fairness are rooted in social ideas about fairness because economics and society and relationships are hard to disentangle. There's strong evidence that in highly regulated, impersonal markets, self-interest dominates but in informal economies where human relationships (what the Chinese might call 关系, guānxì) matter and which are culturally far more important than mere contracts, concerns about fairness loom larger. Consider, for a moment, business arrangements involving friends and relatives, where people tend to want to be scrupulously fair (if they're willing to do business with friends and family at all) because the relationship is on the line if a deal is perceived to be unfair or turns sour.

In managing close relationships, there are other approaches to fairness. Some are based on strict proportionality: 'I spend the same amount of time with each of my partners'. Some might be based on need: 'I spend more time with José because he's been struggling since losing his job.' It might be reciprocity: 'I choose to spend more time with Enemene because she is always there for me.' Or allotting time based on the closeness of the connection: 'David is my soul mate so naturally I spend most of my time with him. Abby is a more casual thing and, anyway, she has other partners she's more committed to.' There's also self-interest, which isn't really about fairness at all: 'I mainly hang out with Janine because she's hot, she has a high disposable income and she's super fun.'

Many people work on a mix of some or all of the above. It's not a precise science. Most people seem to go with what works. However, what works when everyone is doing okay may stop working when they're not, and at that point people are forced to confront their limitations. With cake, biting off more than one can chew is rarely a bad thing, but with relationships it can lead to disappointment and sometimes to people being badly let down.

How many relationships can you manage?

It all comes down to a simple formula: $x/y^2\text{-}r = w^3z$.

Joke. I just made that up. Truth is, there is no simple formula. Sorry.

However, some academics, notably the anthropologist Robin Dunbar, have investigated the number of close connections we're able to maintain. 'Dunbar's number' has become a near-ubiquitous reference point. He posits that while we (on average) may be able to recognise up to 1500 people, give or take, at any point in time no more than 500 will count as acquaintances, 150 as meaningful relationships, 50 as friends, 15 as good friends, and five as close connections. He argues that this pattern has shown up regularly throughout history, from the structures of Roman legions to the effective units in modern corporations. Company-size military units are typically around 150 strong and subdivide from there, and businesses are starting to cap staff numbers for a given building at around the same number. Dunbar, who started by studying animals and progressed to humans, also posits that the size of any social animal's social group is determined by the size of their neocortex. So for monkeys, the corresponding numbers are found to be lower than for humans.

But whether your neocortex is simply 'small but perfectly formed' or positively 'Oh My God!', you surely have limits to the number of close relationships you can manage. Unless you're Bill Clinton or live in Beverley Hills, those numbers probably aren't too far from the ones Dunbar put forward.

It would be interesting to see some quantitative research into consensual non-monogamy and whether it influences the number and quality of connections that people maintain. My suspicion is that among CNM people, much of the social space typically occupied by close friends in monogamous situations is given over to partners and other intimates—and that rather than people's inner circles expanding, their nature changes.

Clearly some people don't want to maintain a romantic and/or sexual relationship with someone unless they're part of that inner core, while others will settle for a lesser degree of closeness.

It's a useful exercise to look at one's life and ask how many close friendships you can maintain. That's probably a good indication of the total number of close relationships of any sort you can manage. However it's also worth asking whether you're okay with a slot or two or three in your inner circles currently occupied by good or close friends being taken over by romantic partners.

On the other hand, some would argue that having several close, intimate, romantic relationships gives them a degree of support and energy that they simply don't get from close non-romantic connections, and that because of this they have the ability to take on more. Nevertheless, some people in the poly community will turn down new connections by saying they are already 'polysaturated.'

WHAT WE CAN ALL LEARN

IT KEEPS COMING back to the same things in many ways: know yourself, understand the extent and the limits of your capacity to love and support others, make your own needs plain, endeavour to listen to and understand those of others, and above all, communicate.

There's little difference between doing that in a monogamous and in a non-monogamous setting. Where non-monogamous people score is often that they have no choice but to communicate, as we shall see.

CHAPTER FIFTY-ONE

Communication

Instead of offering empathy we often have a strong urge to give advice or reassurance and to explain our own position or feeling. Empathy, however, calls upon us to empty our mind and listen to others with our whole being.

— *Marshall Rosenberg*

I know it's big and scary but just communicate. That is the single biggest tool that all of my relationships have had that have made them better, made them longer, made them more fulfilling. Tell them what you think. If things are going well, you have to communicate it. If things are going badly you really have to communicate it, really, a lot. It's big and scary but it's worth it. It pays dividends.

— *Nathan*

IF THERE ARE superpowers that most consensually non-monogamous people rely on, or try to develop, one of them is surely communication.

Our development of language as a means to communicate complex ideas distinguishes us from other animals, has allowed humans to collaborate with one another and has made us masters of our environment (albeit with mixed consequences). It's generally accepted that we as a species developed big brains because of the need to process and manage both the complexities of group living and the sophisticated communication tools that facilitated it. Consensual non-monogamy certainly puts both of these core human abilities to the test.

Monogamy is complicated enough for most people. Consensual non-monogamy adds to that complexity. But that's not all. As already pointed out, there's no cultural blueprint yet for how to manage a consensual non-monogamous life, no set of unspoken rules that people absorb as they grow up, so none that we can take for granted to guide our dealings with other people. CNM is not a set menu, it's not even a buffet, it's an entire city full of restaurants. You get to choose what and who suits you. However, that also means it's essential to make sure you're on the same page as the people you're dating. Everyone has wants and needs and expectations and, with CNM, there's a very real possibility those could clash. Unless your telepathy is much better than mine you'll need to communicate explicitly and verbally. It also means you'll have to negotiate where people's different wants, needs and expectations impinge on, or conflict with, one another.

There's also the fact that, as Morgan puts it, poly culture typically encourages people to 'do a lot more talking and exploration of the self.'

So communication (along with negotiation) is an essential skill in CNM. It's one that almost all of us assume we already have. After all, we can talk, therefore we can communicate, right? You *would* have thought so, wouldn't you? And yet people constantly miscommunicate, often with unfortunate consequences.

The Dunning-Kruger Effect: As we begin to learn about something we scale Mt. Stupid, but some of us are quite content to stay up there just to enjoy the view.

Though I've been a writer and journalist for most of my life, I've come to accept that not only will I never stop learning how to do what I do better, but also that, however hard I try, there's a chance that what I'm trying to communicate will be misunderstood or misconstrued.

Lots of us need professional communication skills: journalists, salespeople, doctors and nurses and consultants; therapists and teachers; lawyers, politicians, military and business leaders. But does being a communicator mean we can manage a difficult discussion with a partner well? Not necessarily. There are many forms of communication. Just because we've mastered one doesn't mean we've mastered them all. It's a little like learning a language or a musical instrument. Once you've learned one it makes learning another easier, but it doesn't confer mastery. Communicating in relationships is its own skill—one most of us are never taught. We just pick up what we know from our environment: parents, friends, movies and drama.

And though we tend to assume that people are people wherever they are, feelings and the way they're expressed vary from culture to culture and from one age to another. Some are more comfortable with expressing emotion than others. For instance, the Inuit make a point of never getting angry with their children and teach them from a young age not to display anger or frustration.[94]

As a result different people learn different rules and approaches about how to display emotion, what emotions are considered acceptable, and how one talks about them... or doesn't. In a 2013 poll the Gallup survey organisation asked people around the world to record which of ten emotions (five 'positive', five 'negative') they had experienced the previous day. The Philippines scored the most (60% experienced the full range of emotions), Singapore scored the least (36%).[95] Indeed, one element in Singapore's school curriculum is rather unusual: 'emotional and social learning.'

Vincent and Mia both, to some extent, typify that conflicted Singaporean relationship with feelings and their communication. He favours a high degree of disclosure but is not very forthcoming emotionally; she's more private about what she might do but wants to discuss feelings.

> I guess communication is harder for me than it is for her. I come from a family that is more stoic. So my parents don't really talk about things like emotions. They don't express themselves very well. So, between me and her, she is normally the one who's asking me about what happened, how do I feel, what's going to happen next, that sort of thing.

---

94   'How Inuit Parents Teach Kids To Control Their Anger', National Public Radio (US), 13 Mar 2019. https://www.npr.org/sections/goatsandsoda/2019/03/13/685533353/a-playful-way-to-teach-kids-to-control-their-anger

95   The US scored 54%, the UK 49%, Lithuania 37%, Russia 38%, South Korea 42%, India 44%, China 46%, Nigeria 50%, France 52%, Spain 53%, Bahrain 56%. Most Asian countries score low, as does Eastern Europe, most Arab and Latin American counties score higher, while Africa and Western Europe show a broad spread.

For both of them communication has been a learning process. If you don't get it by osmosis from your family and if it's not something that is there in the ether around you, then what's the answer? The alternative is conscious effort.

> What I have done consciously, over time, is to not over-react to everything he tells me. And that gives him a safe zone to talk freely with me as well. I think one of the reasons that he kept a lot of things to himself was that I tend to escalate things very quickly. For instance if he said he really liked the way her boobs looked, it would seem to become 'Oh so you don't like my boobs' when he wasn't actually saying that. So giving him that safe space to speak freely is what I think helped. You need to give the other person the freedom to express themselves.

Again, perhaps modern America has shown its influence. To an outsider it appears, at least superficially, to be a confessional culture. Guests open up on Oprah's couch, celebrity relationships play out on a public stage, seeing a therapist is less a taboo than a conversation starter. It's all very upfront.

Yet the 'let it all hang out' public confession would be alien and uncomfortable to people in many parts of the world. Even for Brits of a certain stripe it's all pretty horrifying. Displays of emotion that are appropriate and encouraged in some cultures can be seen as inappropriate or shameful in others. Many of us are neither given the language nor the permission to discuss feelings. There's no lit pathway.

Even people from the same country and of the same generation may differ in their styles of communication depending on their upbringing. Shyam and Rati are both ethnic Malayalee from India's Malabar Coast and speak Malayalam and English. However while Shyam grew up in a quiet village deep in the countryside, Rati spent much of her childhood in India's hectic business capital Mumbai. Their personalities and their styles of communication reflect that. Rati is passionate and fiery, Shyam's nature far softer and more emollient (they also both make me laugh a lot). It means that Rati has had to adjust the way she talks to Shyam if she wants the two of them to engage.

> *Rati:* There are different ways to approach the communication, but, I think you have to really know when to back away when you're angry or even jealous or even when you tell the other person 'I'm hurt' if you don't say it the right way, in a certain way it's really going to damage the relationship. And it gets even more complex when you have more than one partner.

> *Shyam:* I think, one most important thing is respect. Initially, for me, one of the problems was that she grew up in Mumbai. I pretty much grew up in a village and

even here I don't use, like, even 'fuck you'. I don't use that kind of words in a normal context even to a friend or in a relationship and I get angry.

Rati: I know he's very sensitive about words, but so far I've only been allowed to call
him *pundai*, which is a Tamil word for pussy. And I use it in a funny sort of way. But
if I'm angry, and even if I see like today we actually got into an argument and I said,
'You should be fucking grateful.' And just because I said 'fucking' it was quite bad.

It's interesting, isn't it, how two people who love each other can have very different registers when it comes to communicating. For instance, some of us find swearing
cathartic. It can be a way to relieve pain or stress or to give something emphasis. But
for a person being sworn at, especially if they're not given to swearing, it can feel like
being assaulted.

A lot of the emotion that we can pour into our communications may reflect how
we feel, but it can easily become an obstacle. Confronted by someone in a charged situation we focus on expressing our feelings rather than securing what we need.

For instance, if we feel powerless we might puff ourselves up through anger, or we
might try to bully the other person. If we're hurt we sometimes focus on getting the
other person to feel our pain not by allowing them to empathise but by reflecting the
pain back onto them in the form of verbal barbs and accusations.

Sometimes we ensure that we're heard at the expense of our being listened to.

For this reason, this chapter is going to focus on communication that isn't just
aimed at everyone being heard, it's going to be very much about results. In a relationship, that typically means ensuring that we're understood as well as that we understand our partners. At the heart of that it's about ensuring that our needs and those of
everyone else involved are met.

NONVIOLENT COMMUNICATION

I FIRST MET Chris when we were students together in the 1980s. Even then, though he's
very modest about it, he had great powers of empathy. He was an excellent listener
and one sensed he drew upon an inner well of compassion. Some ten years later, having been a Buddhist since his younger days, he decided to be ordained as a Dharm-
achari monk. He took the name Shantigarbha, which translates as 'seed of peace,' and
he has become an authority on Nonviolent Communication (NVC).

Nonviolent Communication emerged as a peacebuilding tool in the 1960s. The
originator of the idea, the American psychologist Marshall Rosenberg, saw in conflict

not competing needs but competing strategies to obtain those needs. He felt that human needs themselves were not inimical to one another.

The qualities that NVC encourages are **empathy**, **honesty**, **compassion** and **collaboration**. So how to achieve this? Shantigarbha thinks we concentrate too much on getting what we want rather than building the relationships that will turn conflict into a positive process—and thereby get us the best result.

> It means focusing on the relationship, the quality of connection, rather than the outcome, focusing on the quality of connection that will lead to everybody's needs being addressed, everybody's needs being valued.

In Shantigarbha's book *'I'll Meet You There'*,[96] a book I can wholeheartedly recommend, he opens with an account of a mediation session in Nigeria where two communities, one Christian, one Muslim, had been in conflict over the allocation of stalls in a marketplace. A number of people had been killed, and both sides initially saw the attempt to bring them together for talks as an opportunity to air grievances. It was wholly understandable. Everybody had lost someone or knew someone who had lost someone.

What the mediators strove to do was to get both sides to focus on what they needed, not on recrimination. Even so, when one side was finally encouraged to stop blaming the other for long enough to say what it was they were after, primarily security, their foes could only respond with more expressions of anger and pain. It took effort by the mediators to finally get each side to repeat what the other needed, to show they had listened.

It was powerful stuff. You may recognize this practice of repeating back what the other party said, to make it clear that you heard them correctly, as the NVC technique of *active listening*.

We all have needs. When we realise that others have them too and we acknowledge that, we can start to see what *they* need alongside what *we* need.

Shantigarbha is full of stories. He offered me a choice and I chose this one about an attempt to bring together a group of Israelis and a group of Palestinians, people both isolated from one another and at the same time bound together by one of the most protracted, intractable and emotive conflicts of our time.

I chose this partly because it reminded me of Shelly, the Israeli-Jewish academic, and one of her partners who is of Palestinian origin—two people showing in their

96   Shantigarbha, *I'll Meet You There: a practical guide to empathy, mindfulness and communication*, Windhorse Publications, Cambridge UK, 2018. ISBN 978-1-911407-41-6

own small way that when we see our needs as indivisible, not irreconcilable, then peace and love can follow.

> We did a nine-day reconciliation event for about a hundred Israelis and Palestinians. I think it was 2011. And it was a very scary business. I think everybody who came was scared. I'd like to pay tribute to them. The Israelis who came were scared of being ostracised by their families, and the Palestinians who came were afraid of being stopped on the way and also being ostracised by their families and their social networks. So people came because they realised that the political process was not going to result in anything that they were looking for in terms of reconciliation or even just understanding each other in a little more thorough-going way.

> So, they had zero hope in the political process. So that's pretty much what united them. And then they realised that actually they need to go and talk to each other and listen to each other. So we ran an event. We worked very hard helping them to listen to each other. When things broke down, when they got angry or upset, the walls came up, then we paused. We went into smaller groups to listen to them more, listen to people individually. And then we did community activities like dancing and singing and eating. And then we went back to the listening; supporting them to listen to each other.

> And there's one Israeli woman who was in a communication exercise with a Palestinian man in a small group. They were listening to each other. And I think for the first time she was able to hear the pain of the Palestinian man without hearing it automatically as blame of her and of every person of Jewish origin. And it was very, very moving for her. So she was able to cry with him to just acknowledge his pain and his suffering, his upset. And at the end of the session she went up and hugged him, which is very unusual for a middle-aged Jewish woman to do in a semi-public context. So, that was a moment of amazing grace you could say.

> In those kinds of situations connection is a very scarce commodity, so it becomes very precious. Whatever we can contribute to connection, towards mutual understanding, that becomes very, very precious. It helps me to understand and realise just how precious connection and understanding are for me in my life.

Many principles of Nonviolent Communication have made it into mainstream therapy and counselling in the half century since Marshall Rosenberg first set out his stall. They haven't changed much. It's all about establishing and maintaining a connection through empathy and working together with compassion towards a mutually beneficial conclusion.

Does that mean everyone who offers NVC advice is great at this? No. *Knowing* how to communicate better and *applying* the principles are two different things, particularly when we're upset or at a low point. But it's a really useful reference point. Even putting a few of these thoughts into practice should be helpful.

One caveat—these suggestions are intended to help you communicate more productively with someone with whom you are safe both physically and emotionally. Better communication can help, but like almost anything it can be used as a weapon and a tool of abuse. As we'll see in the next chapter, rather than think about radical honesty I suggest that we think in terms of radical vulnerability, i.e. choosing to make oneself (not someone else) vulnerable. If someone else is seeking to make *you* vulnerable and not themselves, there's something amiss. 'You will do it this way' rather than 'I will do it this way' is a warning sign.

As previously mentioned a thought that I really struggle with is the oft-repeated mantra that 'no one can *make* you feel anything'. As we'll see below, framing things in terms of 'you make me feel *x*' is unhelpful in reaching a resolution because it assumes intent—that someone else is intending that an action produce a feeling. However there are instances where that is exactly what is happening—gaslighting, coercive control and other behaviours are all designed to elicit a particular set of reactions.

In such situations, if things are so highly charged that you are unsure of your safety or wellbeing, if your instincts or your friends tell you that you are being abused, then you shouldn't put yourself at risk. That is not a situation in which honest, open-hearted communication can take place. If in doubt, make sure you have support and make your safety paramount.

A BLEEDIN' GINORMOUS LIST OF TIPS FOR BETTER COMMUNICATION

NOT ALL OF these are canon NVC, but all should be worth considering.

Prepare.

Get yourself ready. If you ready yourself for battle you'll be ready for a battle. If you ready yourself to connect you'll be in the right frame of mind to make a connection.

It's quite common to play through scenarios in one's mind as a form of preparation, but that can become a self-fulfilling prophesy. If you're concerned about the possibility of conflict, then rather than psyching yourself up for a fight it's surely better to prepare by focusing on being calm. Calm works for most things. If you need help, seek help. Shantigarbha:

> Before you have that conversation either do some serious self-connection or ask for some support, listening support, or empathy. Ask a friend to listen to you, so you get a chance to get things off your chest in a safe, compassionate way before you go into the difficult conversation.

Make time.

It's not easy to prepare for something if you didn't know it was coming. And marshalling your thoughts when you've been caught on the hop is often difficult. You haven't had a chance to think through what you might like to say.

Anita's idea of setting aside time regularly is an excellent one.

> I've tried to initiate a weekly relationship-check-in kind of setup where we have a set day a week where we would touch base on the phone if we aren't seeing each other, because we only see each other once a week. But he's fairly averse to that because he thinks it's too formal, but I think it would create a space by which we could say this is one point in the week where everyone's safe to talk.

It means you can communicate without it being a big 'Hey, we need to have a deep and meaningful conversation' moment. That can lead to anxiety. A regular check-in can also help to ensure that communication comes slow and steady rather than a whole shedload of pent-up feelings all spilling out at once.

Touch.

Within a relationship, communication can be a means of forging and deepening a connection. Sometimes physically connecting, holding a hand or rubbing someone's foot, changes the dynamic of the conversation. Affectionate touch can be very soothing. More than that, says Shantigarbha, it's a subtle but powerful echo of the emotional link between you.

> What I would suggest is find a way to assure your partner that you wish to stay connected, maybe even make an agreement about how you do that. For [my partner] and I, what that means is usually we keep some physical contact when we're having a difficult conversation; we have a hand or a foot and the hand or the foot says, 'I

want to keep this connection.' It's okay that we disagree with each other. It's okay that we have different ideas, that we were different people. That's okay. We want to keep the connection.

If you can find a way to both touch and be able to look at one another while you talk, maintaining eye contact and a physical link, you may find it leads to more calm and positive discussions.

Empathise.

This is really hard for many of us, particularly when we're upset. If we're anxious or angry, insecure or afraid, it's very easy to be so overwhelmed by our own feelings that it's hard to have the space to listen to someone else's. But this is what we try to do when we empathise. It's about sensing what it's like for another person to be standing in their shoes. That's why picking a time when we're not overwhelmed is a good idea.

Empathy is at the heart of Nonviolent Communication. It's not trying to stage a courtroom battle between accuser and defendant, or a debate between two sides of a legislature. We're trying to build understanding, to find common ground, to resolve issues together. Empathy is a way of moving a discussion from confrontation to collaboration and it often starts when you...

Listen.

Confession: I have a bad habit, especially when interviewing people: I react to something they say before they've finished speaking. Sometimes that means butting in to ask a supplementary question, sometimes it's formulating that next question in my mind as they speak. The trouble is, as soon as I do that I stop listening.

If you really want to listen, then really engage with their words. Don't get lost in them and disappear off into your imagination while they're talking. As Shantigarbha says, be present to the person in front of you.

> When I want to just listen, be fully present with the other person, to give my full attention to the other person, if something comes up for me during that time, then I would just say to myself, okay, Shantigarbha, just give yourself a little bit of space later on, maybe later today for that. Come back to it when you're ready. For the time being I want to give my attention to the other person.

It's worth noting that for people who are used to communication as a form of conflict, someone listening quietly to them can feel remote or disengaged. You might take note of the section further below, 'Repeat back, clarify.'

Stupid things we do when we think we're listening and empathising.

We offer advice. We try to fix someone/something. We offer explanations and excuses, correct their story, show pity, offer consolations, tell a story about us to show them we understand (guilty... so totally guilty), tell people what to feel/not feel, sympathise (it's not the same as empathy and it's often unhelpful); we collude, investigate, interrogate, evaluate, criticise, educate, and indulge in one-upmanship ('Oh, you think you've got it bad, you should have seen what I had....')

Don't do this shit. (Also note to self: Don't do this shit). As Marshall Rosenberg said, empty your mind and listen (and shut the fuck up). List courtesy of Shantigarbha's lovely book *I'll Meet You There.*

Repeat back, clarify.

It's one thing listening well but it's quite another assuring someone that they've actually been heard. Being heard is important. How much of the conflict in our world stems from people feeling unheard and powerless to change that? How much violence is an attempt to gain attention?

Repeating back what someone has said to you is a good way to show that you've listened. It can also be very effective if you repeat what they've said in your own words and use that paraphrase as an opportunity to clarify.

If you do it with empathy and compassion it is also an opportunity to refocus the conversation on needs and substantive issues. For example:

A: You never do the shopping. You never seem to do your share of the housework. It's always me cleaning up after you.

B: I'm hearing that you feel unsupported, that you need more help with the chores, that you are feeling unappreciated for your work in keeping the place together and want everybody to pull their weight. Have I understood right?

That brief exchange has done several jobs—it's an acknowledgement, it shows understanding and engagement, it changes the tone from accusatory to being practical and needs-focused, and it moves the conversation towards a resolution. Demonstrating that you've listened to and understood what's being said does not require you to accept it as objective truth, even if it is the other person's truth.

Ask!

Asking questions is another form of active engagement. Again empathy and compassion are key here. It's not an interrogation. It's not an opportunity to catch someone out, to trip them up or to make them feel stupid. The point of asking questions, says Shantigarbha, is to deepen your understanding of the other person.

> There's a kind of natural curiosity that comes up about other people and about what's going on for them. So we look for that natural curiosity, and we're wanting to connect with specific things about the other person. Like, what are they feeling at the moment and what do they need?

Asking questions in a genuine spirit of enquiry shows that you're interested. Don't forget to listen though. That's the point, yes?

Weigh your words!

Lordy, words really do have weight. Many are loaded and contain implicit judgements. This will be confronting for other people who don't agree with those judgements.

Think about the way people use words to accuse or excuse. Think about the euphemisms we've developed to reduce our own feelings of guilt for what we've done. We don't fire people, we 'let them go' as if we were returning otters to the wild. The military doesn't inadvertently kill women and children by shooting into buildings and blowing things up; 'operations' result in 'collateral damage'. If you phrase it properly it was no one's responsibility. Don't let your words accuse, but do let them take responsibility.

Avoid sweeping, absolute statements.

Lots of words increase the risk of conflict because they're absolute: always, never, everything, nothing, everyone, no one. If you say 'You never help' then it may feel unjust to the other person and leads them to think of an instance when they did help, even if they didn't help much. It derails the discussion because the 'never' statement is, taken literally, not true. If you keep things more relative and less absolute it is less confrontational and almost certainly closer to the truth.

Indeed, in any form of communication, I'd counsel people against using 'always' and 'never'. It makes you a hostage to fortune or simply to facts.

I, not You.

If you need a simple barometer it's the ratio of *I* and *you* appearing in your communication. If you're using *I* a lot you're probably doing okay at explaining your side. If it's predominantly *you* then you might want to take a step back.

Let's talk about using 'I statements'.

When we're talking about I in this context, we can truthfully explore areas like feelings. I can say with factual confidence 'I am feeling upset'. However if I say 'You are being mean' that's firstly much more adversarial, and secondly it may not be true. It's possible that the person felt they said such a thing honestly in an attempt to clarify, not as an attempt to hurt. 'You are being mean' is not just accusatory, it also makes presumptions about intent. Saying 'You're trying to stop me seeing x because you're jealous' makes assumptions about both intent and motive.

Couching things in terms of 'I feel...' changes the dynamic. Difficult things can still be said, but 'I statements' can acknowledge that feelings have arisen out of the perception of someone else's actions. Shantigarbha:

> 'You make me feel such and such'—that's an interpretation or evaluation. It implies that the other person has the power to make you feel certain things. To regain a sense of empowerment (and self-responsibility) you could try saying, 'When I notice how much time you spend with this other person I feel jealous. I feel hurt and sad because I really want to be valued, I want to know that I matter. I want to know that I belong'.

Evaluations and opinions vs. facts and feelings.

Try to stick with the more concrete. You can explain how you feel about things. You can link feelings to events; 'When you did x, I felt y.' 'I wanted you to help with cleaning out the garage. In the end I did it all on my own.'

Try to avoid speculating about the motives of the other or make statements about things that you cannot know - how someone else felt, or why they did something. As Shantigarbha points out, people can easily be wounded by the way others interpret their actions, especially when talking about feelings.

> It certainly helps to reduce the number of interpretations of other people's behaviour, generally speaking, because when you introduce interpretations or evaluations, they tend to be heard as blame or criticism. So, an evaluation might be, 'You make me feel worthless'. It's an evaluation, ascribing responsibility to the other person for what the other person has done to me. Interpretations and evaluations tend to trigger the other person.

So, better in this instance would be 'When you say x, I feel that I'm worthless'.

Be clear. Be specific. Deal with the issue in hand.

Don't try to solve everything at once. Know what it is that you need to discuss and stick to that. Try not to derail something that someone else needs to talk about by talking about something different unless it's directly related.

'I'm worried about money and I feel all the responsibility is falling on my shoulders to support us financially,' is one topic.

'I contribute in other ways; I look after the house and kids while you're working,' is an on-topic response. 'Well you spend plenty of it on Tom, so why should I care?' is off-topic.

Try to keep your focus on an issue, not on the person.

Identify needs.

This is where you should be headed. 'I'm unhappy about x' is a statement but it doesn't offer a path to a resolution. As Shantigarbha says, it helps us to explore behind and underneath the mass of feelings that sometimes overwhelm us and ask what it is that we are actually after.

> I support people to connect with the feelings and needs that they're in touch with.
> So, if you're feeling jealous and needing love or attention or being valued, strip it
> back to the feelings and the needs and take out interpretations or evaluations.

'I'm worried about you and Anna. I'm left wondering how much you care about me. I need to feel that I'm important to you. I would like us to spend more quality time together doing things that we both enjoy. Can we look at our diaries and find three dates in the next two weeks?' That identifies an issue and its impact, and it suggests a concrete direction to go in.

Share.

Without overloading someone, give them background and other information that allows them to understand where you're coming from:

'This is difficult for me because of what happened when I was at college,' followed by an explanation, if necessary, of what happened.

Chill.

If things get heated take time to let them calm down. There's rarely a deadline to resolving the kind of issues that crop up in relationships. Even if there is a deadline the issues are not going to get sorted out better or more quickly for trying to do so while upset, anxious, agitated or angry. As Rati says:

One thing I've learned: If you're angry or hurt... take a break. And it could mean a few minutes, it could mean a few hours. But I think that really helps when you back away, you know, like you can be really pissed.

One piece of advice that is often shared in the poly community is that after an argument, it takes a good 20 to 30 minutes for the cortisol and other stress hormones to clear out of your system, so attempts at reconciliation before that has happened could explode in your face. Say that you need some time alone, and perhaps even set a timer.

Just as people use safewords in kink and BDSM, safewords have a role in communication too. Agreeing on safewords beforehand—they could be the same or different than those you use in other situations—allows people to signal that they've become uncomfortable and are worried about the way the conversation is developing.

Again, communication is almost never better for taking place when people are feeling uneasy. You're looking for empathy, compassion and cooperation. Allowing someone to flag their discomfort gives everyone a chance to pause and to refocus on working together to achieve a positive outcome for everyone.

Own your stuff.
This will come as a shock to some of you who have read thus far... but I'm not perfect. Sorry to shatter your illusions but I get stuff wrong. Sadly this happens far more often than I'd like. Here's my guess (and yes, I know this is speculation, and speculation should be avoided, but it's a hunch based on thousands of years of humans getting stuff wrong, so...) you probably do too.

That's okay. To err is human and all that. However the first step towards putting something right is accepting that you got something wrong.

Politicians and business leaders struggle with this. They don't like admitting they screwed up. Trouble is, it slows down the process of sorting stuff out.

A good place to start is with 'sorry'. However it's best to be clear about what you are sorry for. You are apologising for, and owning, your error. You are not apologising for someone else's actions or for their feelings.

'I'm sorry that you didn't understand and couldn't play your part,' is not an apology. It's passive aggression.

'I'm sorry that you feel that way,' is not an apology. It's just crap. And pathetic. Translated into English it means 'I'm frustrated that you're upset. Frankly I couldn't give a damn but I want to make some sort of noise so you'll go away.' PR people love this stuff. Call them on it. It's not an apology, okay?

'I'm sorry I screwed up. I want to try to put it right,' *is* an apology. See, got there in the end. Gary Chapman of the five love languages also suggests five elements that make apologies work: expressing regret, accepting responsibility, making restitution, genuinely repenting, and requesting forgiveness. It's a useful checklist.

Anita did things in her previous relationship that she heartily regrets. The fact that she's faced up to her mistakes has given her the chance to grow, the ability to help others grow through sharing her experience, and the possibility of self-compassion.

> For me a big part of my growth in this space is about modelling best practice and essentially being someone that has made mistakes but knows the pain caused by those, both to oneself and others... and who does the best one can do in as many situations as possible, whilst giving myself plenty of leeway to still fuck up occasionally.

Accept imperfection. Deal with the important things. Accept what you can accept.

Conflict is a part of human existence. However, too much of it makes life unbearable.

As for me? After getting into far too many arguments with far too many people, I decided 'Enough! From here on I'm going to pick my fights.'

Yes it's annoying getting ripped off for a fiver but, as someone put it, some things you can simply accept as the price of peace of mind. If you're broke and hungry a fiver is a lot, so deciding at what point one can afford peace of mind is a choice we each make in each situation. As Debbie says, it's about deciding what is important enough that you need to deal with it, and letting go of the rest.

> Don't sweat the small stuff! I mean that's a very clichéd thing, but I found that if something seems like it might be bothering me, if I step back and not necessarily sleep on it but like sit on it for a tiny bit.... The smaller things, a lot of times those don't really matter and they're not anything that's going to build up into anything big. But at the same time just remember like hey, to communicate is the biggest thing I've noticed that counts in any relationship. Just make sure that you're on the same page as the other person that you're around or with.

Respect difficulty. Respect difference.

How we feel about outcomes is often a reflection of our expectations. Someone who'd hoped to be paid £7,000 would probably be disappointed with £5,000, but someone who'd hoped to be paid £3,000 would doubtless be delighted.

When we're communicating with someone else it helps to manage expectations. As someone once said, 'Life is hard. Once you accept that, life becomes much easier.'

The same can be said for many things, not least the process of trying to connect with someone else and solve problems together.

Don't pin your hopes on breakthroughs. Don't bank on someone else changing radically. In particular, don't expect someone to change radically the way you'd like them to change.

Where it's possible, accept difference. It is there to be celebrated. Our diversity really is a strength. It's nature's way of giving humanity a fighting chance of making it into the next millennium, and it's way more interesting than everyone being the same. After all, the Borg in Star Trek are many things—but they're not known for being fun at parties.

And, as has been said, accept the possibility that a relationship may indeed end. Sometimes differences are insuperable and those involved can't live with them.

Once you've committed to collaboration, are resolved to use empathy and compassion, and have let go of attachments to particular outcomes, you're prepared for most things. Take it from Nathan. It can be scary but it's worth it.

> Communication is really difficult and it's really necessary. Your communication style will grow as the other person's will. They'll come to understand you better. But start. Fear makes the monster bigger. Don't let fear win; start! I say this, but it's way easier to say than do. There are many times in the past I've caught myself not starting because of fear.

The kitchen sink.

Might as well. I've thrown almost everything else in. So here it is: If it's your turn to do the dishes, perhaps you might want to wash and dry them before you talk. :)

I want to end this section with another story from Shantigarbha, this one more personal. Perhaps we might reflect on it in the light of the above. How could this couple communicate better? How would you do it differently? Is there anything here you might bring to your own discussions?

> One of the first couple-mediations that I did was in London. A young professional couple, a man and a woman, came in. They were probably around thirty. Initially they were quite polite with each other and then they started talking about times when they went out to restaurants. And then the woman said, "You're just sitting there on your phone, you don't pay any attention to me". And then the key phrase, "You never listen to me". She said, "I tell you about my work, I tell you about my

day. You never listen to me!" So that was like the catch phrase. Of course the guy heard this and didn't want to know, didn't want to be involved.

So I encouraged him to listen to her, but he found it difficult and said, 'Look, I'm new to this. I don't understand.' So, I said, well perhaps you could just acknowledge that she wants your full attention. Just to say to your wife, 'Look, I can see it was painful for you because you want my full attention right now.' And so he said this, and she looked relieved for a moment, but then he added something else, and that threw the whole thing again. She went back to, 'You never listen to me and you always try and turn this around and you always try to make it my fault.'

Then I switched tack and said to her, 'How about if he tells you three things that he enjoys about you? And she said, "You know, maybe that might work." So then he started, and it was quite difficult, but he found three things that he appreciated about her. I think he appreciated her dress sense [among other things]. Anyway, he started warming up with these three things. And then after a while she kind of relaxed and could receive him again. She could begin to see him as her partner again, as the person she loved.

That's a very sweet memory of one of the first mediations I ever did.

WHAT WE CAN ALL LEARN

COMMUNICATION ISN'T A non-monogamous thing any more than it's a monogamous thing. It's just a human thing. However, the fact that it's so central to the way that many people practice CNM reflects the fact in the CMN world, fewer assumptions can be made about many things and thus more needs to be discussed.

But that doesn't mean that monogamous relationships don't benefit from better communication. Talking more won't make you less monogamous. It's not a threat.

It's when there are things that we feel we can't discuss that a relationship can become difficult. This is why deceiving a partner, whether through lying or cheating, can be so corrosive. It results in significant things that can't be discussed, and these become a barrier to intimacy. The feeling that we can't wholly open our hearts can lead us to pull back further, rather than talk deeply and risk stepping on one of those lie-mines that we've laid for ourselves because we've forgotten where it is.

A lot of non-communication is grounded in fear: fear of hurting someone, of being hurt, of hearing what one doesn't wish to hear. There is no easy answer to that, however. It requires bravery but if bravery was easy it wouldn't really be bravery[97] would it? But if you believe that it's better to face reality and deal with it than live a half-life that you'll never be able to fully trust is true, then communication is a route to the real.

And, above all, better communication builds deeper intimacy. Life can be lonely enough as it is. Creating safe environments in which to talk with empathy and compassion is a powerful response to those feelings of distance, loneliness and isolation.

---

97   Sometimes bravery looks a lot like stupidity. There *is* a difference. Bravery involves understanding the risks and the possibility of loss and taking a decision to act regardless. Stupidity is based on neither knowing nor caring to know and blundering in all the same. Brave generally wins out over stupid. Generally.

CHAPTER FIFTY-TWO

Honesty, Radical or Otherwise

TRUTH IS INTIMACY and intimacy is truth. Funny how so many of us are prepared to be physically naked in front of someone but fear being emotionally and spiritually naked. And yet just as being skin to skin with someone can build real physical intimacy, so too being soul to soul with someone can build a deeper emotional intimacy, one that with the right people leaves us feeling more accepted and less alone.

Honesty is the foundation of trust. A surprising amount of business is done on trust. It's a great lubricant for the machinery of commerce. There's certainly a correlation between the level of everyday honesty in different countries and their economic success[98], one that was even more pronounced in the days before accountable institutions had developed to enforce things like contracts. Before the watchword of the City of London became 'Fill your boots', it used to be 'My word is my bond.'

This applies to relationships too. Being honest allows the people around you to know where they stand with you. They may not always like what they hear, but at least they understand the basis of the relationship.

And yet how many people get into situations where their intimate relationships are based on a lie, and then compound it with a whole series of lies? Sometimes people in monogamous relationships simply find themselves unequal to the challenge of being someone's everything forever as signed for on the dotted line at the altar. It can get even more fraught when two lives are bound together by children, home and finances. Rather than unravel the Gordian knot of modern life, sometimes it simply seems easier to lie. But one lie may soon require another.

---

98 'Honesty and beliefs about honesty in 15 countries', David Hugh-Jones, University of East Anglia, 29 Oct 2015. 'The link with honesty is clearer for earlier economic growth, as summarized in 1950 GDP levels, than for growth since 1950, consistently with the theory that honesty substitutes for technologies and institutions that ease monitoring and accountability.' https://www.uea.ac.uk/documents/746480/2855738/Honesty_paper.pdf

Before we get into honesty let's briefly consider why people lie and the different sorts of lies we tell. A team of three Polish researchers came up with a grid for categorising lies.[99] There are two axes . One divides lies between those intended for *gain* and those intended to *protect* (avoid loss). The other divides lies that benefit one's *self* from those that benefit *others*. The grid looks something like this:

	For gain	To protect
To benefit self	**SELF-SERVING** To gain status, position, political or social advantage, money, possessions, self-esteem, ingratiation, etc.	**SELF-DEFENCE** To avoid criticism, punishment, blame, responsibility. Covering up shortcomings. Hiding one's past. Protecting or disguising one's feelings or opinions. Avoiding uncomfortable conversations or situations, or damage to a relationship.
To benefit others	**PLEASING** To make someone else feel good: lies to make people feel cherished, valued, worthy, competent, attractive, confident; to promote their wellbeing or happiness.	**SHIELDING** To help others avoid distress, sadness, or hurt. To serve a higher cause, such as preventing someone from coming to harm.

So there are lies that would be considered self-serving and lies that would be considered more altruistic. One could say the same of truth telling.

Consensual non-monogamy changes the relationship landscape by redefining what is acceptable and consequently what people may be tempted to lie about. It's not that people don't ever lie or cheat in consensually non-monogamous relationships. It's still possible to breach understandings, and there are plenty of things that people lie about including infidelities. And, of course, we shouldn't forget that lying or simply withholding the truth denies other people the ability to give active consent, because consent needs to be informed.

When we meet someone new, one of the first things we try to do is establish trust. Of course, in some situations we judge that this isn't possible. When we fall in love we

99 'Motivation and Consequences of Lying. A Qualitative Analysis of Everyday Lying.',Beata Arcimowicz, Katarzyna Cantarero, Emilia Soroko (2015).

tend to suspend judgement and move to a position of trust quickly. It's a key part of the bonding process. We rush to find out everything we can about the other person and they about us. It can be exhilarating.

When someone discovers they've been lied to they're forced to reconcile the mental image they had of the person with a new reality. But what is that new reality? What is real and what isn't? One hears people who've been lied to by their partners say it's as though they never really knew them. Or, 'I don't know what to believe any more.' Or, 'I'm not sure I can believe anything they say.' It creates a strong sense of alienation.

Trust is a little like a precious piece of porcelain. It's only perfect until it's broken. Then, even if you glue it back together, it regains its shape but it's forever flawed. However beautiful it is, your eye will still be drawn to the fractures.[100]

One thing that consensually non-monogamous people treat as a strength is the additional latitude that it gives them to be honest within intimate relationships. It's simply a fact that many, if not most people will occasionally experience attractions to people other than those they're in a relationship with. Some find themselves constantly attracted to people other than their partner(s). Whereas monogamous traditionalists might argue that one should simply repress those thoughts, non-monogamous people tend to see that as bottling-up an internal conflict and would rather acknowledge these feelings even if they don't act on them. Things unspoken produce distance rather than intimacy.

For this reason many consensually non-monogamous people put a high premium on honesty. As discussed earlier, others, such as those who operate a 'don't ask don't tell' policy, prefer not to know. Such agreements aren't dishonest as they are consented to, but neither are they honest on a more profound level and they tend to weigh against intimacy.[101]

---

100 The Japanese have a technique called Kintsugi (金継ぎ) that involves joining the broken pieces of an object (typically ceramics) back together using a lacquer or resin mixed with precious metal powder: silver, gold or platinum. This approach embraces and celebrates an object's history by highlighting the damage and making it beautiful. In human terms one could say an equivalent might be when somebody uses a moment of personal failure to grow and become a better person than they would have been had they not failed. If the old person could not be trusted then perhaps becoming a new person is necessary to reestablish true and profound trust. The scars still show, but they become a reminder of our ability to transcend our flaws.

101 As Jennifer Piemonte and Jennifer Rubin noted in their study, those in open relationships, where 'don't ask don't tell' arrangements are common, enjoy lower levels of relationship satisfaction than those surveyed who identify as monogamous, polyamorous or swingers. 'Sexual satisfaction among individuals in monogamous and consensually non- monogamous relationships, Terri D. Conley, Jennifer L. Piemonte, Staci Gusakova, Jennifer D. Rubin, University of Michigan, *Journal of Social and Personal Relationships*, (2018) Vol. 35(4) 509–531.

Honesty opens the door to a different sort of relationship, one that isn't about maintaining appearances and pretending that all is well when it isn't. And yet, as Kevin Patterson found out, it can be hard to rewrite the social programming people pick up living in an overwhelmingly monogamous world.

> One of my bigger mistakes was I hooked up with a friend and I did not tell my wife about it because the friend was worried that it would impact our relationship. I told my friend, 'It's cool; my wife and I are non-monogamous. It's all good,' But she was still so certain that this was cheating, that she begged me not to let my wife in on the story. I was early enough in my relationship that I hadn't unlearned all of the toxic monogamy I was socialised in. So I lied. I just omitted the truth. I went back home with my wife and when she asked me about my time away, I just left out the part where I slept with a friend. Eventually it felt so ridiculous that I was being needlessly dishonest that I eventually broke and told my wife. She was fine with it. She thought it was funny that I came home without a story, even though she knew full well that I was going to generate a story while I was away, and my friend was upset that I couldn't keep the lie. Eventually it didn't matter. My friend got over it, my wife got over it, they are still friends, we're all still friends, and I realised that if it's something that breaks my integrity, I'm not here for it.

Kevin's wife was understanding of his situation. After all he hadn't lied for personal advantage or to protect himself. He'd found himself caught between the desire to be honest with his wife and a new partner's fear that she'd done something wrong.

So if we consider lying in the light of the grid above, there are lies that are self-serving and there are lies that are well-intended. However there is a school of thought within consensual non-monogamy, perhaps reflecting the fact that there are fewer taboos, that any and all untruths are intrinsically wrong.

RADICAL HONESTY

BACK IN THE 1990s the American psychotherapist Brad Blanton came up with a concept he called 'radical honesty.' Indeed he later trademarked the term. Its first core principle is that 'Lying is the primary cause of suffering.' That's a big statement, and it gives a sense of the ambitions of the radical honesty movement. Of course, some would point out that there are also poverty, starvation and disease, which to the sceptically minded are grounded less in lying than in the vagaries of climate and inequitable economic systems. But Blanton is adamant that the fundamental problem is lying: 'Stress, pain, oppression of self and others, even war... are primarily caused and maintained by various forms of lying.'

There are, as it happens, other opinions out there. Jesus, for instance, taught that suffering often stems from our failure to love our fellow humans as ourselves; the Buddha that it's rooted in desire and ignorance and our attachment to material things. Others would argue that life is complex and messy and that the irreconcilable needs of the living things that inhabit this small planet lead, all too often, to conflict.

And yet, like many virtues, honesty can become a vice if used with ill intent. My old friend Shantigarbha has brought his skills in Nonviolent Communication to conflict resolution around the world. He refers to two different approaches to honesty: one that involves tearing someone to pieces and another that requires sticking one's neck out.

> I identify two kinds of honesty, and for convenience we call them *Jackal honesty* and *Giraffe honesty.* These are playful terms from Nonviolent Communication. Jackal honesty is the language of disconnection. It's where someone says 'I'm going to be honest with you right now. You're a complete loser and I never should have let you in my life'. You know, that sort of judging and blaming honesty, and it's usually preceded by the person saying, "Look, I'm going to level with you' or 'This may hurt but I'm doing it for your own good'.

> With Giraffe honesty, the crucial difference is that it involves vulnerability. Rather than diagnosing what's wrong with the other person, you express how you're feeling and what needs of yours are not being addressed in this situation.

> Both are kinds of honesty. However they have very different intentions and very different outcomes.

There's a long history of people being attracted to the idea of a single bullet that solves a whole host of problems and Radical Honesty has something of a loyal, some might say 'cult', following not least in CNM circles.

The trouble is, as with many things, absolutist philosophies included, radical honesty is wide open to abuse. There's radical honesty that's applied mindfully, but, as Nathan has found, there's radical honesty that's just dumping your stuff on someone else and not taking responsibility for it.

> In the wrong hands radical honesty can be a bit of a dangerous thing. The idea sounds really good except it seems like it could be used as a cover for people being

dicks. They're saying 'No, no I'm just being radically honest, I'm telling you exactly the way it is,' or visiting their unsatisfied feelings onto the situation, under the guise of radical honesty. Like 'No, no babe I'm not being a dick, I'm just telling you how it is, like this is the truth'.

No, *you're* being a dick. There is truth in what you say but you're also being a dick, you could be a little kinder about it.

Amongst the people I interviewed Radical Honesty is perceived quite negatively, less the ideal than the execution. It's associated with people who use what Shantigarbha would label 'Jackal honesty'. Joreth, Franklin and Eunice:

Joreth: Radical Honesty with capital letters, from what I know of it, comes with a whole philosophy attached to it and I'm only superficially familiar with it, but most of my exposure to people who follow the philosophy tends to be those who use it as a blunt object with which to bludgeon people over the head.

Franklin: "I'm just being honest!" Honesty is an essential component of any kind of reasonable consent-based interaction between human beings. Radical honesty is mean-spirited bullshit.

Joreth: So I am in favour of honesty, but I don't think honesty by itself is a virtue. I think honesty is a vehicle for experiencing intimacy.

Franklin: The *virtue* is consent, honesty is the tool that gets you there.

Joreth: And even though I have bias against the whole radical honesty thing, I am still honest in all of my relationships. I tempered my honesty with compassion but it's still always honest. So, it's not so much the philosophy of radical honesty that I'm opposed to as implementation of it.

Franklin: And on paper that's the way it's advocated, if you read books on radical honesty that's precisely what they're talking about; but it's the practitioners that make it go somewhere else.

Eunice: They see little white lies as [merely] being kinder, so they decide that to go for the honest thing they should lose the kindness.

If we take a more nuanced view of honesty we recognise that it can be used to inflict harm, and dishonesty can be used selflessly as an act of love. But *regardless of the motive* it's unavoidable that when telling untruths, even out of the deepest kindness, you risk limiting someone else's agency and ability to consent. And if one is operating on a consent-first basis, lying is always problematic in that respect. For that reason alone some people will always prefer honesty.

However I think there is a different kind of radicalism that we can pursue that can light the way to a greater intimacy. As Eunice puts it; "'Compassionate honesty is better than radical honesty.'"

Compassionate honesty is an essential element if we're to move beyond Jackal honesty and towards Shantigarbha's Giraffe honesty. Jackal honesty is a seizure of power, a weaponizing of honesty. If we're to do something radical it should be a radical stepping away from power to make ourselves vulnerable. After all, as people say, 'To love somebody is to become vulnerable' and, notes Joreth Innkeeper, that scares a lot of people.

> I think one of the reasons why honesty is so difficult for people is because it leaves you vulnerable. That's one of the reasons why it's a vehicle to intimacy, because it leaves you open and vulnerable and people don't like feeling vulnerable.

If we're to really pursue honesty and the benefits it can bring within relationships, we need to overcome those fears and accept the fact that the best sort of honesty goes hand in hand with vulnerability and that vulnerability is a reality check against misusing honesty. So is what I would like to propose is ***radical vulnerability,*** and that we combine it with ***compassionate honesty*** to strengthen our connections with one another.

Putting compassion first in our dealings with others means that we're using honesty with love, and by making ourselves vulnerable rather than exploiting another's vulnerability we can radically upend the way we often explore deep feelings while ensuring that we never disempower someone else.

Of course, it needs to be said once again, if you are already vulnerable and disempowered making yourself more so can be a risk. If so then tread carefully. Taking a decision to make yourself vulnerable to someone is a huge act of trust, a reaching out in the hope that someone will join you in that emotionally naked state. No one would or should suggest you do this with anyone you don't, or can't, trust to respond to your vulnerability with love, compassion and vulnerability of their own—much less if they abuse trust. Many people develop, or rebuild, trust incrementally. This is a perfectly reasonable approach. Vulnerability should be balanced; two or more people stepping out on a path of vulnerability together, dropping their armour piece by piece.

So let's consider what we might want to achieve with honesty.

Firstly, if there is a right moment in a relationship to start being completely honest it's right at the beginning. It can save a lot of time and heartache to find out about any serious incompatibilities at the outset. If we don't share values, interests and goals then it can be hard to make a relationship work, and the faster we find that out the faster we can decide if the emotional investment will be worth it. Some people ache for a relationship so badly that any connection is better than none, but even then it's better to begin fully aware of what one is entering into.

Secondly, as already mentioned, truth is intimacy and compassionate honesty is a good route to building deeper connections.

Thirdly, as Kevin Patterson says, it helps maintain respect for oneself, they for you, and you and they for them.

> The biggest lessons I have learned? Number one is integrity. And that's not to say that I always get that right, but just maintaining it, even if the answer is going to be 'no', even if you're going to get a negative result, you have to be honest with yourself. You have to be honest with the people around you. 'Cause when you're not, everything goes to shit the second you break your integrity.

Fourth, lying is really hard work. It's harder to remember what you said you did than what you actually did. Our real memories and our memories of stories we concoct imprint differently. It's why lies, especially complex ones, unravel so easily. And lies beget more lies. It can become a habit. It takes much more time and energy trying to maintain a false reality, even if we build that false reality though misdirection and omission rather telling an actual lie. It saps energy that could otherwise go into the relationship.

So does being unable to drop your guard around someone that you're in an intimate relationship with. Lies you've told can weigh heavily. They act as a barrier, even if the other person doesn't realise they've been deceived. Lies are isolating.

LEVELS OF DISCLOSURE

As Seb observed earlier in the book, there are some things one would simply rather not know. For some people it can be incredibly erotic to share explicit details of their sexual encounters with other partners;, for others it can just be uncomfortable. As Alice puts it:

> I want to know enough. I would like to know that the girl you're with is beautiful and smart and makes you happy. I want to know that you're happy. Which makes me incredibly happy to know that you're happy. I would not like to know the details of how you have sex. Don't go into details telling me how you threw her across the room and pulled off her clothes and things like that.

Alice says her ex-partner wanted a high degree of disclosure. She says he more or less wanted to know everything. However she found that problematic.

> [It was] pretty awkward because he had a huge thing about anal sex. I don't like anal sex, but I was comfortable enough to explore that with [another] sex partner, in Hong Kong. So the whole rule of tell me everything, how am I going to tell him that I have anal sex or I am exploring anal sex with [that] partner in Hong Kong? Because he would flip out and he would be just incredibly insecure, so that rule kind of didn't work.

Eventually Alice told her ex what she'd done with that other lover, and it apparently contributed to the breakdown of the relationship. Obviously it was far more complicated than just issues around that particular sex act. It was about security, and being required to share intimate details challenged that.

Nathan's take on disclosure is similar, except he has a useful rule of thumb:

> I don't need to know everything. Are you happy, are you having fun, is there something interesting that you want to bring me, will whatever information you bring me make our relationship better, will it make me as a person happier?

So this isn't about unfettered disclosure, it's about telling people what they *want* or *need* to know. Yes, it may take you to difficult places sooner rather than later, but those places already exist. Honesty helps one address them. If your preferred strategy is to hope things will go away if you refuse to acknowledge them for long enough, this sort of honesty will be hard.

Eunice likes to weigh up three considerations: what one partner is willing to have shared *about* them, what a second partner is willing to *hear*, and what you are willing to *talk* about. You defer to the comfort level of the person with the greatest privacy concerns around information sharing. Obviously if you're very open and a partner is exceptionally private or vice versa it may reach the level of incompatibility.

For me the answer is relatively simple; if it's something I might talk about with my best friend or closest confidant other than my partner but don't want to share with my partner, I will ask myself why. There's almost always something interesting at the end of that question.

CHAPTER FIFTY-THREE

Rules, Agreements and Boundaries

LET'S TALK ABOUT three related things that all have a bearing on relationships: rules, agreements and boundaries.

Life is full of rules. Indeed it's likely that complex societies and civilisations couldn't have emerged without them. The earliest set of laws for which we have a written record, the Ur-Nammu code, was set out around 4000 years ago and would probably delight modern-day conservatives.[102] And though many of us have become a wee bit more nuanced, even humane, in the four millennia that have followed, there are still rules. Lots of them.

Rules or laws make possible the societies we live in. But think for a moment about the etymological tie between a rule, a ruler, and the ruled. Ultimately rules are imposed, usually by force (overt or implied), for reasons both good and bad. We are subject to laws and rules that we have not necessarily consented to. Few of us have a role in shaping them other than in the crudest sense that most of us get a vote every few years.

Monogamy is often quite strongly rules-based, both legally and even more so, socially. It's not so much a formal set of instructions (albeit the Ur-Nammu code begs to differ: cue more getting stoned for adultery – basically paleo sex, drugs and rock n roll with real rocks). It's more something that most of us simply absorb from the around us. The worst part of it is that these rules are often unspoken, which means that until you find yourself in a position where one or the other of you has transgressed these invisible lines, you've probably never bothered to discuss them. Dr Liz Powell:

---

102 'Then did Ur-Nammu the mighty warrior, king of Ur, king of Sumer and Akkad, by the might of Nanna, lord of the city, and in accordance with the true word of Utu, establish equity in the land; he banished malediction, violence and strife, and set the monthly Temple expenses at 90 gur of barley, 30 sheep, and 30 sila of butter.' It generally goes downhill from there.

The closer you get to monogamy, the more that the way you do your relationship is structured on the basis almost solely of assumptions. Very few monogamous folks have explicit discussions about what they consider cheating; very few monogamous folks have explicit discussions about what they can expect of each other in terms of when they will give way and when they will hold to their ground. And I think that the further away from that structure you move, the more you have to have those discussions because you can't operate on assumption anymore.

However, in consensual non-monogamy, there is quite a lot of resistance to rules in relationships. Back in 2010 Kassia Wosick-Correa surveyed more than 300 people[103] and found that 39% of them, almost two in five, were antipathetic to terms like 'allow,' 'restrict,' or 'rules' that suggested some degree of control over a partner.

To many people's ears 'rules' sound a lot like one person or one group imposing their will on another, and in the context of relationships, that's generally a red flag.

However, as we all know, relationships don't have to be about one person asserting themselves or dictating terms. Rather than having rules we can have *agreements*. Unlike rules, says Franklin Veaux, agreements are negotiated and multilateral.

The way I look at it, rules and agreements are very different things but their difference is not something that a lot of people are really cognisant of. So, they tend to confuse the ideas. Rules are restrictions that I put on your behaviour: 'you must...', 'you may not...', 'you cannot...', 'you have to....' Agreements are things that we explicitly negotiate that everybody who is touched by the agreement has a voice in.

Joreth Innkeeper also recognises this distinction. However she's conscious that people aren't above dressing one up as the other.

I'm very gun-shy about the phrases 'commitments' and 'agreements', because in my experience people use them as substitutes for the word 'rules' but they don't want the stigma that comes with rules, so they just rebrand them as agreements and commitments. And so I get very nervous because I'm not sure what they mean by that.

The touchstone for such things is ultimately consent. If all those involved in making an agreement wholeheartedly consent, bearing in mind that for there to

---

103 'Agreements, rules and agentic fidelity in polyamorous relationships,' Kassia Wosick-Correa, *Psychology & Sexuality*, (2010) 1:1, 44–61.

be consent a person has to be in a sufficiently clear state of mind and able to make decisions for themselves, then one could fairly say it's not imposed from without. With some of the agreements we make, such as in business, we can appeal to an external body like a court or a panel of arbitration to enforce the terms. With relationships it's more complex. When a relationship agreement has legal force, such as a legally constituted marriage, a court can intervene. However the scope of other legal contracts in relationships, such as prenuptial agreements, is limited in many countries and the justice system is circumspect about when to get involved. If both parties consent it's even more loath to get between them.

Clearly there are occasions when society and the law beg to differ on the primacy of consent, and on occasion they do intervene to stop certain 'consensual' acts where, in their eyes, a consensual agreement isn't possible. Extreme examples[104] aside, the authorities have in some countries intervened to criminalise and prosecute some consensual BDSM activities.

Some CNM relationships within the BDSM sphere are founded on agreements that essentially allow someone to hand out rules. That's pretty much the whole point of them. Master/slave or D/s dynamics are very much about the surrendering of control and responsibility for the gratification of all involved. However, there is considerable emphasis in the BDSM community on consent (which doesn't mean there aren't violations) and the conditionality of that consent. A submissive who is tied up and is being flogged has to be able to use a safeword if a scene that was pleasurable veers into undesired territory. Even a slave in a 24/7 relationship with a master needs to be able to call a halt if the arrangement is no longer working for them.

Clearly BDSM relationships (and there's a significant intersection between many BDSM and CNM communities) can look strange, even disturbing, to those outside. It's still legally marginal in the UK and Italy and could fall foul of the law in some US states. So, in these cases, an agreement may not be enough to convince a court.

However, the critical distinction between rules and agreements, Veaux argues, is all about where power lies. If actual (as opposed to play) power is distributed equally then you have the conditions necessary to negotiate an agreement. But if power lies with one person or with only some of those affected, then you have a rule.

> So, for example: if I say you are not allowed to have sex with anybody else, that's a rule. If you and I get together and we say, the two of us agree that as long as we are with each other we will not have other lovers, that's an agreement. The difference is

---

104 An extreme case would be that of the 'Rotenburg cannibal' Armin Meiwes, who killed and ate his victim Bernd Jürgen Armando Brandes with his apparent consent. He was eventually sentenced to life imprisonment without the possibility of parole.
In the UK restrictions on some consensual sex acts and on the filming of certain consensual sex acts still remains in place.

the locus of control; in an agreement the locus of control is with all of the parties involved, with a rule the locus of control is with me. I have the control over your behaviour. The deal you get with agreements, though, is that it has to include the voice of everybody who is affected by the agreement.

It's important not just that consent has been given but that it can also be withdrawn at will, however annoying that may be for the other parties. That's an essential element of agreements in relationships; people can withdraw from them or renegotiate them.

There's a third category that's also important here: *boundaries*. What boundaries have in common with rules is that they are unilateral. One person can make them. However, a boundary is generally taken to mean a rule that someone applies to their *own* person or property. Xena sets out how she sees the distinction.

'Rules' is implying that you're forcing your opinion, what things are allowed and not allowed. Rules is implying that it is putting [restrictions] onto somebody else. I don't see my boundaries as a rule and [one of] my boundaries has always been that I don't date friends or friends of friends, and in the past [another] was not posting to the Facebook of your partners.

Basically it boils down to the idea that boundaries are healthy statements of self-respect, while rules are attempts to control other people. It's worth bearing in mind that ultimately the main means of enforcing boundaries is to withdraw. However, even that is open to abuse. If you say to someone 'If you don't stop seeing *x* I'll leave you,' you could try to pass that off as maintaining good boundaries, but it's actually simply an attempt to bend someone else to your will through emotional blackmail. Kevin Patterson experienced a breakup where one of his partners couldn't accept another. However in this instance she acted honourably not using blackmail but simply withdrawing leaving them both sad but, critically, with their integrities intact.

I actually had a breakup which really hurt. And the breadth of the purpose of the breakup was because I started seeing somebody who another partner refused to be a metamour with. And I understood their reasoning behind it, but they decided to set a boundary. They said, 'I can't be a metamour to this person. I have to go.' And as much as that hurts, I get that. I'd feel a lot differently about it if they were like, 'You need to break up with that person'. The results would've been the same, but then there would've been an animosity there regardless of whether I did or didn't break up with this person.

Perhaps the innate tension between consensual non-monogamy and rules is right there in the terminology—the difference between a rule and an agreement is that the latter requires engagement, participation and consent. That is a long way from maintaining that consensual non-monogamy is innately un-boundaried. McFadden argues that in this respect non-monogamy and monogamy have a lot in common.

> I think that the parameters of non-monogamous relationships, in the way that those parameters are negotiated, are not actually fundamentally different from monogamy. It's just that the underlying tenet of [sexual] fidelity is absent, as an explicit or implicit agreement, from non-monogamous commitment and negotiation.

> [I think that there is] a most ridiculous fetishization of non-monogamous relationships, that somehow that they're qualitatively different from dyadic relationships and I don't actually think that they are. I think that ultimately one-to-one and one-to-many relationships are really negotiated in the same way. The fundamental difference is in acceptance to one extent or another of the fundamental insecurity of reality.

I agree with McFadden to a degree. Polyamorous and other consensually non-monogamous relationships are open to being, and indeed often are, fetishized by people who'd like to think that there is something more evolved or idealistic about them. As he says, it really boils down not to being more evolved but perhaps to being more accepting of life's uncertainties, especially the uncertainty of human love and desire. However, monogamous relationships are also fetishized to an extraordinary degree by a society that reveres the goal of two people enjoying lifelong happiness and contentment free from conflict. Both risk erasing the messiness of human relationships, dooming us all to failure.[105]

---

105 The pioneering psychologist Carl Jung (1875-1961) asserted that 'American marriages are the saddest in the whole world because the man does all his fighting at the office.' He's generally taken to mean is that the American ideal promoted in his day was one of conflict-free relationships, and that consequently in that culture people weren't given the tools with which to disagree or 'fight' constructively.

Where I disagree is that I see the issue of fidelity as only one difference in how monogamous and non-monogamous relationships function. Another significant difference is surely the sheer amount of communication and negotiation necessary to make most CNM relationships work. The absence of a set of rules that everyone has been socialised into, that literature and music and movies have reinforced, means that non-monogamous people can't live by unspoken and commonly held assumptions. Nathan's agreements with his partners sum it up really quite neatly

> All [our] 'previously discussed [agreements, those where] now there's no need to discuss them anymore because they've already been established' [come down to] 'Don't bring any bugs home, and talk about everything and let me know what's going on, talk to me and if life happens then talk to me, and if life isn't happening then talk to me, but above all else talk to me.'

So the explicit understandings are pretty minimal. The rest is down to all concerned agreeing to communicate, hopefully well. That's something that Nathan's monogamous partner Debbie appreciates:

> I'd have to agree that it's the communication part, and I think that's what I like about it so much—it's nice to have somebody who actually tells you what's going on.

There is a perception amongst its critics that consensual non-monogamy is a way of throwing off the shackles of commitment, that it's a world of casual dating and casual relationships and casual sex. And of course there will be people for whom it is, and others who will simply adopt the language of CNM because it gives their desire to fuck around some sort of cultural cachet.

However, as Joreth Innkeeper says, it's simply wrong to suggest that because there's no single, universally accepted set of rules for consensual non-monogamy, it precludes agreements and commitments.

> I have a lot of conversations with monogamists who are confused about 'how can you not commit to anything?' and then we start going around in circles. I do commit to things, I just don't commit to being sexually fidelitous. I asked them what part of their wedding vows included sexual exclusivity and did they not have anything else that they talked about? Surely, their relationships can be summarised or described by things other than who they're not fucking. So, monogamous people make all kinds of agreements and commitments and so do I.

So what do commitments and agreements in CNM look like? The answer is that they look however the people who make them want them to look. There's a phrase on currency notes issued by the Bank of England: 'I promise to pay the bearer on demand the sum of...' Bank notes are simply promises. What distinguishes them from other pieces of paper and gives them value is trust. Ultimately the only true currency in the world is trust and, as Dr Liz Powell says, it's the first point of appeal of all agreements.

> When I was in the military you had to be able to rely on the people in your unit, even if you don't like them, even if you think that they're a piece of shit as a human being, you still rely on each other and trust that the other person's going to be there when you need them because that's the pact that you've all made with each other.

> And so, when I have non-monogamous relationships I have much more of that military model [in mind]. I trust that the agreements that we're making about how we're going to support each other and that we're going to be there for each other, are going to hold and I know that they may not. And you have to hold that seeming contradiction in the understanding that that is the only way that life is. Like the only way to guarantee that someone is never going to cheat on you or break one of your rules is to handcuff yourself to them and never sleep.

Perhaps unsurprisingly a lot of CNM agreements are about sex and other relationships—unsurprisingly because this is an area where every person has their own particular preferences and because there's less guidance from the wider culture. Therefore it's better to have these things explicitly stated.

Obviously agreements can cover things like household finances, chores, and not leaving the toilet seat up. Non-monogamous couples broadly handle such things the same way as others, albeit perhaps with a greater propensity to negotiate and agree on them explicitly.

Eunice notes that the diverse nature of non-monogamous setups and arrangements is reflected in the diversity of agreements.

> There's such a variety in polyamorous relationships. Part of the joy is that you can negotiate every aspect, even those that would be assumed in monogamous relationships. So some people might say, "Hey, I'm not comfortable with you having sex in the bed that I sleep in." That's one form of boundary that they might prefer. Obviously there's always context—for instance if this means that their partners can never [have sex with anyone else] because there's no other [place]—that can

be the thing that takes a particular form of boundary from ethical to unethical, for example.

But there are other things. Such as 'Please tell me within 24 hours/ three days/ a week if you have sex with someone new', that can be a boundary. Or, to say 'I would feel comfortable and secure in this relationship if you do X. Can you please do X?' That can be an agreement you make. But other than some things about sexual health, keeping the dates you make, and general courtesy things, there's very little that specifically encompasses all polyamorous relationships.

The author Anita Cassidy arrived at an understanding with her primary partner, who is younger than her and who dates quite widely.

The core agreements we have is that there really aren't any rules as such, certainly no rules about certain acts or behaviours that are exclusive to us. What we do absolutely value is absolute honesty and openness about our feelings towards each other and other people; absolute transparency around arrangements. So, if you're seeing someone you let another person know how long for and where, because a coffee date in Starbucks for two hours is a very different setup to four hours spent over dinner in someone's apartment. So, [we're] very clear about location and timing and the nature of certain dates and other relationships. But apart from sexual rules in terms of practicing safe sex with other people because he and I are fluid bonded, [that's about it].

Vincent and Mia's agreement is not atypical in being very informal.

Vincent: I don't think we have an agreement in a contractual sense, maybe more a memorandum of understanding. There are clear bright lines where we understand what each other's requirements are, and what each other wants out of this arrangement, and we work from that perspective where she, for example, wants to be updated what's going on and she knows what I want out of this. So we meet those needs rather than having clear rules about what each of us has to do.

Mia: I think the only rule we have is that we have to not fall in love and not to have the other party fall in love with us. So whenever that happens I think our expectations are that we have to be upfront with each other.

Their arrangement has a lot to recommend it in so far as they're careful to prioritise communication rather than putting the onus on one another to behave in certain ways. However, in other ways it's potentially setting themselves up for failure.

One: they're setting out rules for people they haven't yet met. Okay, no one has to sign up to these rules, but third parties must either agree or must go forth and multiply with someone else.

Two: as already pointed out, all the rules in the world don't stop people falling in love or experiencing other feelings. Least of all people you've not yet even met. Putting such rules in place risks causing damage whatever the outcome. Even the strictest rules (i.e. laws) only really work when they concern actions. We're not yet able (thank god) to police thoughts and feelings effectively.

In Vincent and Mia's defence their approach is far from uncommon. Couples opening up are wont to create rules about feelings to defend their relationship. 'No falling in love' rules are very common in parts of the swing scene, for instance, and when people do fall in love despite their best efforts not to, then they can find themselves without the tools to navigate the 'What next?' Sometimes, in the absence of other options, they simply keep it quiet and lie about it.

Kevin Patterson argues that rather than make rules, we'd do better to look at the underlying issue that a rule or agreement is trying to fix and deal with that instead.

> If I say; 'Hey, I don't want you to date such and such a person' or 'This type of person, I don't want you with them', it shouldn't become a rule. It should be 'I'm trying to understand what my aversion is to that person'. I'm trying to figure out what my insecurities or my fears are and work them out so that we don't have to have these rules or agreements in place anymore. Rules don't fix insecurity, they just put a wall around it so that it basically protects your insecurity instead of fixing it.

Of course, as a number of my interviewees pointed out, there are circumstances where rules and boundaries blur because of the potential for some people and situations to cause problems that spill over into the lives of those not directly involved. Thus one could get agreements along the lines of 'No dating people with serious drug issues, gun nuts, anyone likely to bring the police or social services knocking, or Vogon poets in the vicinity of Earth pending the construction of a new interstellar bypass in our corner of the galaxy. If that does happen I will have to leave.'

What often happens is that rules or agreements or boundaries made in the abstract at some point butt heads with reality, and in the face of reality they often change or at least flex.

In a small way, that was the case with Shelly and Moshe.

SHELLY'S STORY

I don't want to offer you Shelly's story as a 'how to do it' when it comes to agree-ments. There is no single right way. You will need to find yours. Rather I share this be-cause of the people I interviewed for this book, Shelly is one of those whose thoughts, experiences and advice I particularly enjoyed, and because I find the way that she's gone about things quietly inspiring.

She fizzes with positive energy that makes her almost luminous. And I love her story. When she met her husband in Israel neither of them knew that they were go-ing to end up being consensually non-monogamous. They explored together, first in their imaginations and with their intellects and then in the wider world. They didn't rush. They were together eight years before the question of non-monogamy arose. They have a family. They patently love each other enormously. But there's also a real-ism there about the impermanent nature of everything and the fact that we change and grow.

> To start with, we did the contractual thing. We actually got married before we opened up our relationship and we decided after three years of deliberations to open up.

> Just anecdotally, the three years of starting to talk about changing our relationship structure started by me randomly picking up Ester Perel's *Mating in Captivity* in a bookshop, bringing it home, and us very boldly deciding to read it together in bed. As in lying together, holding up the book between us. Each one grabs one side of the book and we read it at the same pace, the same chapter. That was a very con-fronting thing to do because sometimes you really want to nod at something, being at that vulnerable space of admitting that yes, you do feel something, or sometimes you are not attracted to your partner, or sometimes you do fancy other people. Or sometimes all you want to do is... I don't know, something that's not acceptable in a normative relationship, being in that space right next to a partner and being a witness to their reactions to those things.

> So we talked about it for three years before doing anything. But when we did we got married again as in we rewrote... well, not rewrote... we wrote a contract between us, which I have in my purse and he has in his.

And what's nice about it is that if you read our original wedding vows, none of what we do now contradicts them because we never said monogamy in our wedding vows. We just said love. And luckily love is still around. And even those five or six bullet points in our kind of second vows—even though we have evolved greatly from the moment that we decided this is the journey we're going on—now six, seven years later, none of those are contradicted either, because we built in, as tech people would say, flexibility, agility and scalability.

When you strip it down to the core of it, at the core is a mutual desire for freedom, a mutual recognition of our separateness, and a joy in choosing to spend some of our selves with the other person. And the amount and the quality of the way that we spend some of us with the other person has changed, but the core is still there, I think.

This is one of the important relationships that I have in my life. It also has the symbolism of being important. Yes! We co-own property. We co-parent children. And, by default if we haven't made other plans, we will end up in the same bed in the evening. And we like that. We enjoy that. We're also very conscious that sometimes we don't choose each other and that one day we may not choose one another anymore for extended periods of time. I don't know. Who knows? I think it's an exercise in presence. So we're this; I love you now, right? I live with you now. Who knows? I think that acknowledging the uncertainty around it is important.

The third thing is that I think the processes, the emotional and intellectual processes that I've experienced in the last few years, were so profound that they extend way beyond romantic and sexual relationships, but also beyond relationships in general. I think the skill set that you need to go on this journey—it's kind of basic, but it's being willing to ask the questions with a really open question mark at the end and not know. It's being willing to unlearn a lot of things that you knew before or felt before or ever talked before. It's being able to have empathy even in situations which are very emotionally trying. All of these things are relevant to everything, are relevant to how we relate to, I don't know, politics, refugees, climate change, relationships with our children, relationships with our parents. They're all the same skill sets, and I feel I've evolved as a person in ways that have nothing to do with our sexual and romantic selves or parts triggered by those emotional, intellectual processes around polyamory or non-monogamy.

As Shelly and I sat in a café opposite Bush House on London's Aldwych, drinking coffee and sharing cake, she takes out the piece of paper that lives in her wallet and looks back through the bullet points. It's a journey back in time for her too. She's right that she and her husband built in space for the two of them to grow and change, and she acknowledges than in the years since they drew up their list they have done just that.

Yeah, it was January 2013, so coming up to six years following three years of talking about it.

So this says: 'Home is the centre,' and by home we meant our children. Meaning their wellbeing is really important. Any... I'm translating as it's written in Hebrew... anything will be done only for enrichment and positive flows or—what's the word? Like when you regenerate something. So the idea is whatever we do, this is to bring more good into our lives.

Mutual respect and fairness at all times.

Money and mood. That means don't bring your shit from anywhere and dump it on the kids or on the relationship, which is I think a general truism for anything. Don't spend money without consulting. You know, don't buy a house with a partner without consulting, things like that.

Social circles. Which basically meant at the time, don't fuck my best friend without consulting, or don't have sex with parents from school because that is potentially risky. I think this one has probably evolved because many of our close friends now are from the circles of non-monogamy. So don't sleep with my friends doesn't make sense anymore. But this was the risk management [at the time], and we didn't have any clue what we're doing and we have a lot to lose because we have three kids.

Expectation management *vis-a-vis* anyone who was involved. So anyone who's involved knows where we are, knows that we are married, knows that this is like a consensual thing and so on and so forth.

I don't know if this one is directly translatable: It means keep fingers on the pulse. So yeah, you can like check in.

Transparency, which doesn't mean I need to know every time you take a pee, but it means like, let's share the important things.

Safety, which was about no germs, viruses and things.

This one is a break clause that says if we feel that anything is harmful, we have the ability to say 'Let's stop and re-evaluate'. So just an ability to say, Okay, there's a crisis. Let's unilaterally stop.

Upon reading those, again I probably haven't looked at them in a few months or a year or so, I think probably what we thought these would mean has evolved a little bit. So still now if there is a crisis, I'm sure that we would treat it same way but I don't think that either of us would now say you must break up all of your relationships and be only with me, because I think all of these have evolved into a single rule, which is be awesome to each other.

Be excellent to one another. See, we're back to Bill and Ted and Jesus of Nazareth and maybe the Gautama Buddha as well.

That was a long spiel from Shelly, but reading that I'm right back there with her in that café. I can hear her voice, the voice of someone telling how she and her husband forged an agreement with love that's stood them in good stead over the years.

Agreements that liberate rather than constrain our spirits, that allow room for change, that are made with trust and good intent, these things aren't a guarantee of success, but they're a better foundation than fear and insecurity and the instinct to cling onto someone for dear life.

In the next section we'll look at the art of negotiating and see what we can learn about this from others.

WHAT WE CAN ALL LEARN

IN MONOGAMOUS RELATIONSHIPS it's not uncommon for agreements to be:

i.   Off the shelf: you borrow someone else's.
ii. Made at the outset and not revisited: all that stuff at the altar when you're distracted by the dress and your mum in the front pew and worrying whether the caterers are drunk.
iii. Unspoken: you both think you know what the other thinks you've signed up for but you've never actually spelled it out.

It doesn't have to be like this. It is actually possible, as non-monogamous people have found, to thrash things out explicitly, just as it's possible to keep these things under review.

The message, once again, is this: you can have a fantastic monogamous relationship that simply doesn't have to look like anyone else's monogamous relationship. It's your relationship, you get to make the rules, or rather negotiate the agreements! Even if you've agreed the monogamous bit everything else can be up for negotiation as well. Just try not to rely on assumptions or telepathy. Neither are terribly reliable.

CHAPTER FIFTY-FOUR

Negotiating

HOW TO NEGOTIATE?

Well, plenty of books get written about exactly that, often by CEOs and the big-swinging-dick brigade. Indeed if you look on the internet for advice about how to negotiate, very little of it either applies to or is specifically about interpersonal relationships; rather it's about salaries or business deals or property purchases and such like.

That's pretty telling of itself. The skills that business leaders or salespeople or (real-)estate agents would have you learn are often dire liabilities when applied to ongoing intimate relationships.

We're neither expected to nor taught how to negotiate with the people with whom we have the deepest connections. How much of parenting eventually comes down to 'Do as I say. I'm your mother/father'? That's fine if you're trying to stop your child running out into the road, but terrible as a life lesson. Negotiation in any context is a skill, and the skills vary according to context.

I'm not going to pretend it's easy. For instance, no advice on negotiation will help much if you're in a very unequal relationship. It's hard to negotiate if the other person is prepared to take a scorched-earth approach because they simply don't care if everything goes up in a great ball of fire. However that, of itself, tells you something.

In relationships that are worth preserving, negotiation, while it can be hard, ought at least not be pointless. As we saw, the way you communicate is important. So here are a few suggestions that may help you and your partners and your metamours end up in the place where you all want to be.

1. Choose your moment. Even better, create a good moment. While rarely is there a perfect time to do anything, some times are unarguably better than others. If you're ill or your partner has just crashed their car or you've both had three nights in a row where you've not slept well (children, drunks singing outside your window at 2 a.m., road drill starting at 5 a.m., biscuit crumbs in the bed...) that's probably not a good time. As Dr. Liz Powell puts it:

> Negotiate when you're well-resourced. So, when you're well-fed, well-rested, you're not in the middle of a conflict, your emotions are relatively level. I think that the less well-resourced you are the more likely it is the negotiation will go poorly.

If you are in a position to set aside time, make sure you're both fed, rested, relaxed and prepared; it can only help.

2. Don't rush, but don't let the process slide. Occasionally events impose their own time frame, often they don't. Take the time you need. Don't necessarily try to re-solve things all at once. The first session may cast light on problems or raise questions. You may need to sit with that for a while before answers start to take form.

By the same token, don't launch a process without an end. Aim to come to a reso-lution even if it's only for a limited time. Negotiations can be hijacked to become an end in themselves. Better to focus on reaching a positive conclusion.

3. Create buffering. While you're negotiating it can be useful to have a holding agreement. As Kevin Patterson observes, 'I think if you're going to have rules and agreements you should not picture them as a solution. They're more of a buffer until you can create solutions.'

However, be aware that temporary agreements have a habit of becoming perma-nent or at least entrenched. You might want to time-limit them. Limits can be extend-ed more easily than open-ended agreements can be rescinded. They also give you a time frame to work within.

4. Assume no malice. It can be very hard to negotiate positively if you've reached such a difficult pass that you feel a partner is out to harm or punish you.[106] You're charting a route back from stormy waters to calmer seas. You both need to be in agree-ment that you want to reach a resolution or at least improve things. If what you or a partner want is primarily an opportunity to express anger or hurt, then it's probably best done separately from any negotiation. That doesn't mean your hurt can't have a voice in the negotiations, just that if you need that hurt to be heard, it may require time both in preparation and also after talking so that everyone can settle and talk without their fight/flight/freeze/fawn responses being activated.

---

106 This is not intended to apply to situation where there is the risk of abuse or intentional harm.

For situations without this degree of animosity, it's generally easier to start from a positive place. As Liz Powell says, you can disagree with someone and still wish them well and want to secure a positive future together.

> When you find yourself assuming poor intentions on the part of your partner, ask yourself 'What's the kindest explanation I could come up with for what they're doing?' and try to operate from that as long as you can. Assume no malice, because for the most part, outside of people who are acting in abusive ways or who have very specific things going on for them, the majority of folks are not purposely trying to hurt you.

> It's absolutely possible to be abusive without being malicious. Assuming no malice allows you to evaluate whether it isn't actually malicious, whether instead it's just someone messing up. Because we're all going to mess up, we're all going to hurt other people, and that's just part of being human and part of being imperfect. And the more that we give each other the benefit of the doubt and try to stick with each other as much as we can, the better it's going to be.

5. Be kind. Aim to be as kind as you can. This is something that people get wrong. Sometimes they're aiming to be kind but get confused about what kindness is. More from Dr. Liz:

> Kindness is not the same as niceness. Kindness is about doing what is best for everyone involved, which sometimes means calling someone on their stuff. Which sometimes means drawing a line in the sand.

Kindness is about compassion and generosity of spirit and wanting the best for someone. *Niceness* is about being agreeable. We can be nice by smiling while seething inside. Niceness is what you get from people you don't really know and who are trying to be polite (or who are very confrontation-averse). Your real friends will do you the profound kindness of telling you what you may not want to hear but what you need to hear, and of telling it to you with love. That's a big deal.

6. Listen. Listen a lot. Ask questions if it helps someone explain or helps tease out their thoughts and feelings. Asking questions shouldn't mean conducting an interrogation or a cross examination. Questions are to help someone clarify or illuminate a situation. Try to avoid leading questions, those that steer or push someone towards a particular answer. Don't presuppose their answers. Don't assume: either that they know what you mean, or that you know what they feel. In particular don't assume motives. If in doubt clarify, clarify, clarify.

7. Don't box yourself in. Big sweeping statements don't help. As McFadden says, these are difficult to row back or for someone else to move forward from.

> If we make declarative statements we have excluded the possibility of amendment by the other person. In any kind of relational conflict, and non-monogamy especially, if we bring a spirit of curiosity and a formulation of inquiry to those negotiations we wind up closer to the place that we would all like to get.

8. Know thyself. It's such good advice that the Greeks had it inscribed on the temple of Apollo at Delphi so that people would see it as they went in to visit the oracle and also on the way out again, knowing less than they did 30 minutes earlier. McFadden says that for him, understanding his feelings, desires and motives was a turning point.

> I would say the first watershed for me in terms of being a successful participant in non-monogamous relationships was owning the things that I wanted and needed and owning the feelings that I didn't want, and just simply accepting that I had those feelings and starting from where I was at.

It's a cliché, but it's very hard to be honest with other people if you're struggling to be honest with yourself, and if you can't be honest with people when you're negotiating, you've undermined your best basis for success.

9. Be clear about your boundaries. This is a toughie, because as Liz Powell says, having boundaries means having a plan if someone crosses them.

> It's important when negotiating to be very aware of, and firm on, your own boundaries. One of the things I see people mess up the most is agreeing to things they're not actually okay with, and that are outside of their own boundaries, because they're afraid of losing the relationship. And as soon as you are unwilling for a relationship to end, you're no longer in a relationship, you're in a hostage situation.

You cannot adequately negotiate a relationship if you are unwilling to face the possibility that it could end.

Like most of this chapter it comes down to 'that's not a non-monogamy issue, it's a human issue'. Plenty of us have been in situations where we'll do pretty much anything to keep a relationship going. It's a horrible position to be in, but you don't want it to let it be a vulnerable position as well. Knowing that we can, if necessary, exist happily by ourselves—not investing all our hopes for happiness in another—gives us a much better chance to be happy sharing a life with other people. Sounds easy, doesn't it?

10. Be honest. Be plain. Tell people where you stand and what you actually want. Take it from Seb. He's an international lawyer and negotiates deals worth tens and hundreds of millions of dollars. This may go against the popular conception of lawyers, but mostly what contract lawyers seek is clarity—because clarity helps preclude the unforeseen and the unwanted. And clarity is hard to achieve without honesty.

> You should be as honest as possible. In fact, as a lawyer, I would say my style of negotiating tends to be a very honest, open one when I'm negotiating professionally because I think you avoid a lot of issues and misunderstandings that way. I don't think you really gain much of a strategic advantage in negotiations by concealing things, even professionally. And that idea is reinforced a hundredfold when you're negotiating anything personal.

If you want more quality time with your partner, just say that. Don't second guess what *they* might want so that you end up saying you'd really like to take them to that restaurant they mentioned or the film they sent you a review of. They may have been suggesting that because they thought *you'd* like it. All too often people end up doing things for each other because they think their partner would like it when actually neither of them does. Better to explain the real thing you're after. 'I really want to spend some time with you when we can connect' would be a start. You could then explain what that might mean. 'I really like it when we share experiences that bring us closer and give us things to talk about like the time we went to that Thai restaurant and couldn't speak after that insanely spicy papaya salad or when we went to see that German movie neither of us could make sense of.' Okay, this may not be your idea of a bonding experience but it's probably someone's somewhere.

11. Aim for a win-win (or in more complex poly constellations, a win-win-win-win-win). Some people, particularly some business leaders, seem to see negotiation as a form of rutting. They get to lock antlers with some other old dear and see whose break first. This isn't very sensible in a business context let alone when you're negotiating within a relationship.

The smarter outcome is to try to forge an understanding where everybody gets what they want, or at least as much of it as possible.

12. Consider negotiating issues as a bundle. There are times when it might work better to negotiate several things at once as a package (though there are times when it might not). If someone is unhappy at the way cleaning duties are distributed, you might consider looking at the way all the labour within your household or relationship is distributed. One of you may like cooking and consequently takes care of that and is happy to do the grocery shopping, while another is particularly concerned about cleanliness and tends to be the first to reach for the vacuum and the mop so they might also be happy doing the dishes. Parcelling related issues together can give a better overall picture and allow for a wider range of possible trade-offs to achieve a happier balance.

This might also apply, for instance, to things like how you spend your free time. One person asks that you go to the theatre more often, another wants more picnics. Hint—summer, Shakespeare, a stately garden somewhere and a hamper. God that was easy. Next!

You should probably be wary of conflating major issues with minor ones or simply with very disparate ones. 'Yes we can have a baby so long as I can build myself a man cave' has huge potential to end up going horribly wrong, as would 'Sure Bob can move in just so long as I can use our savings to buy a Porsche'.

13. Remember that value is subjective and relative and will change. Something that is very important to you might be of marginal concern or value to someone else or vice versa. This cuts both ways. It can mean that the person you're negotiating with doesn't *see* the value of something that matters to you. If they do, it might mean that they're happy to concede it to you because it costs them little. Or it might mean they're unwilling to concede it because it costs them quite a lot and they can't grasp its significance to you.

It's always helpful to explain *why* something matters to you. By the same token, it's always a positive to look for things you can give away cheaply in negotiations that mean a lot to the other person and areas where they can do the same for you.

14. Negotiating can be fun. Seb, our lawyer, learned a new trick from an old hand—the sex educator Midori—at an under-the-radar kink conference in Singapore.

> What she showed, and she did show it rather than talk about it, was how to negotiate in a way that was fun and wasn't made out to be a serious and stressful task that had to be accomplished before you got on to the good stuff. I think there's an important lesson there, which is that the negotiating and the discussion which is a key part of healthy non-monogamy does not need to be unpleasant.

Midori's talk was about working negotiation into a scene, almost making it part of the foreplay. Of course negotiating a scene or sex has much more latitude to be playful than many discussions about one's relationships; nevertheless Seb's point holds. It can be an opportunity for mutual exploration and something that can be done very much as a 'together' thing rather than an isolating one.

WHAT WE CAN ALL LEARN

PRETTY MUCH EVERYTHING here is as applicable to monogamous relationships as to non-monogamous ones. If you want to get the best out of a relationship, be prepared to discuss things and negotiate an amicable solution at the drop of a hat.

Some monogamous people absolutely do that. Jonty, who works as a science educator in the UK, has seen that first hand.

> I think that having a clear, negotiated relationship where everyone involved understands where everyone else is coming from is the most fundamental part. I have two friends, a man and a woman, a couple, but they're not poly. They are aware of poly, they have negotiated their relationship, but to them, exclusivity was important. And in that negotiation, they discovered actually, no, we don't want to be poly, we want to be exclusive to one another. But they've reached that point, not through it being the societal norm and it just being understood, but through full discussion of all of the options.

> It's not whether or not you're poly that I think of as, like, the main differentiating factor. It's whether or not you have a negotiated relationship where you are fully talking about what [the relationship] means.

This point has been made several times already: that negotiation is healthy however your relationship works. Just because it's just the two of you doesn't mean that everything else has to follow the standard playbook. Negotiate the relationship that you both want. Don't assume.

CHAPTER FIFTY-FIVE

Veto

IN POLY CIRCLES veto agreements almost always produce a sigh. *Veto* is Latin for 'I forbid'. A couple's veto agreement (it's almost always a couple) typically allows either to forbid the other to start or to continue a relationship or course of action. In other words, 'If I don't like it you can't do it' and vice versa.

Oh dear.

As the author and educator Kevin Patterson puts it:

> Somebody said that a veto is forcing somebody to break their own heart, and that's sort of how I feel about it. I'm not a big fan of a veto.

People introduce restrictive clauses and vetoes into CNM relationships perhaps because they want a degree of control over somebody else or, as Dr. Liz Powell sees it, to deal with their own insecurities.

> There are certain types of rules and agreements that people put into their relationships that make them feel more secure. Things like 'You will always have this date night with me' or things like… promises to allow each other to veto partners, or not to date someone the other person doesn't like.

There is a fairly narrow range of situations where this might conceivably be healthy. Morgan has told her partners that they have an effective veto over her choice of new partners if they think someone poses a genuine risk to her wellbeing while she's lost in the throes of NRE.

I think in our specific circumstances, they both have an unspoken, but I've told them, veto power thing, because they are the people in my life who have the best taste in people. And I'm like oh! If they don't like them, there's got to be something that I am fucking missing. The Dunning-Kruger effect, idiots don't know they're idiots because they're idiots, is the simplest way to describe that.[107]

Whenever I do get into relationships I do try to make sure that they meet both [my partners] so that if either of them goes 'Oh! No, that person's crazy' and it's just that I haven't seen it because I've been experiencing Dunning-Kruger, they can just pull me to one side and go 'No, don't do that'.

In truth this doesn't quite amount to a veto, it's more Morgan's own request for a second (and third) opinion that will carry a great deal of weight, probably delivered with a Paddington hard stare. Moreover, this was not Morgan's partners putting a mechanism in place to protect her from their own insecurities. They are *so* secure with Morgan that Morgan trusts them to give an objective assessment of someone she falls for.

'I need to protect him/her from bad peoples' is a common justification for someone claiming a right of veto. However, as Joreth Innkeeper points out, it's readily misused.

People who make rules for their other partners, who impose their own will, who decide what somebody else's behaviour should be, often fall back on the abuse argument. 'We have rules where I have a veto over my metamours because I need to protect my partner from abuse. If I see my partner being abused, then I want to be able to veto their relationship to get them out of it.'

There are plenty of people practicing consensual non-monogamy who say that exercising a veto is simply wrong. If you find yourself looking to impose a veto, or are having one applied to you, it's an opportunity to ask what the underlying issue is.

---

107 A slightly more measured summary of the Dunning-Kruger effect is that it's a cognitive bias that leads people, particularly those not yet familiar with the complexity of the field they purport to understand, to vastly overestimate their level of expertise in it. With continued study this inflated self-confidence fast falls away until a low point is reached, after which a degree of genuine expertise starts to support confidence again. Ultimately a true expert will have a much greater level of self-awareness and appreciation of both the extent and the limits of their knowledge and skills.

After all, the assumption is that we're all adults here. It's rare that someone subjected to a veto will be so vulnerable that it's warranted for their protection. If they are incapable of managing their life to that extent, one might reasonably wonder whether they're in a position to consent to sex or relationships in the first place, including with the vetoer.

Much as Kevin Patterson pointed out, Dr Meg-John Barker thinks vetoes raise big questions about underlying issues.

> I guess you're going to ask yourself, if you're vetoing somebody else's freedom, what do you actually want for your partner? Do you want to constrain the people that you love or do you want to expand their possibilities? But it's complicated territory because we're all insecure. We all fear the loss of people we love, and it seems like controlling what the people we love do is a way to keep them and to keep us safe. I guess I would argue that quite a lot of the time it's the opposite. The paradox is the more we try and constrain people, the more likely we are to lose them. Whether it be that they finally end the relationship, or whether we're basically in a relationship with a zombie because we've constrained them so much that they aren't this free person that we fell in love with. I think that's the kind of place we have to be really careful with vetoes.

And that is one of the great paradoxes of human relationships. I'm not the biggest fan of the Indian guru Rajneesh (or Osho as he rebranded himself) but he summed up that paradox pretty well:

> If you love a flower, don't pick it up, because if you pick it up it dies and it ceases to be what you love. So if you love a flower, let it be. Love is not about possession. Love is about appreciation.

The more invested we get in a relationship, the more we plan a future around it and the less we experience it in the present, the more we fear its loss. And it's from this fear of loss that so much of the pain we cause ourselves in our relationships stems. It's an attempt to control the uncontrollable: the changeable nature of our fellow humans and the transient nature of all living things. We want certainty in an inherently uncertain world.

As we've said many times, there's an important difference between good boundaries intended to protect the self and rules that are ultimately about controlling others, often in hopes of achieving a semblance of certainty or security. The veto, as it most commonly manifests itself both in consensually non-monogamous relationships, and indeed in monogamous ones, is generally about that need for certainty and security. But experience suggests that it's at least as likely to destroy a relationship as preserve it.

CHAPTER FIFTY-SIX

Commitments

COMMITMENT IS ONE of those slightly confusing words because it has two closely related but subtly different meanings.

In one sense a commitment is a measure of loyalty, dedication or devotion, faithfulness and fidelity: a commitment *to* something or someone.

In another sense it's a responsibility, an undertaking, a duty or obligation—a commitment to *do* (or to *not do*) something.

Quite often commitment *to* a person or thing also entails commitments *to do things*, and how faithfully we carry out our commitments *to do* is used as a yardstick to measure the quality of our commitment *to*. As in 'If you really loved me you wouldn't have forgotten to do the washing up,' and 'If you really loved me you wouldn't have gone to see Igor when I wasn't feeling well.'

So when Eunice, the London-based events organiser, says; 'People tell me I'm afraid of commitment. My answer to that is that I like commitment so much I want more of it,' she's talking about commitments *to*. At various points over the last few years she's had three, four and five partners. Her current relationships date back as much as twelve years. There's no lack of commitment, just an absence of exclusivity. Here Eunice is very much talking about loyalty and devotion—how committed people are to her and she to others—though there's a slight irony that Eunice is one of those people who also takes on more of the other sort of commitments, *to do*, than most of us.

Some people assume, as she says, that those who practice consensual non-monogamy are shy of long-term involvements—as though monogamy equals commitment in the sense of devotion and dedication and the alternatives do not. That's not borne out by the evidence. Plenty of people flit from one monogamous relationship to another, sometimes with periods of overlap. There's equally no shortage of non-monogamous people who remain deeply involved with multiple partners over years and decades. There are certainly those who see in consensual non-monogamy an opportunity to sidestep the contractual commitments that they associate with marriage (which, in a way, turn commitments *to* into commitments *to do* and *to not do*), there are plenty who, to borrow Andie Nordgren's phrase from the Relationship Anarchy Manifesto, are happy to 'customise their commitments'.

Dr. Liz Powell has an interesting take on things. The commitment *to* that she describes here is actually loyalty to a set of principles that guide how she treats others. And then when she talks about 'minutiae', she's talking more about specific commitments *to do*.

> When I think of the commitments that I have with people, a lot of them are ones that I make to myself rather than to them; commitments about how I will treat them, how I will interact with them, how I will think about them and how I will conduct myself if and when things end. What I want to have for myself is a clear set of values that guides the behaviour I have throughout the rest of my life and that applies to everything, not just my relationships. And so, the commitments I make with individual people tend to be more about minutiae than about principles, because the principles I hold to, I hold to for me, and I hope that the other people hold to similar-ish ones.

Liz feels that having a central overarching commitment *to* a '*how to*' helps her ensure that everyone in her life is treated fairly and consistently.

McFadden likewise is insightful about that relationship between commitments *to* and *to do*. In many ways our commitments to someone or to a set of principles can be rather nebulous in the abstract. We ourselves might not even be wholly sure just how committed we are *to* someone until the time comes to act on that commitment. It's in the doing that we get a shape of the feeling.

> The question I have, the question that's present in my mind over the long term, is who's going to come fetch me from the emergency room?

> We can laugh about that but I actually did have what I thought was a primary partner in the past who failed to come and fetch me from the emergency room. The broader version of that question is who has your back when the chips are down, right? When things are unpleasant for all concerned, who shows up for you anyway?

So, as you see, our loftier commitments are often put to the test by the practicalities. Does the 'Of course I'll always be there for you, babe' actually translate into being there when it's 3 a.m., you're bloody tired, and that particular babe is in the accident and emergency room after falling over in the street after two glasses of pinot noir too many? I mean, is it 'I love you n'all but not that much, know what I mean?' Or is it jumping in a cab so you can help them home and the only comment passed is a Roger-Moore-style raised eyebrow? Sometimes you only find out when it happens. By the same token, time and again you hear people say you only find out who your real friends are when things get tough.

In much the same way, specific commitments *to do*—to raise a family, to maintain a mortgage, to support someone in their career—are all expressions of a deeper impulse: an impulse to stick together, to survive together, which are all in the realm of devotion and loyalty, of commitments *to*. McFadden again:

> We bring a series of ideals to each relationship, but then there's how do we deal with each other in practice on a day to day basis, and come to grips with each situation, however challenging, as it comes up? It takes a lot of courage to be willing to accept a measure of uncertainty. If your other partner is also in the hospital, to whose rescue do you come, right?

> It's the difference between what one aspires to in principal and what one chooses to do out of love. Human beings who are acting out of love find a way to make things work.

There are various ways that we arrive at our commitments *to*. Some are chosen, some arise out of a mutual need for support and to survive (the kind of bond our ancestors might have had with their tribe), some arise by accepting others' expectations of one's duty, and some arise from the human equivalent of what, in titi monkeys, Karen Bales would call pair bonding and the parent-child bond.

McFadden is highlighting the dilemma that people face when they have deep and bonded relationships with more than one person. It's not unique to the consensually non-monogamous. Parents certainly ask themselves the same thing. If I had to make an impossible choice between my loved ones, parents, partner, children, how and who would I choose? It's the kind of choice that movies are written around precisely because it's the kind of choice that we dread.

And yet, for the most part, we rarely or never find ourselves in that position. We are presented with manageable choices. You ask a partner to take care of your child on this occasion because another partner fell ill and needs care and support. As McFadden says, 'Human beings acting out of love find a way to make things work.' You could try writing that into an agreement but it's the doing of it that actually brings it into being.

I think there's a case for us understanding commitments through the prism (haha) of Maslow's hierarchy of needs.

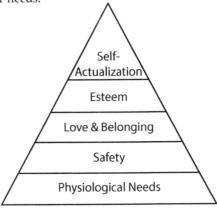

Our relationships are an important means by which we and others meet our needs. We're social, not solitary. We look for commitment from people who will do things for us, and there's a not unreasonable expectation that we'll reciprocate. In a precarious past without social safety nets, people's loyalty and their determination to make good on things expected of them were all that kept people from destitution and death.

Traditionally, commitments such as marriage have been about formalising commitments *to do* as part of meeting a range of needs. But because people have to meet the needs at the bottom of the pyramid before they can attend to those at the top, these commitments were primarily about food, warmth, shelter and safety first. Love and belonging were a bonus, and esteem only if you were marrying into a privileged class. Only recently in human history has a wider segment of society entered into committed relationships for the purposes of self-actualisation. Historically that was open to few people, the most privileged of the elite, because few had the security to aspire to self-actualisation. Even Leonardo and Michelangelo had to work to pay the bills, just like ninja turtles everywhere.[108]

---

108 In 1482 Leonardo wrote an outstanding speculative letter to Ludovico, Duke of Milan, asking for a job. Of course Leonardo was hoping to corner the bedroom poster market not quite five hundred years before Andy Warhol, but in the meantime art be damned, he'd build weapons of mass destruction to pay the rent: "If needs be I will make big guns, mortars, and light ordnance of fine and useful forms, not the everyday sort. If bombardment operations should fail, I will design catapults, mangonels, trabocchi, and other contraptions of marvellous and endless variety and means of offence and defence. In peace time I believe I can offer perfect satisfaction equal to any in the practice of architecture and the construction of public and private buildings, and in guiding water from one place to another. I can execute sculpture in marble, bronze, or clay, and also in painting I do the best that there, as well as anyone, whoever they might be."

So when Liz Powell talks of her reservations about the limitations of the tradition-al lifetime marriage ideal, she speaks as someone who, as a woman of her background and circumstances, is capable of meeting her own physiological and security needs in-dependently and who sees commitments more in terms of realising her higher needs.

> I think that the idea that you can make a commitment that will last for that long is interesting and cute as an aspiration but not particularly practical. The person I am today is not the person I'll be in 20 years or 30 years. And yet the model that we come from, most of us, is one that says that the only successful relationship is one that ends in death.

The thing about commitments *to do* (or not) isn't so much what you commit to—so long as that's clear and agreeable—it's the doing of it. You could commit to doing anything from the dishes once a week to spending a lifetime caring for someone. Clear commitments *to do* give people an idea of your level of devotion; in the performance, they see whether your commitment means anything.

The 1978 movie *Same Time, Next Year* starring Alan Alda and Ellen Burstyn is about two lovers (both married to other people) who meet up once a year for 26 years to continue their affair. At the end of the movie Alda's character, by now widowed, proposes to Burstyn's and stomps off when she refuses him, only to return whereupon they renew their commitment to meet every year for as long as they're able.

Notwithstanding the fact that they're probably not honouring their commitments to their respective spouses by having an affair, it's an illustration of an enduring com-mitment to something quite specific and limited but nevertheless meaningful to them both. It's what would be called a comet relationship.

One problem with traditional marriage vows, until people started pointedly re-writing them to reflect their own circumstances, was that they were an off-the-shelf collection of societal expectations and other people's pledges, not the couple's own commitments to meet one another's needs. Marriage vows have also institutionalised some very challenging commitments. 'I will look after you for the rest of my life' is tough enough but it's a commitment to do something. 'I will *love* you for the rest of my life' simply creates an impossible burden. It's a beautiful aspiration and a romantic declaration, but we don't have the same degree of control over our feelings as we do over our actions. People fall out of love even when they don't want to.

The fact that some people don't think very carefully about the vows they're making, or sometimes promise what they find they can't deliver, is a good illustration of what consensual non-monogamy, with its high levels of regular, ongoing communication and negotiation, can offer as a model for monogamous people.

It's also clearly possible to make and honour commitments *to* multiple people beyond the monogamous norm. However, monogamous or not, it's generally better—to borrow from business-speak—to under-promise and over-deliver.

MAKING COMMITMENTS

I HESITATE TO offer hard and fast guidelines for making commitments. They're very particular to people's personalities and circumstances. But here are a few thoughts:

- *It's almost always easier to make a commitment than to fulfil it.*
- *Commitments to do something are generally more realistic than commitments to feel something.*
- *Fulfilling commitments is more important than making them.*
- *Some commitments, such as to those who are dependent on us—for instance, children—are treated differently because the other party can't negotiate.*
- *Power differentials matter when making and honouring commitments.*
- *Failing to honour a commitment we've made costs us emotionally and in terms of self-esteem.*

CHAPTER FIFTY-SEVEN

Celebrating Poly Relationships

IT'S EASY TO be cynical about wedding ceremonies. They've evolved into an opportunity for parents to display their wealth, for the wedding-industrial complex to skim off a fair bit of that wealth, and for the bride and groom to say in public, like Bilbo Baggins, 'I don" know half of you half as well as I should like, and I like less than half of you half as well as you deserve'.

Consensual non-monogamy is, if nothing else, an opportunity (here we go again) to write your own rules or to have none. In many cultures marriage, or even a formal commitment, is a matter of choice and not a social requirement. Even where there is a commitment, that doesn't mean there has to be a public confirmation. Take Ivan and Alexandra, for instance. Ivan isn't averse to ceremonies, he's already married after all. It's more that he and Alexandra don't see the need.

> *Ivan*: Celebrations are nice and when there are more reasons to celebrate that is great, but I don't think I have a need to formally profess my love for her and my commitment in front of other people. I don't really need their approval or even them being informed of this. This is between us, that I feel. I am content with this but if you think this is something we should do I am open, we can talk about this.

> *Alexandra*: We are very private people and I don't see a need to celebrate it with friends and other people or family. I don't need that sort of recognition, or statements to say that he loves me.

But many people do like to mark their relationships, so that they can be witnessed by the people who are important to them. There are plenty of templates be they

444 A WORLD BEYOND MONOGAMY

Christian, Muslim, Hindu, Sikh, Buddhist, Taoist, Humanist, or just plain consumerist. However, because of the nature of consensually non-monogamous relationships and the fact that traditional models don't always fit, people often design their own.

One popular option is handfasting. Handfasting has ancient roots. It functioned as an engagement ceremony in the British Isles in the mediaeval period. In some places it served as a temporary marriage, with a couple being married for a year and a day.[109] If the arrangement was extended a third time it became permanent; a sort of suck-it-and-see approach to marriage.

One advantage of handfasting is that it is an old tradition but one about which relatively little is known and that largely fell out of use four hundred years ago. So it's a mostly blank canvas which a couple can use to devise a ceremony to suit them while borrowing a little from an ancient past.

Most cultures have ancient traditions, whether it be the native American blanket ceremony, the Chinese wedding procession, the Javanese *midodareni*, the Indian *mehndi* ceremony, or African dowry and bride-price rituals. This shouldn't need pointing out, but if it's not part of your tradition then it's generally appreciated that if you must borrow, borrow with respect. Meaning that at a very minimum you understand the cultural and spiritual significance of what you're doing. That's not always easy with other people's cultures, so if in doubt, probably better to borrow from your own. Hey, we're pretty free to mix and match as we like with our own traditions.

Handfasting has been adopted by what are often termed neo-pagans, people who've created pagan rituals from the little we know about older pre-Christian European traditions and who've adapted them to invest them with new meaning. It wasn't Charlotte's cup of tea, but she still appreciated the significance it had for her friends.

> Some of my friends got handfasted a few months ago, and that was a really lovely ceremony and really meaningful to everyone who attended, because it was very meaningful for them that they made this obvious if not legally binding commitment to each other in a public ceremony. But equally, like, I'm not particularly het up on public, wedding-ceremony type things for myself, right, but I'm still planning to marry myself for my 40th because I want the party and the cake, and the dress damn it!

And you shall go to the ball Charlotte, cake and party, and cake and dress, and cake and all. Save me some. As I mentioned at the start of the book I too went to a

---

109 The origins of handfasting at Scottish weddings: 'When Scots 'married' for a year and a day', *The Scotsman*, 14 Feb 2019.

handfasting ceremony. Popular choices of dates are around the solstices, equinoxes and the great Celtic quarter days that fall between them: Beltane (May Eve), Lughna-sadh (Lammastide), Samhain (All Hallow's Eve) and Imbolc (Candlemas). My friends chose Imbolc. My hot tip here—or at least a temperate one—Beltane, Midsummer and Lammas are nice times of year to get hand-fasted.

As well as being a therapist, DK Green is also a celebrant, helping to design and lead ceremonies for two or more people wishing to find a way of honouring their relationship.

> It's about marking a binding of relationship. It's about marking the relationship as an important function in your life, that person as a desperately important person in your life. And the answer to that in poly circles is often handfasting. I've performed many dozens of handfastings between two, three or more. For example, [my partner] Rachel and I handfasted in 2003 and then [partners] Rachel, Lou and I handfasted in 2004. For us it was the marriage. It was simply that there were more than two of us.

Perhaps it's something deeply human that transcends time and culture, but all the ceremonies, just as one might expect with more mainstream celebrations, feature common elements.

> In my experience every handfasting I've ever done, people surround themselves with family and friends as witnesses. And we gather in a circle and bear witness to that joining. It's a tribe recognition. It's literally a community or a tribe recognition and holding this relationship as important to these people.

However, the fact that there is a thread that runs through almost all these events shouldn't obscure the degree to which people work to make them very personal, something that is also increasingly common with church and civil weddings.

> The handfastings are all very bespoke because I meet with a couple beforehand. I have to make sure that there's no element of coercion. I speak to them individually to make sure that everybody is entering into this agreement or covenant with each other, absolutely, eyes wide open with consent and with the best heart and intent. And then we decide what sorts of celebration and ritual they want and they desire. I show them my sort of smorgasbord, this board of, "this is what I usually do. A, B,

C, D and E, which bits of it would you like? How would you like to change any of it and make it quite individual?" So I'll send them one over, recognising that it's one set from the shelf and there are lots of different palettes.

So, a few things to remember:

As DK says, it really only works if all involved really want to do it.

It's your ceremony. By all means get ideas from those who've been there before, but do make it your own.

Think about what you want to come away feeling you've done; made a pledge before your people, made a commitment one to another, forged a spiritual link, become part of a bigger tradition, done something romantic, thrown a huge party—different people want different things from a ceremony. Figuring out what it is you want as early as possible will help—but don't be surprised if something else hits you right in the middle of the ceremony. These things can surprise us.

Spending money on it won't make it special, though it will sort out the catering. You bring the 'special' yourselves for free.

CHAPTER FIFTY-EIGHT

Scheduling

Part of the reality of consensual non-monogamy is time management. It's hard enough dating one person if you've both got busy working lives and don't live together. When you're dating two, three or more then it becomes a greater logistical challenge. Indeed the complexity seems to grow exponentially as you factor in more people.

There is no single right system. Every relationship is different and the circumstances of every relationship are different. Moreover, as an oft repeated poly saying goes, love may be infinite but time is not. Neither is emotional bandwidth. For Xena time and scheduling effectively set the limits on her romantic involvements, bringing her to what some call the polysaturation point.

> The most difficult thing is time management, because when you live in two different places... that was tough for me. I would usually make it two days because luckily my husband is working from home so I can have him during the weekdays, and because my boyfriend had an office and had to go to work every day usually I would spend the weekend with my boyfriend. So, whatever it is that fits to individual needs. Luckily both of my men have a different background and work schedules, so every week has a weekend for my husband. Basically you just have to look how it works for your boyfriends and your partners' schedules.

Sometimes part of the attraction of a new connection is that this new person fits neatly into one's life. For instance, you're busy, you live with a partner and you have limited time for a second relationship. However you live in New York and work in your firm's London office for a few days every couple of months. You happen to meet someone you like in London. They're very happy to have a relationship with someone who is only around occasionally... and bingo! Sometimes these things feel fated, when it's actually just our brains going 'Hmm, handy *and* convenient!' Never underestimate the human capacity to make practicality a romantic feature (or, to be fair, the opposite, depending on your complexity orientation).

Nathan is lucky. His partners' demands on his time (and body obviously) happen to dovetail perfectly.

> One of the millions of metrics that I have is time that she likes me around. I've noticed that Debbie likes me around for about two weeks minus three days, like it'd be really nice if I could bug off for three days about every two weeks. Joreth is the opposite; really likes her peace and quiet and her time away from everybody, but would like me to show up every two weeks for about three days.

So that suits everybody. However, as Debbie says, the fact that there's more planning involved does limit the 'wild and free' vibe a bit.

> Me-time does help, it helps a lot, and I think the only frustration that I ever have is like I kind of missed the spontaneity of less structured relationships. You know, where you can go 'Hey! Let's go away,' for whatever and I don't have to look at a Google Calendar to decide if we've got free time together. But at the same time, I like being able to schedule 'Hey, you know there's this big event going on such-and-such a date', and the fact that he relies on his calendar so much helps to make sure that he won't forget such-and-such a date.

To be frank, to a lot of people with children all this will sound quite familiar. It's the question of How do we get 'us' time in a world of commitments?

As Debbie says, technology definitely helps. One day someone will do some research to see how closely the popularity of consensual non-monogamy grew in parallel with the use of online calendars and scheduling apps.

DK Green is as open to relationships as his diary allows.

> I am probably as poly as poly gets; I have discovered or found over many years that I can equally be in love with more than one person and that doesn't seem to have a lid on it. I think for me it's a bit like children, and just 'cause you have another child doesn't mean you stop loving your first one or love them any less or any different. But you know, it was just exponential for me. So I can be in love and sexual with whomever I can fit into my life. And to be fair, the only limit is Google Calendar.

So is Google Calendar the oil that makes the wheels of DK's love life go round?

Absolutely 100%. They all have access to my diary and they can book a slot. If you are on the ball for an afternoon off or an evening off, someone will message or call me and say, "Can I have that?" That's how it works.

For Penny, whose love life has occasionally been frantic, it's also been about making sure her husband and children also get their share of her.

I think mostly the issue is about time management, how we manage the time between work and family and the primary partner and the partner outside.

In some ways the scheduling is the easy part. Making sure everyone's needs are met can be more challenging. Where choices have to be made, most people aim to ensure that everyone gets some of what they need. But having tools to solve the practical side of complex emotional equations certainly allows people to focus on the emotional.

It's Political, Innit?!

CHAPTER FIFTY-NINE

The Politics of Consensual Non-Monogamy

A REMARK IN a newspaper article a while ago really caught my eye. It was written by a woman talking about not just the lack of female voices in public life, but the sort of female voices we're presented with. What she said, and I paraphrase, was that 'The female voices that we hear are those of women who have learned to play nicely with men.'

It was one of the most thought-provoking things that I'd read in ages. And it doesn't just apply to women. It was a comment I put to Meg-John Barker as we spent a very chilled few hours chatting in a seaside cafe on Britain's south coast, and one that they concurred with.

> I think as a trans person, I really resonate with that and I hear that from people of colour. Even if you're doing a training on trans as a trans person or on race as a black person, you have to be the nice one. You have to be the reasonable one. You have to hear the slightly transphobic or racist things that people are saying and be really gentle and kind about them because as soon as you show the pain that you feel from structural racism or from structural cisgenderism, then you're put in that category of the angry black person or the angry trans person or the angry disabled person, any marginalised group, and then you're not listened to. And I think that's really accurate and extremely sad.

I've already ventured so far as to suggest that in today's Britain, as in much of the West, the only acceptable sort of anger is white, cis, male anger. This is not a political cringe, just a reflection of the way that anger is used by the powerful to silence other people or to keep them in line.

Of course there are many angry white men who feel anything but powerful. But the genius of modern capitalist society is that it turns one group against another in order to distract attention from the forces within society that actually disempower and marginalise people, regardless of their gender, ethnicity, orientation or disability.

It's almost a joke, with the benefit of more than a decade's hindsight, how fast the anger at the cavalier bankers who brought about the 2008 financial crisis, and the decade of economic blight that followed, was deflected towards immigrants and minorities. Never mind the people we bailed out to the tune of a trillion dollars or more, what about those brown people who want to grab an extra hundred here and a hundred there in welfare payments?

What, you might ask, does any of this have to do with non-monogamy? Plenty. The world we live in, an angry world where countless millions feel acute insecurity in the face of climate chaos, economic change and the growing gulf between a tiny coterie of super rich people and almost everyone else, is inevitably an environment that shapes our relationships. Class matters to relationships. Economics matter. Societal crises matter.

There are such things as structural biases. Often people who live in relative privilege don't want to hear about these. A lot of the time it's because they don't feel very privileged themselves. Ask a white working-class man in a post-industrial town in Northern Europe or North America whether he feels privileged, and he'll almost certainly tell you to... um... take a hike. He's worried about his own future. People in such circumstances feel left behind and ignored because they *are* left behind and ignored. Past promises of increasing prosperity and security are being laid waste by globalisation as jobs, increasingly skilled jobs at that, disappear to South or East Asia or to Latin America. How are they to fulfil the roles they've been socialised for as breadwinners and heads of their households if they can't bring home a pay packet that commands respect?

In this position being told that you're privileged can feel insulting and disrespectful. You don't see it. Nor do you necessarily care much about the plight of those worse off than yourself. Migrant workers and refugees? Cheap labour keeping your wages down. Women? Dave the manager at work has been replaced by Brenda the manager. For some raised in conservative cultures it can be hard to feel like the man you were brought up to be if you're being bossed about by a woman, especially one still in her 20s with an MBA who knows nothing about anything.

You get my drift. This is not a defence of people's resistance to acknowledging their privileges, more an attempt to remind ourselves that we don't always stop to think about the battles other people are fighting.

And yet there are countless people from backgrounds like those mentioned above who are completely switched on to the unequal and arbitrary distribution of power in our society, and who see their own struggle as indivisible from those of people who also have to deal with additional discrimination because of the colour of their skin, their gender, their culture, their orientation, their age, and so on and so forth.

Likewise, there are people from minorities who see beyond the anger and hate and reach out to those who have assailed them and find common ground. People can be and often are bigger than the things that divide them and bigger too than those who seek to promote division.

Yes, but what does this have to do with non-monogamy and why are you dodging the bloody question?

It would be easy to say that the non-monogamous world mirrors the monogamous one, but in certain key aspects I'm not sure it does. I've interviewed dozens of people from San Francisco to Shoreditch to Singapore to Sydney to try to include a wide range of voices and perspectives. However I'd have to concede that the vast majority, though they may be female and/or queer, and though their skin is more likely to be brown than white, are nevertheless disproportionately educated members of an increasingly global culture that takes its inspiration from black American music one day and Korean television drama the next.

How and whether non-monogamy is done does seem to be influenced heavily by people's circumstances. Gender, ethnicity, orientation, disability and generation are all very much part of that picture, but I suspect that the biggest influence is economic.

Being financially independent gives people choices. Being financially dependent or insecure limits them. To a great extent non-monogamy is lubricated by disposable time and money just like many aspects of monogamy or decisions about whether or not to have children. Lack of money never stopped people falling in love or having babies but it has certainly always made the options broader and the practicalities easier.

Wealth also helps to insulate people against social disapproval. The aristocracy has been flaunting its sexual experimentation since time immemorial. In much the same way being from more privileged parts of society makes it easier to be out about one's relationship choices. The less wealth you have the more respectability becomes a valuable part of your social capital.

And yet, according to a team from the Kinsey Institute for Research in Sex, Gender and Reproduction at the University of Indiana; 'Studies show that more than one in five participants report engaging in CNM at some point in their lifetime. This proportion remained constant across age, education level, income, religion, region, political affiliation, and race, but varied with gender and sexual orientation.'[110] The studies' samples were reportedly designed to mirror the US census. So perhaps the impact of economics may be more to influence the way people from different backgrounds practice CNM and their relative visibility.

---

110 M. L. Haupert, Amanda N. Gesselman, Amy C. Moors, Helen E. Fisher & Justin R. Garcia (2017) Prevalence of Experiences With Consensual Nonmonogamous Relationships: Findings From Two National Samples of Single Americans, Journal of Sex & Marital Therapy, 43:5, 424-440, DOI: 10.1080/0092623X.2016.1178675

Gender, ethnicity, orientation, disability and age also have a profound influence on the formation of relationships, and the principles of intersectionality apply. Just to restate these briefly, intersectionality, simply put, argues that the impact of the different sources of discrimination we face is cumulative rather than discrete. For so long as people are discriminated against for being non-monogamous then it becomes another layer in that pancake stack of prejudice and some, who have enough on their plate already, may choose to forgo yet another source of stress and grief. They may wish to be non-monogamous, or at least not to have to keep it hidden, but frankly they have enough shit to deal with as it is. Best opt for the quiet(er) life.

So, in the chapters and sections that follow we'll look at various social factors that have an influence on relationships.

One would like to think that the ostensibly switched on, 'woke' people who have chosen non-monogamy would have created a community that deals with diversity well. That's not necessarily the case. Educator and author Kevin Patterson, who is African American, is pretty clear-eyed about how far short of the ideal poly communities tend to fall.

> Generally I don't think it's very good, but there are people who want to do better. There are people who will listen when you tell them how. I sold thousands of copies of *Love's Not Color Blind*. There's gotta be a reason why. Every once in a while I still get emails, and messages, and people saying, 'I read your book, I read your blog, I've made some changes to the community, and they went over really well.' And other times they're more like, 'I tried to make changes to my community and they didn't go over well at all because the older cis-het white men, who make up most of my community, pushed back on it pretty hard.' So there are people who want it. There are people who don't. But that's life. That's everything. That's not just polyamorous communities. It's every community.

As Kevin says, these issues aren't peculiar to non-monogamy or to a particular community. If you're monogamous and in a relationship with someone who is subject to some of these considerations, then it's useful to be aware. It never hurts to set out some of the issues so we can all reflect on them.

None of the sections that follow even aspires to be comprehensive. Each subject could fill a book on its own. However it's a start. Read on.

CHAPTER SIXTY

Money, Class and the Social Divide

CAN YOU BE poor and poly? It's an awkward question, one that provokes strong feelings and also one that the consensually-non monogamous community can be exceptionally sensitive about. We live in a system where economic status is a major determinant of outcomes: education, career, housing, health and, yes, relationships.

Almost all the people I've interviewed for this book, whether they're from Europe, Asia, Africa, Australasia or the Americas, are educated, articulate, professional. They would broadly be described as middle class.

Magick may be most of those things, but middle class he's not.

> I come from a working-class background but I went to a grammar school and I've got a double-barreled name so I've always been in this weird place where people assume I'm kind of middle class but I actually came from a fairly poor background, my dad worked in the factory and stuff.

If you look through the biographies of my interviewees at the end of the book, you'll find that they're not a representative cross section of humanity. Yes, I've made a point of interviewing people from around the world to broaden out the wave of writing about CNM that is quite culturally specific to the United States. But almost everyone I've included has gone to university. At the small gathering of an international polycule where I met Magick, about half the people there had PhDs, mostly in STEM subjects. As he says, it's easy to get the impression that being educated and having some financial resources are the norm in poly circles.

I think that it has a role insofar as, if you look at the scene, most people are reasonably comfortable financially at least to the extent where they don't have to rely on somebody else and are reasonably well educated, at least the extent where they have been taught to think and analyse things. Personally, I'm reasonably well educated but I'm fucking penniless.

The fact that I've not found many people who would identify as working class in the groups I've interviewed shouldn't be taken as an indication that they don't exist. As Maxine says:

No evidence of something happening is not the same as evidence of it not happening. Tales of historical working-class non-monogamy... if nobody's writing history about someone, how do we know?

The answer is that we don't, really. Much of the research that has been done on poly-identifying people[111] (predominantly in the United States) has included very few who haven't been to university (typically under 10% haven't attended university at all) or who come from minority groups (also well under 10%). The Haupert, Gesselman, Moors, Fisher & Garcia surveys mentioned earlier, designed to sample the general US population more accurately, found consensual non-monogamy happening at similar levels across almost all economic classes and other divisions.

So what's going on here? Is there an issue of representation or simply one of visibility? That's difficult to say but there are certainly a number of factors at play here.

Firstly, lack of money inevitably makes most things more difficult. As Kevin Patterson puts it:

Polyamory costs money and people try to pretend like it doesn't. People try to say, "You don't always have to do stuff with your partners that requires money." But in a capitalist society, anything you're doing that isn't making you money, is costing you money. If I've got to work two jobs, how am I supposed to manage two relationships? When me and my wife both want to go to a thing, or if both want to go to separate things, we've got to figure out babysitting and gas money. Having excess resources can really boost your polyamory. If you don't have that, it can really limit what you're able to do.

---

111 Including: 'The Privilege of Perversities: Race, Class and Education among Polyamorists and Kinksters', Elisabeth Sheff and Corie Hammers (focusing on kink/BDSM) (2011), 'Gender, Family and Sexuality: Exploring Polyamorous Communities'; Sheff, 1996-2003; 40 in depth interviews and the Polyamorous Families Study; Sheff, (2007)

As in Philadelphia so too in Singapore, says Billie.

> The only other poly people I know other than my own 'family' is this other one couple, and they were upper-middle-class and they were a bit douchey. I think education and open-mindedness and the ability to research certain subjects, it comes with being privileged, so I think it's mutually exclusive. If you're poor and worried about money, struggling all the time, I think it's quite hard to decide 'I want to support another partner'.

Or as Mawar in Jakarta has it:

> I think non-monogamy people from the marginalised group, they have probably other important things to worry than ethical non-monogamy.

Quite.

The forms of consensual non-monogamy I've tended to encounter do require resources of time and money—time to engage with multiple people, time to travel to see them—and time, to use the cliché, is money. Many people who have time don't have money and vice versa. As Kevin says, if we're working all the hours, time is limited. If we're not working, money is limited.

However much we like to think that love can transcend all obstacles, it's in the nature of obstacles to make things harder.

A difference in income creates another barrier. Kevin again:

> So many times when people speak about what their experiences are, they try to separate partners with this financial barrier. 'We only go to this restaurant together, but I go to some other restaurant with my other partner.' Or we take separate vacations with separate partners. I'm supposed to be taking a partner to see that Avengers movie tomorrow night. And the first thing that she told me was, 'I don't have the money for that'. So, even though I was the one who asked her out, there's a level of insecurity, a level of fear, and worry about being able to be financially responsible for a date. It would have been just as easy for her to say, sorry, I can't make it.

Simply put, even if one person doesn't mind paying the lion's share of the expenses involved in maintaining a relationship, and even if the other doesn't mind being, in the nicest possible way, subsidised, it can still affect the relationship dynamics. People generally prefer to interact as equals. It usually makes healthy relationships easier. Financial disparities can really screw around with that.

Then there's the issue of perception. As Liz Powell notes, the instances of consensual non-monogamy that make the news are often studies in privilege.

> You'll see in the media every once in a while a sensationalist 'These people live together and they're all having sex' kind of article and it's generally upper middle class white folks who likely live in California.

And, as Magick and Ivan say, if it's not the privilege of wealth, then it's the privilege of not having to care what other people think.

> *Magick:* That it's a very sort of middle-class bourgeois thing doesn't mean everyone involved is, but it's become a bit of a hipster thing much like BDSM has as well. It's kind of artists in turn-of-the-century left-bank Paris, Jean Paul Sartre, very open ...

> *Ivan:* Maybe this is about conforming to norms of society, and that you can afford not to conform to them after you have a certain level of comfort in your life. Basically if you look at polyamory and living in larger-than-two groups of people, it is actually beneficial to having children if you have four parents. If you have more than one income from just one father it's easier to bring up more kids. It's weird, if you look at it this way, that polyamory is not more of a working-class thing, because it's easier to survive if there are six of you. But here is where I think the social norms kick in, and if you're starting [having] other people in your shack you are a slut and the witch and we should burn your field blah blah blah.

And that's the other thing; it's not just money. Consensual non-monogamy is, at present, very much the choice of a minority not in the mainstream. There's still a lot of prejudice. If you already face discrimination there's a big disincentive to take on more. As Morgan puts it:

> There is a theory that as a child you learn an optimal level of [your total] risk. So people who feel safer in the home will drive more like maniacs; it's all of that balancing out. I think that it applies to this situation. People who are less privileged are less likely to be found in poly circles because there is no legal protection, it is an additional risk on top of everything else.

So, in the plainest possible terms, if you already have enough on your plate why would you want to make life harder for yourself?

What's more, there are easier ways to be non-monogamous than being polyamorous if you are facing or concerned about facing social disapproval. Swinging, for instance, tends to be something that couples keep quite separate from their vanilla social lives. Monogamish and open relationships, with their tendency towards 'don't ask don't tell', allow for greater discretion. Equally, certain poly styles, such as all-together-under-the-same-roof arrangements, can make economic sense and, managed discreetly, can be made to look very vanilla to the outside world.

Indeed, as Ivan inferred, a more communal approach with more social solidarity, more pooling of resources, traditionally benefits the lower-paid disproportionately. To borrow from Franz Kafka and Frank Zappa; 'When it's just you against the world, back the world.' That's why we join together to stand a fighting chance. For this very reason, it's simply not something that capitalism encourages. The power of the collective, whether in the form of public services, cooperatives, collective bargaining, trades unions or political movements, is something that those who wield the power of money have always seen as a threat.

No wonder Margaret Thatcher extolled the virtues of the nuclear family and declared 'there's no such thing as society'; it's much easier to push two isolated people around than an entire village, even a metaphorical one. But, despite all that, there are what Liz Powell calls 'movements towards creating greater inclusion,' and, says Dr. Meg-John Barker, alternatives to the 'standard' solo poly model.

> We always have to think about the practicalities and the economics of it, how easy is it to live alone, for example. But there are other options for Solo-ness within community. Like co-ops and shared housing for example. I recently was living in a co-op for a while and that seemed to be quite a nice example of somewhere where you had the solitude of having your own room but also the communalness of having people around you. So I guess there's a way of doing it relatively cheap, but again, to what extent you can escape a capitalist model if you live in a capitalist society? That's a bigger question.

> I suppose we mustn't assume that solo poly necessarily means living alone, like there may well be ways of cohabiting. Again, it's hard to buy somewhere or rent somewhere as a polycule or as a group of people, but it's not impossible. People are finding ways around these things.

But I'll give the last word to Maxine and Magick in turn. While both enjoy the privileges of education, neither is financially secure and both have found their poly networks to be a safety net in time of crisis.

> *Maxine:* There are a number of articles that have gone viral around the community about how it's not possible to be poor and poly and it's not possible to be ill and poly and it's not possible to have a long term disability and be poly.... I don't think I would be alive now if it hadn't been for polyamory, because of the periods when I'd gone through an abusive relationship, I have a chronic illness, I was homeless. Polyamory effectively saved my life, because I would have been on the streets and probably dead otherwise. Had it not been for the fact that I had these connections that I considered to be family, like I'd built family through polyamorous relation-ships and had people who were capable of supporting me and helping me out through that time—that's made my life possible. So, this idea that it's not possible to be polyamorous and poor is just utterly shocking to me, because without it I wouldn't be here.

> *Magick:* Absolutely the same here—when I was in trouble two or three years ago, if I hadn't had connections with people I have played with and the BDSM scene I'd have been fucked, absolutely.

It's something we see again and again: that solidarity is the secret weapon of those on the margins. That's when the strengths of the 'tribe' really come into play. Poly networks are simply another expression of this phenomenon, one that we find across cultures and across time. And for some people, when it counts, being part of that bigger thing, that extended family, makes all the difference.

CHAPTER SIXTY-ONE

Gender, Gender Roles and Feminism

PLENTY OF PEOPLE would argue that consensual non-monogamy in general and polyamory in particular are fundamentally feminist. They have a case.

One could start with the observation that since the emergence of polyamory in its modern form in America in the mid- to late 1980s, a significant majority of its organisers, opinion leaders, media spokespeople, book authors, conference planners, bloggers and podcasters, as well as most academic researchers into the subject, are women.

Traditionally marriage and property were inextricably linked. As we've seen, it's only in the last century and a half in the West that women have had any real degree of control over the their lives. Before the advent of women's rights women usually passed from father to husband almost as chattels and their legal identity was subsumed into that of their husbands.[112]

As for monogamy, it also seems to be bound up, at least historically, with ideas about property and ownership. Prof. David Barash speculated that monogamy could have emerged as a form of redistribution of women in response to social unrest amongst single men in societies where 'harem forming' (powerful men monopolising the pool of available mates) was the norm. Others would argue that it emerged along with private property as men wanted to know that their land and goods would go to their biological offspring. Prof. Joanne Begiato sums up the standard view of traditional marriage as emerging because 'monogamous relationships are easier to manage. They are tied very much to our kind of patriarchal society in which property statuses

---

112 Through much of human history women have been treated as chattels: possessions of their fathers or husbands. The principle of couverture essentially subsumed a woman's rights into those of her husband. It wasn't until 1870 that the British parliament published the Married Women's Property Act, which enshrined in law women's rights to earn money and to inherit property in their own right. One of the virtues that some see in CNM is that it further dismantles the notion of woman as possession.

of various kinds are distributed through marital relationships.' Still others argue that monogamy was the result of lower status men devoting more time and resources to one mate than a powerful man could to many. In all these cases the assumption is, at least in part, that women traded sex (and unpaid labour) for protection, food, shelter and security for their offspring.

Most forms of consensual non-monogamy trample all over those conventions insofar as they return an individual's ownership of their sexuality to them and this, Joreth Innkeeper argues, benefits disproportionately those who don't identify as heterosexual men and gives women freedoms that don't exist in monogamous culture. Mawar also sees CNM as both feminist and liberating:

> I think being in a non-monogamous relationship is basically not only you're feminist, but also, you know, in a sense human rights because you are responsible of your own action, kind of. I feel empowered. I feel like I'm free. I'm free of the sort of traditional convention of how women should act, what women should be, because I am my own person. I'm responsible of myself and I can do whatever I want as long as it's not hurting anyone's freedom.

But intrinsically feminist? Alice, for one, has her doubts.

> I don't necessarily think it has to be a feminist thing, but it is liberating that you can make decisions outside of what society dictates, i.e. to be this one man, one woman plus children kind of couple. Feminism to me is just equality for men and women. This, for me, it's not really equality of any sort. It's just the consent that you negotiate with your partner.

On the other hand, many of the women Meg-John Barker has talked with over the years see polyamory as being a more feminist way of doing things. It certainly encourages people to build alliances rather than to be alert to rivalries. It lends itself to being collaborative and collective. It requires the skills that women, rather than men, tend to be encouraged to develop as they grow up, such as communication and empathy. Perhaps CNM is thus easier to navigate for those (men, women and non-binary people) who've learned them rather than those who've been discouraged from doing so.

> We talked to a bunch of poly women back then and found that people were talking definitely about polyamory as feeling like a potentially feminist way of doing relationships. I remember people talking about how it enabled child rearing with

multiple adults involved and that took the pressure off. Some women talk about being really like the hub of their networks. Often you get the sense that it was them who were quite the driving force within their poly cluster or polycule. People talked about the excitement of being desired multiply and being able to act on those desires.

The key word has to be 'potentially'. The hope that poly people might somehow be inherently more egalitarian or inclusive is probably a vain one. Anyone can call themselves consensually non-monogamous or polyamorous. Plenty of people will claim to be whatever they reckon they can get away with if they think it will get them what they want: 'feminist', 'egalitarian', 'ethical'... You can label yourself however you please but 'by their deeds you shall know them' and all that. Understandably Meg-John advises caution.

> We've got to be careful. I think there's this idea that maybe somehow polyamory would be inherently feminist or that sexism would disappear. Sadly, it was really not my experience.

MJ did chuckle when they said that... so perhaps there is some cause for hope. In many CNM circles there's a higher degree of accountability to the community. People talk; it's that communication thing. If there's a problem it's perhaps that people don't always talk enough, something I deal with in the section on 'the broken stair'. However, says Joreth Innkeeper, we shouldn't be surprised that while the poly community may be separate to a degree, it's not separate to the extent that it can barricade out all the attitudes and behaviours that are pervasive in the wider world.

> Unfortunately, there is always going to be influence from the culture from which we come, which means a lot of the outside pressures that are put on the culture, and then the people who join the poly community, who are still products of the culture, are going to be bringing in all of those ideas. So, there are corners of the poly community that are not as liberating for everyone.

What polyamory does do is encourage people to communicate, including with their metamours, and to see them as friends or at least allies rather than rivals. Maybe it's Kevin Patterson's low-key 'We're all teammates on Team [Shared Partner]', or Seb's sense that metamours create a whole that is greater than the sum of its parts. Without a willingness to communicate and negotiate, consensual non-monogamy can fail or become toxic pretty fast.

So what of gender? Some traditional gender roles don't fit very well into polyamory and other CNM styles. Most people arrive at it having grown up in a culture that offers a narrow view of gender roles and a limited range of role models. Dr. Liz Powell:

> Men are allowed to feel happy, angry and turned on. Those are the only emotions men are allowed, particularly in American culture. Those are all generally powerful emotions. Happy is good because good things are happening, anger means you can punch some shit and ruin things, and turned on is you can go take the person of your desire in a manly way. There's a lot of power associated with [those]. They're all outward focused and have a direction that includes some sort of action.

Don't knock 'happy, angry and turned on.' It's the emotional palette that made possible Chuck Norris's acting career. But for many of us it's an emotional gag. Men are constantly up against the idea that to have feelings, let alone express them, is to be seen as weak. As McFadden observed, for men to have emotional needs is taboo. But men do, and those feelings end up somewhere. All too often they come out as rage, often with tragic consequences for others, or as inwardly directed anger which is associated with depression. Traditional masculine stereotypes don't offer men much guidance for having a healthy relationship with their feelings or, frankly, with others.

Women meanwhile, argues Liz Powell, are left having to do the emotional heavy lifting for their male partners, because men tend to have a smaller network of people (if any) with whom they feel able to share deep feelings. Meanwhile women are left to find outlets outside the relationship for their feelings.

> Women are given a lot of space to feel in some ways but not necessarily in others. Particularly in modern dating culture, women are supposed to not have many feelings aside from having feelings that are okay with the dude they're dating. If you have more feelings than the dude that's a problem. If you have less feelings than the dude that's a problem. If you have feelings that you need his support on, that's possibly a problem. And if you don't want to support his feelings, that is also a problem.
>
> Particularly in American culture, straight men can only get their emotional needs met by the woman they are having sex with, that is the only place they can talk

about their feelings, the only person who is expected to support them on their feelings, the only person they can talk to about their problems.

So, women aren't really allowed to have a lot of emotions that they display and are a part of the relationship. They just technically get to have them mostly with their girlfriends or their gay friends. And I think that that's one way in which women have a leg up in some ways, that they tend to have a lot of people with whom they can discuss their feelings who are not their male partners.

It's worth pointing out that it's quite possible to recreate these traditional patterns in a non-monogamous context. CNM does not bar the doors to people who want to stick with traditional gender roles, or for whom communication and emotional engagement are uncomfortable. And I have to agree with Julie Bindel that CNM in and of itself is not necessarily a force for change.

My scepticism about polyamory is not about being anti-sex or stuffy, and I wish good luck to those in relationships, for love, sex or whatever, with five, six or 20 other folk. But let's not pretend it will bring on the revolution any time soon. A true sexual revolution will have happened when there is consent and equality in every sexual encounter.[113]

But consensual non-monogamy is also very welcoming of those who have departed not just traditional gender stereotypes but who've also transcended simple gender binaries. Transgender and genderqueer people seem, at least anecdotally, to be overrepresented within polyamory, though perhaps somewhat more so in the UK (and possibly in the groups I interviewed in Asia) than the US. A number of those who contributed to this book are nonbinary.

I've been left wondering whether people who've had to come to terms with genders or orientations outside the mainstream have, in the process, been left better equipped to deal with the complexities of consensual non-monogamies; not least an ability born out of necessity to be able to explain difference and state particular needs.

Nor does CNM limit you to one expression of your gender. Different relationships can give voice to different aspects of one's personality including the gender-related. As Meg-John says, one connection might bring out a more masculine you, another a more feminine one, a third conceivably something quite androgynous.

---

113 'Rebranding polyamory does women no favours', Julie Bindel, *The Guardian*, 26 Aug 2013.

Having multiple close relationships enables me to be in differently gendered sides of myself. So being a non-binary trans person, my experience of non-binary or trans is that there are, for want of a better way of putting it, more masculine, more feminine sides. And having relationships with more than one person of whatever kind can enable those to embody or experience those differently gendered ways of being. Primarily what it opens up for me is that potential.

But what about masculinity?

There's been a lot said and written about a crisis in masculinity (particularly, in the UK, in *The Guardian*). Men in particular seem to have been struggling for the last forty years or so to find an expression of their masculinity that serves them in a changed world where both men and women work and find purpose and fulfilment outside the home.

One issue seems to be that many men aren't looking to new models of masculinity that fit into a world we live in now. Instead they're insisting on a return to a world that has ceased to exist, oblivious to the fact that economics and the need for skills alone would have drawn women into and promoted them in the workplace, regardless of wider demands for social, political and economic equality.

The growth of the so called 'men's rights' movement, of inceldom, 'Men Going Their Own Way', pickup artists, and a whole collection of groups that seem to be at war with women (encouraged and exploited by the far right for its own ends) is surely symptomatic of this crisis of masculinity. The male stereotypes we've inherited are from an age that largely accepted the lethality of childbirth and the unpaid labour of women without question. They're from an age when men were lionised for taking all the risks in a world in which they could be conscripted to fight in bloody industrial wars or be killed or maimed in mines or foundries. It was an age when the responsibility of putting food on the table often felt like theirs alone and the shame too if they failed.

Yet the world of men as lone, horny-handed breadwinners or smoking-jacketed masters of their own wine cellars isn't coming back.

Instead, we're a society where communication and negotiation are needed to thrive and people without those skills struggle. And yet many men see globalisation not as a phenomenon that allows capital to dodge taxation and western labour costs while handing ever more money and power to the super-rich, but as a plot by women to neuter and emasculate them.

At the same time as most men find themselves with less power than their fathers enjoyed, women have gained agency, albeit agency still constrained by the same disempowering system.

Hardly surprisingly, then, it looks to many men encountering consensual non-monogamy as though women are having all the fun, are in sexual demand, and that non-monogamy just plays into female hands—with predictable scenarios playing out in the poly scene. Franklin Veaux, Joreth Innkeeper and Maxine:

> *Franklin:* So, the thinking goes, if you are a man and you have a female partner, well she is going to be able to just run around and have sex with anybody she wants but there's no way that you could ever keep up. Because, you know, men just have to work so hard at it. I've seen so many cis het white dudes in the poly scene whining about this. You know, 'Oh My God! My girlfriend has 'mumble frotz'[114] lovers and I just can't get laid because this is all about women, and women can get laid anytime they want just by asking for it...' And have you considered maybe being a little bit less entitled about access to sex?

> *Joreth:* Like maybe nobody is going to have sex with you because we just don't like you. It's not because you're a man and we have it out for men, it's because you're not a nice person and we are finally in a community where we have other people we can have sex with.

> *Maxine:*—And probably because you're not very good at sex.

> *Franklin:*—Because your penis is so small; if you had a bigger penis you wouldn't have this problem.

> *Joreth:* Who is that comedian? DeAnne Smith? Yes women love your cock. We're just so tired of everything else that's attached to it.

That's not every poly activist conversation. Everyone knows that men are indeed quite capable of navigating the world of consensual non-monogamy if they choose— it's full of them!—and they aren't all 'alphas', whatever that's supposed to mean.

Again I return to a thought I find myself expressing throughout this book: Consensual non-monogamy's flexibility and the way it encourages people to rethink convention and to write their own rules makes it easier for it to accommodate difference. So when it comes to questions of gender rights and identity, fewer of the traditional constraints are inherent. It's up to people to choose not to put them back in.

---

114 Ancient geek for an indeterminate number.

CHAPTER SIXTY-TWO

Poly and Orientation

The roots of consensual non-monogamy can be followed in many directions, and some of those routes are definitely queer.

That's hardly surprising. In a 2018 study[115] a team of researchers found that queer people were strongly over-represented in a sample of almost 2500 polyamorous people, where almost two thirds identified with an orientation other than heterosexual as against only a quarter of the monogamous control sample.

Orientation	Polyamorous (2,422)	Monogamous (539)
Heterosexual	882 (36.4%)	399 (74.0%)
Lesbian/Gay	95 (3.9%)	31 (5.8%)
Bisexual	788 (32.5%)	73 (13.5%)
Pansexual	435 (18.0%)	19 (3.5%)
Other	222 (9.2%)	17 (3.2%)

What's also striking though is that lesbian and gay people are under-represented in polyamory compared to the monogamous population at large. And yet, in many ways, gay men and lesbians were as instrumental in shaping modern consensual non-monogamy as was sixties counterculture, perhaps more so. Julie Bindel, although sceptical of modern polyamory, was nevertheless quick to claim it for her contemporaries who were at the forefront of the women's movement of her youth.

115 'Demographic Comparison of American Individuals in Polyamorous and Monogamous Relationships', Rhonda N. Balzarini, Christoffer Dharma, Taylor Kohut, Bjarne M. Holmes, Lorne Campbell, Billie J. Lehmiller & Jennifer J. Harman *Journal of Sex Research* (2018). DOI: 10.1080/00224499.2018.1474333

It was radical feminists in the 1970s onwards that developed the notion of non-monogamy as a way to challenge patriarchal heterosexuality. One could have as many sexual partners as desired but everything was honest and above board, with no one being deceived. The type of non-monogamy radical feminists developed and practised involved no men. We were all lesbians starting off on a fairly equal playing field.[116]

But even more than the lesbian connection, contemporary CNM owes a huge debt to the gay scene of the 70s and 80s. As Amy Moors and Jes Matsick noted in their research;

Contemporary CNM has its roots in the activities of gay communities. Gay men's engagement in consensual sex outside their primary relationship was documented first in the early 1980s . This research—some of it now 30 years old—does not appear to have been especially controversial, perhaps because dominant groups have less interest in regulating the sexuality of marginalised groups than of other dominant-group members.[117]

In other words, the further you are outside the mainstream the more the mainstream leaves you alone to get on with it. Before attitudes started to shift in the 90s, GSRD (Gender, Sexuality and Relationship Diverse) people were so far from social redemption that they were damned any which way. So, on the principle that you might as well be hung for mutton as lamb, people just got on with things as they thought best, 'no rules but our rules' fashion.

The evolution of gay consensual non-monogamy owes a great deal to the prevailing attitudes of the time. Prior to the 1970s it was far harder for gay men to have both romantically and sexually committed relationships; after all, two single men seen regularly in one another's company, let alone being affectionate in public, were likely to attract attention and outright hostility. It's easy for people outside the gay community to forget the violence as well as the disapproval routinely directed at gay men.

Instead, bathhouses and gay bars gave men who had sex with men a place to meet and have sexual encounters. While tolerance, and later acceptance, grew and men found it easier to have relationships with other men openly, the culture retained its sexual openness.

---

116 'Rebranding polyamory does women no favours', Julie Bindel, *The Guardian*, 26 Aug 2013.
117 'Investigation of consensually nonmonogamous relationships: Theories, methods, and new directions', Amy C. Moors, Jes L Matsick *Perspectives on Psychological Science* (2017), Vol. 12(2) pp 205–232.

One factor, according to Charlie, a gay man in his early sixties living in Colorado, was that thirty years ago and more, when gay men often came out later in life, there was a lot of making up for lost time to be done.

> People of my generation experienced a lot of repression with our sexuality—I didn't come out until I was in my late twenties—so we didn't go through the same kind of relationship development or experimenting as young people, as teenagers, and learning how to have relationships and such. And we were not sexually fulfilled; all that's repressed for people that are closeted. And then when you come out, it's like, woo hoo, you know, you want to catch up. You have a lot of repressed feelings that you want to explore or just do everything.

But as LGBTQIA activists like James Finn recall, when in the early nineties he and others were pondering what a queer-friendly future might look like, monogamy wasn't part of the picture. By then the culture of consensual sexual non-monogamy was seen as a feature of the gay scene, not a bug.

> Monogamy, in my experience, was not a highly valued commodity. Relationships could be permanent relationships, loving relationships, but the activist set at the time and the people who were envisioning a new way of being post-Stonewall, we never assumed that we were going to be emulating straight people, as we talked about it then. We didn't have any notion that there was going to be a groundswell and a push for equal marriage. That was on no one's radar. So we were interested in building something new and different, and what we probably then would have called better, and it didn't envision monogamy, and it never did.

And yet, while sexual non-monogamy remains common amongst gay men, romantic non-monogamy apparently is not. If there is a prevailing norm it's probably the open relationship. When Charlie came out as polyamorous back in the early 2000s it caused way more ructions than when he came out as gay.

> It was amazing to me that all of my progressive friends... When I came out as polyamorous—gay and straight—I lost a lot of friends, because that was less acceptable to everybody than my sexuality, you know. And longtime friends straight rejected me and just stopped being my friend when I came out to be polyamorous. They thought it was wrong. That's all that they could tell me, that it's just wrong. What do you do with that when somebody says that. You can't even have a conversation about it?

James Finn too has noted that the apparent hostility to polyamory extends into some LGBT circles, something that he was surprised to encounter.

> When I go on social media and promote articles and other people's articles, people who are talking about polyamory, I get tremendous, bitter pushback sometimes. People are really hostile and that surprises me. I wouldn't have thought that. I mean, when I'm out there pushing articles and engaging with the public, it's mostly in the LGBTQ focused places and I would expect maybe a little more tolerance, and I find that there's a great deal of intolerance. [Some] people really do just instinctually believe because of how they're brought up, I suppose, that poly lifestyle is simply wrong and they feel it fiercely and they lash out.

Finn makes the interesting observation that some people who would completely reject the notion that being queer is a matter of choice nevertheless see being inclined towards non-monogamy as a matter of choice and make it a moral issue in exactly the same way that some religious or conservative people continue to treat being queer as a moral issue.

Perhaps it's a sign of how far the LGBTQIA community has come in terms of acceptance that some queer people now feel inclined to seize what they feel to be the moral high ground and pass judgement on CNM people.

That progress, if you call it progress, cuts both ways. If gay men were largely left to do their own things while they were outside mainstream society, that started to change when queer people increasingly found themselves accepted and adopted as a totem for liberal values. Could it have been the prospect of social contagion that led to the surprisingly rapid acceptance of same-sex marriage? After all it's one thing for a pariah group to have unusual sex lives, but if those people start to become objects of admiration and to be seen as good, regular people, might not that lead to an acceptance of the way they organise their relationships?[118]

As LGBTQIA people have been co-opted by the mainstream, the more that both the pressure and the opportunities to conform have increased. Same-sex marriage was a huge step towards equality, but it's hard not to see a subtext that 'You got marriage, dump the bathhouses.' Charlie again:

> There was a lot of pushback within the community when the struggle for gay marriage was going on. A lot of them felt like they didn't want to have any part of

---

118 Arguably this is, in part, exactly what's happened. Some elements of straight culture have always been influenced by queer culture. Flirting with queer style now seems less edgy than it once did, and queer culture has gained in influence.

that, in part because it's old-paradigm that dates back to a time when women were chattels. And so they felt like 'We want to be liberated and free and be able to have whatever relationships and sex we want; we don't necessarily want this old system that we should buy into to be 'normal''. But ultimately more and more people felt like it was just a matter of civil equality than anything else.

This situation differs in different countries. In the US, wariness about polyamory in the LGBT community seems to have diminished substantially in the wake of same-sex marriage being legalised throughout America in 2015. Until then, conservatives had long argued that gay marriage would be a slippery slope to legal polygamy (not to mention bestiality and marrying trees[119]). In this environment, it worried some same-sex marriage activists that people maintaining multiple relationships might play into the hands of slippery-slope scaremongers and hinder the cause. In the US at least, that particular type of timidity is apparently now largely history.

The important things remain choice and consent. Equality, surely, for queer people doesn't just mean equal marriage, it means dignity and respect regardless of whether someone's choice is marriage, unwed monogamy, or whatever form of CNM pleases them. As James Finn puts it:

Being queer—to me—means having the freedom to explore and invent ways of being, to create family, to live fully, to live differently from convention. To set our own rules and define our own happiness.

Charlie and James were both born in the early 1960s, so I wondered whether the resistance from their peers to romantic consensual non-monogamy might be a generational thing. Simon Copland was born in Australia in the late 1980s and is almost three decades younger. He sees sexual CNM as the norm amongst his gay contemporaries in the antipodes—gay couples are well represented on hookup apps for instance. But even now he is sceptical about whether there's more acceptance of multiple romantic relationships in Australia's queer community.

When I first entered into a polyamorous relationship, that was back in 2014. Australia was in the middle of the marriage equality debate and I got a lot of pushback from within the gay community and also from lesbian women because of fears that polyamory was just too out there and that it would be used by conservatives to target the marriage equality campaign to hold back that sort of legislation.

---

119 Remarkably the number of people in the United States marrying trees has never been lower.

Simon still finds himself particularly running into flak when he speaks about his relationships publicly, although Australia legalized same-sex marriage in 2017. He sees the criticism he gets from within the LGBT community as much the same as gays and lesbians had to put up with before there was a shift in public attitudes.

> I think it's 100% respectability politics. It was, 'You're going to give us a bad name. You can have your relationships but please be quiet about it, please don't talk about it publicly.' What I find extraordinarily ironic is that a lot of those messages are exactly the same messages that conservatives have said to gay people for a very long time, and they do that without thinking about the history of that language and how they're now directing it at a different group of people. And that's very disappointing.

Consensual non-monogamy still largely precludes respectability. These days, in much of the West at least, being LGBTQIA doesn't. If there are stereotypes around modern lesbianism they're probably more likely to conjure mild women hanging a chandelier than wild women swinging from one. Indeed, Charlotte, who identifies as a lesbian, feels most others are disconnected from today's CNM culture.

> It's really fucking hard being a non-monogamous lesbian because lesbian culture is incredibly monogamous. I mean like those U-Haul jokes aren't really jokes.[120] I do know couples who are now married who like moved in together on the third date. So, non-monogamy is far less of a thing in the lesbian community. I think it's just like women get so heavily hammered with the monogamous narrative. Because the lesbians I know who are poly are the best at poly because no one likes discussing their feelings like lesbians.

BISEXUALITY / PANSEXUALITY

MANY PEOPLE ARRIVE at consensual non-monogamy out of a desire to explore other aspects of their sexuality. For some people who are either bisexual and/or biromantic, pansexual and/or panromantic, monogamy can feel like having to choose which expressions of that to pursue and which to abandon.

Just how prevalent that is becomes obvious from the research I referenced earlier, where half of those polyamorous people surveyed identified as bi- or pan-sexual, compared to around one in six of the monogamous sample.

---

120 *Q:* What does a lesbian bring on a second date? *A:* A U-Haul (a rental removals van). rofl, checks scatter cushions, rofl again....

However, the perceptions of bi men and bi women within CNM varies. Bisexuals have long faced prejudice even within the gay and lesbian community; stereotypes include bi people being greedy or indecisive or even simply in denial of their 'true' orientation.

The semi-mythical hot bi babe is often an object of fantasy, fetishization, and ardent pursuit. The equally hot bi guy, not always so much. Indeed, as the author and broadcaster Cooper Beckett observed, while swinging is almost predicated on female bisexuality, the swing scene's attitude to male bisexuality is often equivocal, suspicious or unwelcoming. Although, in some circles that is changing and efforts are being made to make swinging more friendly to queer men.

That same double standard is sometimes evident within poly groups, though attitudes vary from place to place and from generation to generation. For instance, some polyamorous Americans I've interviewed were struck by how queer the UK scene is compared to that in the States. Conversely, some poly Brits find the US scene far more sex driven than their own. UK polyamory can verge on the cerebral at times... with a lot of tea and a lot of books and not much sex.

Anecdotally, younger people discovering polyamory are more likely to identify as queer (millennials and Gen Z are increasingly adopting 'queer' as more generally inclusive than LGBTQ+) and also to be comfortable with male bisexuality.

Jonty, a 40-something science educator living outside London, identifies as bi. While he's aware of the perceived bias against bi men in the swinging scene he says his experience of being bi and poly in the UK is very different.

> I find that in the BiCon[121] world, in the poly world, in the queer world, you almost get a reverse effect. I remember snogging a guy at BiCon and I have a stranger come up to me and say, 'Oh, it's so nice to see two guys being bi, rather than it always being two girls'. At Polydays, BiCon, things like that, there's always the worry that you're going to get infiltrated by effectively cis-het, white, middle-class dudes coming in and being idiots. So, as a man, if I'm showing affection or interest in another man in that kind of queer London bubble, I find everyone else sort of loosens up and is more accepting.

By and large the CNM world seems more alive to, and more accommodating of, variations in orientation than many other spheres. In the last couple of decades, the way orientation is thought about has shifted away from the more binary or ternary perceptions of straight, gay and bi, towards understanding sexuality as a spectrum and our romantic and sexual desires as multi-dimensional. Consensual non-monogamy has broadly reflected that.

121 BiCon is the UK's annual bisexual-positive event.

CHAPTER SIXTY-THREE

Ethnicity

RACE EXISTS. IT'S a thing. Race, at least in the way we tend to think of it, has no basis in science. Any DNA test will tell you you're a unique mix of genes from all over. And those genes all have a common origin in Africa. But it's right there in our minds and how we see other people, and it's there when we decide whether or not to give other people shit or just, consciously or unconsciously, avoid them. The existence of racism, whether structural, unconscious or intended—and people's experience of it, whether within consensual non-monogamy, the wider community, at work or dealing with institutions—is far easier to prove empirically than any half-arsed idea about race.

Look at any genetic map and there's no clear line that delineates one group from another. Genetic researchers think that 10,000 or so years ago there were no people with blue eyes. All blue-eyed people are supposedly descended from a single person with that particular gene mutation born somewhere between 8000 and 4000 BC.[122] Yup—I'm mutant spawn but I'm okay with that. When the first ancestors of modern Britons crossed the land bridge from continental Europe around 10,000 years ago, their skin tone was probably very dark.[123] It's probably the lack of sunlight and the need to make more vitamin D, but we white Brits and other northern Europeans seem to have adapted over the years to become the generally delightful, slightly pasty hodgepodge we are today. Our direct ancestors looked quite different.

Yet people still persist in seeing the human world, with all its physical and cultural variety, in the terms shaped by the instinctive human fear of the stranger, the one from outside the tribe, dating from our hunter-gatherer past—a fear that continues to stoke itself today with misconception, stereotype and lazy thinking. Self-identifying with a particular race can be an act of solidarity. Having it imposed upon you is another thing entirely. Too often it's about excluding others or asserting superiority over them.

---

122 'How one ancestor helped turn our brown eyes blue', *The Independent*, 31 Jan 2008.
123 'First modern Britons had 'dark to black' skin, Cheddar Man DNA analysis reveals', *The Guardian*, 7 Feb 2018.

This is obviously a huge subject, far better covered by Kevin Patterson in his book *Love's Not Color Blind*, which I would urge you to read. Kevin, and Ruby Bouie Johnson, who we'll hear from again shortly, are both African American. African Americans aren't the only ones facing discrimination. But their continued fight for the same rights and the same dignity as their fellow citizens—in a nation that purports to believe 'that all men are created equal, that they are endowed by their Creator with certain unalienable Rights, that among these are Life, Liberty and the Pursuit of Happiness'— has become a global touchstone for those seeking justice and respect everywhere just as the struggle against apartheid was a generation earlier. So let's start the ball rolling with Ruby and Kevin.

If you're from a minority group *and* consensually non-monogamous you're increasing your chances of facing discrimination or prejudice. It comes back to the principles of intersectionality: Prejudices layer and accumulate like sedimentary rock strata. You get grief for being a member of an ethnic group and you get grief for being non-monogamous. For every additional marginalised group to which you belong, there's another layer weighing down on you. Given that many people from minority groups earn less than their majority peers, there's another one right there.

Society, of course, subscribes to crude stereotypes about many different groups. Ruby Bouie Johnson says those used to label and constrain African Americans have a long history and are so pervasive that they've even been unconsciously bought into not just by Americans at large, but also by some in the community.

> There's these four archetypes about black women: that we are Jezebels, you have [the aggressive] Sapphire, you have the Matriarch, and you have Mammy. And so those also set up how you see us as women. And so on the black male side, you have the hyper-sexual: the bull, the one with the big dick, the one who has a certain persona. They were, you know, the bucks and they were there to have sex with slave women and produce more slaves. And it was all based upon [the stereotype of] our butt and our hips, you know, that we are ready to be bred, we are savages, we are hedonistic.

There are a host of others from the Sambo and Uncle Tom of yesterday to today's angry black woman, and the 'magical negro' beloved of Hollywood, and they crowd out other, more positive models. Kevin Patterson:

> There's always a representation gap when you're black. In America there's always this representation gap. There's always this limit of what people think black people can and can't do, can and can't be. And sometimes that's easy to really internalise.

And this in turn means African Americans, just like members of other groups, are offered limiting ideas about what they can be and achieve, what they can participate in, and what is appropriate.

> Like with being non-monogamous, if I bring it up to people who don't really know me, one of the first questions I always get is like; 'Isn't that just white people shit?'

The hostility from some in the community toward consensual non-monogamy is hardly surprising when, as Johnson argues, African Americans are trying to shake off white America's prejudiced view of them.

> It's viewed that we don't have sustaining relationships, you know, 'missing fathers and all of the mothers are single, they're all out to get money and be taken care of and not use birth control' and all of that, coupled with people's already having personas about polyamory and open relationships, I mean it's the perfect storm.

So there's trouble on multiple fronts. Consensually non-monogamous African Americans, like other members of minority communities almost everywhere, are trying to push back against age-old majority prejudice. At the same time they're having to fight a rear-guard action against traditionalist views in their own community, which worries that CNM will jeopardise its attempts to prove itself moral and worthy. KP again:

> Cunning Minx podcasts Polyamory Weekly. I love her podcast and I've hosted it a bunch of times and they end every episode with, 'and remember it's not all about the sex...' To some extent, we're trying to prove that we're normal to the normies, and we shouldn't have to do that in order to be respected as people or as an identity. It plays out in working class situations. It plays out among black folks or people of colour. There's always this idea that if we pretend that we're less than we are, people will respect us more. We really want people to respect us regardless. Do you want people to see us as a full and vibrant people just as we are? I don't play into respectability politics. I work my hardest to not do so. But it shows up from time to time. But it's all bullshit and it's everywhere.

'If we pretend that we're less than we are, people will respect us more'. Isn't that just a perfect summary of the fallacy of respectability politics, where the debate has some-

how shifted to whether someone is the 'right kind' of black/Asian/queer/working class person? But at least there's the poly community, the liberal, welcoming, broad-minded woke folk who are as right-on as they are kinky? Well, when Ruby Bouie Johnson first got involved in the CNM scene some ten years ago, not everyone was exactly enlightened.

> I would go to events here in Dallas and there were about 75 people. I was one of two people that were black or of colour. And when I walked into the room it was like I was on that block again, it's a given that I would expect to hear people moaning, talking about my butt, talking about 'I've never been with a black woman'. I'm like a piece of chicken in the frozen food section.

Let's give this a little extra context. African American women students are more likely to complete a university degree than any other ethnic-and-gender demographic in America. Yes, any.[124] You hear it time and time again from people from minority backgrounds: you play by the rules, you get qualified, you do a skilled and demanding job, and still some person with half your talent and less than half your ability looks straight through you and asks you to fetch them more ice for their drink. Like most nonsense that people have to put up with repeatedly, the first time you shrug it off, but by the 1000th time it's starting to get a little old. Don't be surprised if that ice ends up down your shirt.

And still there are times when the poly scene in the US can apparently be a bit tone deaf on these issues. Both Kevin and Ruby have been invited to speak at events about 'black issues' rather than any other area of their expertise and have found themselves either the only person of colour there or in a small minority. If one's not careful, it becomes more about the semblance of inclusivity than ensuring the real thing—and at worst a form of diversity porn.

Joreth Innkeeper is a member of another American minority; she's Chicana.[125] However she passes for white, so some people are surprised to discover that she's not 'one of us'.

> I'm assumed to be any number of things so people treat me that way, which means I get to hear them talk the way they talk when they don't think any oppressed are listening. And so they will say things assuming I'm one of them and then I'll reveal something of myself to them and then there will usually be surprise and a backlash

---

124 Black women become most educated group in US, The Independent, 3rd June, 2016 quoting the National Centre for Education Studies.
125 Chicano/Chicana is the chosen identity of Mexican-Americans in the United States.

akin to betrayal. Betrayal is a much stronger word than what they're feeling or what they're reacting to, but it is.

The United States isn't alone in having to deal with racism. However of the three major centres covered by the interviews in this book it seems to loom larger there than elsewhere. Kerilyn, born in Zimbabwe but very much a Brit, having grown up in Birmingham and studied in Southampton and Liverpool, encounters more issues with gender than with her ethnicity.

> I'm possibly one of those people of colour who, being very comfortable in some ways in my identity as a British person, has not felt the colour part as much as perhaps other people. I notice my being a woman more than I notice my being a person of colour. Non-monogamy, when you first look at it, seems to be structured more in favour of men. There are things that lean towards that kind of shit; one penis policies and crap like that but you don't have anything like that comparatively when it comes to colour. London is a very vibrant diverse place where it's very easy to feel at home.

London is one of those places where it's very hard to pick out the locals from the visitors (though Hawaiian shirts can be a bit of a giveaway). Nevertheless people of colour still get stopped and searched way more often than white Londoners.[126] There are many other metrics that underscore the fact that the UK still has a long way to go before ethnicity is no longer an issue. At its best though the London polyamory scene seems to reflect the fact that it's a city that increasingly belongs to the world, drawing in both temporary and permanent residents from around the globe. However, not all parts of the UK are as diverse and inclusive.

Like London, Singapore also has race issues, but has worked hard to defuse tensions, though minority groups still suffer from economic marginalisation and semi-benign neglect. Again, the poly scene there, such as it is, seems to be very mixed. There's less apparent demand for munches and meetups just for people from minority groups, though that could be a reflection of the fact that the scenes are too small to make forming sub-groupings practical.

Back in the States, however, the sheer size of the scene makes that possible. Ruby Bouie Johnson again:

---

126 Black people nine times more likely to face stop and search than white people, The Guardian, 27 October, 2020

There's a black and poly group, it has approximately 21,000 people within it. We have DFW (Dallas - Fort Worth) Polyamory & Black. And we are literally a family, right? Reason being is that there's safety there. We're not asked about the texture of our hair. Right. We can talk about racism and we can talk about it like no one else is listening that's non-black. I don't have to prove myself or my experience or try to explain an experience that is based in a place that unless you're black, you won't understand.

Up in Philadelphia, Kevin Patterson thinks there's good reason for getting together as a community within a community, for much the same reason: the comfort and confidence that comes from having common reference points and things that are simply understood.

I like being able to have events where I don't have to worry about that, where that doesn't have to be a fear. Netflix put out a show called 'She's Gotta Have It' based on Spike Lee's movie. I hosted a person-of-colour exclusive watch party for that. Part of the 'why' was so that I didn't have to explain myself when I felt a certain way when certain things happened on screen. There were some really touching cultural references in that first season and I didn't want to have to explain to my white friends why they brought me to tears. I didn't want to have to share that with people who didn't just understand.

And yet these safer spaces and tolerance from one's own crowd can have their limits. After taking flak from the world at large, including the African American community and white poly people, you might hope that other African American poly people would cut you some slack, yes? For the most part certainly, but not always. It's safe, for instance, to talk about colourism, the prejudices that are sometimes applied within communities on the basis of how dark or light someone's skin is, something by no means unique to African American society. But one can still run into taboos and prejudice even amongst poly people of your own background, as one African American interviewee who preferred to speak off the record explained:

I do feel respected within certain communities. Now I say that, but let me date interracially, right...! And this happened at one big poly event where [a black friend] was thrown under the bus because he was with someone who was not black and she shared that she was with him, and so he lost people behind that....

The pushback that some African American people experience, especially it appears African American men, when they date people of other backgrounds requires a degree of context. Firstly, for some, it runs counter to the sense of solidarity that they feel a community that faces so much discrimination owes itself. Then there's the unavoidable fact that the US criminal justice system incarcerates young African American men at far higher rates than young men from other backgrounds, out of proportion to the frequency and the severity of their offences. That's had a noticeable impact on the numbers who are living free and available to date in the prime of their young lives. And lastly, there's the bias against black women that's shown up in research by the dating site OkCupid, which suggests they're rated as less attractive than women of other ethnicities. The same OkCupid data similarly suggests a bias against Asian men.

That's evident, to some extent, even in Asia. There is certainly a sort of reverse prejudice, perhaps based on bad experiences, where people positively avoid dating people of a *similar* background to themselves. Xena, for instance, tends not to date fellow Indonesians.

> I want to feel that my opinion is valued. I feel like with Asian men, you are not as valued as a man in the same position. I like dating white guys because guys in Indonesia, whenever we have discussions and they always think they are right and they don't value the woman's opinion. This assumption is always 'What do you know?' That's kind of the look they're going to give me; 'What do you know anything much about the man world, the world in general?' Well I probably know more than you, but it's because generation to generation the men have never been challenged before, hence they always put the women's opinion to the side. With the western men I feel listened to even when maybe I'm not right. For me it's important to be recognised.

So what to do about all this? I tend to assume goodwill and the absence of malice, though my ability to do so is probably a reflection of my relatively privileged position. And while there is a lot more racist behaviour than there are consciously racist people and while many people who discriminate don't do so consciously, that's doubtless scant consolation to anyone on the receiving end.

We remain highly attuned to difference, far more so than to sameness. We pick up first on what makes people stand out from the norm rather than what they have in common with us. To an alien coming to Earth we'd probably all look weird in much the same way. Being alert to difference evolved as a survival trait. Walk into your messy work space and if someone has moved something while you were out, the chances are that you'll home in on that one thing. If you're staring at a largely static landscape you'll notice tiny movements or something there that shouldn't be. Those of our ancestors who had this skill were more likely to survive and pass it on to their children than those who didn't. So too is our ability to draw general conclusions from a small amount of data hopefully to cover what we don't know. We spotted that thing moving through the grass. It's a snake. We don't wait to find out if it's a nice friendly snake or a deadly poisonous one, we assume the worst and bash it with a rock or run. That's not a million miles from how we react to those human unknowns we run into. But what serves us well in some situations serves us very badly in others.

And then there is the miasma of messages and information, much of it faulty, in our environment. Meg-John Barker sees this as less of a failing of us as individuals than as an inevitable consequence of the world we live in.

> When people are pointing out racism nowadays, they're trying to emphasise this is a structural issue. When you've grown up in this culture where it's just pounded into us all, all the time, you're not going to be able to escape it as an individual. So it's not that if you get called out for racism that you say to yourself, 'I'm not racist'. It's like, no, 'I live under structural conditions of racism. This is bound to happen.' And all of us do. Even people in the marginalised groups often will still have internalised homophobia, transphobia, racism, sexism, etc. because we live in these cultures. What can we do about it? I think it's important not to be defensive about it and to say I own it, recognise it in ourselves and be mindful of it.

We should also bear in mind that those who actively promote a racist agenda target people who feel marginalised, neglected and forgotten, for recruitment. Our need to belong is strong. Hate groups hold out the prospect of belonging to those who lack that. After all, for the most part, happy people don't hate.

Look at any cult, perhaps at any social movement, and you'll see people adjusting their thinking to that of the group. It's the price of admission and membership and it's much easier than changing the thinking of others to match one's own. Sometimes it's easier than finding other groups to belong to. People of liberal outlook who look down their noses at those without skills or education or cultural capital need to realise that they play a part in this dynamic too. Surely a better response to people who have joined a hate group because they want to belong is not rejection but offering something better to belong to, a something that rejects bigotry.

So in certain ways, making prejudice wholly an issue of individual responsibility is counterproductive. Most people don't *want* to be sexist or racist or ableist or homophobic, or at least most don't want to think of themselves that way. We can expend a lot of energy either in denial, because of the shame of admitting it to ourselves, or in self-recrimination. Neither of those makes us happier or tackles the problem. Tackling it would involve busting ourselves when we find we're not relating to and interacting with the unique person standing in front of us, but rather with a bunch of assumptions that have been foisted on us over the course of our lives.

There's no easy answer to this other than to be aware, and when one finds oneself doing it, pushing one's preconceptions to one side and returning to the person actually in front of you. The best way of overcoming old prejudice is through new experience, and the only way to have new experiences is to come to them afresh.

Meg-John says the old adage of walking a mile in someone else's shoes, even if it's only their Twitter shoes, can broaden our perspectives.

> Something really simple I do is follow folks on Twitter who are from very different backgrounds from me, often activists in particular areas around disability and race, for example. So that every day I'm looking at my Twitter feed and seeing what it's like to be a person in a wheelchair or seeing what it's like to be a person of colour in this country, just immersing myself in that as well as reading books or listening to podcasts. I think just having regular incoming information is helpful, but not with the view that we're ever going to escape because it's just there all the time.

> And then I think a really good early conversation in any relationship would be, 'What are the power dynamics between us? In what ways am I in more of a position of power in our culture? In what ways are you?' It's always going to be complicated. It's always going to go in multiple different directions, but you know what the impacts of that are on how possible it is for us to be consenting in this relationship.

Better still, be an ally. Stop one moment! Don't put on your bloody superhero cape and go out the door to save people just yet. If you want to be an ally ask the people you want to support how you can be an ally. Pass the mic, amplify their voices, support them when they march, join them if they feel it's appropriate. Listen. Listen some more. Don't stop listening. Am I great at this? Not always. The thing is to keep trying.

Kevin mentioned that he saw the movie *Frozen* with a friend (don't judge, ha has young daughters). And there's a character turns up with the line 'I'm here. What do you need?'

'That's you,' Kevin's friend said to him. If we want to be a friend, an ally, we should be asking the same and listening for the answer.

THINGS TO BEAR IN MIND

IF YOU'RE THE only person in your circle who's polyamorous and out, you may find your-self being asked to explain poly or open relationships. You may find yourself going on dates with monogamous people who aren't actually interested in dating but want an educator or someone to be a poly ambassador for an evening for their research project into the wilder side of life.

Firstly, especially if that sounds like waaaay too much work, you can tell them to buy this book. Thanks. But secondly, and more importantly, you can pause for a mo-ment and reflect on the fact that for someone from a minority community, this can be a very common experience. You become the instant explainer for all things African, African American or Latin American, East Asian, South Asian or whatever, likewise trans-, queer- or disability-related. If there's something that happens in your country or community you're somehow expected to explain. 'How come people like you do *x*?' This gets very tiresome, and after a lifetime of it people get ground down. It's not just your question, it's all the other questions just like it that have gone before. Mostly people want to be treated as themselves, as a unique human being—not an avatar for a faceless crowd. Just bear that in mind next time.

If you run a group or are a member of a group or team, it's worth asking yourself, 'Does my group look like the society I live in in microcosm?' If it doesn't, if there are people conspicuous by their absence (or perhaps not conspicuous if you never notice these things), there are two questions to ask. The first is 'Why?' and the second is 'What can I/we do about it?' Seriously, why cheat yourself of the chance to meet awe-some people just because no one thought to make sure that everyone feels your group or event is for them?

Kevin Patterson, in *Love's Not Color Blind*, puts it very pithily; 'If you aren't being actively inclusive, you *are* being passively exclusionary.' Making spaces inclusive for people disempowered in our society takes work. But it's worth it. You have so much to gain.

A hint (and I am slightly head in hands wondering whether it's really necessary to point this out): Being welcoming means welcoming the whole person to your gathering, not allotting them the aforementioned role of ambassador. In various parts of the world I've met people who've asked me if I know a particular person because 'He's from England too.' Obviously there is a good chance that he's one of my 56 million personal friends. Doh. Now apply that to someone from a minority group. Just talking about their cultural background, orientation or even gender gets pretty dull.

I heard it put wonderfully by the BBC broadcaster Peter White. His heart sinks whenever he's at a party and someone says 'Peter, I want you to meet so-and-so. You two have so much in common.' Will it be a fellow football fan? (I think I recall he supports Southampton FC.) Maybe it'll be another craft beer aficionado? No. Almost inevitably it'll be someone else who's blind. Same same. Just focus on stuff you have in common, not what makes the person you're supposed to be welcoming feel different. It ain't rocket science.

As mentioned above, just accept that we're not colour blind and that we shouldn't aspire to be. As ever, the poet Nayyirah Waheed puts it beautifully (and regretfully I must, for reasons of copyright, paraphrase); 'don't trust those who say they don't see colour because it suggests you're invisible to them.'

Being 'colour blind' erases a huge part of someone's identity and experience. Embrace yourself and others in your and their wholeness.

FETISHISATION

"It's not a stereotype!" he replies. "Black men are built differently. You have to acknowledge nature. Number two," Wayne continues, "black men have better rhythm in bed. That's also a fact. And thirdly, they are just more dominant. You know, a lot of these women are not satisfied by their husbands, who want them to do all the work. They want to feel a strong man inside them, dominating them. They want an alpha male. That's what they get here."[127]

So goes Afua Hirsch's encounter with a black British man in a venue hosting an evening called the Black Man's Fan Club that caters to white women swingers wanting to have sex with black guys. A regular guy, Wayne is happy with his lot. 'Where else can you go and have sex as many times as you like?' he says and makes it clear he doesn't feel judged.

He's not alone. Ruby Bouie Johnson had a very similar encounter with a fellow African American at an event in New Orleans.

We had that exact conversation about him being fetishized, and for him it was a source of pride that he can be at an event and he can have sex with any woman he wants. He said he can go down a hotel hall [there] and just go into anyone's room. And he did that for 10 rooms. He just went into one after another. There's also one that used to be called The Chocolate Room. I mean, think about that name.

127 "'As a black woman I'm always fetishised": racism in the bedroom' - Afua Hirsch, *The Guardian*, 13 Jan 2018.

And so basically, he's a bull in the cock fantasy. I said, 'Do you recognise what is happening? You're just your dick. I mean, there's no other pieces of you. You're there as an attempt to fulfil someone's fantasy.' And he said, 'What's wrong with that?' I said, 'So this is your belief system. And so you tell your son, which he has, hey, you're going to go through the world and people are going to value you for your dick.' I mean, this guy was super intelligent.

And there's a female corollary. Black women are stereotyped as assertive and stroppy and voracious and animalistic, so when people approach Ruby on kink sites there's a certain predictability to it.

Being a black woman, there is fetishism with me based upon, you know what, I'm bloody dominant, right? And I'm telling you on Fetlife. I used to get like 10 messages a day from a white man asking me to dominate them.

It's worth reflecting on the fact that there's a porn category label 'interracial' and it's pretty much exclusively about sex between black guys and white women. That tells you a lot about the society that produced it insofar as it's reflected in the US porn industry. Then there are a couple of billion people in China and South East Asia—they get the generic label Asian, or 1.2 billion people in India—Indian—or the other porn 'race' categories out there; Brazilian, Japanese, Korean.

It's a pretty stark reminder of how some people consume sex: as a shopping list of superficial features. In the same article referenced above Hirsch encounters members of Britain's Windrush generation, migrants from the Caribbean who recall how, in the 1950s, white English men would express interest in sleeping with them but not dating them. Zayna Ratty (my co-presenter on our podcast *Beyond Monogamy with Zayna and Jonathan*), who is a therapist specialising in helping GSRD people and a person of colour herself, talks about people collecting stamps in their ethnicity passport.

And these attitudes persist. For Kevin Patterson it's just a matter of being treated as a human rather than an object.

My polyamory is pretty sexual. It's pretty easy to get in my pants. But there's so many different ways to approach me. You can say, okay, I'm into the same sports or the same geek shit or video games. I'm into education, you know, I'm an academic too. Let's have a conversation about those things. Let's express some common interests. But there are people who would approach me and just say, 'Hey, I'm into black dudes.' It doesn't matter what else I'm into or who I am as a person. They're just into black.

Jonathan: So, you're black, you have a penis, you will do.

Kevin: Exactly. And it's a really dehumanising thing by people who think they're being welcoming and approachable.

That's the soul crushing thing—some people clearly think that saying 'I'm really into black guys,' or 'I love Asian girls,' traditionally followed by the polite enquiry 'Where your people from?' is friendly and affirmatory.

Over in Jakarta, Mawar, the arts administrator, has had her share of people hitting on her because she ticks certain boxes and, surprise surprise, she's not particularly wild about being reduced to one or two superficial characteristics either.

I was chatting this guy on FetLife and he just mentioned that he likes Indonesian girls. I am assuming by Indonesian girls, he means tan skin, subdued and ready to be dominated.

This wasn't one of those conversations that led inexorably to a meeting of hearts, minds, or even reproductive organs. Rather it quickly took a turn for the terminal.

Oh, I said, 'fuck you!' End. And I blocked him. Easy. I hate that. I hate being acknowledged just by my skin colour or just because I'm Indonesian and have cute accent or weird accent in that sense. But like patriarchy, it's still very much there. And no matter how hard you yell, there will always be some douche bag that will annoy you and makes you angry. I'm tired of having to deal with these peoples where if I'd met them, I would just shut the door. I don't have the patience to have a civil conversation with them.

Nor is fetishization just about 'race', though it's one of the most commonly fetishized characteristics. People are fetishized for their age, their body shape, the colour of their hair, their tattoos and so on. People will fetishize most things. If you've lost a limb someone out there will lust after you because of it. Some people find being fetishized infuriating. Some empowering. Others don't care.

Penny, also in Jakarta, another smart and educated woman with a distinguished career in media, can give as good as she gets. She's dated scores of foreign guys over the course of three or four years and if they find her attractive for how she looks rather than who she is, then, to a great extent, it's mutual.

I would never think that I'm just one of those Asian girl that those guys found exotic and all available. And even if people think that, I will think the opposite. I mean [Indonesian] women, they also fancy foreigner, like typically European or Caucasian. I mean I would think the same too. You know what I mean? I wouldn't think that I'm just someone's fantasy and then they tick the box. Even if even if they do, I don't think it matters for me.

Consensual non-monogamy does give people the chance to explore. Dating people from backgrounds other than one's own offers an amazing opportunity for experiences beyond the confines of place, culture, class etc. and to grow as a person in the process.

There's no easy way to say this, so I might as well say it bluntly. Forming a relationship with someone and coming to care about them, seeing the world through their eyes, seeking to understand their culture and upbringing, to meet them half way and create something shared to which they and we each bring the best of ourselves can be magical. It's not without pitfalls. Dating someone from a different background than ourselves does not suddenly confer immunity from all the assumptions and prejudices that we've absorbed from the society around us. But it does offer a route away from them.

But it's quite possible to date someone from a different background without making the effort to connect, without valuing the person rather than the packaging. Some of us will still date a someone who could be an anyone insofar as anyone who ticks the same boxes could fill those shoes.

And yet, most of us, in relationships as in life, want to feel unique. Fetishization negates our uniqueness and renders us generic. And if that's possible in a relationship, it's far, far easier if it's a casual sexual encounter. We're reduced to being just another flavour in a box of sweeties and some people just want to try all the flavours.

That's bad enough for any of us, but if someone is from a background that means they don't enjoy equal status and power, it risks being just more of the same old shit. So when your well-intentioned compliment about liking their skin or hair or body because that's your thing goes down like a cup of cold sick, it's not necessarily because you're uniquely awful but possibly, just possibly, because you're the two thousandth person to treat them like an object and not a human. Meg-John Barker:

> Philosophically the existentialists, the Buddhists, and many, many philosophers have pointed out that we have a tendency to treat people as objects, treat people as things, for our own benefit. Either in terms of trying to make them something for us, [or] trying to make ourselves something for other people. So right there,

we're already as human beings struggling in this area to actually treat ourselves and others mutually, and as equally valid. Then we have millennia of patriarchy, all of the years of capitalism, colonialism, white supremacy; our wider culture is based on treating some bodies and lives and labour as more valuable than others. And so, we're swimming in a soup of non-consent as [San Francisco-based poly activist] Pepper Mint puts it. We're culturally and existentially primed not to treat somebody else as valuable as us or vice versa too. And that's where bell hooks and intersectional feminism come in; 'The only way to really do love is to see ourselves and others as equally valuable.' But it's a big ask. It's a really hard one to do, given the wider culture.

CHAPTER SIXTY-FOUR

Neuroatypicality

If you've met one person with autism, you've met one person with autism.

Dr. Stephen Shore's much-quoted observation, made by a man with autism and a professor of special education to boot, captures a vital point necessary better to understand *neuroatypical* (Na) people: those whose brains work differently than most. The autism-spectrum disorders, including autism and Asperger's syndrome, are less a specific condition and more a list of traits. Almost everyone has some of the traits on the list. This means that neuroatypicality is a matter of degree, and thus we are all somewhere on a spectrum of neuro(a)typicality , and also that neuroatypicality will present in a myriad different ways. There is no cookie-cutter person with autism. Some people who are profoundly autistic need complete care. Others thrive by finding ways of using their neuroatypical traits to their advantage and can navigate a neurotypical world with relative ease.

Anecdotally, neuroatypical people seem to be well-represented in consensual non-monogamy. Charlotte, for instance, is not untypical of people with autism because she finds nuance, context and reading between the lines more difficult than most.

Certainly, because I am autistic, I find poly a lot easier than monogamy basically because communication is so much a given. I find poly a lot easier because there is much more of an expectation of you will talk [to me] about your feelings rather than [me] having to assume. I mean, you will talk about the rules. And also I had some reasonably significant anxiety issues, and poly's a lot more useful for those as well, because, again, with communicating things clearly and having clear expectations of each other, it makes life a lot easier for me basically.

For those people who struggle to pick up on references to implicit knowledge—knowledge gained where inference and expression provide context—consensual non-monogamy can be a revelation. In a CNM relationship it's okay to ask 'How does it work?' or 'What do you expect from me?' With monogamy we're often just supposed to know or intuit. For some neuroatypical people, intuiting isn't easy or even possible.

In Charlotte's case she finds people hard to read.

> I am very bad at inferring things, especially emotional things, especially if these emotional things involve reading people's faces when they're making a complicated emotion face.

Charlotte's partner Morgan has occasionally found that the most innocent things have caused her utter confusion.

> There was literally a time when I was just sat in the kitchen watching her cook thinking, 'God damn I love this woman' and she turned to me and went, 'Your face, it's doing a thing. What's it doing?'
>
> 'I literally just love you,'
>
> 'Okay, then continue what you're doing.'

To which Charlotte responded:

> That's not an easy face to read, okay, but you know, I do occasionally have to give up and be like 'I'm really sorry, I have no idea what your face is doing. Please, can you tell me this in words.'

Luciano has challenges different from Charlotte's. He works in Germany as a software engineer for a tech giant. Unfortunately his challenges are almost expressly designed to drive the average German person nuts on a date. In Luciano's experience dates in Germany are highly planned and structured. That would certainly fit with the stereotypical picture that some people have of Germans. Although Luciano is quite remarkable in many ways and is an exceptionally talented coder with a real facility for mathematics and a prodigious memory for facts, he at times feels significantly disabled by his autism. He certainly finds German dating protocols difficult.

I have problems with executive function. So being able to be on time, being able to deal with weird bullshit that life throws at you and being on top of it, this takes a heavy toll on me. And in Germany you are expected to be able to deal with all of that. And so every time I'd been going out with a German person, if you don't have your date planned or if you try to, like, wing something, it is going to make them very stressed and it's just going to be a point of conflict.

So are there common traits that partners of people with, say, Asperger's will encounter? Possibly, though they aren't universal. Fairly common is a lack of social filtering. In other words, some neuroatypical people can be very blunt. They often find social subtexts opaque or untranslatable. Unable to figure out the right thing to say, they often opt for the unvarnished truth. This actually fits a lot of styles of consensual non-monogamy quite well. Occasionally, however, it comes across as tactless. In situations when a neurotypical person might tell a white lie or soften the truth to save someone's feelings, someone with Asperger's, for instance, might not. Nor does small talk or giving people compliments always compute, whilst most neurotypical people are socialised into such things for the sake of lubricating the wheels of human relations.

Another relatively common trait, to the extent that it's often cited as a factor in diagnosing some forms of neuroatypicality, is that when neuroatypical people get into something, they *really* get into it. We're talking expert level here. Their ability to focus and commit can be awe inspiring. If you want to enter a new world, whether that be steam locomotion, opera, the complexities of the US electoral system, or the use of statistics in epidemiology… you could find yourself with a very knowledgeable and loquacious guide. Alternatively it could just be more information than you ever wanted.

Some people simply can't handle those who are neuroatypical, and far too often Na people get bullied or abused or socially isolated. The world is set up for people in the middle of the bell curve, those outside the fat middle are too often discounted or ignored. However, if you have the time to invest in someone who may need a little more effort to understand—if there's nothing you like more than someone with an unusual mind, perhaps finely tuned and high octane or simply quirky and surprising—a neuroatypical person can make an awesome playmate. You may feel that you've stumbled across a diamond overlooked by everyone else who has passed by.

So, let's assume you're lucky enough to find yourself dating an amazing someone who has been diagnosed as autistic or who has traits consistent with autism. A good first step, as Luciano says, is to find out more about how they deal with the world.

Early in the relationship, as soon as things start becoming serious, try to find what's hard for them and then ask [yourself] if that's a big thing for you. Then try to work together to make that more bearable. Like someone who has ADHD might have a hard time with a different set of things than someone who has autism or autism plus ADHD or bipolar disorder. So just ask them what frustrates them and figure out if that is something that you can deal with and, if not, try to find a middle ground.

Sadly, some people simply find themselves out of their depth with someone who thinks in unfamiliar ways. It can be a case of the sooner you realise that the less hurt is caused. Conversely, the sooner you find out that you can rub along with each other with certain adjustments the happier everyone will be.

Do watch out for a couple of things that neuro*typical* people tend to do, with the best of intentions, that often really don't work for Na people. For Luciano, one is people 'helping' him without knowing whether help will be appreciated.

> The biggest thing is to ask the person *how* can you help them. Do not assume things and try doing them. This was actually something that came to life for me when a friend of mine was in a wheelchair. I asked him at some point like, 'Oh, how should I help you?' And he's like, 'Okay, please don't open doors for me. I can do that just fine. If people keep going out of their way to open doors for me I feel that I'm annoying people and this makes me feel slightly worse, even though you're trying to do something good.' So try to see what the other person can deal with and what they cannot, where they need help and when they don't. Because even if it looks like they're struggling, the fact that they can do that thing, even while struggling, it's something that makes them feel powerful. If you don't give them the chance of even trying, it just feels [to them] like they're incapable.

The second is trying to be sympathetic with someone whose experiences really don't mirror your own, the old 'I know how you feel' or 'I went through something like that' when you actually didn't because you haven't understood how your partner experienced it. What they actually experienced may be hard to relate to, but listening can help bridge that gap.

> I find that neurotypical [N] people, a lot of times they assume things based on their own life experience. I find that the N people, they tend to project—you talk about something and they try to empathise by putting [in] something from their own experience, and a lot of times they end up, like, having a wrong idea of how your mind works or how you function because it's very different.

I think that "Na" people, they tend to just assume that you're going to be weird in other ways. So they tend to be a lot more like, Oh, how do you actually function? Because [their experience is that] 'My whole life has been worrying how other people function because I do not understand them. So I'm going to assume that I also don't understand other [Na] people.'

It's wrong to assume that two neuroatypical people automatically 'get' one another simply by virtue of their both being atypical. Doesn't work like that. As I said, there are commonalities but few universals and a world of variety in how people experience their neuroatypicality.

This obviously isn't intended to be a comprehensive guide to non-monogamy for neuro-atypical people nor for those dating them. It's a mere toe in the water, a prompt to find out more. As both Charlotte and Luciano would stress, while background information about the broad sweep of neuroatypicality is useful, you're interacting with the unique person standing before you. Engage with them. Explore them. They'll explore you. Have fun.

If you're neuroatypical and reading this—welcome to a world where straightforward communication is prized and much less is taken for granted. May you be properly appreciated.

CHAPTER SIXTY-FIVE

Faith and Beliefs

NONE OF THE great faiths sit comfortably with consensual non-monogamy. Most faiths started from a place of love but almost all, at some point in their histories, were hijacked by the unkind. Nor is organised religion typically very welcoming of those women who baulk at the subservient roles allotted them. Too often religion has been used as a tool to keep women on their feet in the kitchen, on their knees in the public sphere, and on their backs in the bedroom.

As for sex positivity, the major faiths diverge somewhat. Islam, at least until recent history, had a vibrant debate about sex and sexuality. Some of the Hadith (the collected sayings of the prophet) were strongly supportive of a wife's right to sexual pleasure. Judaism, like Islam, places a similar emphasis on a woman's fulfilment. Hinduism embraces sexuality but again, generally only within the confines of marriage.

Buddhism and Christianity are rather more ambivalent about sex. Buddhism because its teachings about non-attachment shape its attitudes to sex, so that it is seen as an obstacle rather than as a blessing. As I suggested earlier, Christianity arguably owes as much if not more to St Paul than the historical Jesus. And Paul is deeply, deeply conflicted about sex to the extent that he is celibate and would like others to follow his example, though at least he recognises that most won't. However, lest I give the wrong impression, most religious *texts* aren't obsessed with sex. Indeed many barely touch on the subject. The four Christian gospels, for instance, simply don't dwell on it.

But whatever the original intent behind religious teachings, they've been readily co-opted by people who have used them to work out their own issues—and to use decrees of acceptable sex to gain control and power over followers. While there are very inclusive and accepting religious groups, many others have been shaped by powerful people who seem to have had issues with women and with their own sexuality. The result is that, for many people, finding a healthy expression of their sexuality while remaining faithful to their religion is hard.

Vincent and Mia live in Singapore, a fairly conservative society where religion in its many forms looms large. Many of the ethnic Chinese majority are Christian, and evangelical churches are very influential. Campaigning by evangelicals has led to restrictions being placed on Singapore's annual pride event, Pink Dot. Vincent isn't particularly religious but nevertheless feels very much a product of that environment.

> Before I started seeing Mia and before we entered into an open relationship I used to think more like conservative Singaporeans think, and Chinese Singaporean male society in particular, with regards to relationships and commitment and marriage and all that. And I guess if you come from a historical perspective or socio-economic perspective, they drum that message into us of the [traditional male-led] family as the cornerstone of society. I guess I did buy into that a little bit when I was younger.

Mia, meanwhile, had been involved in her church but at the same time is aware of her own kinks and desires.

> I think for me it was a lot more difficult. I became a Christian when I was 16. So there I was at 16, a Christian but still very kinky. It was really bad. I definitely felt a conflict. So I would [switch] between staunch Christian and going back to being very kinky. It was always like this back and forth. I could never reconcile the two sides of who I was. I was either this or that. I could not accept myself being both.

The messages that the evangelical churches she attended put out about sex were very restrictive. It's not as though Mia didn't try to reconcile the two, or even to walk away from her sexuality. In the end she left the church albeit not her faith.

> As a Christian you are brought up not to have premarital sex. You are not supposed to have multiple relationships. You are supposed to save your virginity for the one. Over time I have realised that it is more of a social construct that churches have put in place. I didn't have that level of enlightenment but also there was a lot of guilt. That went on for many years and whenever I got into a relationship with a Christian person I would fall out of the BDSM scene. I would disappear for maybe one or two years and then when I'm out of that relationship I'm back.

> Vincent is the first person that I was really open, truly honest with in terms of my religious background as well as my kink inclinations. All my other partners,

whether they were romantic or kinky, they never knew who I truly was. It was in this relationship I started to try to have both sides meet. It's not fully there yet, I really do want to go back to church, but I think I might burn up, combust, the moment I do.

To be fair to Mia it's more than a social construct. It's rooted in scripture, or at least in a particular reading of it, and we all know how it's possible to use the bits we prefer and conveniently forget the rest. Mia's solution has been to segment her life. Many of her friends are people she knows through church or through work, and she keeps them separate from her kinky and non-monogamous friends.

Is there a degree of cognitive dissonance here? Do people who like fluffy little lambs still eat shepherds' pie? It's perfectly understandable to want to be a good person in the way that you were taught growing up and yet find yourself in conflict with that teaching. A lot of people end up resolving simply to do their best especially insofar as they don't hurt anyone else.

Muslims face many of the same issues as Christians, arguably to a greater extent as current Muslim society is generally more conservative. Growing up Muslim in Indonesia, Xena was confronted by the fact that men could take four wives but she couldn't have four husbands.

As I got older I started thinking why is only happening to guys? And even up until today I ask my boyfriend why is it only guys who get to have more than one woman? Why can't women have more than one or two guys? Why is it so bad in the world today and when normal people will think that you're such a slut? And somehow I think oh well, is not so bad to be a slut.

Emma is Singaporean but her upbringing was Muslim, unlike Vincent and Mia's. It's quite common for Islam in South East Asia to be performative in that there's pressure to maintain a public piety that doesn't always square with how people behave in private.

Emma's parents, however, buck this trend by seeing religion much more in terms of a personal relationship with God than of earning the admiration of their neighbours. Consequently she grew up in, by Singaporean standards, an unusually open-minded environment.

They're religious but not pious. Very open. They go through the motions. Faith is just faith. It's not about the actions that you do, the places that you go. That's why my dad doesn't believe in that. He says that what you have with God is a direct connection you don't have to pray to. At the end of the day you have to be answerable to yourself, not answerable to anyone else.

Has that influenced the way she grew up? Probably. Her parents are very accepting. However, that doesn't necessarily mean they want all the details.

I just had a Chinese new year lunch last weekend and I was being very open about the people that I see and this was obviously packaged in a way that "Yes I'm having sex with them", that kind of relationship. They nod their heads to say I am listening to you, I am receiving the information, but as to giving an opinion I don't think they do have very much foundation to say anything. My parents are very open about things but no parent wants to know about who their daughter is fucking.

When I was reporting from South East Asia I stumbled upon a phenomenon that neatly illustrated the tension between the need to comply with the pressures of a religious society and human sexuality. In the mid-noughties when phone cameras started to become ubiquitous, it became quite common for Muslim teens and twenties in the region to swap naked pictures of themselves or their girlfriends. Women were also under more and more pressure to wear the tudong, a tight-fitting headscarf that frames the face and completely covers the hair and neck. The result: a lot of these pictures featured women completely naked apart from a headscarf.

David was brought up Catholic in Singapore. His mother fell out with the church during his teens but didn't lose her faith. What is interesting is that, though she's accepting and open minded, he doesn't feel able to come out to her, something that perplexed his partner Laura.

She's given me that room to explore. I go wherever my interests take me. And I don't have to feel guilty about it. My brother is homosexual and he also took a long time to come out to my parents, but when he did come out they were very accepting. Now he has his boyfriend over, in fact we're going to meet later for family dinner, and it's not typical of a Singaporean family.

Laura: But why would you not tell mom that we see other people?

David: Because she's an Asian mom and we do not tell such things to Asian moms! Maybe one day I'll tell her but it doesn't feel right.

Laura: If they don't need to know there is no need to tell them. I come from a Christian background. I'm Methodist. So my entire education up to university was Methodist. I had chapel every week. And all my school friends are very staunch Christians. None that I would ever imagine my sharing this side of myself with. I am not close with many of them anymore but when I do see them I am a different person.

Laura faces much the same issue as Mia. Maintaining one's faith, or simply just maintaining friendships made through church, mosque or temple, requires them to segment their lives. That's pragmatic and sensible but marginalising for partners and lovers and frustrating for those who want to be their authentic selves with all those they care about.

Hell is Other People

CHAPTER SIXTY-SIX

Community: Being Part of the Tribe

NEVER, IN ALL of human history, have people lived such separate and parallel lives as they do in developed nations in the early twenty-first century. For all that our on-line social networks give us a simulacrum of community and the illusion of engagement, we're more isolated than ever. In many countries around the world, one-person households are now more common than at any time on record.[128] As countries industrialised, traditional extended-family households' links with more distant relatives weakened to leave only the isolated core nuclear family: mother, father, their kids. And many nuclear families have shrunk further to being one-parent.

McFadden terms it 'atomised,' a perfect word to describe modern life. This, in historical terms, is an aberration. Across the globe and throughout history humans have thrived in groups, sharing social connections, child care, and the economies of scale, exchanging skills and resources, and providing mutual safety nets. The forms have included extended families and clans, guilds and unions, clubs and social organisations, churches and gangs. And when people meet informally at the pub, its American cousin the bar, the Indonesian *warung*, the Chinese *kafei dian/kopitiam* or the Indian *daru ka theka*, they join a wider community of happenstance.

In the UK pubs are closing. Even before the pandemic of 2020 they were struggling. A century ago most Brits' parlours or living rooms were cold, dark, damp, and boring. The pub provided light, warmth, company, entertainment and good strong ale. These days the average living room is centrally heated and as bright or dark as one might wish. There's a sofa or two to sink into, a TV with as many channels as you like, distractions beyond previous generations' imaginations, cheap supermarket beer and microwavable snacks in the fridge. All the pub has to add is other people, but since we can now hang out for hours online with our humans of choice, why bother?

---

128 https://ourworldindata.org/living-alone

And yet, for all this previously undreamed wealth of comfort, levels of depression are higher and loneliness is epidemic. We're wired for sociability but are increasingly organised away from it.

People typically don't come to consensual non-monogamy seeking a social experience. They arrive at it because they would like more than one relationship, or sex beyond the confines of coupledom. But having discovered it, many people clearly find that one of the most compelling aspects of CNM, and polyamory in particular, is the connections they build beyond their immediate intimate relationships. I touched on this in the chapter on metamours.

Researchers Amy Moors, Jes Matsick, and Heath Schechinger note that for a lot of people, consensual non-monogamy meets a need for wider connection.

> Whether CNM provides greater opportunities for social bonding and enjoyment than monogamy remains an empirical question; however, recent research supports the idea that those engaged in CNM embrace the nonsexual activities that are involved in their relationships.

> Perhaps, this benefit is particularly salient for people engaged in CNM because they may not be experiencing dyadic withdrawal. For instance, research on people in monogamous relationships has shown that as a couple progresses toward living together (and becoming more committed), they tend to withdraw from their social networks (M. P. Johnson & Leslie, 1982; Kalmijn, 2003). It is unclear whether this phenomenon also happens among people who engage in CNM (this remains an empirical question).[129]

Many of those I've interviewed who practice CNM have found in it a new form of community. However Joreth Innkeeper's own experience is different but very telling.

> I don't see it as being different from monogamy because I think monogamy is also similarly varied; it depends on what style of monogamy you have. I don't have an isolated, nuclear-family history. The complexity aside, it is not any different to me with all my extended cousins and great-aunts; my family is very tribal. My family has an immigrant history and as I recently discovered, people from immigrant backgrounds tend to form very complex networks of interdependent relationships

---

129 'Unique and Shared Relationship Benefits of Consensually Non-Monogamous and Monogamous Relationships: A Review and Insights for Moving Forward', Amy C. Moors, Jes L. Matsick, and Heath A. Schechinger, *European Psychologist*, (2017) vol. 22, pp 55-71.

and families and support structures, which is where I think [I got] those skills from in my poly community.

She's right about immigrant communities. They often offer strong support networks both for those who are established and those who've just arrived. This can be in the form of jobs or a pool of potential employees, it can be as business opportunities, purchasing clubs, solidarity in adversity, friendship, or potential romantic partners who literally get where you're coming from.

So perhaps she's right about the social side of monogamy and consensual non-monogamy looking similar if your life is already rich in social and familial connections. Could it be that the more people have lacked a sense of community, of being part of that thing bigger than themselves, the more that certain forms of CNM appeal and meet a need?

Nathan chooses an interesting phrase: 'like a family reunion'.

One of the real strengths of poly is that it exposes you to a whole pile of metamours and meta-metamours you can draw on. It's like a family reunion. Everybody gets together and wants to know how you're doing and how things are. Somebody said to me a while back that there is no thing in life that is not people; buying a car, having a job, hanging out, there is no thing in life that is not people-based.

I have the sense of being around my tribe. I'm free to move about, free to do my own thing, but there are friendly people within reach that will help me out if I get myself into a pickle, which I do frequently. And it just makes life easier, it makes life better, it makes things richer, having mad scientists around and people that can knit. It takes a village. We are that village, strange as it may seem.

McFadden experienced something similar. He's not someone who comes across as overly sentimental, rather he's quite evidence-driven, logical. And yet he was struck by how his intimate relationships, and through those his relationships with metamours, brought him together with people who shared interests and values. He compares it to the experience of using the dating site OkCupid.

The original OkCupid was driven far more than now by a set of questions users could choose to answer relating to pretty much any interests or values. Particularly telling was a popular question about which was worse, burning a book or a flag. It divided the world neatly into tribalists and universalists: it's the kind of thing that if you don't see eye to eye on could result in a wasted or even a painful date. Because OkCupid was adaptable and users were effectively able to programme in their own values and desired attributes, the polyamory world flocked to it—even choosing it, for several years, over dating sites that were poly-specific but much smaller. You couldn't count on any sort of chemistry, but since you shared an unusual and important special criterion, your chances of clicking over a coffee or a bottle of wine were higher.

As McFadden says,

> The very first non-monogamous relationship that I was in was [part of] a transitive graph of people who had intimate relationships or friendships that involved the five other people. And each of the three men and the three women in this, what I referred to as the benzene ring, each had intimate relations with each other and they were all friends.

Benzene ring

> I thought that it was funny, I guess as a person who was new to non-monogamy, to have a very relaxed attitude towards this. [It] really defined that it was sort of novel and fun rather than anything that was troublesome.

> And the thing that it gave me, actually probably more than anything else, was a sense of belonging, that here was a group of people distributed across the West Coast of the United States with whom I had a bond of almost like kinship. And, I would add, a more robust feeling of being supported socially and emotionally than I think people in dyadic relationships or nuclear families really get to enjoy typically.

That sense of belonging and kinship isn't compulsory. Some people would posi-tively rather avoid it. As it happens, all the interviews in this chapter and a few more besides took place at the biannual gathering of members of a transatlantic polycule. It was held in a converted barn in a rural location in the English East Midlands and most people stayed around a week.

Some thrived on it. Others preferred the periphery. The atmosphere was affable going on friendly going on intimate. It was not dissimilar to a family gathering or village celebration. People found their own level.

It's not necessarily typical of consensual non-monogamy. But what is likely, if you are non-monogamous or thinking about it, is that some form of community is on offer. For many people it's the unexpected bonus that keeps them engaged.

CHAPTER SIXTY-SEVEN

Abuse

THIS IS THE saddest chapter in the book. It's also one of the most important. A lot of people are drawn to consensual non-monogamy for the best of reasons and some for the worst. And some people, regardless of where they wash up, end up causing harm, intentionally or unintentionally. Meg-John Barker is all too aware of that.

> Oh, I'm afraid we've seen a lot of that in poly and kink communities, but I suspect it's true of all communities. As you know, certainly I'm a Buddhist and most of them, as communities, are now having their #metoo moments.

At its heart, Meg-John says, #Metoo is about abuse of power: power that allows people to cow their victims into submission. It's the difference between being able to say no because you don't want something and the inability to say no because, although you don't want something, the consequences of saying no are so horrendous that the less bad option, especially in the short term, appears to be to give in to abuse. In the CNM community the same power structures apply as in the wider world: People who are of European descent, men, cis-gendered, educated, well-off, middle-aged, able-bodied, and straight have the advantages that they bring with them from wider society, and people who are women, brown, queer, trans, poor, disabled, young, or very old bring their disadvantages and relative lack of power. Barker says that being in positions of influence or enjoying a degree of celebrity, even in a small community, adds to concentrations of and imbalances in power.

> Unfortunately when somebody has the huge amount of power of an organiser in a community they can often abuse that power in various ways. It boosts somebody's

ego to be seen as the great expert or the organiser. They're getting a lot of people being interested in them. It must be very tempting. But again, that power imbalance from being an expert or organiser, it's even bigger than all the other cultural power imbalances. And often those people are older, often they're white men, so they've already got a whole bunch of power and they've now got this power as organisers/ experts and people are often reinforcing that sense that they're somehow particularly awesome. Those are the scenarios in which we see people abusing their power just as in mainstream society, just as in the kind of situations that the #metoo movement drew our attention to.

Part of the problem is the tendency to assume that because the consensual non-monogamy community aspires to be enlightened and consent-aware, this attitude is universal. Or that sufficient checks and balances exist. Or that because of the number of people involved, the number of connections, the amount of oversight all around, abuses must be rare. If only that were the case. Indeed, the more this myth is perpetuated the more cover it gives to the ill-intentioned to get away with bad and harmful behaviour.

Some in the community have identified a pattern where some people will be drawn into an inner circle of a group and others are kept at a distance, a situation that an unprincipled but charismatic figure can exploit by pointing to an 'enemy' on the periphery to bind his chosen insiders closer. It can lead to the in-group effectively gaslighting the 'other' and sets up the potential for all sorts of deeply disturbing abuse.

And that's not the only complicating factor. Parts of the CNM scene are, as Joreth Innkeeper says, cult-like. It may be the presence of people who are effectively unchallengeable or simply skilled manipulators. However, the collective dynamic is also very powerful and people can adjust their opinions and beliefs to fit in with prevailing attitudes. It takes considerable mental toughness to withstand group pressure.

> Abuse in poly in relationships takes on this weird combination of traditional abusive dynamics and cult behaviour. It's not either one or the other; it's not a cult and it's not one-on-one abuse but it's a mixture of the two. And discovering that was horrifying. We've never seen anything like that before, so teasing out which part is one-on-one abuse and which part is cult behaviour, and teasing those things apart from what is healthy group dynamics and healthy one-on-one behaviour is really tricky. I think we're only just now starting to look at it.

We tend not to accept just how much one person can exert control through manipulation or simply through charisma. In a monogamous situation the end of a relationship means you lose one person (and sometimes friends). In a group situation exclusion can result in the loss of multiple relationships (or even your entire community), not all romantic but nevertheless important. It can be like losing an entire family. We know how people will hang on in an abusive monogamous relationship. That effect can be amplified in a non-monogamous group. Joreth Innkeeper again:

> I was in one group dynamic that was particularly awful. There were a lot of consequences to disagreeing [with one particular person]. In the end everybody just stopped disagreeing with him because it was easier, though at first it looked like everybody agreed. Eventually he and I had quite a big argument and everybody else stayed silent. It was very isolating and disheartening. Later other people came up to me individually and said, 'I just wanted to let you know I agree with you but it's just not worth arguing with him.'

> Now, with hindsight, I can see that was a big red flag that ended up carrying over into much darker places. He would have a disagreement with one of his partners, then he would go back to the rest of the group and say 'My partner said or did this thing, isn't she wrong'. And the group wouldn't disagree, so then he could come back to the partner and say we all think you're wrong. And this would then isolate his partners, at least one of whom became an abuse victim, because they would now see this division; it's us against you, you alone are wrong, we all have the same idea.

Another well-known figure in the CNM community from a minority background has seen how both smaller groups and the wider community can react, not rationally but like a mob—especially online—when someone refuses to adopt the prevailing groupthink or dares to defend someone who has fallen out of favour, let alone someone who has been accused. The principles of natural justice are thrown out, out come the pitchforks, and everyone wants to be the first to tie a noose.

> We can character assassinate and villainize someone so quick just because of social media. And I mean people get annihilated within like large groups like virtual polyamory groups. You'll have one person who has a dissenting opinion, I'm just talking about opinions right now, and you have 20 people tell them that they're

wrong. They can't have a different opinion. Also, we tend to side with a person who has been violated. We tend to side with [a] victim and we don't hear two stories, both sides. And then an entire community will gang up against the person who has been accused of the violation.

The danger here is that it prompts a rush to be the first to claim victimhood. A smart and manipulative abuser, when facing possible exposure, may do exactly that. Or, probably more often, the abuser *really **does*** believe that they're the victim. Their abusive behaviour comes from a place of genuine fear and pain. The result is that whoever first declares themselves the victim gets to shape or even control the subsequent process. If an abuser yells 'I'm a victim' then people don't listen to the actual victim, because there's a tendency to dismiss their claims of abuse as an attempt to distract and derail the process.

Of course, it shouldn't need to be said that claims of abuse must always be heard and that we should start from a presumption that people don't step forward to tell lies. Such research that has been done into the prevalence of false claims of rape, for instance, finds them to be rare, typically about one in twenty, though the way figures are recorded doesn't make the estimates wholly reliable.

Putting someone alleging abuse through the sort of aggressive cross examination that one encounters in adversarial court settings is clearly distressing not just for the person being interrogated but also for the wider community. That sort of approach is more about the means lawyers are prepared to use to clear their clients come what may, and less about truth seeking and community protection. And many people understandably want to spare an abuse survivor that ordeal. However that shouldn't mean that differing accounts shouldn't be examined and witnesses sought. Organising this sort of process in a community is both a skill and a heavy responsibility.

One challenge is that not every situation is black and white, with one person acting badly and another meekly accepting it. Quite often two people in a relationship are acting in ways that, from the outside, look equally bad. Sometimes that is indeed the case—however it's one thing for someone powerless to behave in a certain way and quite another for someone powerful to do so.

When you have two people pointing at one another saying 'They abused *me!*', a useful tool is to examine where power lies and who is trying to exert the greater degree of control. Who has power and control over someone else in a relationship? Who makes decisions about finance and who doesn't? Who determines the people their partner can see and who can't, who has been afraid and who hasn't? People resist, and in resisting may act in ways that look unreasonable. But here's the thing: resistance to abuse is not the same as abuse.

The basic quandary for the CNM and especially the kink/BDSM scenes is that people who wield power in a community are hard to hold to account. For the reasons Joreth Innkeeper describes, most people find it easier to hide from someone abusive than to take them on. Even if someone is known to be accusing their victim of abuse, if the cost of opposing the abuser is too high there's a very real chance that people will simply stay silent and just pray it's not them next. Whatever systems are put in place to deal with abuse in minority communities, they surely must have the ability and the will to hear everyone concerned and put all testimony under the microscope so it's examined without prejudice. The consequences of not doing so, says Ruby Bouie Johnson, are that miscarriages of community justice can occur.

> Someone can be unheard and accused and misunderstood. And we ostracise and we kick people out of their families. They become the black sheep and you know how that feels, you know what they talk about, you know, that one kid who was not the hero or the one kid who was the hero and they get knocked off their pedestal or something because of whatever. Right? And so we have love be conditional rather than unbiased, you know, loving, caring, compassionate. So I have watched, and, to be honest, Jonathan, I just don't know. We just don't have these conversations.

Finally I'm going to leave you with the words of one quite well known female figure in the CNM scene in the United States. I'm not going to name them because, although they didn't ask for anonymity, the occasionally febrile atmosphere in parts of the community means that those who speak out fear becoming targets.

> I don't leave my fucking house because I'm scared. I am scared because I'm a public person. Right now I want to date, I want to do things, but I can't in my local community because I'm afraid because of social status or perceived mini celebrity that I'm going to coerce someone or someone is going to perceive it as coercive. I am one person's accusation—no matter if it's true or false—away from losing my entire [world], that I spent two decades building. And that scares the shit out of me because I have witnessed it. I have watched it and I'm like, I don't want to be that person. And it's simply the truth. And I want to say that polyamory, it's more individualised than we think. And I want to say that I have a community that will love me unconditionally, but they will love me as long as I act the way they want me to act.

THREE THINGS TO LOOK OUT FOR

WITH POLYAMORY AND other forms of CNM becoming increasingly acceptable and even fashionable anyone can announce a poly munch or a meetup and many do. Most are doubtless sincere, good-hearted and possibly rather idealistic. When you're checking out a new group, however, poly organisers offer some points to watch for.

1. Is there a charismatic leader? Is there someone who does most of the talking, gives the impression of knowing it all, and to whom others defer? Beware signs of cult behaviour.

2.   Look instead for a comfortable egalitarianism among the regulars. In particular, look for *distributed leadership:* several people making things happen and passing jobs and decision-making around, and asking for input from each other when making decisions.

3. A good reputation in the community. How long has the group been around? What do other polypeeps in the area think of it? Get thee to thine interwebs and enquire about it, and invite people to message you privately if they prefer.

In the next section I'll consider what a community might do to tackle instances of bad behaviour. First let's look more closely at what abuse is.

ABUSE RESOURCES

BELOW ARE A number of examples that offer a yardstick by which to assess abuse. They're only indicative, not definitive. One can set the bar for 'abuse' as low as one likes. Any line drawn to distinguish abuse from non-abusive behaviour will be blurred, contextual and, to some extent, arbitrary. These things also tend to reflect prevailing attitudes, so what is considered abuse in one place or time may not be in another.

A line needs to be drawn in order to highlight and focus on boundary violations a society or community feels are serious and damaging. Hence, if the bar encompasses too much there is the danger of reaching a point where 'everything is abuse' and then, by extension, 'nothing is abuse'. The point is to avoid trivialising a serious matter or enabling allegations to be dismissed. Drawing this line is never easy.

As an initial reference point, here is a list of coercive and controlling behaviours in relationships based on statutory guidance from the UK Home Office, issued in 2015. The behaviour listed may not be criminal in isolation or in its own right, but under current law a pattern of behaviour including a number of, but not necessarily all, of the below might constitute coercive control, which is a criminal offence in England and Wales.

- *Isolating someone from their family and/or friends*
- *Depriving them of their basic needs*
- *Monitoring someone's time and activities*
- *Using spyware or surveillance technology to monitor someone*
- *Controlling behaviour over someone's everyday life, denying or managing their movement or association, their appearance or even when they eat, wash or sleep*
- *Preventing their accessing specialist support, medical or other services*
- *Repeatedly using degrading or negative language to attack someone's self-esteem and to make them feel worthless*
- *Enforcing rules and activity that humiliate, degrade or dehumanise the victim*
- *Forcing the victim to break the law; this could include anything from tax evasion or theft to drugs offences, or criminal treatment of children, in order to attack the victim's self-worth and deter them from seeking help*
- *Financial abuse; controlling someone's finances, or using financial or resource starvation as a form of punishment*
- *Making threats to assault, injure or kill*
- *Making threats to a child or regarding a child*
- *Threatening to 'out' someone, to make private information public or to 'report' them*
- *Assault*
- *Damage to property (such as destruction of personal property, household items or even abuse of pets)*
- *Rape*
- *Preventing a person from having access to transport or from their place of work.*

Look at what all of these have in common: *exerting control* over a person.

Next, here are other instances of behaviour that are adapted from the widely used Duluth model. The model is gendered; its creators have been criticised for erasing male on male and female on male violence. That exists and it's significant. However the proportion of women who've experienced abuse at the hands of men is far higher, abuse against women recurs more regularly within a relationship, is it typically more serious, and is far more likely to end in murder. These additional areas of abusive control include:

- *Blocking access to legal or criminal justice systems*
- *Gendered abuse—enforcing traditional gender roles, exclusion from decision making, mocking someone's sexual performance*

- *Making threats to leave or of suicide*
- *Minimising one's responsibility or unreasonably justifying one's actions —'you make me jealous'.*
- *Using undermining psychological tactics that cause someone to doubt their sanity*
- *Threatening displays of weapons or of physicality.*

Also, as a matter of guidance, here are some samples based on quotes from abuse survivors.

'I was constantly on a hair trigger. I'd could never tell if he was going to be Jekyll or Hyde, loving or a monster.'

'In public he could never do enough for me, in private he was totally different.'

'He wanted me to take on the role of mother and housewife – I had to do everything in the house or he'd go mad.'

'Even little things would set him off. He'd tell me I wasn't cleaning the house or that he didn't like my cooking. I was always on guard.'

'He was completely obsessed with the idea I was having an affair. What with work and looking after our daughter I just didn't have time even if I wanted to. It was crazy, but he'd even ring up my colleagues to keep tabs on me.'

'I got really badly into debt because he wouldn't let me work. It all ended up on credit cards.'

'He would take away my debit card. He wouldn't let me have more than small change. He'd check every day to make sure I wasn't hiding money away.'

'It's ruined my life. I don't have a social life. I don't have a sex life. Boyfriend? Forget it. He keeps me isolated. If I went to work he'd harass me so I don't go to work.'

'He threatened to shoot me because our son didn't want to see him. Shoot me. Stab me. He said he'd kill me and all the police said was 'Don't let him in.'

These quotes and reference points are for guidance only. Abuse is a complex subject and I would urge you to contact local support services if you think you are being abused or know someone who is.

Where can you find those services? In the UK you can call the National Domestic Abuse Helpline, 0808-2000-247. In the US call the National Domestic Violence Hotline, 1-800-799-7233. In Europe see https://ec.europa.eu/justice/saynostopvaw/helpline.html.

THE BROKEN STAIR

THERE'S A METAPHOR, originally called 'The Missing Stair', coined by blogger Cliff Jerrison on his blog The Pervocracy, that has widespread currency in the CNM world. People in BDSM, kink, queer, and consensually non-monogamous communities often use it to illustrate the way that those groups sometimes (perhaps too often) tolerate and sidestep abusive or other problematic people within their circles rather than confront them and stop the problem. A reluctance to exclude is quite common in marginalised groups.

The analogy runs like this. There's a house where an extended group of friends often gather. Perhaps you or one of your friends lives somewhere like that. It's your social circle's venue of choice. New people are always turning up. There's always food on the kitchen table and coffee in the pot. But the house has a quirk. One of the steps on the staircase is broken. Everyone knows about it. No one has bothered to fix it, so whenever someone new comes to the house they are told about the stair. 'Careful, if you step on that one you might twist your ankle or fall down the stairs.' So everyone avoids that step—until one day someone doesn't.

Then everyone is surprised. 'Everyone knew' about the problem and avoided stepping on it. Why, it's so well known that sometimes the house is known to others as 'the house with the broken stair.' But it was easier to step around the problem than to face up to it and solve it.

In communities, the broken stair is a problem person. Everyone knows about Joe. He brings a really decent bottle of wine, everyone knows him, just don't go out into the garden with him alone. Joe is Joe, just take care and you'll be okay.

Then something bad happens. The neighbours say they knew it was only a matter of time with the house with the broken stair, and those in the house wonder, guiltily, 'Why didn't we replace the stair? We all knew.'

Perhaps the 'broken stair' in their circle isn't as bad as Joe but is just irascible, or a bit of a bully after a drink or two. Maybe, as Jerrison says, they're absolutely fine so long as no one upsets them. Consequently much effort goes into not upsetting them—rather than into calling them out, holding up a mirror to their behaviour, and asking them, nay requiring, that they address it.

In more dangerous situations the broken stair is violent or violates consent or both. Rather than 'Mind the third step' it's 'Don't go with Greg to his place on the lake', or 'Don't get into a private scene with Andi' or 'They're great so long as you're not in a relationship with them.'

Members of a minority or a stigmatized community often develop a strong sense of solidarity and want to keep it. For some, that's part of the attraction. For others, who are members by default through their culture, orientation, skin colour or whatever, it can be a matter of survival. If you can't look to the majority overculture and its institutions to help, you take care of things and each other yourselves. Abusers know this, and the smart ones plan on it. They know that people can be very reluctant to cause 'problems' from the inside when a community faces so many from the outside.

Self-policing aside, one doesn't have to listen to too many ugly accounts from women who've gone to the real police after a sexual assault, or from people of colour who've been victims of crimes and call the cops only to be treated with suspicion or hostility or worse, to understand the dynamic of keeping quiet. Non-monogamous people or kinksters may well fear they won't fare much better.

A person might imagine possible responses at the police station:

"You say you allowed this man to tie you up naked and flog you, but you didn't want him to have sex with you? Surely it wasn't unreasonable of him to conclude you wanted sex?"

Or,

"Just how many 'partners' do you have, Miss?"

Or,

"Well Sir, if you choose to hang around with such people, it's inviting trouble isn't it?"

Or,

"Well, you may say that but I can't imagine a jury of twelve *normal* people agreeing with you."

So, what is the answer? That's rather harder than setting out the problems.

First, take a broken stair seriously. Point at it, tell the people in charge they have to fix the problem. As I've already mentioned, false allegations of rape or sexual assault are fairly rare. A series of studies in the US between 1977 and 2010 found that the percentage of cases investigated where the allegations were found to be untrue was somewhere between 2% and 11%.[130] False allegations of domestic abuse also appear to be fairly rare (though it has been suggested that they could be skewed in very specific

---

130 'False Allegations of Sexual Assault: An Analysis of Ten Years of Reported Cases', David Lisak, Lori Gardinier, Sarah C. Nicksa, and Ashley M. Cote, *Violence Against Women*, 16 Dec 2010; Vol. 16 issue 12, pp 1318-1334.

circumstances).[131] Just to be clear, where there's a serious allegation appropriate action needs to be taken. Normally that would mean involving the authorities. Where that is not a safe option there need to be other processes in place that meet high standards of justice.

Secondly, professionals are trained specifically to deal with such situations, whether they be social workers, victim support case workers, investigating police officers (they're often better than they used to be), or prosecutors. Indeed if it's possible to insist on a specialist, do. The fact that these professionals sometimes fail should not detract from the fact that they have considerable experience and relevant skills that communities often lack internally.

I hope this disheartening chapter hasn't left you unduly worried. But awareness when you're exploring new places and getting involved in scenes is always a good idea.

---

131 'Thousands misusing abuse orders to get legal aid, says parenting charity', BBC News, 3rd July 2018 https://www.bbc.co.uk/news/education-44628179

CHAPTER SIXTY-EIGHT

Leadership and Justice

CONSENSUAL NON-MONOGAMY SEEMS to have grown remarkably quickly in North America and Europe since 2010 or thereabouts. During the decade and a half prior to that, the spread of the internet had enabled those drawn to consensual non-monogamy to find others like them, to discover that they were not alone, and to connect and organise. Especially in the United States, polyamory in particular has reached a critical mass that has given rise to more formal structures, extensive networking, regional conventions, and hundreds of local meetings and events.

One thing that communities often do is choose, appoint, or elect leaders. In the case of the community in Philadelphia, where Kevin Patterson lives, the issue came to a head because he and other community members felt a number of issues, including that of partner abuse, needed addressing urgently.

> When I joined the local community here in Philadelphia it had a reputation for being unwelcoming to queer folks, unwelcoming to people of colour and for harbouring abusers. Me and a handful of others really pushed back against that. We actually like forced an election for new leadership to address all of those things.

> That leadership has turned over a couple of times since back in 2017 when I held the leadership position. And you know, they keep documentation on abuse reports and when possible, I believe they started taking more steps to communicate with other leaders in the kink and swing communities so as to make sure that people who are harmful or problematic aren't just bouncing from one place to another.

Kevin Patterson and Ruby Bouie Johnson, both African American, know from hard experience about marginalisation. Belonging to the wider CNM community makes them members of an additional marginal group, one that hesitates before turning to the mainstream for help. Both, by virtue of having highlighted the need for more minority leadership within US CNM groups, found themselves pushed towards assuming those positions themselves. This is Bouie Johnson:

> I did a brief needs survey in a leadership group that I'm a part of. The survey looked at how we become leaders. And the issue within the non-monogamous community is that we are a migrant group. We are a group that lives on the periphery because of the shaming, the stigma, et cetera.
>
> Now media representation is making it more visible, there's a lot more people coming into my office that are folks of colour that are curious about it. But that's not really what is needed with a community that's about relationships. That's actually leadership development. And I think that's one of the shortcomings is that just by someone saying they run a local event, that means that they're a leader within the community. The poly symposium that I've run for five years, PolyDallas Millennium, I actually own that. It was automatic. I became a leader. But it wasn't something that I asked for.

She isn't the only one who has had responsibility thrust upon them. Joreth Innkeeper has long run an influential website and blog TheInnBetween.net.

> I've always been an activist. I had angry feelings and I needed to vent them out somewhere where they would do something rather than internalising my anger which turned to self-destruction. So, I started writing my anger so that other people could see and people who felt like me but who didn't have a voice could have a voice through me and people who didn't feel like me could feel a consequence for the things that they were doing.

Joreth describes the experience of regularly being idolised one moment and villainised the next. It's a hazard of being handed responsibility without actually having power or there being robust systems of accountability. People gravitate around better known names and faces and expect them to do something. Then, because there's no formal, let alone legal, framework and often no mandate, people are angry at these figureheads when they don't get the outcomes they want, even if no one was ever in a position to deliver that outcome in the first place.

This mix of idolisation and demonization even extends to some of the relationships she's formed within the community, where even people with whom she's been intimate can't see past the public persona.

> A lot of my breakup conversations end with, what part of blank did you not understand when we first started dating? Because I seem to date a lot of people who don't like me very much. They seem to love me or they seem to idolise me but they don't seem to like me very much.

In this situation leadership is often an unenviable task. There's little upside and a great deal of downside. However, as Ruby Bouie Johnson says, the community has to start somewhere in building the capacity to provide accountability and justice.

> With that comes a whole lot of responsibility and accountability when there's issues around consent violations, when there's issues around people being ostracised. And for me that is so important because there are consent violations, but there's no understanding. Okay, you told me what happened, what's the next step for us to not ostracise someone out of an already marginalised community? Right. And how can we do some restorative and transformative justice here? And so there is an entire summit that we're doing here in Dallas, based upon that express need, on leadership and justice because we don't have those conversations at all.

That's something that Joreth Innkeeper echoes.

> We're finally in the poly community starting to have conversation about the responsibilities of community leaders and the types of partners we choose because you have a power imbalance when somebody is a figure, somebody is a name, somebody has a persona in the community.

JUSTICE

WHAT SEEMS TO have taken place in the CNM scene, at least in the US, are moves to put in place at least minimal protections to prevent abusers gaining a toehold. However any closely interlinked community faces problems of accountability.

In many places, not least in the States, there's a reluctance to turn to those outside. Just as black, latinx, Asian, indigenous, queer people, not forgetting women and many more, look at the justice system and see an institution that is overwhelmingly white, male and straight, the CNM community may be understandably wary of a justice system assumed to be mainstream regarding monogamy and all the other norms. The intersection of religion, politics and the politicisation of justice in the US makes it difficult for many people to get a fair hearing. Likewise in other countries there's a perception that the criminal justice establishment is unrepresentative and disconnected from the worlds inhabited by those they pass judgement upon. Who could arbitrate on issues within a community they don't understand and may disapprove of?

One response has been to turn to *transformative justice,* a system of, ideally, peacemaking and reconciliation that bypasses the criminal justice apparatus. But it still faces the question of ownership. Whoever owns the process controls it. Just as mainstream criminal justice can be unduly beholden to those with political power, an alternative justice process risks being skewed by the politics of the community. If an individual holds the power to make or break the reputations of others within that community, or to cause them to be ostracised, who then can hold that individual to account? It's a brave person who risks their own wellbeing to stand up for someone else's.

So we must ask, as Juvenal put it, *quis custodiet ipsos custodes*—who will guard the guards themselves? Accountability necessarily applies equally to all involved in a justice process, without fear or favour. A system of accountability that automatically exonerates one person over another simply because they're the first to say they've been the victim of an injustice is hardly a justice system worth the name. There needs not merely to be neutrality but also checks and balances, so that any analysis of a situation, any questioning of those involved, any attempt at resolution and restitution, is transparent and open to challenge.

Therefore recourse to people outside the community, people who have nothing to lose in terms of reputation or relationships within that community and who are able to reach an informed but disinterested conclusion free from the fear of losing their livelihood or friends or reputation, seems necessary. The question of course is who?

All I would counsel is not to deviate too much from the principles of justice (as distinct from the way they're often applied). These have evolved over hundreds of years because, in most cases, bitter experience has proven them to be the least imperfect options we have.

In terms of finding new ways of doing justice I'd refer you to a maxim known as Chesterton's Fence:

> In the matter of reforming things, as distinct from deforming them, there is one plain and simple principle; a principle which will probably be called a paradox.

There exists in such a case a certain institution or law; let us say, for the sake of simplicity, a fence or gate erected across a road. The more modern type of reformer goes gaily up to it and says, "I don't see the use of this; let us clear it away." To which the more intelligent type of reformer will do well to answer: "If you don't see the use of it...go away and think. Then, when you can come back and tell me that you do see the use of it, I may allow you to destroy it."[132]

I'd put it like this: Most ways of doing things have a 'why': some reason why they were put in place or why they just grew. Understanding the why of a thing before throwing it out, may keep you from disaster. You may find that the why once applied but no longer does, or that it wasn't a very good why in the first place. Or that there is a better way of fulfilling the need that drove the why. Or, possibly, that it's the best available answer.

The fundamental principles of justice in societies around the world have increasingly converged at least since the Magna Carta was signed on a small island in the Thames in June 1215.[133] They're about redress, but they also require that evidence is tested and weighed and that a ruling, where no consensus is available, must be fair and transparent. The person making the ruling must be truly disinterested, that is they have no interests at stake in the outcome. They must also be above being swayed through inducement or threat.

Whatever form of justice one chooses, however, the problems tend to arise more with the performance than the principles.

The two traditional approaches to justice in the West have been the adversarial system that originated in English common law, where each side would be argued before a judge, and the inquisitorial system that's rooted in Napoleonic systems, where a presiding judge or magistrate has much more latitude to lead an enquiry so that while all sides are represented, those representatives don't necessarily monopolise the questioning.[134]

There are also more recent variants such as restorative and transformative justice, which seek to move away from traditional systems to produce better outcomes both for the parties involved and for society.

---

132 G. K. Chesterton, *The Thing* (1929).

133 For those of you unfamiliar with Magna Carta, let me refer you to the late Mr. Tony Hancock: "Does Magna Carta mean nothing to you? Did she die in vain? Brave Hungarian peasant girl who forced King John to sign the pledge at Runnymede and close the boozers at half past ten! Is all this to be forgotten?"

134 The United Nations Office on Drugs and Crime offers a good summary: 'Adversarial versus inquisitorial legal systems', online at unodc.org.

Restorative justice examines the hurt, its causes, and the needs of those who have suffered harm, and it looks for agreement between the parties on restitution and reform. However it has faced criticism for not including properly trained and qualified people in the process.

Transformative justice aims to avoid some of the institutional problems in the traditional criminal justice system that adherents believe promote further criminality and violence (including the violence of the system towards those who are found guilty). Violence reduction is, instead, at its heart. It tends to be community based and aims to promote healing, accountability and safety rather than cause exclusion or alienation.

The appeal of transformative justice to a marginal community such as a consensually non-monogamous network is clear. It can tackle situations that don't amount to outright criminality. It also avoids involving a conservative framework prone to making hostile moral judgements against the community itself that would impede rather than aid justice.

Its weaknesses potentially include a lack of independence and neutrality in a highly networked community. Justice is usually depicted as wearing a blindfold because it's supposed to stand back and be impartial without regard to status, wealth or connections. I would worry how possible that is if the process is not overseen and guided by someone with no possible conflicts of interest. The potential for conflicts within the CNM community are legion. Furthermore there is very little quality control within transformative justice. People can claim to be practitioners without training, qualifications or oversight, and without any guarantee that they don't have conflicts of interest themselves or are on a campaign to impose a personal agenda or world view. In traditional systems judges and prosecutors with conflicts of interest are required to recuse themselves—something that doesn't always happen, though often it does, but at a minimum it's a legal requirement.[135]

Nor are restorative and transformative justice approaches designed as truth-seeking processes. They require that the facts are largely agreed upon so that a healing resolution can be found. They are ineffective and inappropriate where the facts are disputed.

There is an opportunity, some might say a pressing need, for a suitable process to be devised, founded on transformative-justice principles but including the best principles and practices of traditional justice systems, designed by the community but independent of it. However, any such process would surely need to reflect universal

---

135 The murder of Ahmaud Arbery, shot dead in the US state of Georgia in February 2020, is a case in point. Two prosecutors that handled the case had links to the two men accused of the killing and not only failed to disclose those and recuse themselves, but recommended that no action be taken to prosecute the accused.

standards for persons involved in overseeing justice, such as those set out in the Bangalore Principles in 2003: requiring judicial independence, impartiality, integrity, propriety, equality, competence and diligence. For instance, the restrictions imposed on the extracurricular activities of judges in England and Wales follow these principles and preclude anything that might lead to the mere perception that these principles are not being honoured.

Without a robust framework based on these, and without an overriding attention to facts and evidence over personalities, the CNM community will, with a likelihood verging on inevitability, preside over miscarriages of justice. These will inevitably reflect badly on the entire community and undermine faith in its ability to police itself or provide justice worthy of the name. The result, as we see all too frequently, are contested claims or disputes polarizing and splitting apart an entire region's CNM or kink community with embitterment all around and no resolution.

CHAPTER SIXTY-NINE

Healing

PERHAPS THE HARDEST part of being an abuse survivor is admitting that that's exactly what you are. For a lot of people it feels like an admission of failure. 'I let it happen.' Rather than accept that we have been abused we blame ourselves. In many ways that's easier than accepting that one was unable to protect oneself.

A little while ago I was chatting to a young woman in Massachusetts. She was hinting at a bad dating experience, 'a bit of an issue' she'd had with someone she'd met on the dating app Bumble. She and a guy had been talking online for a few weeks. They'd arranged to meet up and have sex. However when it came to it, this young woman changed her mind.

Her date, however, wasn't about to have his expectations dashed. 'He wouldn't listen,' she said. 'I said no, but he wouldn't listen.' She had indeed said no repeatedly. Then came those words that you almost know you're going to hear. You can feel your heart sinking before they're even spoken. 'It was my fault.'

To me, that sounded a lot like rape. I almost didn't say anything but honesty seemed preferable to letting someone blame themselves for having suffered a sexual assault. It all perpetuates the culture of non-consent that surrounds us.

Most of us like to maintain an illusion of security and control. Life is unpredictable and it can turn in an instant. Sometimes denial helps us to carry on rather than to accept that we are vulnerable and not always able to defend ourselves.

It's hard to heal before you accept that you've been wronged and wounded. Assumption of responsibility for someone else's actions is an obstacle to that.

It's not unusual for someone to experience delayed rage and anger, and it's not unusual for people to work out their experiences in a variety of ways. They have dark fantasies of revenge. As Meg-John Barker has pointed out, people often sexualise their trauma. It all needs to be acknowledged and accepted. Indeed sitting with our feelings about having been abused is important even if it can be very uncomfortable. Pushing these feelings away doesn't generally avoid a reckoning but merely delays it, and in the meantime many trauma survivors find the traumatised parts of themselves, rather than their regular coping selves, reacting to things. It can leave one feeling rather out of control.

Having a violent revenge fantasy, for instance, is very different from acting on one. Fantasy is often a way of reasserting control, if only internally. If it can't be done easily in reality, then the privacy of one's own thoughts offers an alternative. However, such fantasies can be disturbing for the survivor. A non-judgemental therapist should be able to offer guidance, ideally one who is GSRD/kink friendly and who has experience of helping people heal from trauma or abuse. Brief advice about finding a suitable therapist can be found in the chapter on mental health.

I have come across other advice that includes seeking to forgive one's abuser. This may sound counterintuitive or just wrong, but it's important to stress that forgiveness is not absolution nor does it mean forgetting. Nor should forgiveness take the place of a proper justice process—justice isn't solely about the survivor, it also seeks to deter criminal behaviour and protect potential victims by removing people who pose a danger to others from society.

However, what forgiveness *is* is a very powerful way of releasing *ourselves* from the past. It offers freedom to the person offering forgiveness. Being trapped in resentment and bitterness may feel just but it also risks extending the trauma and preventing us getting on with our lives. Guidance from a counsellor or therapist, or at least a support network, may be very helpful.

Two quotes come to mind. The first is from an interview that my late friend Rehman Rashid did with the legendary writer Kurt Vonnegut. Vonnegut's final words to him, Rehman wrote, as he shook hands and prepared to leave, were 'Abandon revenge.' It's one of those simple thoughts that has stuck with me and remains powerful, gaining ever more meaning and relevance.

The other is from the IRA hunger striker Bobby Sands, who famously said 'Our revenge will be the laughter of our children.' To me, knowing that one's children will be able to live and laugh and love freely isn't revenge in the normal sense of the word. It's triumph. It's vindication. It's transcendence. These things are a worthy riposte to abuse and oppression.

There surely can be no better response to someone who has sought to belittle, control, threaten, beat and abuse than to live one's life as one wants to live it—the very thing that consciously or unconsciously, they sought to prevent.

If forgiveness of the other can help, even more important is one's forgiveness of oneself. It's so easy to get bogged down in self-recrimination. We can end up making it all about our own failure to protect ourselves or invent a narrative in which we're somehow deserving of having been abused.

Again, some of the best advice I've been given is that we need to be our own best friends. It's a fairly simple reality check—if it were your best friend in your position, would you give them the hard time you're giving yourself? Absolutely not! If we saw someone treating our besties as we often treat ourselves we'd give them a bloody earful. So, oi! You! Stop beating yourself up, or I'll be round to have words! Got it?

Lastly there are some excellent books out there by people who have written about just these things. Janina Fisher's *Healing the Fragmented Selves of Trauma Survivors* and her mentor Bessel Van der Kolk's *The Body Keeps the Score* are both insightful.

CHAPTER SEVENTY

Raising Children

TO BE A parent is to fail; it's to amass a litany of 'could have done better', 'what was I thinking?', 'God I was an idiot', 'if only we'd...', 'I'm so sorry', 'we really didn't mean to', and 'grownups can be human too'.

Most of us who have children hope not to re-embody the shortcomings of our own parents and the imperfections of our own childhoods and instead create a charge sheet of our own. Even being a perfect parent has its downsides, aside from the fact that it means becoming a mythical creature. One's idea of perfect is not always one's children's idea of perfect. The more we cleave to the idea of perfection the more we disappoint ourselves.

And yet overwhelmingly people do their best as parents, and their children launch themselves into the world to forge lives, win victories, make mistakes and ride the rollercoaster, all of which are the pen strokes of their own stories.

Parenting while consensually non-monogamous is much the same as parenting otherwise, save for the issue of how you help your children navigate the fact that you have more than one relationship at a time.

It's always a matter of judgement what to tell children and what to keep private. Every parent necessarily makes that judgement for themselves because they are almost always better placed than anyone else to know their children, their circumstances, and the wider context.

The first issue is disclosure. Openness may build intimacy with a partner, but it can have a very different impact on children.

These questions of what and when to tell are faced not just by consensually non-monogamous people but any parent who is dating. Plenty who are single, divorced, separated or widowed have to pilot these waters. Do you want to keep your dating life and your children completely separate? Do you want your children to meet a recurring date before you're sure the person will become a fixture? Do you want to show your children that you're human and that adults need adult companionship?

Nor is there a lot of difference between the questions faced by a single monogamous parent and one or more non-monogamous parents. Such as, 'Who is this new person, will they be sticking around?'

Children need stability. They benefit enormously from routine, reliability, and predictable love and security, and the absence of these, in what social workers call a 'chaotic household' can cause children considerable harm. Obviously, at the heart of this are their parents. Children thrive on close bonds to their caregivers. However, in historical and global terms, the self-contained western nuclear family with two parents and one, two or three children is an aberration. Traditionally we've lived and raised children in far more interconnected networks of people: extended families and communities. The saying that it takes a village to raise a child captures the notion of the way that close communities keep many eyes on young members of the group and assume a degree of collective responsibility for their safety, support, and a successful upbringing. As McFadden wryly observes, rather than represent a threat, people with a wider range of close connections offer their children an advantage.

> In contemporary atomised western society, networks of non-monogamous relationships offer the kind of intimacy and mutual commitment that is often lacking in suburban nuclear families.

In these more communal settings there are, of course, more adults that careful parents need to watch for any signs of trouble around children and screen as appropriate. A more common issue is the fact that a near-family member with whom children develop a bond may depart. This is a recurring complaint from children who are interviewed by sociologists following polyfamilies. But then most people don't need telling this. They understand how to manage their children's expectations and they know when they'll experience a sense of loss if an adult they're attached to goes away. There were adults who used to visit my parents when I was a young child, probably around four or five, who I looked forward to seeing because they were fun and they talked to me. And, yes, I was disappointed when they stopped coming.

When, in my twenties and early thirties, I lived on a canal boat in the midst of a lively and close-knit community, there were children who ran in and out of the boats and were treated like small fellow floating citizens. They seemed positively to thrive on having a wide range of adults to talk to, adults who would, in turn, look out for them.

DK Green had children of his own when younger, and close relationships that brought others into his circle. DK found parenting in a collective environment to be a source of strength, inspiration and joy.

> I have several others in my chosen family, and their kids were raised with my kids and we all have gatherings. My house is sort of the community hub. So everybody comes there, the kids grew up together. My kids are all grown up and have kids of their own now practically, and they are still friends with those kids that they were brought up with. You know, it's really been quite delightful.
>
> I think it gives children a far richer environment if there are more persons and personalities about. For example, [my partner] Rachel's a writer and a painter and like a brain, I mean she's like the Brain of Britain. Lu is a classic American gregarious funster. Basically the kids, if they wanted to know anything they'd see Rachael, if they wanted to have a laugh they came to Lou, if they needed to talk about life and everything, have a hug, they come to me. It was a very mixed bag and they had further people, in our chosen family, who also had their own skills or would be available at two o'clock in the morning if somebody needed this or whatever.
>
> So, it really was a choice to bring my children up like this, and I'm very blessed because they are very open minded, they're incredibly warm hearted, they're very generous. They're as free from bigotry and -isms as they could possibly be really in this culture. They're just really beautiful people and I'm very fortunate. I think that's because I wasn't their only parent, they were parented by the whole family, the chosen family.

Those sentiments are echoed from the other side of the fence by Dr Liz Powell. As someone with no children of their own but with plenty of connections to people who do, she is a significant someone to a wide range of small people.

> I have several friends and lovers who have kids, and a lot of those kids think of me as 'Auntie Liz'. One of them calls me her ultra-mom. And what I see is that they have all of these adults in their lives who love them and give them snacks, and all that they care about is that there's all these grown-ups who have their best interest at heart and who care about them. And for the parents, it gives them a lot of opportunity to have breaks from their kids to be able to pass it off to someone.

That if there's an emergency there's someone to pick the kid up from school who isn't just that person.

It's perfectly possible for children to thrive in an environment where their parents are maintaining multiple romantic or intimate relationships. However they still have to navigate the wider world, one that's often hostile to consensual non-monogamy. There have been instances of courts taking children into care simply because their parents didn't conform to societal norms. DK Green was investigated by social services in his part of England after being reported by a neighbour. He and his partners were not only exonerated but the social workers wrote to say, in an implicit apology for the ordeal, they had provided an outstanding environment for their children to grow up in.

However children also have to deal with their peers, and children can be cruel. Many are desperate not to stand out. For this reason Shelly, the academic, and her husband have been very careful not to let their personal lives bleed over into, for instance, the social circle that's linked to their children's school. Their kids, meanwhile, have taken their parent's choices very much in their stride.

> I once had a conversation with a women's group that I'm part of and they said, do you consider your family, the family home that you grew up, normal? And do you consider the family that you have now normal? And so I said, well, I'm going to ask my family. And I asked them, do you think we're normal? And they're like, 'no'. And I said, do you want to be normal? And they said 'no'. So, I was like, yeah, okay, I'm doing something right.

The key thing here is that the children should know enough to be able to make their own judgements, and that they're in control of the information. Children are sometimes sufficiently astute, even when fairly young, to decide to whom it's safe to disclose details of the family friends, or the family structure, and to whom it's not. They don't have to tell friends, and their parents may be discreet enough to ensure that they won't have to face questioning from anyone else.

Then again, some would say that it places an unreasonable burden on a child to be asked to keep a secret. Not to mention unreliable. So this balance of disclosure is something that many consensually non-monogamous parents wrestle with. Just how much do you tell your children?

The first point to underscore is to be age-appropriate. To a six-year-old a family friend is a family friend. A 12-year-old is likely to figure things out for herself and live in fear that her parent(s) are cheating and it will lead to divorce—unless her parents have already explained about healthy consensually non-monogamous adult relation-ships with everyone approving and getting along. That, however, doesn't mean Too Much Information.

Kate, the swinger from Toronto, has grown-up conversations with a grown-up son—but that doesn't mean they have to be explicit.

> I have a 19-year-old son who is also sexually active and I'm very open with him, but I talk about it in, again, an abstract way. I let him know there are lots of different ways of being, sexually, so you can like boys, you can like girls, you can like both. You don't have to have a relationship with someone to have a caring sexual connection. You can have that in one night. You'd move on. We don't have to be monogamous in the traditional way. So I just talk about these things as options that are all equally valid and I don't really feel the need to say 'x', that's what we do. So I feel like you can have the conversations without going the next step and letting them into your sex life.

Her partner Liam, though, would rather be upfront about other things with his children.

> If I believe in exercise, I share that with my kids and model it to them, and I believe in eating well and I share that and model it to my kids, and a bunch of other things. But one of the most important things I do for our relationship health, for my own mental health, from my own life satisfaction, is our non-monogamous lifestyle. And I don't share that with my kids. So I feel like I'm being a not-great parent in that regard.

It's a truism that every generation, despite a myriad of evidence to the contrary, likes to think that it's the first to discover sex. Many if not most children would rather chew off their own toenails than talk with their parents about either of their sex lives. Many parents feel pretty much the same way. Penny and her husband in Jakarta are less frank with their children than Shelly and her husband, but the Indonesian capital is a much more conservative environment than London.

> We just don't talk about it with the kids. When they're mature enough or they understand it enough, they will know. Sometimes we introduce them to our each other's partner, but not as in 'this is my boyfriend' and 'this is my girlfriend', but

more of like, 'Oh, this is my friend.' But we're not really shielding them. We just don't talk about it. I think it's good that we kind of slowly giving them an understanding that their parents are different and have different kind of relationship. It's more than just the relationship. Like it's more values in life and I think that is more important. So especially living in the environment like this in pretty much conservative society to make them understand that their parents' values are kind of different from other parents' is important. So they have this acceptance.

Kevin Patterson in Philadelphia walks the same tightrope as everyone else. He's conscious of how he behaves around his daughters. They know what is going on with their parents but he takes his responsibilities as a father very seriously and that includes recognising what information his children can and can't manage and comprehend.

My kids are pretty in the know to an age-appropriate extent. I don't bring up, like, sexy stuff around them at all. They might see me like hugging or holding hands or kissing somebody, but that's about as far as that really gets. They know that we're not monogamous. They understand that's a different thing than what other families do. But for them, it's not really a huge factor. It's just more adults around. And sometimes the adults are interesting or they want to be interested in these adults, but that's really about it. You know who's going to bring them for ice cream? That's what they care about. They don't care about what I'm doing with my relationships.

But what happens when you lose control of the information, when your children find out more than you'd like them to? It happens. Let's not pretend that it never happens in monogamous families or that children are oblivious to arguments or antipathy between their parents, or even that one or both are having affairs without the knowledge of the other. However, in consensually non-monogamous relationships things that people would prefer to be as discreet as possible about, if only because they're concerned about social disapproval, sometimes come out unexpectedly. Shelly had to deal with just that when her son found her husband in bed with his girlfriend.

Sex aside, we never hid anything from them, strictly. We took caution in our serious relationships in the beginning. So when people started sleeping over, this is one significant person at a time as per our parents' sort of thing, because that's just what our relationships look like. We took care not to be seen in the same bed with our other partners, until one night our son couldn't sleep and walked in to my partner and his girlfriend, not having sex or anything. He was maybe 10 or 11 at the time and his dad went downstairs and assured him that everything was fine and he went to sleep and I came home later that night.

I wasn't supposed to come home, but we agreed that this would be a better way of dealing with the situation. So my partner's partner went home to her husband and kids and I came back home to talk to our son in the morning. And I asked, 'Hey, what was, you know, what's going on? I heard that you were upset last night,' and he was like, 'Ask Daddy, he will tell you.' I was like, 'Well, I know the facts. I'm wondering not what happened, I'm wondering why you were upset.' And he really struggled. I asked him, 'Do you think anyone was wronged in this?' And he's like, 'Yes, I think you were.' So then I said to him, 'No one was wronged here because this is agreed on'. I gave him the basics of 'We don't think that you only need to love one person. So we've decided not to tie each other down and guess what? Both of us are staying very happily and consensually and lovingly', and he was like, 'Oh, okay, okay.' We asked him if he had any questions. He didn't, a week or two later I checked in. I was like; 'Hey, that thing that I told you, is there anything you thought about and you'd want to ask me?' He was like, no, it made perfect sense.

Children are remarkably adaptable. Most advice on parenting boils down to accepting that your children are their own people and not simply clones of you, and guiding them through life's challenges and complexities until they're ready to face them alone.

The 'experts' stress the need for emotional consistency, love (and lots of it), attention and engagement, good boundaries, and showing by example what good, healthy, loving adult relationships look like.

And, of course, if you have children and more than one partner, then you *really* need to beef up those time management skills—as Penny in Jakarta knows all too well.

Scheduling, that is the most important; putting the priority, which is the kids and the family and also the scheduling. We have this rule, like don't spend too much time outside [away from home]. Like each of us has to stay at home for the kids. So it's not like both of us outside and then nobody will be there for the kids.

Of course parents get it wrong. Back in the let-it-all-hang-out 70s there was a school of thought that suggested adults should be a walking sex manual for their children. And though one would think that common sense would have dictated that this was a bad idea, this was a generation that, having grown up in a sexual false vacuum, was busy trying to redress its parents' shortcomings without having access to a successful blueprint. The blueprint they inherited often amounted to 'Don't, not until you're married, and even then don't enjoy it too much or you'll be a slut', alongside an loud cultural undercurrent of 'Boys, get it where you can, have fun and then tell all your mates, and girls, snag one and get them to marry you.' It hadn't dawned on far too many members of that generation that, for children, who are unable to process the emotional and psychological context of sex, too much explicit information could be confusing, scary and traumatising.

Many years ago I knew a young French woman whose parents had been swingers. More than once she'd returned home to find her living room full of people, including her parents, all having sex. Years later she was still deeply scarred by the experience and conflicted about her own sexuality.

Thankfully, few would consider going down that road today. Talking to a range of parents practising consensual non-monogamy, it seemed to me that they try to bring their best judgement to parenting and simply want their children to grow up happy, fulfilled, able to make their own decisions and choose their own path. Could any parent do more for their kids?

NON-MONOGAMOUS PARENTING FOR MONOGAMOUS PEOPLE

YOU DON'T HAVE to be non-monogamous to avoid a cloistered life. CNM people are often highly networked, and that means that their children have access to a wide range of adult role models. But of course people create a similarly rich and stimulating environment in a monogamous setting. Listening to children of parents in the arts or science or politics who had a never-ending flow of fascinating people pass through their childhood homes, I'm inevitably envious. No one has to rethink monogamy—just question the overly self-contained model of the nuclear family that we're presented with.

Likewise you don't have to have multiple relationships to present your children with an example of what a close loving intimate relationship looks like. The tragedy is that so many children grow up with parents unable to model healthy affection.

If that's not something you're able to do and you're concerned about the impact it's having on your children, just remember, you can rewrite the rules your way. You can use communication and negotiation and a willingness to think outside normal bounds to try to find a better way. Of course this is glib, but most parents would do pretty much anything for their children's well-being; just dare to think differently about what 'anything' could mean.

CHAPTER SEVENTY-ONE

Legal Considerations

LAWS AGAINST FORMAL multiple marriage in the West have a long history and pre-Christian roots, going back to ancient Greece and Rome (where they often went unenforced). In England in the early 17th century, jurisdiction over the crime of bigamy was taken out of the hands of ecclesiastical courts and put into the hands of the civil courts. These days, certainly in Western Europe, the rationale for maintaining such laws probably owes as much to issues concerning tax, inheritance, property ownership and so forth arising from people marrying more than one wife or husband without the other knowing as it does to any desire to discriminate against people who consensually choose more than one relationship. The picture has been further complicated by growing unease over the wellbeing of women coerced into marriages both monogamous and polygynous. Much of this concern is wholly genuine and well founded, some is thinly disguised racism and is particularly focused on the Islamic world, and some is based on misunderstandings of other cultures. In any case there doesn't seem to be any huge pressure for laws to change.

Legislators generally prefer to pick their battles. Pressure from the CNM community, which is still marginal socially and politically, is minimal. Many of those in polyfamilies are sceptical given the legal restrictions and state interference that might result. Those well enough off to hire a lawyer sometimes draw up their own legal documents about property ownership, child guardianship, inheritance, hospital visitation rights, and other things that marriage normally covers, as we'll see below.

Meanwhile opposition from conservative and religious groups is generally vociferous when the idea is raised. Never underestimate the pleasure that frustrated, unhappy and downright sanctimonious people can get from buggering things up for others. If you can't be happy yourself, the least you can do is to force others to join you in misery. McFadden's way of putting it is rather more forgiving.

I think the resentment at having made sacrifices while other people have refused to do so underlies a lot of the discomfort and prejudice that you find against non-traditional models of relationships and marriage. So, the result is that we're more or less forced to resort to corporate legal structures in order to accommodate our relational practices legally. So things like limited liability corporations and explicit assignment of powers of attorney are ways in which non-monogamous people are able to form financial and legal structures that accommodate the complexity of those relationships.

The legal position of those in polyamorous or other consensually non-monogamous relationships is challenging to report on. It's not just that the law is a moving target—it is constantly being updated—it's that its multiple moving targets: every jurisdiction is different. Some parts of the world, Europe and the Americas for instance, have generally been much quicker to extend basic human rights and recognition of relationships to LGBT people, while Africa and Asia have been much slower.

At the time of writing in the early 2020s, consensual non-monogamy is in a position not so very different than that experienced by LGBTQ people before the 1990s. Yes, there are precedents for groups of more than two people getting legally documented civil partnerships, such as cases in Brazil[136] starting in 2012 when a man and two women had their family unit officially recognised by local authorities.[137] But these are still rare, and in Brazil doubtless rarer still since the accession of a far-right, anti-LGBT government.

Elsewhere the consensually non-monogamous are vulnerable within the criminal justice system. Most of my Asian interviewees would put considerable effort into ensuring that they came nowhere near the criminal justice system and stay below the radar. In the United States, where many CNM people want to live openly, you can face direct discrimination within the law and even from professional bodies, as both Drs. Amy Moors and Liz Powell note.

Amy: You can be fired from your job for being consensually non-monogamous. In most States in the US actually you can be fired for being gay or lesbian.[138]

---

136 "Couples" of Three or More May Obtain Civil Partnerships in Brazil," Folha de S.Paulo, 26 Jan, 2016

137 'Three-person civil union sparks controversy in Brazil,' BBC News, 28 Aug 2012.

138 On 15th June 2020 the US Supreme Court ruled that it was illegal to fire someone on the grounds or orientation or gender identity. It's a great example of the challenges of writing about CNM and the law, because that profound shift came after I interviewed Amy and while I was doing the second draft of the book.

Liz: My license is in California. There are psychologists in states like Arizona who have lost their licenses for being non-monogamous. Not for going to sex clubs, not for any kind of sexual assault, not for having sex with a client, but because they are not monogamous and when the board found out, they lost their license. So, it's remarkably backward and it's, again, variable state-by-state.

In some ways the fact that things changed quickly for queer people in places like the United States offers a degree of hope to the CNM community. But, as Amy Moors points out, there were compromises.

In order to get there, there had to be a lot of public campaigning and tailoring different messages, and kind of the rhetoric that stuck, to get same sex marriage on the public's mind and palatable to vote in favour of, was this idea that gay people were just like straight people. So 'love is love', and it was this assimilation model where you don't think about the sex, you just think about the heart, and it was always coupling. It was always monogamy, even though consensual non-monogamy has had a long queer history and it has been a part of queer lives for decades, if not centuries.

You could argue that, yes, queer people gained a degree of equality but that it was equality on straight society's terms; what Moors calls 'respectability politics at its finest,' echoing Simon Copland's take. There has also been some pushback against the widening of the marriage franchise, not just from blood-red conservatives but also from some queer and poly activists who see in 'marriage equality' an attempt to both co-opt LGBT people and to erase some of their queerness, their difference. Indeed, some CNM people reported feeling silenced in the debate over same-sex marriage.

So it's not really clear what this tells us about the prospects for the recognition of consensually non-monogamous relationships. Queer people may have secured rights by 'acting a bit more like conventional monogamous society', though seems likely to be scant consolation to the consensually non-monogamous, given that to be more like monogamous people CNM people would have to be less like themselves.

However Moors thinks the shift in public attitudes towards same sex marriage has also shifted the wider debate about relationships and sexuality.

I think because of same sex marriage and the public being more accepting of queer relationships, we're now having an opportunity where our thinking can be more critical and more nuanced about multi-partner relationships.

That greater nuance isn't apparent everywhere. Family courts can be particularly problematic. Because of the difficulty of legislating specifically for complex family matters, judges in family courts are often accorded considerable latitude when ruling on cases. Until consensual non-monogamy is legally recognised, there's little to stop judges in some jurisdictions treating CNM relationships as detrimental to a child's wellbeing regardless of what impact their intervention might have on the child's wellbeing. Amy Moors again:

> Cases have already been popping up [in the United States] where sometimes people might lose custody of their children because a relative finds out that they're polyamorous, like a grandmother or something, and there have been cases where people are losing custody of their children.

One possible avenue for greater recognition, in Europe at least, is through Article 8 of the European Convention on Human Rights (ECHR). It states that:

> 1. Everyone has the right to respect for his private and family life, his home and his correspondence.

> 2. There shall be no interference by a public authority with the exercise of this right except such as is in accordance with the law and is necessary in a democratic society in the interests of national security, public safety or the economic well-being of the country, for the prevention of disorder or crime, for the protection of health or morals, or for the protection of the rights and freedoms of others.

In recent years Article 8 has been a powerful influence on European law and has been cited in the overturning of countless deportations and separations. The definition of what constitutes private and family life seems to be widening. Indeed the Commission to the ECHR has criticised the narrow approach of some jurists, instead arguing:

> In the opinion of the Commission, however, the right to respect for private life ... comprises also, to a certain degree, the right to establish and to develop relationships with other human beings, especially in the emotional field for the development and fulfilment of one's own personality.

A private life isn't restricted to the notion of an inner circle, so the right to pursue such relationships as one wants extends to pretty much anyone. The ECHR seems to have embraced the top tier of Maslow's hierarchy of needs and affirmed our right to self-actualisation and to the relationships that bring that about. Nor is the concept of family narrowly confined to family defined by marriage. It extends to 'legitimate' and 'illegitimate' family, presumably to children born outside marriage (though the very distinction seems barbaric).

Will this, in the future, extend to poly families? The possibility is there. However, just as one of the arts of politics is knowing how far ahead of or behind public opinion you can legislate, judges too have half an eye on the prevailing culture and public attitudes, not least because their own views and understanding are shaped by the environment in which they live.

In the meantime, poly people in particular use various hacks to achieve some of what monogamous couples take for granted under the law. Formal recognition of poly relationships may generally be out of reach at the moment, but not necessarily the protections.

Take wills for example. Debbie is based in the US state of Florida:

> It's made it a little bit difficult for now, legally when it comes to wills and all that kind of stuff. If you have a lawyer write up your will for you and if you follow the proper procedure, you won't end up with as many complications. [Even] if you have a lawyer do it properly, the [legal] family can still contest anything you leave in a will for somebody and things like that, but if you have it drawn up in a certain way its legal standing is similar to a contract. So there are ways to work around that, though not everybody can afford a lawyer, that's the problem.

If, as McFadden intimated, you want to go the whole hog and create a corporate entity to take responsibility for you and partners, you will certainly need to be able to afford lawyers. As Morgan says:

> It's much easier to create a company and name everybody as directors, so that you all have that same level of protection and then get everything through the company name, than it is to have a multiple marriage at this point. It's just common sense that people want these things.

There are indeed plenty of legal instruments, such as trusts, that the wealthy have long used to protect the interests of their families and to avoid taxes. These vary from jurisdiction to jurisdiction and will change as the law changes. The only (near) constants are that so long as the wealthy remain influential there will be vehicles and loopholes designed to help ensure that they remain wealthy, and that you will best be able to take advantage of them if you're wealthy too.

However it's also fair to say that reproducing the complex web of benefits and responsibilities that has evolved to support couples in default monogamous circumstances—mostly married, but increasingly the unmarried but partnered—would be time-consuming and complicated.

Consider just a few of the issues to be settled: the default provisions for life assurance beneficiaries, insurance payouts, property ownership, pension benefits, state (and insurance) benefits for unemployment and sickness, inheritance, married people's tax allowances, child benefits, healthcare cover, power of attorney in the event of incapacitation.

As Sandy, a polyamory activist and blogger in the US, points out, the varied nature of CNM relationships and their fluid nature makes legislation a challenge and could open up ways for the unscrupulous to exploit loopholes in the law.

> Good law responds to reality rather than precedes it. Twenty or 40 years from now when poly households are commonplace and their issues are well understood, an appropriate body of law will surely have grown up organically to handle the issues that arise. At least that's how it works when civil society is allowed to go about its business, free of religious or ideological compulsion.

Forming a corporation or limited company may get you some of the way there already—it does have certain advantages though of course these too vary between jurisdictions. But it won't replicate all the benefits that have accrued to married people for centuries, including the myriad default protections that marriage law supplies in the absence of wills, agreements, and other deliberate legal arrangements requiring lawyers.

And while, in parts of Europe and North America, life is becoming easier if you're unmarried or queer, in other societies laws are explicitly designed, indeed socially engineered, for a cookie-cutter couple plus their 2.4 kids or a reasonable facsimile thereof. And, as Rati found, that can have a profound impact on the dynamics of consensually non-monogamous relationships.

If you want to have kids in a country like Singapore, you need to be married or you're gonna fall under a category that is not beneficial to you at all. Single mothers' kids don't get the kind of benefits that most married couples' children would get. So when we were in a triad and [one partner and I] wanted to get married for that purpose, so that when we do have kids there's nothing to worry about, that caused a major amount of insecurity for the third partner. Even though we did say that it's not going to change anything or it's just a legal consideration, [it still] sort of affects how the third person sees themselves within the relationship.

Until there's an effective lobby for consensually non-monogamous people that's unlikely to change. Look back at the gay liberation and women's' movements of the 70s. There were magazines and spokespeople and a huge sense of solidarity all driving demands for change. And even then change took decades. It's still a work in progress. Do women, the disabled, people from cultural minorities and LGBTQIA people enjoy complete equality before the law and within society? Do they hell! Inequality and discrimination are still widespread.

Aside from organising and campaigning I sense the major route forward will be in finding common cause with others. For instance, in the UK and in many other countries, significant relationships other than marriage are undervalued, under-legislated for, and under-protected.

Grandparents who are raising grandchildren find they have no rights to see them if an estranged son or daughter returns and takes them away. People who want a best friend to have power of attorney rather than a spouse find their wishes frustrated. If someone falls sick hospitals can exclude non-family. A scheme by which it's possible to register significant relationships outside marriage and civil partnership would benefit a wide range of people in a wide variety of circumstances, those who practice consensual non-monogamy not least amongst them.

On one important level all these struggles are the same struggle. They're the struggle to have our common humanity and the right to make choices for ourselves acknowledged and recognised. They're a struggle to be ourselves insofar as being ourselves does others no real harm (offending someone simply by existing does not constitute 'harm'). Your right to be your own wonderful flavour of weird underpins my right to be mine. If I let yours be taken away, what hope is there for me?

When some respond to the black lives matter campaign by declaring that 'all lives matter' or even 'white lives matter', they are of course right but are wilfully and often maliciously missing the point. Raising money for an underfunded cancer treatment unit doesn't mean that people with diabetes don't count. That would be ridiculous.

When, in the United States, you can routinely get shot out of hand for the crime of 'jogging while white', or when children of white parents are seized and locked in cages on the Canadian border, that will absolutely be the moment to highlight just how much white lives do indeed matter. The spotlight needs to fall where there is darkness to be dispelled.

However it's only by protecting the rights of every individual that you can guarantee the rights of any individual. Our humanity is the one thing that we all possess, and it can only be taken away if we allow the idea that not all humanity is equally valuable. That idea is a moral weapon of mass destruction, and if that weapon is allowed to exist, we can never be sure it won't one day be turned on us. That's why solidarity matters.

So until CNM rights are recognised specifically, this marginal community should think about how it can stand with others and forge an inclusive framework of human rights that protects everyone. Your polycules, your swinger communities, your monogamish bubbles are unlikely to conform sufficiently to a norm as to be enveloped by specific legislation other than in a few very liberal jurisdictions.[139] Let it be enough that you are human, and that your fellow humans enjoy the same rights and protections as you.

---

139 A Massachusetts City Decides to Recognize Polyamorous Relationships, *New York Times*, 1 July, 2020

CHAPTER SEVENTY-TWO

'Trivial' Problems

TRIVIAL PROBLEMS ARE just that... until they're not.

For instance, the metamour who comes round while you're away and drinks that bottle of Brunello you'd stashed away for a special occasion. The partner who never does the laundry, leaving you and your other partner to clean up after them. The partner who is always late, disrupting everyone's plans. Consensual non-monogamy clearly just adds more people with their bad habits that drive everyone else nuts, right? Over to Nathan:

> When I'm standing there going 'Jesus Christ, Jesus Christ, can you please do your dishes?!' and I'm standing there in front of the sink, it's not a poly problem, it's a people problem. Like, maintain your vehicle, pay your bills, do your damn dishes and I'm working on the dishes. Like we both have our weaknesses. I genuinely enjoy vacuuming, she can't stand it, she doesn't seem to have a problem doing dishes, and I can't stand it. So, we'll come towards the centre but these are not poly problems, these are people problems.

And there you have it. Lots of problems in CNM are standard human problems. If you've decided to shack up as a quad, all that stuff with the kitchen cleaning rota—how is this different than four students sharing a house while at university, except that you're all five, ten, twenty years older now and (theoretically) have had all that time to get your shit together? Plus you now have Google Calendar to help you, which might not have been a thing when you were a student?

Exactly.

Or you go round to a partner's house and use their stuff or their other partner's stuff. Remember what your mummy said, 'Treat other people's things as though they were your own?' Obviously that doesn't apply to their 18 year old Lagavulin unless you replace it.

It comes back to the golden rule—do as you would be done by—unless you're an absolutely terrible slob and don't give a damn about your own stuff, in which case raise your game to the level of those around you where *their* stuff is concerned. Actually that's effectively the platinum rule: treat others as *they* would have you treat them—though you can reasonably expect similar treatment back or it's a recipe for pandering to the worst instincts of entitled wankers.

But hey, this all applies whether it's your metamour's whisky or your mate's skateboard. It's just doing Hooman 101. If this is all new to you, frankly this is probably not the book you should have read first....

(And feel free to remind me of that next time I'm having a meltdown...)

CHAPTER SEVENTY-THREE

Going Monogamous

THE ROAD FROM monogamy to non-monogamy is not one way. In a world of choices that allows you to choose to do things differently you also have the option to take the more conventional path having explored the scenic route for a while. People do.

I'm highly skeptical when people say things like 'once you've done that you'll never want to go back'. Yes, it's definitely true of some things. I was once dragged by a date into the M&Ms superstore on London's Leicester Square. I never want to go back. Seriously.

But relationships are thankfully not like that. If they were there would doubtless be a surge of interest in the monastic life. Consensual non-monogamy may be the promised land for some but for others, meh, not so much. Some will take one look and turn around, others will dip a toe in the water and decide it's not for them, others may, as Maxine recalls, be wholly committed but then have a different sort of epiphany.

> One of my partners had been a poly activist for about 10 years and left fairly abruptly having suddenly admitted to having fantasies about a monogamous white wedding for the entire time... ran off into the sunset and got married. So, it was a bit of a surprise. But at the end of the day I believe that loving someone means wanting them to be happy and if that's without me, then that's fair enough though I didn't quite understand it.

For many of those I interviewed the CNM scene is a community; tight-knit and supportive. They don't just have intimate relationships with partners but also close relationships with metamours. However, as with many marginal groups, there's often a sense of solidarity, of sticking together against the world. It is a lot to give up.

Thankfully, for the most part, it seems to be an understanding group. After all everything starts and ends with consent. People float in and out. Where there's exclusion it's often unintended exclusion. However, for those who choose to return to monogamy the wish to 'leave it all behind' can be strong, especially after heartbreak or where someone has struggled with the difficult feelings that consensual non-monogamy can provoke. This is hardly unique to CNM but will be very familiar to anyone who has given up a network of mutual friends after a break up.

Doubtless, should consensual non-monogamy become more accepted the route in and out will be less like passing through an airlock and more like negotiating a revolving door. Indeed, for people who consider themselves ambiamorous, equally open to monogamy and polyamory, that will just destigmatise their reality, recognising it as a simple life choice and one not so heavily freighted as it is now.

Until then, whether or not to be consensually non-monogamous will feel like a big decision to many people which is a pity because in all matters of the heart is not the ideal to be sufficiently unburdened that we're free to explore others and grow into our greater selves as we do so?

CHAPTER SEVENTY-FOUR

Where Does It Go From Here?

WELL, THERE'S A lot to be learned from those who've gone before.

Almost every movement for social change in the last century or so has had to organise to achieve its goals. That goes for women's rights, civil rights, gay liberation, the environmental movement and many others.

There were periods where the wheels grounds slowly and there were moments of catalysis. 1968 was a year of political unrest that, in the West, arguably defined the rest of the 20th century. There was the Prague Spring, *les événements de Mai* in Paris and anti-Vietnam War marches just about everywhere. It saw the rise of the 'new left', of green politics and environmentalism. The Women's International Terrorist Conspiracy from Hell (WITCH) put a Halloween hex on Wall Street, and American cities exploded in the wake of the assassination of Martin Luther King. 1969 brought the Stonewall riot and the founding of the Gay Liberation Front. For many people—women, people of colour, gay men—it was a moment when they had to decide whether to stand up and be counted or opt to continue life as it was: to be oppressed or closeted or marginalised.

Consensual non-monogamy hasn't had its Stonewall moment or found its Martin Luther King. There has been no single egregious instance of discrimination that has prompted people to come out and take a stand and, though some US poly activists are apparently actively awaiting that moment, plenty in North America, Europe and elsewhere are content to be dismissed as 'mostly harmless'.

The lesson from the gay liberation movement is that taking a stand brings first visibility and then accelerated acceptance. And the numbers involved are comparable. The percentages of the population identifying as LGBT and identifying as currently in a CNM relationship are quite similar at around 5 percent. (Indeed, there's long been a considerable overlap between the two groups.) Seen one way, that's a small proportion.

Seen another way, that's a whole lot of people. Yet while only 2.1 percent of the US population self-identify as either gay or lesbian and only 3.1% call themselves bisexual, according to a 2020 Gallup poll[140], same-sex experiences are far from unusual and attitudes towards them have also flipped dramatically. In the UK, Natsal (the National Survey of Sexual Attitudes and Lifestyle) found that among women aged 16–44 the proportion agreeing that 'same-sex relationships are not wrong at all' went up from 28% in 1990 to 66% in 2010.[141] In the US, Gallup found that overall public support for whether same-sex relations 'should be legal' rose from 47% in 1990 and 53% in 2000 to 58% in 2010 and 73% in 2019.[142]

The shift in attitudes towards race in the United States between 2010 and 2020 was also startling. And the Black Lives Matter protests following the murder of George Floyd spread around the world highlighting discrimination elsewhere.

Consensual non-monogamy isn't at that stage yet. Not only is prejudice still quite pervasive, but there's also precious little awareness of the variety within CNM. Much of such awareness as there is, is still at the rather prurient 'Really? They *do* that?' stage. Nevertheless, from his perspective McFadden thinks the liberal San Francisco Bay Area, where he lives, is an outlier:

> Culturally I think it's mostly invisible frankly. I really don't feel like there's a whole lot of poly visibility in the US. In San Francisco there's a kind of a presumption of non-monogamy, particularly in certain sub-cultural circles, and in fact monogamy is regarded as a bit, sort of out of style, I guess, or a bit old-fashioned. But I think that that the San Francisco Bay Area again represents one very sharp end of the bell curve, and that the kind of cultural propensity that has been growing there over the last decade or so is not even close to normative in most of the rest of the country.

What other movements have had is a goal, often protections or legislation that criminalises hate or discrimination (though hate speech and some forms of discrimination are broadly protected under the US constitution this is far from universally the case in Europe for instance). Consensual non-monogamy has hitherto lacked a

---

140 LGBT Identification Rises to 5.6% in Latest U.S. Estimate, Gallup, 24 Feb 2021. Gallup found that 5.6% of those surveyed identified as LGBT in 2020 as against 4.5% in 2017.

141 'Is 10% of the population really gay?' David Spiegelhalter, *The Guardian*, 5 Apr 2015. 'Drawing on the widest survey of sexual behaviour since the Kinsey Report, David Spiegelhalter, in his book *Sex By Numbers*, answers key questions about our private lives. Here he reveals how Kinsey's contested claim that 10% of us are gay is actually close to the mark.' https://www.theguardian.com/society/2015/apr/05/10-per-cent-population-gay-alfred-kinsey-statistics

142 10 Major Social Changes in the 50 Years Since Woodstock, Gallup, 16 Aug, 2019

campaigning focus. Perhaps it could be a push for the sorts of legal changes needed to recognise a range of significant relationships that I mentioned in the chapter on CNM and the law. There are already very early moves in the US to advance CNM rights within legislation.[143] Whatever it is the CNM community needs something that draws people together to bring about change. It also needs more visibility. How that comes about, how consensual non-monogamy gets accepted as a choice worthy of respect rather than prurient curiosity I have no idea. In the early 2020s it still seems some way off, and yet, as we've seen with attitudes towards the queer community, trans people and on the issue of racism, attitudes can change fast. They just need a spark to light the tinder.

---

143 In early 2021 the Polyamory Legal Advocacy Coalition was formed Based at the Harvard Law School it aims to press for anti-discrimination ordinances and for legal recognition of multiple domestic partnerships around the US.

THANKS AND ACKNOWLEDGEMENTS

ANYONE WITH AN ounce of humility realises that our individual endeavours are often, to an important degree, collective enterprises. Many people have played a part in helping bring this book into being.

Firstly I have to thank Alan my editor. Working with him has been an amiable fencing match. He's reined in many of my excesses and helped ensure that my more incomprehensible idiosyncrasies were left on the spike.

Thanks also to Irfan Yang for the effort he poured into his execution of a cover that gives me a small thrill every time I look at it. It's a bit of a luxury for an author to be able to work with an artist on a cover. It's been an exciting and ultimately rewarding process.

Also thanks to my old friend Shaun Streeter for the infinity symbol and frontispiece. He's a far more talented man than he's prepared to admit to himself. He's also a great listener, something I've relied on a great deal in recent years.

To Eunice, not just for reading things through but also for being a font of CNM knowledge who has challenged me regularly to examine my assumptions and opinions, much love and a big squeeze. Likewise Sean for legal advice, wise counsel, warm friendship and being a rock when one was needed.

To all of my interviewees, I owe a huge debt for your time, your sharing of your professional expertise, your personal experiences and for your trust. I hope you feel I have done them justice.

Lastly to the Piglet, bless your little trotters; thank you for your love, faith and occasional adoration. The sun has shone more brightly, life's colours have been more vivid and its songs undoubtedly sweeter since you wandered into my world. This book is dedicated to you.

Appendices

Less Common Poly Configurations

The Y
Dave and Bob both think they're in a relationship with Fatima. However Fatima only has one relationship: with her dog Fluffles.

The WWWWWWW
It looks like a relationship configuration. It also looks like a conga line. No one is quite sure which it is.

The VW
There could be three of you. There could be four of you. There could even be five or six or more of you. It's all down to how much lube is needed to actually squeeze you all into the car, and whether or not you get pulled over by the cops.

The X
Alexandra is in a relationship with Michelle. Zul is in a relationship with Vladimir. They're all cross with one another.

The P
It's kinky and we don't ask questions.

The T (primarily found in England)
Cecily would rather have a nice cup of tea. Peter would rather have a nice cup of tea. Charles would definitely rather have a nice cup of tea. Daphne would rather have a nice cup of tea than anything in the whole wide world. However they've run out of Darjeeling...

The I
Self-absorbed, narcissistic, solo poly.

The R
Strictly hierarchical poly. Zora is Captain. Chantal is First Mate. Will is the Bosun. Daisy is the Cabin Boy. Ahmed has been designated ship's figurehead and is dressed as a mermaid. They're all afloat on the high seas in pursuit of the good ship Unicorn. Prepare to be boarded.

The O
We went looking for love but all we found was the screaming void at the heart of human existence.

Resources

Books

Anapol, Deborah M. *Polyamory in the Twenty-First Century: Love and intimacy with multiple partners*

Bancroft, Lundy. *Why Does He Do That?: Inside the minds of angry and controlling men*

Barash, David. *The Myth of Monogamy: Fidelity and infidelity in animals and people*

Barker, Meg-John. *Rewriting the Rules: An integrative guide to love, sex and relationships*

de Becker, Gavin. *The Gift of Fear: Survival signals that protect us from violence*

Beckett, Cooper. *My Life on the Swingset*

Bellemeade, Kaye. *Swinging for Beginners An introduction to the Lifestyle*

Bergstrand, Curtis R., and Sinski, Jennifer Blevins. *Swinging in America*

Bisbey, Dr. Lori Beth. *Dancing the Edge to Reclaiming Your Reality: Essential Life Skills for Gaslighting (and Trauma) Survivors*

Block, Jenny. *Open: Love, sex and life in an open marriage*

Chapman, Mim. *What Does Polyamory Look Like?*

Creation, Koe. *This Heart Holds Many: My life as the nonbinary millennial child of a polyamorous family*

Deri, Jillian. *Love's Refraction: Jealousy and compersion in queer women's polyamorous relationships*

Easton, Dossie, and Hardy, Janet. *The Ethical Slut: A practical guide to polyamory, open relationships and other adventures (3rd edition)*

Fern, Jessica. *Polysecure: Attachment, trauma and consensual nonmonogamy*

Fisher, Janina. *Healing the Fragmented Selves of Trauma Survivors*

Gilmore, Richard, and De Arcana, Elon. *Creating a Line Family*

Gahran, Amy. *Stepping Off the Relationship Escalator*

Jenkins, Carrie. *What Love Is: And What It Could Be*

Johnson, Sophie Lucido. *Many Love: A memoir of polyamory and finding love(s)*

Kristjánsson, Kristján. *Justifying Emotions: Pride and Jealousy*

Labriola, Kathy. *Love in Abundance: A counselor's advice on open relationships*

Labriola, Kathy. *The Jealousy Workbook: Exercises and insights in managing open relationships*

Labriola, Kathy. *The Polyamory Breakup Book. Causes, prevention, and survival*

Linssen, Leonie, and Wik, Stephan. *Love Unlimited: The joys and challenges of open relationships*

McGarey, Robert. *Polyamory Communication Survival Kit*

Michaels, Mark A., and Johnson, Patricia. *Designer Relationships: A guide to happy monogamy, positive polyamory, and optimistic open relationships*

Mint, Pepper. *Playing Fair: A guide to nonmonogamy for men into women*

Minx, Cunning. *Eight Things I Wish I'd Known About Polyamory (Before I Tried it and Frakked It Up)*

Patterson, Kevin. *Love's Not Color Blind: Race and representation in polyamorous and other alternative communities*

Pincus, Tamara, and Hiles, Rebecca. *It's Called 'Polyamory:' Coming out about your non-monogamous relationships*

Powell, Dr. Liz. *Building Open Relationships: Your hands-on guide to swinging, polyamory, and beyond!*

Ryan, Christopher, and Jethá, Cacilda. *Sex at Dawn: The prehistoric origins of modern sexuality*

Shantigarbha. *I'll Meet You There: a practical guide to empathy, mindfulness and communication*

Sheff, Elisabeth. *The Polyamorists Next Door: Inside multi-partner relationships and families*

Sheff, Elisabeth. *Stories From the Polycule: Real life in polyamorous families*

Sheff, Elisabeth. *When Someone You Love is Polyamorous*

Taormino, Tristan. *Opening Up: A guide to creating and sustaining open relationships*

Turner, Page. *Dealing With Difficult Metamours*

Van der Kolk, Bessel. *The Body Keeps the Score*

Veaux, Franklin, and Rickert, Eve. *More Than Two: A practical guide to ethical polyamory*

Williams, Dan, and Williams, Dawn. *The Polyamory Toolkit: A guidebook for polyamorous relationships*

Winston, Dedeker. *The Smart Girl's Guide to Polyamory*

Yuen, Jenny. *Polyamorous: Living and loving more*

Acknowledgements and Biographies

I'M INDEBTED TO dozens of people for sharing their thoughts and experiences and thus making this book happen. Some are academics, some are fairly well known within the CNM world or even public figures, and others want to maintain their anonymity.

When I interviewed them I explained that, regardless of whether or not they reveal their identities, readers should know enough about them to give context to what they're saying. I asked pretty much everyone about where they're from, their ethnicity, their age, their gender identity, their orientation, their profession, educational background and so on.

Some of the academics I interviewed either aren't non-monogamous or simply don't make their private lives public. They are as follows:

Dr. Amy Moors is Assistant Professor of Psychology at Chapman University, Orange, California; a research fellow at the Kinsey Institute, Indiana University; and co-chair of the Consensual Non-monogamy Committee of the American Psychological Association. Her particular areas of interest include gender, sexuality, diversity, and well-being, and she's written more research papers on CNM than you can shake a stick at. Her work has been featured in *TIME*, *The Atlantic*, and *Scientific American*. She enjoys scavenger hunts and hiking.

Prof. David Barash is an emeritus Professor of Psychology at the University of Washington in the United States. He's written, co-authored and edited dozens of books on a wide variety of subjects including human aggression and sexual behaviour in humans and animals. His first book, *The Whisperings Within* (1978), argues that natural selection favours the development of adaptive behavioural traits over long periods of time, while social selection favours the development of other habits in far shorter periods. He's best known in the CNM world for *The Myth of Monogamy: Fidelity and Infidelity in Animals and People* (2002). Prof. Barash is rather partial to baklava.

Dr. Judith Lipton is a psychiatrist and Distinguished Fellow of the American Psychiatric Association. She's written a number of books with her husband Professor David Barash on sex, war, and human nature. Both Judith and David have been stalwarts of the peace movement in the United States. She shares a love of baklava with her husband but can stray from the true path if presented with cardamom ice cream, napoleons, or creme brûlée, or maybe all of them at once.

Dr. Dylan Selterman is a social psychologist and a Senior Lecturer in psychology at the University of Maryland. He has a range of research interests including: close parent/child, friendship and romantic relationships; the experience of emotions related to relationships such as jealousy and love; romantic attraction and sexual behaviour; and the morals and ethics of interpersonal relationships. He blogs on Psychology Today and, while you probably couldn't distract him with pudding, you could get his attention with a good bar of really, really dark chocolate.

Prof. Karen Bales is a much-garlanded Professor of Psychology at the University of California, Davis; Core Scientist at the CNPRC, formerly unit leader of the Neuroscience and Behaviour Unit at the California National Primate Research Center, a past president of the American Society of Primatologists, and editor-in-chief of the *American Journal of Primatology*. Her specialities include the physiology, neurobiology and development of social bonding, with a particular focus on 'monogamous' species such as prairie voles and titi monkeys. Titi monkeys prefer to end their meals with fruit (then again they prefer to start with fruit too, followed by a fruity main course, perhaps with a side of fruit, and a soupçon of insects for variety...) Prof. Bales, on the other hand, has rarely been observed in the wild eating dessert but regularly conducts research into gummy candy of all sorts.

Shantigarbha was born in 1965 in Dorking, England and studied Classics and Philosophy at Keble College, Oxford. He joined the Triratna Buddhist Community and was ordained with the name Shantigarbha (meaning 'seed of peace'). He has taught Nonviolent Communication (NVC) and mediated around the world. He's the author of the excellent guide to NVC, *I'll Meet You There*. You can find out more about him and join his online and in-person trainings at www.seedofpeace.org.

Prof. Joanne Begiato has been Head of the School of School of History, Philosophy & Culture at Oxford Brookes University since 2016. She took her degree and PhD from Durham, was a Junior Fellow at Merton College, Oxford, and a Fellow and Director of Studies in history at Murray Edwards College, Cambridge. Her research focuses on the history of emotions, the family, marriage, masculinities, material culture, and law from c. 1700-1900. She doesn't like dessert [the horror -Ed.], but will eat vegan chocolate cake occasionally.

MY OTHER INTERVIEWEES contributed personal experiences of consensual non-monogamy and, in a number of cases, professional expertise. Those whose names I've changed to protect their privacy I've marked with an asterisk.

Prof. Carrie Jenkins lives in Canada but was born in the UK where she took a PhD from Cambridge. She has been a Professor of Philosophy at the University of Aberdeen and is currently a Professor of Philosophy at the University of British Columbia. She's the author of *What Love Is: And What It Could Be, a reflection on the meaning of love*, as well as *The Philosophy of Flirting, Concepts, Experience and Modal Knowledge*, and other books and articles. She's been openly non-monogamous for a number of years and has a bit of a thing for sticky toffee pudding with custard.

Dr Liz Powell is a psychologist and the author of *Building Open Relationships: Your hands-on guide to swinging, polyamory, and beyond!* They teach, write and consult on areas of sexual diversity and pleasure, non-traditional relationships, and sexual empowerment.

Ruby Bouie Johnson was born in Fort Knox, KY. She studied social work and received her MSSW from the University of Texas at Arlington. She is a writer, activist, and sex therapist with specialty in alternative communities. She founded and is the CEO of PolyDallas Millennium LLC, a BIPOC-centered CNM and polyamory conference. Her favourite dessert (and meal) is cake and ice cream.

DK Green is a psychotherapist, counsellor, celebrant, and poly activist living in the English East Midlands. He was born in the late 1960s into a white background, raised a family and then transitioned. He identifies as a trans man.

Kevin Patterson was born in Brooklyn but grew up in New Jersey, took his Bachelor's in Fine Arts from Howard University and his Masters in Education from Widener. He's an educator, author (*Love's Not Color Blind* and, with Alana Phelan, the *For Hire* series of SF novels), and a former poly community leader in Philadelphia. Kevin identifies as straight, polyamorous and African American. His favourite dessert is rocky road ice cream!

Dr. Meg-John Barker was born in 1974 and grew up north of Hull in the North of England. They took a PhD at the University of Nottingham and lectured in psychology at the Open University. Meg-John wrote the acclaimed 'anti-self-help' book *Rewriting the Rules*, graphic non-fiction books, *Queer: A Graphic History, Gender: A Graphic Guide, The Psychology of Sex*, and shedloads of other books. They co-presented the Meg-John & Justin podcast with sex educator Justin Hancock, which you really have to listen to. It's fab. Meg-John is trans and likes apple pie with clotted cream.

Anita Cassidy was born in the mid 1970s into a white working-class military family and grew up in the UK and Germany before studying at Warwick University. She's divorced with two children and lives in London, where she writes fiction and non-fiction and runs a website supporting alternative relationships. She identifies as bisexual.

Joreth Innkeeper is the scene name of a long-time poly activist and campaigner for civil and economic rights. She runs the website TheInnBetween and lives in Florida. Joreth has a qualification in architectural gingerbread.

Franklin Veaux is co-author of *More Than Two* with Eve Rickert and *The Game Changer*. Born in the late 1960s, he became one of the world's best-known poly activists as early as the late 1990s.

Cooper Beckett is a prominent member of the North American swinging community, the author of *My Life on the Swingset* and a number of fiction titles, and co-presenter of the *Life on the Swingset* podcast. Cooper identifies as bisexual and lives in Chicago with his wife, terrier and cat.

Charlie Wilde is a gay white man, born in Florida in the early 1960s. He took a degree in theology from Mia Curtis Hopkins College. After a long career as an entrepreneur and activist, both for environmental and LGBT causes, he moved to Colorado where he runs a solar energy business.

James Finn is a man of many parts: born into a religious, white, aspirational working-class family in the early 1960s, he took a degree in engineering from Iowa State. He was an intelligence officer specialising in Soviet air defences in the US Air Force, also served in the Marines, has been an LGBTQ and HIV activist through ActUpNY and Queer Nation, and describes himself as a 'middle-aged uppity faggot'. He currently lives in northern Michigan and writes screenplays and YA fiction.

Simon Copland was born in Australia in the late 1980s and grew up in Canberra in an upwardly mobile family. He's a white gay man in a V configuration with two partners. He's currently working on a PhD in sociology.

Kerilyn* was born in the early 1990s in Zimbabwe, the child of professional parents who took manual jobs when the family moved to Britain. She's studying for a degree while working in victim services in London. She identifies as black British, straight and kinky and likes carrot cake.

Seb* was born in South Africa in the mid 1970s. He studied in both South Africa and the UK and has worked in leading law firms throughout his career. He's married, and he and his wife both have other committed relationships. He's white and identifies as heteroflexible. His favourite dessert is crème brûlée.

Shelly* was born in the late 1970s and grew up in Israel, North America and Europe. An academic based in London, she is married, has three children, and identifies as bisexual but largely heteroromantic. Favourite dessert: Majhul dates filled with half walnuts, and glazed in dark chocolate infused with orange zest and cardamom. Wow.

Shyam* was born in Kerala, India, in the early 1980s into a Malayalee family. He took a degree in Computer Security and Forensics and works in IT. He identifies as bisexual and his preferred dessert is tiramisu.

Ivan* was born in Russia in the early 1980s, is a graduate and works as a software developer. He's married, polyamorous, and identifies as white and straight. Ivan doesn't like dessert [sad face—Ed.] but he does like sunflower buns...

Alexandra* was born in Singapore in the early 1980s. She's a graduate and works in advertising. She identifies as Singaporean Chinese and heteroflexible.

Yana* was born in Russia in the late 1980s and dropped out of university. She works as a barber. She's white European and identifies as straight. Favourite dessert: Soviet Souffle Cake. I'm sure there's a political gag in there somewhere.

Billie* was born in Singapore in the late 1980s. He studied in Australia and took a degree in photography and works as a photographer. He identifies as Singaporean Chinese and is straight. Billie likes panna cotta.

Charlotte is from a white, English, working-class background. Born in the late 1980s, she was only the second person in her family to go to university and took a Masters in human rights law. She works in the property sector in London, identifies as a lesbian, has been diagnosed with autism and is partial to salted caramel cheesecake.

Morgan was invented in Ireland in the late 1980s, sometimes refers to herself as a 'gender pirate', has a bachelor's degree, works in IT, has a fluid sexuality and is polyamorous. She's W.E.I.R.D.[144], a member of the proletariat, on the spectrum, transitioning M to F, and likes pretty much all puddings (except for chocolate cake) especially lime cheesecake, baclava, honey cake, coffee and walnut cake, sorbet and a cake from a shop in London's Soho shaped like a boob. Don't ask.

Eunice was born in Essex, England in the mid 1980s. She took a degree in creative writing from University of Leeds and works as an events organiser. She is currently training to be a psychotherapist. She plays a key role in organising many of the UK's poly events. She is British-born Chinese and identifies as bisexual and grey-ace. She doesn't have a favourite dessert, but that's because she's indecisive and/or greedy.

Debbie* was born in the late 1970s into a white middle class American family and took associate degrees in science and commercial art. She's predominantly monogamous and lives in Florida.

Nathan* was born into a white middle class family in Texas in the early 1980s, dropped out of university and works as a technician in the entertainment industry. He lives in Florida.

McFadden* was born into an educated white middle class family in the late 1970s, grew up in Philadelphia, and has lived on both the East and West Coasts of the US. He has a degree in linguistics and has turned an early interest in IT into a career.

Emma* was born in the early 1990s in Singapore. She's from a Muslim background and works in retail. Favourite dessert: molten lava cake...

---

144 'Are Your Findings W.I.E.R.D.?' [pertaining only to Western, educated, industrialized, rich, democratic (WEIRD) societies], American Psychological Association *Monitor,* May 2010. https://www.apa.org/monitor/2010/05/weird

Vincent* was born into a middle class Singaporean Chinese family in the mid 1980s. He has a degree and works in law. He is married and identifies as heteroflexible.

Mia* was born in the mid 1980s in Singapore into a middle class Chinese family. She is a graduate and works in marketing in FMCG. She is married, identifies as a Christian and as bisexual. She likes durian. People do. Get over it.

Laura* was born in Singapore in the mid 1980s. She's a graduate, has worked in education, and works discreetly as a pro-domme. She's ethnic Chinese from a middle class background, raised Christian, divorced and has remarried. Favourite dessert: sticky date pudding.

David* was born in Singapore to a middle class ethnic Chinese family in the early 1980s. He's a graduate, works in PR and is divorced.

Maxine was born in the early 1980s and grew up in various places around the UK, dropped out of university because of health problems, and works as an illustrator. She uses the pronoun 'bunny' and identifies as 'mongrel British', female (??), a gender trickster, a universal adaptor, a unicorn and bisexual. Maxine's preferred dessert is people, which is cheating, Maxine!

Becky was born in Zimbabwe in the late 1970s but moved to the UK as a child. She studied at art college and works in IT. She's a white bisexual trans woman and her favourite dessert is tiramisu.

Magick* is from a white working-class background in the English Midlands. He was born in the late 1960s, dropped out of college, lived around the UK, Denmark and Spain, worked as a musician and more recently as a porn producer and is starting a degree in creative writing. He identifies as straight and male and his dessert choices are mood-dependent, but if pushed he'll have a piece of baked New-York style cheesecake thank you very much.

Xena* was born in Indonesia in the late 1970s and lives in Denmark with her Danish husband. She's worked in marketing in the auto industry and likes mango and jackfruit.

Rati* was born in the early 1990s on Kerala's Malabar coast into a Malayalee family but grew up in India's commercial capital Mumbai. She trained as a psychologist and currently lives in South East Asia. She identifies as bisexual and likes tiramisu.

Luciano* was born in Brazil in the mid 1990s. He holds a PhD and works as a coder with a major technology company. He identifies as white, bisexual and neuroatypical. He enjoys brigadeiro, a Brazilian recipe combining condensed milk, cocoa and diabetes.

Alain* was born in France in the late 1980s. He is from a middle class background, has a masters in computer science, and works in IT management consulting in South East Asia. He identifies as a cis-het male white European. His favourite dessert is mousse au chocolat.

Kate* was born in the mid 1970s and has a postgraduate degree. She teaches for a living and writes fiction. She identifies as white and bisexual. She lives in the greater Toronto area.

Liam* was born in the early 1960s, took a degree in English and holds an MBA. He runs a medium sized business and has a separate career in the arts. He has children and identifies as white and heteroflexible. He lives in the greater Toronto area.

Jonty is a science educator living in the east of England. Born in the early 1980s, he's a graduate and a former rocket scientist (seriously — when I point out that something isn't rocket science, Jonty is an informed second opinion). He's white, middle class, bisexual and married with two children. Favourite dessert: Eve pudding.

Mawar* was born in Java in the mid 1980s. She took a degree in journalism, lives in Jakarta, and works in the arts. She identifies as Javanese and straight. Favourite dessert: cheesecake.

Alice* was born in the early 1990s in Singapore and took a degree in arts administration, the field in which she works. She identifies as Singaporean Chinese and heteroflexible. Alice likes ice cream, ideally chocolate or rum & raisin.

Penny* was born in Jakarta in the late 1970s. She's had a high-flying career in advertising and the media and until recently worked for an international technology giant. She's married with two boys. She identifies as Javanese and is bisexual. Favourite dessert: chocolate pudding, matcha ice cream and fruit...